The Reform of Federal Deposit Insurance

The Reform of Federal Deposit Insurance

Disciplining the Government and Protecting Taxpayers

James R. Barth
and
R. Dan Brumbaugh, Jr.

EDITORS

HarperBusiness
A Division of HarperCollins*Publishers*

International Standard Book Number: 0-88730-530-X

Library of Congress Catalog Card Number: 91-39952

Printed in the United States of America

Library of Congress Cataloging-in-Publication Data

The reform of federal deposit insurance : disciplining the government
  and protecting taxpayers / James R. Barth and R. Dan Brumbaugh, Jr.,
  editors.
      p. cm.
    Includes index.
    ISBN 0-88730-530-X
    1. Deposit insurance—United States. 2. Deposit insurance—Law
  and legislation—United States. I. Barth, James R. II. Brumbaugh,
  R. Dan., Jr.
  HG1662.U5R44
  368.8′54′0973—dc20   91–39952
                                                                CIP

92 93 94 95 CC/RRD 7 6 5 4 3 2 1

For Mary and Lloyd Barth
and
in memory of Estelle and Floyd Arthur Brumbaugh

Contents

Tables, Charts, and Figures

Preface

Deposit insurance is considered a birthright by most Americans. From the creation of federal deposit insurance in 1933 until the savings and loan debacle of the 1980s, the birthright also seemed relatively costless. The reserves accumulated in the deposit-insurance fund from relatively modest premiums levied on depositories easily covered the losses of failed depositories. The benefit from federal deposit insurance—the elimination of the possibility of widespread runs on depositories—seemed obvious and large.

In the 1980s, however, the costless birthright showed itself to be a chimera that imposed huge costs on taxpayers through the failure of thousands of savings and loans whose fragility was a by-product of federal deposit insurance. The same federal statutes that created deposit insurance for savings and loans, for example, eventually led to regulations that required savings and loans to hold long-term, fixed-rate home mortgages funded by shorter-term, variable-rate deposits. The fixed-rate home mortgage from the savings and loan became an important part of Americana. But when interest rates unexpectedly soared in the late 1970s and early 1980s, the savings and loan house of cards built on lending long and borrowing short collapsed.

The collapse of the inherently unstable structure funded with federally insured deposits for savings and loans began to reveal additional manifold shortcomings of the entire federal deposit-insurance system. Most important, the reserves in the insurance fund proved totally inadequate relative to the costs of the insolvencies of savings and loans. Additional insurance premium income levied on the healthier savings and loans was meager. By eliminating depositor scrutiny, moreover, deposit insurance transferred scrutiny to government regulators. Regulators, relying on accounting techniques that grossly obscured true economic financial conditions, allowed insolvent savings and loans to remain open and operating for years in far too many cases.

The overwhelmed deposit-insurance system provided open but insolvent savings and loans with an enormous incentive to gamble for resurrection. The potential gains from greater risk-taking flowed to the savings and loans but the losses, when they occurred, flowed to the federal insurer. In this atmosphere the Congress provided all federally insured savings and loans with the opportunity to lend beyond home mortgages, primarily for commercial real estate, and many state legislatures followed suit or went further for state-chartered savings and loans.

Though the costs associated with the federal deposit-insurance system manifested themselves in liquidations and government-assisted mergers of failed savings and loans throughout the 1980s, the perception of the crisis changed forever in 1989 when the Financial Institutions Recovery, Reform, and Enforcement Act (FIRREA) made the taxpayer directly responsible for part of the cost. For the first time in the 56-year history of federal deposit insurance Americans were told that they would pay a large price for such insurance.

We began planning the conference (which led to this volume) in May 1989, three months before the passage of FIRREA, when the price for cleaning up the savings and loan debacle was being debated. Though the financing mechanism of FIRREA is so complicated that a skeptic might conclude part of its purpose is to obscure the true taxpayer burden, the magnitude of the taxpayer burden was generally perceived: $50 billion "over three years." Nonetheless, many critics, ourselves included, said that the true cost in present-value terms was far greater.

A year later, the day the conference began, the Treasury Department announced that the present-value cost to close failed savings and loans was more in the order of $100 to $150 billion, most of which was to be borne by taxpayers. Suddenly the government was validating private estimates that the cost of the birthright of deposit insurance was outrageously high. The government had protected insured depositors, but had failed miserably to protect taxpayers.

This discussion almost completes the backdrop for the conference and the papers in this volume, but one additional issue must be mentioned—the deterioration of commercial banks. Only the cataclysm of the savings and loans obscured what would have otherwise been a national concern over the condition of banks.

Beginning in 1982 with the deterioration in the quality of loans to lesser developed countries, commercial bank asset deterioration surfaced and widened to include troubled commercial real estate loans, loans for corporate mergers, acquisitions and recapitalizations, and consumer loans. In a pattern resembling the savings and loan debacle, commercial bank performance deteriorated, reserves in the Bank Insurance Fund declined, regulatory laxity and forbearance developed, and the prospect of a taxpayer bill for resolving the banking problem emerged.

This then is the context in which the papers in this volume confront the deposit-insurance issue. The first paper by Charles Calomiris of Northwestern University places the current debate in a historical perspective, indicating what lessons emerge from the successes of the predeposit-insurance era. The paper argues that the rationale for federal deposit insurance is not well grounded in our nation's history.

The next two papers describe and draw lessons from the breakdown in deposit insurance and the regulation of depositories in the 1980s. James Barth of Auburn University and Philip Bartholomew of the Congressional Budget Office demonstrate how the the savings and loan crisis revealed weaknesses in the way the deposit insurance system was structured and insured institutions were regulated. Then the paper by Dan Brumbaugh and Robert Litan of the Brookings Institution critiques the Congressional response in the form of FIRREA to the distress of depositories and the deposit-insurance system, and describes the implications of the flagging financial strength of commercial banks.

The following set of papers evaluates the legislative reforms of the 1980s from the perspective of public choice analysis, using the methodology of economic analysis to evaluate political decisions. First, Edward Kane of Ohio State University argues that the behavior of the deposit-insurance agencies in the 1980s reflects inherent incentives in the current system to misregulate. Thomas Romer of

Princeton University and Barry Weingast of Stanford University analyze the action and inaction of elected officials in reaction to political incentives that thwart economic policies promoting competition and efficiency.

Next, three papers discuss the effect of external forces on depositories, deposit insurance, and government regulations. Gary Gorton of the University of Pennsylvania and George Pennacchi of the University of Illinois discuss how technology and other forces are separating the two sides of the balance sheet that expose banks to panics—financing of nonmarketable loans with short-term liabilities. They contend that the market-driven separation of these two functions is reducing the fundamental cause of banking panics. Robert Chirinko of the University of Chicago and Gene Guill of the Bankers Trust Company discuss how aggregate macroeconomic shocks affect depositories and then argue that approaches to deposit-insurance and regulatory reform that do not explicitly consider the interaction of depositories with aggregate shocks create serious problems. Finally, George Kaufman of Loyola University argues that the Federal Reserve System has quietly become part of the deposit insurance safety net by providing lender-of-last-resort assistance to economically insolvent large banks considered "too large to fail" and then indicates why this is inappropriate behavior that must be corrected.

As we have mentioned, accounting techniques have played a major role in the interaction of depositories and deposit insurance and regulation. Two papers deal with this issue by focusing primarily on the merits of market-value accounting versus historical cost accounting techniques. William Beaver, Srikant Datar, and Mark Wolfson of Stanford University argue that it is the interaction of market-value accounting with regulatory behavior, not market-value accounting by itself, that matters and suggest that with some forms of regulatory behavior market-value accounting can exacerbate problems. George Benston of Emory University, Mike Carhill of the Office of the Comptroller of the Currency, and Brian Olasov of Long, Aldrich and Norman, however, present empirical evidence that even very generic forms of market valuation are superior to the traditional accounting principles.

The FIRREA mandated that the Treasury Department prepare

a study of deposit-insurance reform and present it to Congress with recommendations in 1991. Much of the 1990s will be taken up with the Congress and the nation debating the shape of depositories and deposit-insurance reform. It appears that the debate has begun with the country in a recession, with savings and loans continuing to deteriorate, with commercial banks failing in record numbers and imposing record costs on the Bank Insurance Fund, and with the American taxpayer facing ever larger potential costs. The papers in this volume provide insights accumulated over years of research by some of the nation's most thoughtful economists. Our hope is that the product of their analyses will contribute to a fuller and more thoughtful debate on deposit-insurance reform.

Acknowledgments

The idea that led to this volume came to us following an annual academic conference we both attended in the summer of 1989. Four years earlier we had presented a paper at a previous conference at what we recall was the only session dealing with the problems of insured depositories and deposit insurance. In 1989 there were more sessions on those and related topics than we cared to count or could possibly attend. As much as we were pleased with the growing attention by academics to what we considered an important area, we were dismayed that the ideas being expressed, some new and some not-so-new, had yet to find their way into policy making.

One of us had joined the Center for Economic Policy Research at Stanford University in the spring of 1989 and approached the Director of the Center, John Shoven, with a suggestion for a conference that would present a summation of the ideas developed by academic economists and that would disseminate the ideas widely both to other economists and to policy makers. We thank John Shoven and Ed Steinmueller, Deputy Director of the Center, for encouraging the Center's steering committee to sponsor the conference. Cochaired by one of us, it was held May 18 and 19, 1990, in Washington, D.C. The papers from the conference comprise this volume.

We also thank the Center's Carolyn Sherwood, Vicki Oldberg, Deborah Carvalho, and Carol Pfister for their help in the preparation of the conference.

Joseph Stiglitz graciously accepted the invitation to cochair the conference. His contribution with John Shoven and Ed Steinmueller to the contents of the program, his thoughtful comments at the conference, and his introduction to this volume reflect his keen economic insights.

Each of the sessions at the conference was introduced and moderated by economists who themselves have made contributions to understanding insured depositories and deposit insurance: Andrew Carron of the First Boston Corporation, Kenneth Scott of Stanford University, Mark Flannery of the University of Florida, Catherine England of the Cato Institute, Christopher James of the University of Florida, and Joe Grundfest of Stanford University. Douglas Breeden of Duke University also made a thoughtful presentation. We thank all of them.

We also thank the participants of a special session of the conference designed to sum up the emerging agenda from several perspectives. The speakers were John Anderson of the *Washington Post,* syndicated columnist Warren Brooks of the *Detroit News,* and Barbara Timmer, General Counsel to the House Banking Committee. Joseph Stiglitz discussed the emerging research agenda.

We were also fortunate to have Congressman Jim Leach (R-Iowa) of the House Banking Committee deliver the keynote address on the first day of the conference and Michael Boskin, Chairman of the Council of Economic Advisers, deliver the keynote address on the second day of the conference. We are grateful for their participation.

Finally, we thank the following sponsors and supporters of the conference without whose generous funding it would not have happened.

SPONSORS

- Anonymous
- American Savings
- Cornerstone Research
- Federal National Mortgage Association
- First Nationwide Bank
- Federal Home Loan Mortgage Corporation

SUPPORTERS

- HarperCollins Publishing Company
- California Credit Union League
- Eastbridge Capital, Inc.
- Ferguson & Company
- Glendale Federal Bank
- Goldman, Sachs & Co.
- Merrill Lynch Capital Markets
- Roosevelt Bank
- Seward & Kissel
- Smith Breeden Associates
- SNL Securities
- Salomon Brothers
- State Bank of Ohio
- Wells Fargo Bank

The Reform of Federal Deposit Insurance

INTRODUCTION

S & L Bail-Out

Joseph E. Stiglitz

When we began planning this conference, we had mixed feelings about its timing. Congress had passed the President's legislation bailing out the Savings and Loan industry, in the finest tradition of the previous Administration. The Administration had approached the problems of the S & Ls under the unspoken motto of "Deal today only with the problems that you cannot postpone until tomorrow. Who knows? The deeper problems might go away, and in any case, there is a good chance that they will not reappear during your watch on the bridge." During the early 1980s, Congress and the Reagan Administration had quietly applied Band-aids to the problems of the S & Ls, but it was apparent by the late 1980s that the lack of adequate earlier treatment necessitated what might be viewed as minor surgery: Move an administrative agency around here, change a regulation there, put the right person in charge—that plus the paltry sum of $150 billion dollars—as much of it as possible off budget—and presto, instant solution. The Band-aid used to hold the patient together after surgery—or to disguise the extent of the problem—was bigger than the ones previously applied, but it was a familiar brand.

Though the Administration might think the Band-aid would hold at least until the beginning of the next Administration, most neutral observers were not convinced; but as we planned the conference, even we thought the palliative would hold for at least a while. The interim might be a good time to think about the longer-term solutions—away from the passions of the moment in dealing with a patient obviously in the intensive care unit. We were confident that the Band-aid would not hold, and that a time would soon come when more serious attention would be given to the underlying problems. Our conference, we hoped, might help set the agenda for such discussions and might set into play some solid research which would help provide answers to some of the unresolved questions.

Although we thought this quiet period would be an excellent time to address the fundamental issues, we were concerned by the old aphorism, "out of sight, out of mind." Who wants to discuss issues that are, at least temporarily, "solved," particularly within the policy arena?

Well, we all know what happened: The patient starting hemorrhaging almost before the Band-aid was applied. The $150 billion bail-out began to look more like $200 billion, then $250, and now possibly $300 billion or more. (Had dishonesty or incompetency in government been raised to a new, higher level?) The attendance at this meeting is testimony to the fact that the issue is very much on the minds of Americans. The disadvantage of our timing is that we are afraid the discussion may be less dispassionate than it would otherwise have been, had it been merely a group of academics trying to find solutions to what might appear to be only an academic problem.

There are times when you wish you had been wrong. I think that is the feeling of many of the economists who participated in the conference and whose papers appear in this book. They saw the problems in the early 1980s. They wrote about the inadequacies of the solutions being tried then. They predicted the disaster that came to be known as the S & L crisis. And they predicted that the palliatives of the Bush proposals would not work. I want to emphasize that these are not Monday morning quarterbacks, or the kinds of stock market analysts who constantly predict an upturn, or alternatively a downturn—some day they will inevitably be right.

The S & L crisis, while it is a tragedy for the country, is a triumph for economic analysis, and economic theory in particular. For almost two decades, many of us have been studying closely a broad range of incentive problems, particularly the kinds of incentive problems which arise in capital markets with highly leveraged firms (and financial institutions can be viewed as highly leveraged firms).

The term "moral hazard," borrowed from the insurance industry, where some of these problems were first studied, has now become both widely used and understood. With high leverage, bankruptcy laws, and deposit insurance, individuals and firms need not bear the full consequences of their actions; they may be induced to undertake excessive risks. They are in a "heads I win, tails you lose" situation.

Those financial institutions which Ed Kane refers to as zombies— whose true net worth (not the net worth used for accounting purposes or for regulatory purposes, but the true market value of their assets) is negligible or negative have nothing to lose by engaging in these gambles. If the investments pay off, they are out of trouble; if the investments fail, the government picks up the tab. Deposit insurance results in a process of Gresham's law: Depositors have no incentive to look to what the S & L does with their money. Financial institutions which engage in riskier investments can offer higher returns, and only these promised returns matter to the depositors.

The unraveling of the S & Ls can be viewed as the natural—we might say, almost inevitable—consequence of a "bad" incentive structure. Precisely what was wrong with the incentive structure will be discussed in greater detail in the ensuing papers. The greatest failure of the recent legislation is that it failed to address adequately these basic incentive issues.

The press and politicians have often tried to shift the blame onto two other sources. Private greed, reaching out to public bribery and outright fraud, makes for much better front page headlines than do learned discussions of fundamental incentive issues. The irony is that but a little while ago, bankers were held up as among the more staid and respectable members of the community. Did these staid bankers overnight become the rogues they are portrayed to be in the press? Economists believe that people respond to incentives, and by and large, the S & L debacle is the predictable outcome of an incorrect incentive structure—an incentive structure which may serve to attract some less savory or more risk taking individuals, but these are but a minority.

Politicians have also tried to shift blame onto the regulators. If only we had better regulators! or a better regulatory structure! This is nonsense. Sure, the regulators may have slipped up from time to time—but it is remarkable how few (if any) cases of regulatory corruption have been uncovered, given the seeming opportunities. (The check provided by having three separate regulatory agencies may provide part of the explanation. Surprisingly it is precisely this check that the Bush administration now proposes to eliminate.)

But even though regulators are fallible, like all humans, even doubling their number and requiring that they have advanced accounting degrees and pass tests on church attendance would not change the basic problem: Given current accounting procedures, it is difficult if not impossible to detect and/or deal with problems before they have grown to an almost unmanageable scale. Some of the papers in this volume deal with these problems. It is imperative, of course, that we have as good a regulatory structure as we can get and use the most appropriate accounting procedures. Yet the question is, without directly addressing the incentive issues can these regulatory reforms be viewed as much more than larger, or perhaps more attractive, Band-aids, detracting attention from the underlying diseases?

For almost a decade, successive administrations and congresses have evidenced a penny-wise pound-foolish approach to dealing with the problems of our banking system. The popular discussions have focused on the cost to the taxpayers, but we should be clear that far more than taxes are at stake. The banking system performs a vital role in allocating the country's capital—capital which, given the low savings rate of our country, appears all the more scarce. We cannot afford to squander that capital. Yet, to a large extent, that is the real crime of the S & Ls: Our country's scarce investment capital has been put—or as we economists say, allocated—to uses not only not the most productive to which they could have been put; they cannot repay even a fraction of the amount invested. It is as if a substantial fraction (perhaps more than that) of an entire year's savings went down the drain. It is evident that our financial institutions have not performed well in their central role within a capitalist economy.

Inadequacies in our financial system have important spillovers to other aspects of our economy, which go well beyond the misallocation of capital. In Eastern Europe, there has been considerable discussion of the consequences of soft-budget constraints—of what happens when enterprises do not have to meet a bottom line. More recently, there has been growing recognition that soft-budget constraints can come from financial institutions as well as governments. And there has been growing recognition that soft-budget constraints are like a disease—they are contagious. If financial institutions enjoy soft-budget constraints, they will not have the incentive to force those who get capital from them to make the hard decisions that hard-budget constraints impel. On the contrary, the easy availability of funds induces the same kinds of moral hazard problems, which we have suggested are endemic in the financial institutions, to arise within other enterprises. Highly leveraged enterprises have the same incentives to undertake unnecessarily risky gambles.

The high leverage may also have other serious deleterious effects on the economy, as the highly leveraged firms cut back on long-term investments, including investments in R & D, in order to meet the heavy short-run financial demands of their heavy debt. High leverage can not only inhibit long-run growth, it can also contribute significantly to the short-run macro-instability of the economy.

While we have thus developed a system which has been investing literally hundreds of billions unproductively, we have been unwilling to invest even a few million to support basic and applied research to help us understand the basic economics that led us into the mess. The budget for the National Science Foundation was cut ruthlessly by the Reagan Administration—even as it was setting the stage for the problems before us today—and even today it would be embarrassing to tell you how paltry the budget for basic research in economics remains. A firm that spent as little as the government does on research to understand its operations and where it is going would be marked for a short life. It could not survive the competition. Governments are, in many respects, immune from competition, and this, of course, explains a number of aspects of their behavior.

If we are to have a sound and stable financial system, we need to think carefully about how it should be restructured. All too much of the policy discourse has been dominated by those who have direct vested interests in the outcomes. They can, of course, do an excellent job of explaining why they may be hurt or helped by any proposed change. But try as they may to clothe their arguments in terms of general principles, it is hard for them to see the broader picture. And there is more to the analysis than simply a recitation of the general principles—such as the importance of incentives and the moral hazard problem—though the recognition of these general principles would be a marked advance.

We need to think about the costs and benefits of various regulatory structures. We need to think, for instance, not only about our ability to detect incipient insolvencies early, but also about the effects of changes in the banking system not only on competition within the banking system, but on competition among firms. Will the establishment of large national banks, for instance, lead to a flow of funds to large, national firms, impending the flow of funds to small enterprises? The papers in this volume are written in the hope that Congress and the Administration will see the value of thinking before acting and the value of sound research as an aid to thinking about what are admittedly quite complex issues. The ideas under consideration here are just that—ideas to be discussed and debated, ideas that, it is hoped, some of us will take away to ponder: for those of us in academia, as a basis of further research, for those of us in government, as a basis of new policy initiatives.

AFTERWORD

It is now almost a year since the Conference was held. The intervening months have further confirmed the depth of the losses within the S & Ls. The predictions of experts such as Dan Brumbaugh, arguing that the problems of the S & Ls were in fact more widespread than expected, that the banking system itself was in deep trouble, have been borne out. Concern that weakness in the financial system would have further repercussions on the economy has also, unfortunately, been justified, as the economy slid into a recession in the second half of 1990. How deep are the problems of the banking system, and how disastrous the short- and long-run implications for the entire economy only time will tell. But by early 1991, the problems were sufficiently severe that a new initiative, a reform in the banking system, was being launched by the Bush Administration. That initiative, like the earlier legislation on the S & Ls, seems remarkable in its ability to sidestep the underlying problems. The lessons which emerged from our 1990 Conference seem largely to have gone unheeded. It may be useful, therefore, to review briefly some of the fundamental lessons of that Conference, as reflected in the papers in this volume, and extend them to the ongoing debate on banking reform.

If there is a single lesson that emerged clearly, it is this: Financial institutions must have better incentives. Better incentives necessitate their having more at stake in the outcomes of their investment decisions. This translates into a simple prescription: There must be a *substantial* increase in capital requirements.

A substantial increase in capital requirements would reduce the importance of several other more contested issues. For instance, it is widely recognized that the current system of accounting has many faults. It does not give an accurate view of net worth. If a financial institution has long-term loans and interest rates rise dramatically, the value of its portfolio decreases. This leads to a desire for "marking to market" accounting. Critics of marking to market contend that re-evaluating only part of the portfolio can lead to equally misleading results. Thus, financial institutions often own land and buildings subject to marked changes in market value, often rising in periods of high interest rates. The value of the collateral behind loans can often change, thus changing the true market value of loans. Does it make much sense to measure only part of the firm's assets and liabilities accurately? There is a simple answer to that question: It depends on the purpose of the valuation. If we wish to ensure the solvency of financial institutions, then we are much more concerned with errors of underestimation than overestimation. Our "estimates" are not intended to give us an unbiased estimate of the net worth; rather, they are intended to minimize errors arising from judging a financial institution solvent, when it is really insolvent.

Moreover, there is a natural bias in estimation. The financial institution has some control over the re-evaluation of its assets. If there are assets which are undervalued, it can sell those assets, realizing the true market value. If it is concerned with meeting a net worth requirement, it will do this, but it has no symmetric incentive to sell the assets which are overvalued on its books. Thus, the harm done by marking to market only a part of a financial institution's portfolio is limited.

I find these arguments for marking to market convincing, but the importance of marking to market diminishes as capital requirements increase. With high enough capital requirements, the likelihood of not detecting insolvency from a failure to mark to market becomes negligible.

Consider the issue of deposit insurance. Critics of deposit insurance argue that it has contributed greatly to the current problem, because depositors have no incentive to monitor the financial institutions to which they have entrusted their funds. Critics also argue that the current system, in which insurance rates do not depend on the risks undertaken by the bank, provides a strong bias for excessive risk taking (as I said earlier). Supporters of deposit insurance argue that it is important to maintain the stability of the financial system and to protect small depositors.

To a large extent, the arguments on both sides are red herrings. Deposit insurance is not needed to protect depositors. We now have financial institutions which can provide all the transactions services of banks with the full backing of Treasury bills (for example, money market accounts investing in T bills and brokerage accounts, such as Merrill Lynch's CMA accounts). Use of these accounts would be even more widespread were it not for the subsidy provided by the government to S & Ls and banks through its deposit insurance. In principle, deposit insurance is only available for small accounts (under $100,000); thus the fact that there might be certain economies of scope between business lending and business banking services is irrelevant.

The availability of the Federal Reserve as a lender of last resort is what is truly critical in ensuring against runs on banks that are really financially solvent. (The extension of effective "implicit" insurance to large accounts at the "too big to fail" banks may also help to prevent runs, but under the proposals for reform, this insurance is eliminated; it is obviously not seen as vital to the stability of the financial system.)

On the other hand, the argument that but for deposit insurance, depositors would supervise carefully the banks into which they put their money seems to have little more than a grain of truth. It is now widely recognized that information is a public good, and "good management" is a public good. All depositors, and more broadly, all owners and suppliers of credit benefit. Monitoring banks to make sure that their managers make the right decisions is expensive. It, too, is a public good. And like all public goods, it will be in short supply if left to the market alone. The typical depositor has neither the capability nor the incentives nor the time to inspect closely what the bank is doing. To be sure, there are private firms that provide information services—though their record in predicting, with a substantial lead time, the financial plight of our financial institutions does not seem stellar. As in the case of all public goods, however, there is a potential role for government. In thinking about what that role ought to be, we need to recognize clearly the limits of government's capabilities and the nature of the political process which governs its action—a theme to which I shall return shortly.

Again, having sufficiently high capital requirements reduces the importance of the issue of deposit insurance. With high enough capital requirements, the probability that the government will be called on to make good on a bank should be extremely low. Banks will be closed down when they fail to meet the capital requirements, when they are still solvent. Those who have provided the capital will, of course, lose money.

Accordingly, these last investors will have an incentive to monitor what the financial institution is doing. High capital requirements in effect concentrate the responsibility of monitoring among a smaller number, and this ameliorates the free rider (or public goods) problem. With this greater concentration, not only may monitoring be more effective, it may be easier for these investors to exercise control over bank officials.

There is one more advantage. We noted earlier the importance of having deposit insurance rates reflect the risks faced by the financial institution. It is very difficult for public agencies to set up simple rules (which presumably have to be "fair") for setting the insurance premiums. The riskiness is related not just to the category of lending. Commercial real estate may on average be riskier than home mortgages, but there is huge variation in the riskiness of commercial lending. Lending in the Southwest may be riskier than lending in Minnesota. Is it reasonable to assume that the government could fix premiums for commercial lending in one state at a higher rate than in another?

This is the great advantage of the impersonal marketplace: If a bank in the Southwest engaged in extensive commercial lending, those who supplied it with capital to meet its capital requirement would insist on a sufficient return to compensate them for the risks they bore. The market would set the effective "insurance" premium, and there would be little scope to complain about those rates being "unfair."

At the same time, with high enough capital requirements, and the government bearing only a minuscule residual risk, the inequities and inefficiencies of a failure to differentiate premiums are likely to be relatively unimportant.

It should be noted that the capital requirements could be met either by equity or debt; the latter would mean that the financial institution would simply have a layer of uninsured deposits. From this perspective, the capital requirements reform can be viewed as only a mild change in the regulations affecting financial institutions, an explicit recognition of the absence of insurance on a fraction of the deposits. Although on the face of it, it is a mild reform, it could have profound consequences in affecting the incentives of suppliers of capital and the financial institutions themselves.

In thinking about reforms in the financial system and the role of government, one needs to bear in mind the kinds of political pressures which might arise under various circumstances. We need to be aware of incentive (moral hazard) problems for government, just as we are aware of those problems for the private sector. Given the potentially disastrous consequences to the economy if the government had not bailed out the S & Ls or had not protected large depositors in large banks, its actions were perhaps predictable. But to the extent that such government actions can be anticipated, they have predictable (and undesirable) consequences.

Many critics of the banking institutions have argued that the excessive loans to Third World countries—in some cases well in excess of the net worth of the lending institutions—represented bad business judgment. The banks not only failed to assess correctly the risk of those loans, they failed to take into account the most elementary principle of investment—recognizing the correlation among investments. The kinds of macroeconomic events which did in fact occur (changes in the real interest rate, failure of Third World countries to grow as anticipated, and so forth) would put all these loans at risk simultaneously, threatening the financial solvency of the lending institutions. But perhaps the loans were not a mistake: The lending institutions may have recognized that in such contingencies, there was a high probability of a bail-out from the federal government.

Increased capital requirements may make such government bail-outs less likely. Since banks would be shut down while they are still solvent,

with depositors protected, investors might lose some, perhaps a substantial fraction, of their money; but there is likely to be much less concern with investors—owners of banks or holders of bank bonds—being compensated for losses than with depositors, who so often seem like innocent bystanders. Bank investors are likely to get little more favorable hearing to requests for government to make up for bad investment decisions than, say, the investors in airlines are likely to get.

THE CURRENT DEBATE ON REFORM OF THE BANKING SYSTEM

The current debate focuses on four issues: capital requirements, simplifying the regulatory structure, deposit insurance, and "competition" policies. The Bush Administration's proposed reform begins with a doctrinal belief in competition. If a market isn't working, it must be because of government interference. The cure is immediate: reducing government restrictions will enhance competition and make the market work better. It will also meet the need for more capital because relaxing restrictions on those who can own banks (lowering the barrier between manufacturing and banking firms) will enhance a flow of capital to banks and thus strengthen the banking system. In this view, increased net worth requirements will simply exacerbate the banks' problems, since many of them can hardly meet the current low requirements.

In other respects, too, these proposals seem to have gotten everything backward, including reducing the number of regulatory agencies. The difficulty, I have argued, is not an inadequate regulatory structure. The problems which have confronted the S & Ls and the banking system illustrate how difficult it is to monitor a situation, even in a relatively stable banking structure. There are, in fact, some important advantages to our system of multiple regulators: There have been relatively few charges of corruption on the part of the regulators. Though guarding against corruption is not the intent of the current institutional structure, having three separate regulatory agencies involved in monitoring does provide safeguards against it.

Limiting deposit insurance to $100,000 per individual seems irrelevant. Enforcing such a provision appears to be very costly and since, in the case of Big Banks, the government has acted as if everyone is insured anyway, it is hard to see the relevance of this refinement of current law. Virtually no attention is paid to the more fundamental problems of deposit insurance we discussed earlier.

Attempts to increase competition by reducing constraints will, I think, have ambiguous effects. First, I have argued before that more important than monitoring financial institutions is providing them with the right incentive structures. To a large extent, banks and other financial institutions function well because of reputation. Reputation is essential when trading on "promises." And for reputation to be an effective incentive device, there must be profit.[1] Excessive competition can erode profits, and thus erode incentives to maintain one's reputation, with disastrous consequences.[2] This problem is obviously exacerbated when depositors have no incentive to look to the reputation of a bank because their deposits are covered by deposit insurance.

Advocates of deregulation have focused not on the lower profits that might result from deregulation, but from the increased profit opportunities. Regarding some regulations, they may be correct—restrictions on interstate banking make it difficult to benefit from economies associated with dealing with the same bank regardless of where one transacts business within the country. There are other regulations, however, where the adverse effect on profits is less compelling. Allowing banks to enter into other financial activities (such as selling securities) would only significantly enhance profit opportunities if one believed that there were significant economies of scope, or if one believed that those currently specializing in providing these services were less competent than those who had come to specialize in such services in banks. It is hard to see a compelling case for either of these arguments.

The question that needs to be posed, of course, is whether these regulations serve any useful purpose. If they do, we need to balance off the gains from the restrictions with their costs.

Consider first the restrictions on interstate banking. There seem to be some costs to these restrictions. At the same time, we should be aware of some potentially significant costs that may arise from their removal. There is the possibility that with the establishment of large, national banks, funds would flow more easily to large, national firms: large money center banks have an easier task allocating funds to large money center firms. In the debates on this issue, small local banks have expressed concern that they might lose out in the competition. These concerns have been dismissed by those who believe in the virtues of competition: If they cannot survive, let them die! But there may be further ramifications on the economy. Local enterprises and small, new firms may have a harder time raising capital. Competition, in this broader sense, may actually be impeded. Do the limits on interstate banking impose a significant impediment to economic effi-

---

1. This is the essential message of the reputations literature. See, e.g., Eaton, 1986 or Shapiro, 1983.

2. One could argue that, in the absence of deposit insurance, reputation would act as a barrier to entry, and thus even in the absence of any regulations, profits would be sustained. See, e.g., Stiglitz, 1989. On the other hand, in the short run, firms may enter, overly optimistic about the prospects of profits and the ease of establishing a reputation, and thus erode the profits for all the firms in the industry.

ciency? Or are they opposed because they impose a significant impediment to the accumulation of economic power?[3]

Similarly, the essential issue in evaluating the rules concerning who can own banks is the costs and benefits of current restrictions. The wall between producing firms and banking institutions was originally placed to enhance competition. On the one hand, one could argue that with the enhanced international market in which most firms now operate, concerns about competition have diminished. On the other hand, one could ask what is to be gained from reducing the barrier. The concern has been raised that American banks need more capital. But if individuals, pension funds, and other investors are not willing to put up their money to provide banks with more capital, why should we have confidence that those institutions which they own—the producing corporations—would do so? If they are a bad investment for individuals, they are a bad investment for corporations. There is, of course, one good reason: firms that could not get an honest loan from an unrelated third party might be able to get a loan from a bank of which they are a major shareholder. In short, the proposal to lower the ownership barrier puts the long-run solvency of the banking system into further jeopardy.[4]

America's banks and S & Ls are not just "another" industry. From time to time, one or another industry within our country has trouble. Today it is airlines, a few years ago it was steel, at another time it was shoes. What is at stake is not just the capital of a few investors or a few jobs. Strong

---

3. Formally, we are dealing with the economics of the second best. Financial institutions are important because information is imperfect. Whenever information is imperfect, competition is imperfect. With imperfect information, markets are, in general, not efficient (or, to use the technical term, they are not "constrained Pareto efficient"). See Greenwald and Stiglitz, 1986. Investment by one firm in a small town may create important externalities to others, externalities which a local bank may more likely take into account. Critics of this view might argue that these externality effects are "second order." That may or may not be the case. The loss of efficiency from limiting interstate banking may be second, or third order. What is required is a careful balancing of these effects; and in the presence of imperfect information about their magnitude, some assessment of the consequences of various errors in judgment.

4. There is one other explanation, unconvincing to my mind. The barriers to ownership represent an impediment to the effective working of the market for corporate control. This impediment would be important only if one believed that there were too few potential owners/managers of firms within the banking sector, and/or that those outside the banking sector had a comparative advantage in running banks. Moreover, the experience of the 1980s with the market for corporate control is, at best, ambiguous: There is little evidence that it led to enhanced economic efficiency. For a survey of the recent debate, see, e.g., the symposium in the *Journal of Economic Perspectives*, 5 (2), Spring 1991, pp. 15–110.

financial institutions are essential for the vitality of capitalism, both for its short-run stability and its long-run growth. We need to face the facts: Some of our financial institutions have not been doing a good job. We—and our children—are all having to pay the price. By now, there is a consensus that change is needed. The question is, will the reforms address the underlying and basic problems, or will they be superficial remedies, keeping the system going for a little longer, keeping in place the incentives that have already led to massive misallocations of resources, leaving untouched the root causes?

REFERENCES

Eaton, Jonathan, "Lending with Costly Enforcement of Repayment and Potential Fraud," *Journal of Banking and Finance,* 10, 1986, pp. 281–93.

Greenwald, Bruce, and Joseph Stiglitz, "Externalities in Economies with Imperfect Information and Incomplete Markets," *Quarterly Journal of Economics,* May 1986, pp. 229–64.

Shapiro, Carl, "Premiums for High Quality Products as Returns to Reputations," *Quarterly Journal of Economics,* 98, 1983, pp. 659–79.

Stiglitz, J. E., "Imperfect Information in the Product Market," in *Handbook of Industrial Organization, Vol. 1,* eds. R. Scamalensee and R. Willig, pp. 769–847, North Holland (Amsterdam), 1989.

CHAPTER 1

Getting the Incentives Right in the Current Deposit-Insurance System: Successes from the Pre-FDIC Era*

Charles W. Calomiris

Department of Finance
The Wharton School
University of Pennsylvania

National Bureau of Economic Research

MOTIVATION

There is a growing body of evidence that questions the desirability of deposit insurance, at least in its current form. Careful studies of the recent experiences of federal- and state-insured thrifts by Barth et al. (1989), Brewer (1989), Kane (1988), Horvitz (1989), and many others add credence to the view that insurance itself can be destabilizing. For example, bad initial realizations on investments were translated into a thrift and bank debacle in Texas because they were combined with high initial leverage and increased risk taking by troubled institutions, which responded to the initial adverse shocks by aggressively entering the speculative real estate loan market. High leverage and increased risk taking presumably were tolerated more than they would have been by depositors, absent

---

*I thank the *Journal of Economic History* for permission to use part of "Is Deposit Insurance Necessary? A Historical Perspective."

insurance. By promoting excessive leverage and increased risk taking deposit insurance turned a bad situation into one much worse. The lack of political will by Congress and regulators to close insolvent institutions prolonged the "desperation" risk taking and further magnified losses to the insurance funds.

The renewed discussion of the purpose and proper structure of deposit insurance has focused attention on the history of financial intermediaries and their regulation. Historical evidence on the motivation and performance of pre-FDIC state-level bank liability insurance systems provides more than just additional examples of the sorts of problems observable today. First, the benefits of federal deposit insurance may only be appreciated from the perspective of earlier systems that lacked such protection. The goal of insurance has always been primarily preventative, and thus its successes are inherently invisible. Second, it is more difficult to isolate costs attributable to deposit insurance (in inducing greater risk-taking by member banks) when all banks are insured. Earlier experience with state-level insurance of a subset of banks provides unique "controlled experiments" in which the relative performances of insured institutions can be compared directly, within and across states, with those of uninsured banks under various regulatory regimes.

I will focus on four questions often raised in current debates over regulatory reform that historical evidence seems uniquely suited to address.

1. Was there a legitimate concern that motivated bank liability insurance?

2. Were there possible alternative solutions to this problem that were equally successful at a lower cost?

3. What specific aspects of historical bank insurance schemes contributed to their relative success or failure?

4. Which current proposals for reform are most attractive in light of the "lessons of history"?

WHY HAVE BANK LIABILITY INSURANCE?

Bank insurance in the United States began in 1829 with New York's Safety Fund system, which was inspired by the voluntary coinsurance arrangements of a group of Cantonese merchants. As Golembe (1960) argues convincingly, here and in all subsequent cases (including the FDIC), the primary intended function of liability insurance was to provide protection against the possible collapse of the payments system accompanying a banking panic.

To understand the potential benefits of insurance requires first, a theory of how banking panics occur, and second, an explanation of how insurance, or other preventative measures, can prevent panics. Calomiris and Gorton (1991) review and evaluate the recent theoretical literature on banking panics in light of new evidence from the National Banking era. Calomiris and Schweikart (1991) provide complementary analysis of the Panic of 1857. The salient facts about panics during this period are the following: Few banks actually failed during panics, while practically all banks in the country were forced to suspend convertibility for some period of time (one to three months), during which their claims (notes or cashier checks) circulated at discounts (typically between 0.5 and 4 percent for New York City cashier checks during the National Banking era). Panics occurred at business-cycle, and seasonal, peaks, during which bank leverage was high and the variance of "news" about the state of the economy was greatest. Observable adverse shocks of sufficient magnitude prompted panics. Whenever commercial failures (seasonally adjusted) increased by more than 50 percent, and stock prices fell by more than 7.9 percent, during any three-month period, a banking panic immediately followed (see Table 1.1).

The challenge for theoretical models of banking panics is to explain why observable aggregate shocks with small eventual consequences for the banking system should cause widespread disintermediation and suspension of convertibility. Theory must also explain the optimality of the dependence on demandable debt to finance bank loan portfolios, since maturity-matched debt or equity would eliminate the first-come first-served rule for depositors that makes a panic physically possible.

Recent models have provided explanations for the occurrence of panics, and the existence of demandable-debt banking. Gorton (1989) argues that because bank loans are not marked to market, depositors are unable to discover which banks are most likely to be affected by an observable adverse shock. Under these circumstances, even if depositors know that only a small subset of banks are likely to fail in response to an observable shock, they may find it advantageous to withdraw their funds temporarily until the uncertainty over the incidence of the shock is resolved. Calomiris and Kahn (1991) and Calomiris, Kahn, and Krasa (1991) argue that despite the costs associated with demandable debt (that is, the potential for panics), it was optimal because of the discipline it placed on the banker during normal times, given asymmetric information (between depositors and their banker) about the banker's behavior. It is also possible to argue that demandable debt provided benefits during banking panics. By prompting suspension of convertibility it provided an incentive for banks speedily to resolve uncertainty about the incidence of a particular shock (see Gorton, 1989, and Calomiris and Gorton, 1991).

Thus in the presence of asymmetric information, occasional banking panics can occur "in equilibrium." The possibility of panics, however, is not necessarily inherent in banking. Many banking systems, within and

Table 1.1 Three-Month Periods of Unusual Stock Price Decline, 1871–1909

	Nominal Difference (percent)	Real Difference (percent)	Seasonal Difference Liabilities of Commercial Failures[a] (percent)
1873 (June–Sept.)	−7.9	−7.9	NA
1874 (Feb.–May)	−6.3	−4.0	NA
1876 (Feb.–May)	−7.9	−3.3	30.0
1877 (Jan.–Apr.)	−17.2	−12.9	−8.1[b]
1880 (Feb.–May)	−8.3	−2.6	−11.5
1882 (Aug.–Nov.)	−5.6	−1.1	26.6[c]
1883 (May–Aug.)	−5.4	−0.5	115.8[d]
1884 (Feb.–May)	−12.6	−8.5	202.9
1884 (Aug.–Nov.)	−8.8	−4.5	−6.3[c]
1886 (Feb.–May)	−5.0	−0.2	−27.3
1887 (May–Aug.)	−7.7	−6.5	168.4[d]
1890 (July–Oct.)	−8.4	−13.3	50.3[c]
1893 (Feb.–May)	−12.2	−7.4	428.3
1893 (May–Aug.)	−15.4	−6.6	389.2[d]
1895 (Sept.–Dec.)	−10.2	−8.8	25.2
1896 (May–Aug.)	−13.1	−11.1	71.2
1900 (Apr.–July)	−7.4	−5.0	148.0
1902 (Sept.–Dec.)	−8.8	−13.6	−3.8
1903 (Feb.–May)	−9.5	−4.7	23.3
1903 (May–Aug.)	−12.9	−12.6	22.7
1907 (Jan.–Apr.)	−12.3	−13.1	−7.7
1907 (May–Aug.)	−7.1	−7.9	110.0
1907 (Aug.–Nov.)	−17.0	−14.7	143.5

a. Data on seasonal differences of business failures are for four-month periods ending the month after the corresponding stock decline, unless otherwise noted. Quarterly data exist for 1875–94; monthly data exist after 1894.

b. Uses average of first- and second-quarter data.

c. Uses average of third- and fourth-quarter data.

d. Uses average of second- and third-quarter data.

SOURCE: Charles W. Calomiris and Gary Gorton, "The Origins of Banking Panics," in *Financial Markets and Financial Crises*, ed. R. Glenn Hubbard (Chicago), 1991.

outside the United States, have managed to avoid banking panics. Gorton (1985, 1989), Gorton and Mullineaux (1987), Calomiris (1989, 1991), Calomiris and Schweikart (1991), and Calomiris and Gorton (1991) have stressed that the risk of panics created incentives to form private coalitions or networks of banks to avert panics, or to lessen their costs. Panics could be averted if the coalition could credibly coinsure against the observable shock to the system. For example, if banks as a group agreed to bear the risk of any individual bank's default, then so long as depositors were confident of the solvency of the group, they would have no incentive to withdraw their funds. The mutual benefit of such coinsurance is the avoidance of a banking panic and the consequent disruption to the banking system of commercial payments and credit.

Government insurance, of course, provides an alternative to private coinsurance that similarly removes the incentive for depositors to run their banks during periods when the incidence of aggregate shocks is uncertain. Government intervention is only necessary, however, if private coordination among banks is infeasible. This brings us to our second question: Why did alternative private solutions to the threat of banking panics provide insufficient protection to the banking system, particularly in the case of the United States?

SUCCESSFUL ALTERNATIVES TO GOVERNMENT INTERVENTION AND THEIR LIMITS

Successful examples of the application of the principle of coinsurance by private groups of banks fall into two categories: branch-banking systems and city clearinghouse coalitions.

Branch banking reduced the threat of bank panics in two ways. First, opportunities for diversification for each bank lessened the probability that any aggregate shock would result in bank failures, and hence there was less opportunity for confusion about the incidence of default risk. Second, branching enhanced coordination by limiting the number of banks in any system, thereby promoting coordination during crises. With fewer banks, the incentive to monitor is greater (since the benefits from monitoring are shared). Furthermore, branching increased the ability of banks to monitor one another through multiple overlapping locations.

Within the United States branch banking, when it was allowed, was extraordinarily successful in dealing with the threat of panics. During the antebellum period, branch banking was confined almost exclusively to the South, where it thrived in Georgia, the Carolinas, Tennessee, and Virginia. As early as 1837, branching banks in the South coordinated their suspension and resumption on a regional basis (see Govan, 1936). In the Panic of 1857 there was similarly successful coordination at the state and regional level (see Calomiris and Schweikart, 1988, 1991). Calomiris and Schweikart (1988), and Gorton (1990) argue that the lower risk associated with branch-banking states in the South was reflected in lower discount rates on Southern bank notes in New York and Philadelphia (adjusted for other factors, such as bank leverage and distance). As we shall see below, the successes of branch-banking systems in limiting the rate of bank failure and improving the resiliency of a banking system to adverse disturbances are visible in the postbellum U.S. experience as well.

Evidence from other countries reinforces the view that unit banking inhibits diversification and coordination among banks, and thereby promotes vulnerability to panics. Bordo (1985) provides a useful survey of banking and securities-market collapses in six countries from 1870 to 1933. Summarizing the literature, Bordo attributes to the absence of branch banking the peculiar vulnerability of the U.S. banking system. The panics experienced in the United States in the late nineteenth century were viewed as a curiosity in other countries. Recent studies of the Canadian branch-banking system provide an interesting contrast to the U.S. experience. Unlike the United States, Canada's banking system allowed nationwide branching from an early date and relied on coordination among a small number of large branching banks to resolve threats to the system, with the Bank of Montreal playing a central role in providing and coordinating interbank assistance. Breckenridge (1910) and Williamson (1989) show that bank failures were few, depositors' losses were relatively small, and suspension of convertibility never occurred. Schembri and Hawkins (1988) provide evidence that Canadian branches in the United States often served as safe havens during U.S. banking panics.

Beginning in 1853 with the New York City Clearing House Association, private self-regulating clearinghouse coalitions formed in cities provided many benefits of branch-banking systems. Banks agreed to make markets in each other's liabilities, to make interbank loans, and to coordinate suspensions and resumptions of convertibility to minimize disruption during panics. In all cases, self-imposed regulations and mutual monitoring kept members from "free riding" on collective coinsurance (see Gorton, 1985, and Gorton and Mullineaux, 1987). Moreover, during crises, the fact that a member bank remained in the coalition signaled its creditworthiness to uninformed depositors. Because clearinghouses were confined to cities, and therefore represented only a fraction of the banking system, they were unable to rid the system of panics. Statewide, much less nationwide, self-regulating clearinghouses were infeasible because of the difficulty in coordinating behavior and enforcing regulations among many geographically isolated unit banks. In such a system the costs of monitoring may be prohibitive, and because the benefits of any bank's monitoring another bank are shared with all other banks in the coalition, coalitions of many banks cannot produce incentive-compatible interbank monitoring.

In summary, branch banking and clearinghouse coordination shared the important common features of collective self-regulation and incentive-compatible interbank monitoring, which ensured that banks could protect each other without creating perverse incentives for member banks to take on excessive risks. Member banks invested in interbank monitoring because their fortunes were interrelated, and because the size of the coalitions was small enough that the benefits to an individual bank from monitoring (which were shared) did not exceed the costs (which were private). Self-regulating coalitions of banks typically saw memberships of no greater than 40 banks. Physical proximity of member banks also enhanced interbank monitoring. Clearly, the application of the principle of coinsurance and self-regulation was limited in the United States by prohibitions on branch banking. Unit banking laws meant that as the geographic scope of the economy expanded, so would the number of banks. In a system of several thousand banks, incentive-compatible monitoring becomes impossible. City bank coalitions persisted, and some states maintained state-chartered branch-banking systems alongside nationally chartered unit banks, but such partial coalitions were unable to prevent nationwide panics.

The destabilizing effect of unit banking—which creates more opportunities for confusion about the incidence of shocks, and limits the system's ability to coordinate in response to shocks—was understood as early as the antebellum period in the United States. Indeed, studies of the political history of deposit insurance show that it was the desire by special interest groups to preserve unit banking, and their political influence, that gave rise to the perceived need for deposit insurance, both in the antebellum and postbellum periods. It was understood that branching provided a more stable banking system than unit banking, and deposit insurance was developed as an alternative means to provide stability without giving up unit banking (see Golembe, 1960, and White, 1983). All six antebellum states that enacted liability insurance legislation were unit-banking states. In the antebellum branch-banking South neither government insurance nor urban clearinghouses developed. Similarly, the eight state insurance systems created from 1908 to 1917 were all in unit-banking states.

RELATIVE SUCCESSES OF DEPOSIT-INSURANCE SYSTEMS AND THEIR ALTERNATIVES

The variety of regulatory choices made at the state level allow one to evaluate the characteristics of successful and unsuccessful insurance systems, and to compare the performance of various regulatory regimes (unit banking with or without insurance, and branch banking).

Antebellum Successes and Failures

New York's Safety Fund was established in 1829, funded by limited annual contributions of members, and regulated by the state government. Losses severely depleted the accumulated resources of the fund from 1837 to 1841 until, in 1842, it ceased to be able to repay losses of failed banks, and thus ceased to provide protection to the payments system.

New York in 1838 created an alternative to the insured system through its free banking statute, and allowed Safety Fund banks to switch to that system. The depletion in membership of the insured system kept its losses small during subsequent panics. After 1840 Safety Fund banks comprised a small and continually shrinking proportion of total banks and total bank assets. Losses were also limited by the 1842 restriction on coverage of member banks' liabilities to bank notes, thus excluding the growing liability base in deposits.

Ultimately, the small number of banks that chose to remain in the system, and make continuing annual contributions to its fund, did manage to repay in 1866 the obligations incurred some 30 years earlier; but this "success" was not anticipated in the intervening years (as shown by the high note discount rates attached to failed member banks' notes during the 1850s), and the fund did not protect current bank liabilities or the payments system ex ante, as it was intended to do.

Not only did the system fail to provide protection to the payments system, it suffered unusually large losses due to fraud or unsound banking practices during the period that it did provide protection to member banks. While a supervisory authority was established to prevent fraud and excessive risk-taking, supervision was ineffectual, and fraud and unsafe practices were common. Ten of 16 member-bank failures prior to 1842 (the period when insurance was still perceived as effective) were traceable to fraud or unsafe practices. Moreover, such problems were not detected until after they had imposed large losses on the fund.

The failure of the Safety Fund was not the fault of external shocks, severe as they were. In aggregate, banking capital was large relative to losses, and thus coinsurance among all New York banks would have been feasible (see Golembe and Warburton, 1958). Rather, it was the design of the insurance system that made it weak. Upper bounds on annual premiums prevented adequate *ex ante* insurance during panics, and ineffectual supervision allowed large risk-takers to free ride on other banks. Finally, adverse selection caused a retreat from the system through charter switching to the alternative free-banking system, once solvent banks realized the extent of losses.

Vermont and Michigan followed New York's example and suffered its problems. In Vermont, banks were even allowed to join and depart at will. It took only two bank failures to cause the dissolution of that system, one due to fraud and the other of a bank which joined the system after its prospects had deteriorated. Again, an incentive-compatible, broadly based system could have provided coinsurance among banks, but adverse selection and poor supervision prevented this.

Michigan's system, created in 1836, collapsed because it (like the other two systems) depended for its resources on accumulated contributions to the collective fund, which would be used to support banks during a crisis. The Michigan system had no time to accumulate a sufficient fund prior to the Panics of 1837 and 1839, and thus was unable to provide protection.

Not all antebellum experiments ended so disastrously as these three.

Indiana enacted a different sort of liability insurance plan in 1834, one based on the principles of self-regulation and unlimited mutual liability that would later be imitated by private clearinghouses. The Indiana system did not suffer the supervisory laxity or membership retreat of New York and Vermont, nor the illiquidity of Michigan and New York. Coverage was broad based and there was no problem attracting and keeping members. During its 30-year history no insured bank failed. There was a suspension of convertibility in 1837, and again in 1839, but this was the last time banks were even forced to suspend. During the regional panic of 1854–55 and the national Panic of 1857 all insured banks maintained operations and convertibility. During those same panics 69 of 126 nonmember, uncoordinated free banks failed in Indiana.

The Indiana system relied on bankers themselves to make and enforce laws and regulations through a Board of Directors, and, what was important, gave it authority to decide when to close a bank. Unlimited mutual liability provided bankers the incentive to regulate and enforce properly. The Indiana system was imitated in Ohio and Iowa, with similarly successful results. Ohio's law granted its Board of Control even greater authority than Indiana's Board, allowing it virtually unlimited discretionary powers during a banking crisis, including the right to force banks to make loans to one another. Interbank loans were successfully used during the Panic of 1857 to avoid suspension of convertibility. The insured banks, it seems, even came to the assistance of nonmember banks during the Panic, as indicated by flows of interbank loans. Only one Ohio bank failed during the crisis, and it was not a member of the insured system. Iowa's system was in place for a shorter and more stable period, but its operation was similarly successful.

Like clearinghouses, these three successful insurance schemes aligned the incentive and authority to regulate, and made insurance protection credible through unlimited mutual liability among banks. Like Southern branch banks in the Panics of 1837 and 1857 these systems were able to minimize systemic disruption through a coordinated, incentive-compatible response. They were brought to an end not by insolvency, but by federal taxation of bank notes designed to promote the National Banking System.

The Second, Postbellum Wave of State Insurance

The eight deposit-insurance fund systems of the early twentieth century failed to learn the lessons of the antebellum experience; they repeated and compounded the earlier errors of New York, Vermont, and Michigan. Supervisory authority was placed in government hands, not with member banks, and often its use or disuse was politically motivated (see Robb, 1921). Furthermore, the numbers of banks insured were many more than in the antebellum systems (often several hundred), and as noted above, this further reduced the incentive for a bank to monitor and report the misbehavior of its neighbor banks, since the payoff from detection was shared with so many, and the cost of monitoring was private.

During the halcyon days for agriculture, from 1914 to mid-1920, deposit insurance prompted unusually high growth, particularly of small rural banks on thin capital. The banks in insured states grew faster, were smaller, and had lower capital ratios than their state-chartered counterparts in fast-growing, or neighboring states. Tables 1.2 and 1.3 compare the growth, average size, and capitalization of insured state-chartered banking systems, first by comparing the highest growth insured and uninsured systems, and then by comparing insured-banking systems with neighboring uninsured state-chartered systems, and uninsured national-chartered banking in each of the states. Table 1.4 reports regression results that confirm the unusually high growth of state-chartered insured banks (controlling for other variables) relative to those of other agricultural states. A decomposition among voluntary and compulsory insur-

Table 1.2   High-Growth States: Insured versus Uninsured

	Assets 1914/ Assets 1920		Assets ($000) per Bank in 1920		Capital/Total Assets, 1920	
	National Bank	State Bank	National Bank	State Bank	National Bank	State Bank
Arkansas	.408	.379	1020	456	.084	.085
Colorado	.522	.450	1801	460	.048	.083
Idaho	.341	.316	1088	487	.059	.077
Iowa	.507	.503	1301	562	.057	.067
Minnesota	.509	.406	1979	425	.054	.069
Missouri	.490	.540	5507	572	.063	.072
Montana	.495	.489	761	436	.077	.091
New Mexico	.501	.352	963	347	.073	.119
Wyoming	.314	.315	1365	300	.048	.090
Average	.454	.418	1755	448	.063	.084
Kansas	.463	.380	977	326	.066	.079
Mississippi	.506	.335	1843	664	.069	.066
Nebraska	.537	.335	1566	335	.057	.082
North Dakota	.485	.367	563	248	.068	.081
Oklahoma	.309	.259	1096	346	.060	.070
South Dakota	.400	.351	862	395	.053	.062
Texas	.414	.391	1588	375	.071	.112
Average	.447	.344	1231	391	.064	.078

SOURCE: Charles W. Calomiris, "Do Vulnerable Economies Need Deposit Insurance," in Philip Brock, ed., *If Texas Were Chile: Financial Risk and Regulation in Commodity-Exporting Economies* (Washington D.C., 1991).

Table 1.3   State-Chartered Regional Comparison: Insured versus Uninsured

	Assets, 1914/ Assets, 1920	Assets ($000) per Bank, 1920	Capital/ Total Assets, 1920
Arkansas	.379	456	.085
Colorado	.450	460	.083
Iowa	.503	563	.067
Idaho	.316	487	.077
Minnesota	.406	425	.069
Missouri	.540	572	.072
Montana	.489	436	.091
New Mexico	.352	347	.119
Wyoming	.315	300	.090
Average	.417	450	.084
Kansas	.380	326	.079
North Dakota	.367	248	.081
Nebraska	.335	335	.082
Oklahoma	.259	346	.070
South Dakota	.351	376	.062
Texas	.391	374	.112
Average	.347	334	.081
Alabama	.553	543	.087
Georgia	.412	534	.097
South Carolina	.390	536	.085
Average	.452	538	.090
Mississippi	.335	664	.066

SOURCE: Charles W. Calomiris, "Do Vulnerable Economies Need Deposit Insurance," in Philip Brock, ed., *If Texas Were Chile: Financial Risk and Regulation in Commodity-Exporting Economies* (Washington D.C., 1991).

ance laws reveals that the incentives to grow were especially pronounced in the compulsory insurance systems (where the potential for cross-subsidization, or free riding through excessive risk-taking, was highest).

When agricultural prices fell, insured banking systems suffered higher rates of decline than uninsured state-chartered banks in agricultural states, and showed an even greater difference in the asset shortfalls (relative to deposits) of insolvent banks. All the insurance-fund systems collapsed during the 1920s (see FDIC, 1956, for details). Insured systems also saw greater delays in closing and liquidating insolvent banks, foreshadowing the politically motivated delays during the current thrift crisis (see Calomiris, 1991).

The three states that had long-lived, free-entry, compulsory deposit insurance (which provided the worst and most prolonged incentives for

Table 1.4   Regression Results: Early Asset Growth of State-Chartered Banks[a]

Dependent Variable: Growth in Total Assets of State-Chartered Banks, 1914–20

Independent Variables	Coefficient	Standard Error	Significance Level
Intercept	0.156	0.468	0.741
National Bank Growth	0.682	0.147	0.000
(Reserve Center)× (National Bank Growth)[b]	−0.115	0.063	0.080
Growth in Land Values, 1914–20	0.526	0.334	0.127
Ratio of Farm to Nonfarm Population	−0.328	0.655	0.621
Presence of Voluntary Insurance	0.327	0.251	0.205
Presence of Compulsory Insurance	0.609	0.189	0.004

$R^2 = 0.683$
$R^{-2} = 0.607$

Dependent Variable: Growth in Total Assets of State-Chartered Banks, 1914–20

Independent Variables	Coefficient	Standard Error	Significance Level
Intercept	0.101	0.465	0.829
National Bank Growth	0.681	0.147	0.000
(Reserve Center)× (National Bank Growth)[b]	−0.132	0.060	0.038
Growth in Land Values, 1914–20	0.555	0.333	0.107
Ratio of Farm to Nonfarm Population	−0.283	0.654	0.669
Presence of Voluntary or Compulsory Insurance	0.518	0.165	0.004

$R^2 = 0.670$
$R^{-2} = 0.607$

a. Asset growth is defined as the log difference of total assets. All variables are defined at the state level for a sample of 32 agricultural states.

b. National bank growth in each state is used as a control for state-chartered bank growth. In reserve-center states, national bank growth may be larger, as it reflects growth of correspondent banks outside of the state as well. To control for this difference, I interact national banking growth with an indicator variable for states with reserve centers.

SOURCE: Charles W. Calomiris, "Do Vulnerable Economies Need Deposit Insurance," in Philip Brock, ed., *If Texas Were Chile: Financial Risk and Regulation in Commodity-Exporting Economies* (Washington D.C., 1991).

risk-taking) experienced the most drastic losses by far among the state- and national-chartered systems. While several state-chartered systems experienced shocks comparable to those of the three (North Dakota, South Dakota, and Nebraska), in no other cases were the asset shortfalls of insolvent banks nearly large enough to threaten the capital of the banking system as a whole (see Table 1.5). In contrast, these states showed shortfalls of between one and a half and five times remaining bank equity of state banks.

Contrasting the Performance of Insured and Branch Banking

The failures of deposit insurance systems stand in sharp contrast to their perceived political alternative, branch banking. States that allowed branch banking saw much lower failure rates, reflecting the unusually high survivability of branching banks, and responded well to the agricultural crisis by consolidating banks and expanding branching systems, where this was allowed.

From 1921 to 1929 only 37 branching banks failed in the United States, almost all of which operated only one or two branches. Branching failures were only 4 percent of branch banking facilities, almost an order of magnitude less than the failure rate of unit banks for this period. In states hard hit by the agricultural crisis, branch banks' failure rates were roughly a fourth those of unit banks. In Arizona, Mississippi, and South Carolina—three hard-hit states with statewide branching networks—existing branches survived especially well, and new entry into banking (allowed only in Arizona and South Carolina) was especially strong (see Calomiris, 1991, for details).

Table 1.6 reports regression results on bank growth from 1920 to 1926, and 1920 to 1930. States that permitted expansion of branching saw substantially higher (and statistically significant) asset growth relative to other states, controlling for other influences. A comparison across the two time periods shows that the influence of branching persisted, and grew stronger with the passage of time. The effect of the presence of deposit insurance was negative, but this mainly reflected a temporary retreat from the state systems until after the insurance laws were repealed. By 1930, previously insured state systems had recovered to roughly the same levels of assets as other unit-banking state systems.

Contemporaries often remarked on the unusual survivability and growth of branch banks in the face of the crisis. Many states altered their branch-banking laws in response to these observations. From 1924 to 1939 the number of (full or limited) branch-banking states rose from 18 to 36. Four of the eight states that previously had opted for deposit insurance were among those liberalizing their branching restrictions during this period.

Table 1.5 Estimated Asset Shortfalls of Failed Banks Relative to Remaining-Bank Equity in "Severe Failure" States

	National Banks					State-Chartered Banks						All Banks	
	Deposits of Suspended Banks ($000), 1921–30[a]	Number of Liq. Relative to Suspensions[b]	Avg. Size of Liq. Bks. Rel. to Susp.[c]	Rate of Asset Shortfall[d]	Estimated Shortfall[e]	Total Bank Equity ($000), June 1930	Deposits of Sus. Banks, 1921–30[a]	Liq./ Susp.[b]	Size Ratio[c]	Rate of Asset Shortfall[d]	Estimated Shortfall[e]	Total Bank Equity ($000), June 1930	Ratio of Shortfall to Equity[f]
Arizona	1,256	.67	.83	.50	349	3,815	15,056	.80	.06	.09	65	8,496	.03
Colorado	11,003	.94	.45	.40	1,862	13,776	12,187	.95	.95	.32	3,520	10,273	.22
Georgia	16,538	.84	.09	.49	613	39,064	46,318	.75	.70	.56	13,618	39,805	.18
Idaho	10,601	.81	.65	.53	2,958	4,612	9,185	.85	.63	.51	2,509	4,983	.57
Iowa	55,984	.79	.50	.31	6,855	35,750	138,995	.75	.66	.46	31,649	74,935	.35
Minnesota	28,338	.97	.59	.42	6,812	69,387	80,634	.77	.47	.52	15,174	38,417	.20
Montana	16,287	.87	.44	.66	4,115	9,999	31,361	.89	.47	.48	6,297	9,947	.52
Nebraska	13,695	.80	.94	.56	5,767	26,083	78,093	.85	1.04	.65	44,872	27,760	.94
North Dakota	17,438	.84	.80	.55	6,445	9,210	45,199	.92	1.05	.83	36,240	9,695	2.26
Oklahoma	27,364	.72	.70	.57	7,861	41,251	38,986	.79	.28	.44	3,794	11,493	.22
South Carolina	12,153	.92	.57	.49	3,123	11,665	50,970	.91	.58	.34	9,147	17,069	.43
South Dakota	21,109	.93	.60	.49	5,772	8,477	91,619	.77	1.00	.76	53,615	10,848	3.07
Wyoming	9,154	.91	.45	.30	1,125	4,819	7,536	.80	.48	.46	1,331	3,844	.28

a. Deposits are defined at the time of bank suspension.

b. The number of bank liquidations relative to suspensions measures the proportion of suspended banks that were liquidated.

c. The average size of liquidated banks is divided by the average size of suspended banks to produce this ratio.

d. The rate of asset shortfall equals 1 minus the ratio of the value of liquidated assets to deposit liabilities.

e. The estimated shortfall is the product of the preceding four columns.

f. The all-bank ratio of shortfall to equity divides estimated asset shortfall for state and national banks by the equity of surviving banks of both types.

SOURCE: Charles W. Calomiris, "Do Vulnerable Economies Need Deposit Insurance," in Philip Brock, ed., *If Texas Were Chile: Financial Risk and Regulation in Commodity-Exporting Economies* (Washington D.C., 1991).

APPLYING HISTORICAL LESSONS TO CURRENT REFORM

The Best of All Possible Worlds

I conclude that the most desirable means by which to achieve banking system stability would be unlimited branch banking, combined with the sort of privately administered formal insurance programs of antebellum Indiana, Ohio, and Iowa. Such a system would be adequate to protect the payments system from exogenous disturbances that could produce banking panics (Ely, 1990, has also proposed a bank coinsurance plan; see also related arguments in Calomiris and Kahn, 1990a, 1990b). The greatest threats to systemic stability historically were unit banking, and ill-conceived attempts to promote stability through government-controlled insurance that actually had quite the opposite effect.

The problems of moral hazard and adverse selection which arise in government-controlled deposit-insurance systems are likely to be much more pronounced in today's federal insurance system than in the earlier state programs I have examined. The state insurance systems of the 1920s limited interest paid on deposits, typically required ratios of capital to deposits in excess of 10 percent, and were funded only by the accumulated contributions of member banks. Today's federal insurance, in contrast, does not restrict interest, requires a trivial proportion of capital to deposits, and is supported by the full faith and credit of the federal government. Thus today's financial intermediaries can maintain higher leverage and attract depositors more easily by paying higher interest with virtually no risk of default. From this perspective the unprecedented losses of Texas banks and thrifts in the 1980s should come as no surprise. As in the 1920s there was a risky "upside" to bet on (this time oil rather than agriculture) and any "downside" losses would be shared through the put option inherent in deposit insurance.

Although it is likely that such a coinsurance system of branching banks, if allowed, would develop in the absence of government regulation mandating it, government involvement in regulating such a system still might be desirable. The government's role would be to regulate entry into coinsuring groups of banks, and encourage competition among multiple (say, three), groups of nationwide coinsuring branch banks. These groups would operate like today's futures market clearinghouses, with members regulating each other's behavior and insuring each other's commitments. If the banking system—like today's futures markets—consisted of several groups competing nationwide for business, problems of monopolization that would come from a single nationwide coinsuring group could be avoided.

One might also argue, notwithstanding the evidence from the 1920s

Table 1.6   Regression Results: Late Asset Growth and Bank Size of State-Chartered Banks[a]

Dependent Variable: Growth in Total Assets of State-Chartered Banks, 1920–6

Independent Variable	Coefficient	Standard Error	Significance Level
Intercept	0.544	0.450	0.239
National Bank Growth	0.602	0.235	0.018
(Reserve Center)× (National Bank Growth)[b]	0.178	0.098	0.084
Ratio of Farm to Nonfarm Population	−0.404	0.346	0.254
Growth in Land Values, 1920–5	0.037	0.541	0.946
Business Failure Rate, 1921–5			
Business Failure Rate, 1917–20	−0.040	0.038	0.308
Presence of Deposit Insurance (excluding Nebraska)[c]	−0.190	0.126	0.146
Out-of-city Branch Banking[d]	0.179	0.124	0.163
Within-city Branch Banking[d]	0.204	0.132	0.136

$R^2 = 0.601$

$R^{-2} = 0.462$

Dependent Variable: Growth in Total Assets of State-Chartered Banks, 1920–30

Independent Variable	Coefficient	Standard Error	Significance Level
Intercept	1.539	0.449	0.002
National Bank Growth	0.124	0.200	0.539
(Reserve Center)× (National Bank Growth)[b]	0.078	0.115	0.502
Ratio of Farm to Nonfarm Population	−0.936	0.405	0.030
Growth in Land Values, 1920–30	−0.386	0.551	0.490
Business Failure Rate, 1921–9			
Business Failure Rate, 1917–20	−0.072	0.044	0.118
Presence of Deposit Insurance (excluding Nebraska)[c]	−0.065	0.140	0.647

Table 1.6 (*Continued*)

Dependent Variable: Growth in Total Assets of State-Chartered Banks, 1920–30

Independent Variable	Coefficient	Standard Error	Significance Level
Out-of-city Branch Banking[d]	0.398	0.150	0.014
Within-city Branch Banking[d]	0.428	0.161	0.014
$R^2 = 0.625$			
$R^{-2} = 0.495$			

a. Asset growth is defined as the log difference of total assets. All variables are defined at the state level for a sample of 32 agricultural states.

b. National bank growth in each state is used as a control for state-chartered bank growth. In reserve-center states, national bank growth may be larger, as it reflects growth of correspondent banks outside of the state as well. To control for this difference, I interact national banking growth with an indicator variable for states with reserve centers.

c. Nebraska's insured banks remained open long after they were known to be insolvent. Thus data for Nebraska on total assets of state-chartered banks overstate actual state-chartered bank assets for the 1920s. For this reason Nebraska was excluded from the group of insured states in these regressions.

d. The indicator variable for out-of-city branching takes a value of 1 for states that allowed branching outside the home city of the bank, 0 otherwise. The within-city indicator takes a value of 1 for states that allowed branching only within a bank's home city, 0 otherwise.

SOURCE: Charles W. Calomiris, "Do Vulnerable Economies Need Deposit Insurance," in Philip Brock, ed., *If Texas Were Chile: Financial Risk and Regulation in Commodity-Exporting Economies* (Washington D.C., 1991).

reported here, that government should provide some ultimate protection against systemic collapse of the banking system—that is, against shocks greater than those that could be absorbed by banking group capital. To this end the government might establish an insurance arrangement with a "deductible." For example, coinsurance among banks would be relied on entirely for reimbursing depositors of the first banks that failed; the government would share increasingly in subsequent losses of failed banks. This would provide incentives for interbank discipline and for market discipline of banking coalitions as a whole without risking systemic collapse.

Moreover, it is likely the government would intervene in such crises even without an explicit commitment to do so. It would be best to have that commitment, and the conditions under which it might apply, spelled out in advance. This would limit ad hoc congressional intervention to serve special interests. Recent reform of deposit insurance in Chile provides an example of specific state-contingent government commitments for aid that depend on coinsurance from private parties (see Ramirez and Rosende, 1989).

An additional advantage to interbank coinsurance is the incentive it would create *ex post* for banks to encourage the speedy closure of failed institutions. Historically, privately administered coinsuring groups of banks have acted promptly to close failed banks and thereby limited desperation risk-taking. If banks were given a stake in the losses of failed banks, they would close them rapidly; lacking the authority to do so, surviving group members would lobby politicians and regulators to close them. This would provide an important countervailing lobbying group to the failed bankers.

Would the existence of limited insurance of banking groups lead whole groups of banks to adopt high-risk strategies to take advantage of government insurance? It is extremely unlikely that an entire group of banks would opt for high risk. So long as banks' risks of failure remain somewhat independent, a coalition that would encourage risk would result in some banks subsidizing the large losses of those at risk of failing first. Any bank within the coalition would find it advantageous to have a riskier portfolio than the other banks in the coalition (to maximize the value of the put option). This would not be a tenable equilibrium, and thus one would expect coalitions to regulate and monitor in a way that discourages excess risk-taking.

Assessing Other Regulatory Options

The proposal for reform outlined here is, of course, not the only reasonable possibility for improving the current insurance system. It is one of many possible ways of introducing private market "discipline" into the deposit-insurance system. By placing someone other than the taxpayers at risk when a bank fails, and by giving the actions of those parties some weight in determining whether a bank may continue operating, my proposal, like many others, reduces the potential for excessive risk-taking *ex ante,* and improves the procedure for closing banks *ex post.* It may be useful to compare and contrast my proposal with other means of introducing market discipline, and with proposals that try to resolve the incentive problems of deposit insurance in other ways.

Two of the most popular alternative proposals for introducing market discipline are those of the Federal Reserve Bank of Chicago (Keehn, 1989) and the Federal Reserve Bank of Minneapolis (Boyd and Rolnick, 1988). The Boyd-Rolnick proposal is essentially a resuscitation of the original (unimplemented) permanent plan for the FDIC, with some alterations. This plan would allow each citizen a single banking account insured 100 percent by the government, up to a limited amount. Beyond that, all accounts would be insured 90 percent.

It is important to note that the successful implementation of this plan would not require all depositors to monitor banks. Depositors could take out private policies with insurance companies specializing in monitoring and rating banks, to cover their 10 percent exposure, and would pay varying premiums that would reward holding deposits in low-risk banks. An advantage of this plan is that it would not require the changes in the industrial organization of banking and the role of government regulation envisioned in my more radical proposal. Another advantage of the Boyd-Rolnick proposal is that it makes state-contingent government protection explicit, and thus does not invite *ex post* ad hoc policy intervention. A disadvantage of the plan is that it does not address the problem of *ex post* risk-taking, and the need to establish a credible closure rule for insolvent banks. The main disadvantage of the plan is that it may be very hard (perhaps impossible) to phase it in. Implementing the proposal would require a retreat from the protection currently provided to depositors. Not only would protection have to be reduced to one deposit per depositor, but to achieve a significant reduction in deposit risk exposure the government would have to limit coverage far below the current cap of $100,000. Once such legislation became likely depositors in questionable institutions, or depositors who lack sufficient information to judge their banks' viability, would have an incentive to run their banks and place their funds in a safe haven.

The Chicago Fed subordinated-debt plan shares the Minneapolis Fed plan's advantage over my more radical proposal (no need for drastic reform of institutions) and avoids the main problems of the Minneapolis Fed plan. It also provides explicit rules for government insurance. According to the Chicago Fed proposal, banks would be forced to maintain subordinated debt equal to some percentage of outstanding deposits. Overlapping generations of maturing subordinated debt would provide an automatic means for shrinking or closing undesirable banks (they could no longer attract subordinated debt holders to replace maturing obligations). And existing subordinated debt holders could exert their influence to ensure that regulators would not prolong closure of banks with insufficient subordinated debt. By requiring increased capital in the form of subordinated debt, rather than equity, the proposal ensures that the increased capital of the banks will be held by investors who desire low risk. Banks too small to issue their own subordinated debt could rely on correspondent banks to serve the role of subordinated debt holders, with interbank risk leading to higher subordinated debt requirements by correspondents of small banks. This plan would be easy to implement, since it could be phased in over time without creating any incentives for runs. Furthermore, it would remove the "middleman" and allow informed institutional investors, rather than depositors to directly hold claims on banks (rather than insure the claims of depositors).

I am quite supportive of the Chicago Fed proposal, but I think a system of coinsuring self-regulating coalitions of branch banks provides a somewhat superior mechanism for protecting the system. Banks have lower costs of monitoring one another, and are better informed regarding trade-offs between monitoring a particular activity and constraining it by regulation (see Calomiris and Kahn, 1990b). Finally, banks could act more quickly to force an insolvent bank to close by excluding it from interbank clearings and other dealings.

Other popular proposals for reform that do not introduce market discipline into the deposit-insurance system fall into essentially two categories: improved government regulation and reduced coverage ("narrow" banking). In my opinion, neither of these provides a viable alternative to introducing market discipline.

Proposals for improvements in government regulation (risk-based capital requirements, market value accounting where possible, and so forth) do not deal with one of the central problems identified by the historical (non)performance of government regulators. Regulators systematically commit errors of omission (because they lack incentives to spend resources on gathering information), or errors of commission (because the benefits to the regulator of remaining silent about violations exceed the benefits of reporting them—see Kane, 1988). Proposed changes in regulation will only be as good as the information regulators choose to collect and report. Unless something in the incentive structure of regulation changes, there is no reason to think these reforms will prevent another debacle in the future.

Narrow-banking proposals suffer from a similar political naiveté, and may be criticized on theoretical grounds, as well. These proposals advocate government insurance only for essentially riskless accounts (say, those backed by Treasury bills). The theoretical basis for this proposal is the view that the function of deposit insurance is to provide riskless assets to those who desire them. But other recent models discussed above—and historical evidence—run counter to this view. Deposit insurance is desired not only (or even primarily) because it provides a riskless asset to a segment of the population. Rather, some form of insurance (private or public) of risky bank liabilities is useful in averting panics. Isolating a small portion of the banking system's accounts and insuring these does not solve the problem of protecting the banking system from panics. Specifically, so long as banks provide liabilities of shorter maturity than their assets (as the analysis of Calomiris and Kahn, 1991, and Calomiris, Kahn, and Krasa, 1991, suggests they will), and banks hold portfolios that are not mark to marketable, banking panics will be a possibility. Unless the government removes the constraints on private coinsurance (unit-banking laws), or itself provides some means of insurance, it will leave unresolved the central problem deposit insurance was designed to deal with. Narrow-banking proposals also fail to provide an *ex ante* rule for government intervention in support of "uncovered" liabilities. As I have argued, this is undesirable because it invites ad hoc, politically motivated, discretionary policy by Congress.

Political Considerations

One of the grim lessons of the last 150 years of banking regulation in the United States is the political power of the antibranching, prodeposit insurance political lobby, which has successfully defeated numerous attempts at reforming the banking system, and has succeeded in promoting and continuing unit banking with deposit insurance, regardless of its apparent costs. Certainly the policy debates of the 1930s which culminated in the establishment of the FDIC were informed by the failures of deposit insurance in the 1920s (see, for example, American Bankers Association, 1933). As in earlier cases, deposit insurance was chosen despite prior visible benefits from branch banking and costs from deposit insurance. Is there any reason to think substantive beneficial reform of deposit insurance or branch-banking laws, of the kind described above or any other kind, will be forthcoming?

I see three reasons for being hopeful. First, the unprecedented costs of the current thrift debacle are something new, and the consensus among regulators and economists (and legislative aides I have spoken with) is that substantive reform is necessary to limit costs in the future. Advocates of "market discipline" can help their case by emphasizing historical evidence for consensus in favor of this approach, as well. As Boyd and Rolnick argue, the original permanent plan for federal insurance and the stated intentions of Franklin Roosevelt indicate that insurance was never intended to provide complete government protection to banks.

Second, as the U.S. banking system faces increasing competition internationally and domestically from other intermediaries, the attraction of removing some restrictions on the activities of commercial banks becomes increasingly apparent. At the same time, the potential for excess risk-taking increases as the range of activities banks can pursue expands. Thus, absent substantive reform of deposit insurance, legislators will be forced to choose between growing costs due to excess risk-taking or declining competitiveness of U.S. banks. This should encourage legislators to solve the incentive problems inherent in the current deposit-insurance system.

The third point is of relevance to my more radical proposal for bank group coinsurance. The special interest group which has systematically (and successfully) opposed branch banking in the past has recently fallen on hard times. The silver lining in the cloud of banking difficulties recently has been a decline in the value of unit-bank charters, and a forced liberalization of unit-banking restrictions (often as a means to promote entry or acquisitions in the face of existing bank failures). Declining charter values and relaxation of some branching restrictions has reduced the power of the prounit-bank lobby. At the very least, declines in charter values have reduced unit banks' abilities to make continuing large political contributions. The history of U.S. banking regulation has been a sequence of long-term regulatory responses to short-term disasters. Maybe this time that is good news.

REFERENCES

American Bankers' Association, *The Guaranty of Bank Deposits* (New York), 1933.

Barth, J. R., P. F. Bartholomew, and C. Labich, "Moral Hazard and the Thrift Crisis: An Analysis of 1988 Resolutions," *Proceedings of a Conference on Bank Structure and Competition,* Federal Reserve Bank of Chicago, 1989.

Boyd, John, and Arthur Rolnick, "A Case for Reforming Federal Deposit Insurance," *Annual Report,* Federal Reserve Bank of Minneapolis, 1988.

Breckenridge, R. M., *The History of Banking in Canada,* National Monetary Commission (Washington, D.C.), 1910.

Brewer III, Elijah, "Full-Blown Crisis, Half-Measure Cure," *Economic Perspectives,* Federal Reserve Bank of Chicago, November/December, 1989.

Calomiris, Charles W., "Deposit Insurance: Lessons from the Record," *Economic Perspectives,* Federal Reserve Bank of Chicago, May/June, 1989.

————, "Do 'Vulnerable' Economies Need Deposit Insurance: Lessons from the U.S. Agricultural Boom and Bust of the 1920s," in *If Texas Were Chile: Financial Risk and Financial Regulation in Commodity-Exporting Economies,* ed. Philip Brock, (Washington, D.C.), 1991.

————, "Is Deposit Insurance Necessary? A Historical Perspective," *Journal of Economic History,* June 1991.

Calomiris, Charles W., and Gary Gorton, "The Origins of Banking Panics: Models, Facts, and Bank Regulation," in *Financial Markets and Financial Crises,* ed. R. Glenn Hubbard (Chicago), 1991.

Calomiris, Charles W., and Charles M. Kahn, "The Role of Demandable Debt in Structuring Optimal Banking Arrangements," forthcoming, *American Economic Review,* 1989.

Calomiris, Charles W., and Charles M. Kahn, "The Efficiency of Cooperative Interbank Relations: The Suffolk System," working paper, 1990a.

Calomiris, Charles W., and Charles M. Kahn, "Cooperative Arrangements for the Regulation of Banking by Banks," working paper, 1990b.

Calomiris, Charles W., Charles M. Kahn, and Stefan Krasa, "Optimal Contingent Bank Liquidation Under Moral Hazard," Federal Reserve Bank of Chicago Working Paper—1991/13, 1991.

Calomiris, Charles W., and Larry Schweikart, "The Panic of 1857: Origins, Transmission, and Containment," *Journal of Economic History,* December, 1991.

Ely, Bert, *Making Deposit Insurance Safe Through 100% Cross-Guarantees,* National Chamber Foundation, 1990.

Golembe, Carter, "The Deposit Insurance Legislation of 1933: An Examination of Its Antecedents and Its Purposes," *Political Science Quarterly,* June, 1960.

Golembe, Carter, and Clark Warburton, *Insurance of Bank Obligations in Six States During the Period 1829–1866,* Federal Deposit Insurance Corporation, 1958.

Gorton, Gary, "Clearing Houses and the Origin of Central Banking in the U.S.," *Journal of Economic History,* June, 1985.

———, "Self-Regulating Banking Coalitions," working paper, 1989.

Gorton, Gary, and Donald Mullineaux, "The Joint Production of Confidence: Endogenous Regulation and 19th Century Commercial Bank Clearinghouses," *Journal of Money, Credit and Banking,* November, 1987.

Govan, Thomas, *The Banking and Credit System in Georgia,* Ph.D. dissertation, Vanderbilt University, 1936.

Horvitz, Paul M., "The Causes of Texas Bank and Thrift Failures," working paper, 1989.

Kane, Edward J., "How Incentive-Incompatible Deposit-Insurance Funds Fail," Prochnow Educational Foundation, Report No. PR-014., 1988.

Keehn, Silas, "Banking on the Balance: Powers and the Safety Net," Federal Reserve Bank of Chicago, 1989.

Ramirez, Guillermo V., and Francisco R. Rosende, "Chilean Banking Legislation," working paper.

Robb, Thomas B., *The Guaranty of Bank Deposits* (New York), 1921.

White, Eugene N., *The Regulation and Reform of the American Banking System, 1900–1929* (Princeton), 1983.

Williamson, Stephen, "Restrictions on Financial Intermediaries and Implications for Aggregate Fluctuations: Canada and the United States, 1870–1913," Federal Reserve Bank of Minneapolis, Staff Report 119, 1989.

CHAPTER 2

The Thrift Industry Crisis: Revealed Weaknesses in the Federal Deposit Insurance System

James R. Barth

Lowder Eminent Scholar in Finance,
Auburn University

and

Philip F. Bartholomew

Principal Analyst,
Congressional Budget Office

[With the establishment of federal deposit insurance] the task of preventing banks from developing an unsound or embarrassed condition looms larger than ever before among the duties of the supervisory and examining authorities. They should, therefore, be given adequate powers, and be required to make full and effective use of them, in order that an incipient unhealthy condition may be immediately corrected, and that uneconomic banks may be closed before they reach a state where liquidation would involve losses. (Bremer, 1935, p. 140)

The authors are grateful to Dan Brumbaugh for helpful discussions as well as to Teresa Brown, Sherree Durham, and Donna Wood for their excellent assistance in the preparation of this paper. The views expressed are those of the authors and not necessarily those of the Congressional Budget Office.

The thrift industry has just completed the worst decade in its 160-year existence. More than 500 institutions were closed at an estimated present-value cost in excess of $50 billion. Still another 500 or more institutions were open but insolvent at the end of the decade. These remaining candidates for closure will cost an estimated $100 billion or more (see Barth and Brumbaugh, 1990). There are hundreds more thrift institutions that are financially weak and attempting to survive the massive consolidation, shrinkage, and restructuring that is sweeping through the industry.

Shortly after taking office in 1989, President Bush proposed legislation to resolve the crisis in the thrift industry once and for all. Although the Congress was asked to take action within 45 days, it was not until August 9 that the Financial Institutions Reform, Recovery and Enforcement Act (FIRREA) was signed into law (for a chronology, see Table 2.1). Perhaps the most important feature of this legislation was the recognition by both the Administration and the Congress that the problem was so severe that taxpayer dollars were required to make whole all insured deposits at troubled thrift institutions. The most serious shortcoming was its failure to restructure adequately the federal deposit insurance system. The major culprit in the thrift crisis is the current structure of the insurance system, as will be argued here.

WHAT HAPPENED AND WHAT WILL BE THE COST?

The thrift industry was ravished by all the adverse developments that occurred during the 1980s. Table 2.2 shows that there were 3,993 thrifts in 1980, whereas there were only 2,878 by 1989. And 281 of these were in conservatorship. This 28 percent decline includes 525 institutions that were closed (that is, liquidated, sold, or stabilized) at an estimated present-value cost of $54 billion.

Despite the tremendous decline in the number of thrifts and all the closings, there were still insolvent institutions open at yearend 1989. Indeed, as Table 2.2 shows, there were 517 tangible insolvent institutions with $283 billion in assets. Furthermore, 122 thrifts with $60 billion in assets had a tangible capital-to-assets ratio of less than 1.5 percent.

The cost of resolving all the seriously troubled thrift institutions has been a source of considerable controversy, ever since the first estimate was published in the mid-1980s (see Barth, Brumbaugh, Sauerhaft, and Wang, 1985). As Chart 2.1 shows, all the cost estimates have increased over time, but the official estimates have always been substantially below private-sector estimates. The most recent cost estimates of resolving all remaining seriously troubled institutions substantially exceed the $50 billion provided by FIRREA. Table 2.3 shows that such estimates range from $75–80 billion to at least $325 billion.

Table 2.1   Chronology of FIRREA

February 6	President Bush announced his plan to resolve the crisis in the thrift industry and to place federal deposit insurance on a sound basis. As proposed, the plan would create and fund a new corporation to pay the cost of closing all insolvent thrift institutions, reorganize the regulatory structure of the thrift industry, and reform federal deposit insurance.
April 19	The Senate approved its version of the thrift rescue and reform bill (S774) that was very close in spirit to the Administration's plan.
June 15	The House adopted its version of the bill (HR 1278), including budget financing, tough capital standards, and housing programs.
July 27	Congressional conferees completed their work on the bill and agreed to put the $50 billion funding program on the federal budget while exempting the resulting three-year increase in the federal deficit from the Gramm-Rudman anti-deficit law.
August 3	President Bush wrote a letter to House GOP leader Robert Michel of Illinois, threatening to veto the bill if the funding program was placed on budget.
August 3	Despite the veto threat, the House approved the conference report.
August 3	The Senate turned down the conference report when it failed by a vote of 54 to 46 to achieve the three-fifths majority needed to grant the budget treatment an exemption from the Gramm-Rudman anti-deficit law. The bill was immediately returned to conference to resolve the only remaining point of contention—the financing plan.
August 4	The Senate accepted the revised conference report that placed $20 billion on budget in 1989 and $30 billion off budget in fiscal years 1990 and 1991.
August 5	The House accepted the revised conference report with the House leadership placing many of the proxy votes for members that had begun the summer recess.
August 9	President Bush signed FIRREA into law.

SOURCE: Office of Thrift Supervision.

WHAT CAUSED THE THRIFT CRISIS?

As many have observed (see, for example, Barth, Bartholomew, and La-bich, 1989), a relatively unique set of circumstances gave rise to the thrift crisis of the 1980s. First, interest rates rose to unexpectedly high levels in the early 1980s and have remained quite volatile since then. This development followed a change in operating procedures in October 1979 by the Federal Reserve. Second, thrift institutions were required by law and regulation to operate on the basis of gathering deposits at variable rates and lending those funds for home purchases at fixed rates. The higher rates in the early 1980s drove up deposit costs without a corresponding increase in revenues from mortgage loans. As a result, the fundamental flaw in the design of the thrift industry was finally and openly exposed. Profits vanished and capital—regardless of how measured—was seriously eroded. Indeed, 85 percent of all savings and loans lost money in 1981 and, as Table 2.2 shows, tangible capital declined to only $4 billion in 1982 from $25 billion in 1981. Third, the interest rate problems were followed almost immediately by a deterioration in the quality of assets as regional economies experienced serious difficulties, particularly in the Southwest. Thrift institutions reported steadily increasing nonoperating losses from 1986 onward, reaching a record $15.4 billion in 1989 (see Table 2.2). Fourth, state and federal authorities provided thrifts with greater asset and liability powers and phased out ceilings on deposit rates over the period 1980 to 1986. For adequately capitalized institutions this meant an opportunity for greater diversification. For inadequately capitalized institutions, on the other hand, this meant more degrees of freedom with respect to risk-taking. Fifth, substantial improvements in informational technology, rapid growth in asset securitization, and greater overall competition among financial service firms in the 1980s significantly narrowed the net interest margins for thrift institutions. Sixth, the Tax Reform Act of 1986 reduced the depreciation benefits from investing in commercial and residential property, limited the offsetting losses on passive investments that affect limited partnership syndications, and eliminated the favorable capital gains treatment. These changes in tax laws adversely affected real estate values and thereby thrift institutions. Seventh, fraud and insider abuse, not to mention mismanagement, are always a concern, especially during a period of turbulence and lax supervision and regulation. Eighth, and most important, the structure of the federal deposit insurance system creates a moral-hazard problem, whereby an insured institution has an incentive to engage in riskier behavior than otherwise.

WHAT IS THE INCENTIVE TO ADOPT A HIGH-RISK STRATEGY?

As stated at the outset, it is our view that the major culprit in the thrift crisis is federal deposit insurance. Other factors such as deregulation and fraud certainly contributed to failures and the cost of resolving those failures. But the scope of the crisis was magnified by the way the federal insurance system was structured. The insurance system was established to protect small depositors against loss and to protect the payments system from collapse by providing sufficient depositor confidence that widespread runs on depository institutions would be eliminated. It accomplished these

Table 2.2 Thrift Industry: 1980–89

	1980	1981	1982	1983	1984	1985	1986	1987	1988	1989
Number of Institutions	3,993	3,751	3,287	3,146	3,136	3,246	3,220	3,147	2,949	2,878
Total Assets ($ Billions)	604	640	686	814	978	1,070	1,164	1,251	1,352	1,252
GAAP Net Worth ($ Billions)	32	27	20	25	27	34	39	34	46	25
Tangible Net Worth ($ Billions)	32	25	4	4	3	9	15	9	23	10
Net Income ($ Millions)	781	(4,631)	(4,142)	1,945	1,022	3,728	131	(7,779)	(12,057)	(19,172)
Net Operating Income ($ Millions)	790	(7,114)	(8,761)	(46)	990	3,601	4,562	2,850	907	(2,913)
Net Nonoperating Income ($ Millions)	398	964	3,041	2,567	796	2,215	(1,290)	(7,930)	(11,012)	(15,449)
Taxes ($ Millions)	407	(1,519)	(1,578)	576	764	2,087	3,141	2,699	1,952	800
Percent of Home Mortgages to Total Assets	66.5	65.0	56.3	49.8	44.9	42.4	38.9	37.8	38.6	40.7
Percent of Mortgage Backed Securities to Total Assets	4.4	5.0	8.6	10.9	11.1	10.4	13.1	15.6	15.4	13.7
Percent of Mortgage Assets to Total Assets	70.9	70.0	64.9	60.7	56.0	52.8	52.0	53.4	54.0	54.4
Stock Institutions										
(% of Number of Institutions)	20.0	21.0	23.0	24.0	30.0	33.0	37.0	40.0	44.0	43.0
(% of Total Assets)	27.0	29.0	30.0	40.0	52.0	56.0	62.0	70.0	74.0	71.0
Federally-Chartered										
(% of Number of Institutions)	50.0	51.0	51.0	51.0	54.0	53.0	54.0	56.0	58.0	62.0
(% of Total Assets)	56.0	63.0	70.0	66.0	64.0	64.0	64.0	65.0	71.0	76.0

TAP Capital-to-Asset Ratio

< 0%										
Number	43	112	415	515	695	705	672	672	508	517
Total TAP Assets ($ Billions)	0.4	29	220	234	336	335	324	336	283	283
0% to 1.5%										
Number	63	178	291	310	327	266	227	194	160	122
Total TAP Assets ($ Billions)	4	50	81	88	153	135	144	143	182	60
1.5% to 3.0%										
Number	230	524	592	569	526	460	354	277	281	245
Total TAP Assets ($ Billions)	39	113	136	185	168	212	191	196	244	206
3% to 6%										
Number	1,956	1,766	1,202	1,091	945	1,009	995	891	864	814
Total TAP Assets ($ Billions)	379	348	190	222	227	259	316	356	418	480
> 6%										
Number	1,701	1,171	787	661	643	806	972	1,113	1,136	1,180
Total TAP Assets ($ Billions)	181	101	59	84	62	95	156	188	196	206
Resolutions										
Number	11	28	63	36	22	30	46	47	205	37
Total Assets ($ Millions)	1,458	13,908	17,662	4,631	5,080	5,601	12,455	10,660	100,660	9,662
Estimated Present-Value Cost ($ Millions)	167	759	803	275	743	979	3,065	3,704	31,180	5,608

NOTE: Data for 1989 is for all thrifts. At year-end, there were 281 institutions in conservatorship with assets of $92.6 billion. Resolutions in 1988 do not include 18 "stabilizations" that had assets of $7,463 million and tangible net worth of negative $3,348 million, and an estimated present-value resolution cost of $6,838 million. Resolutions in 1989 do not include 7 FSLIC resolutions (reportedly at no cost to FSLIC) and 2 RTC resolutions (reportedly at no cost to RTC).

SOURCE: Federal Home Loan Bank Board and Office of Thrift Supervision.

Chart 2.1   Selected Estimates of Thrift Insolvency Costs

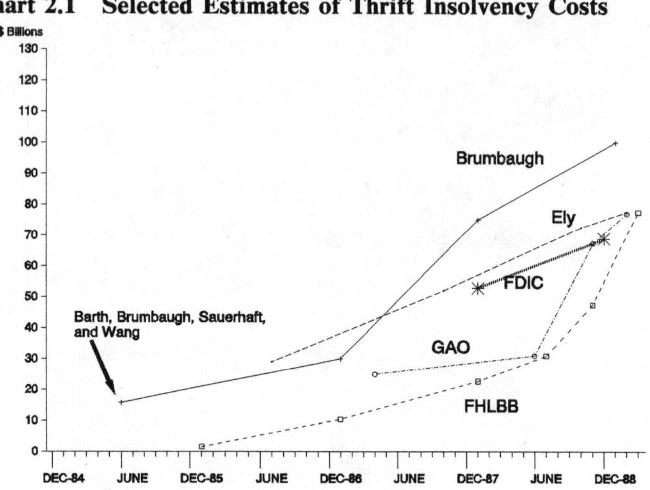

SOURCE: Federal Home Loan Bank Board.

All estimates are on a present-value basis, except as noted, meaning that this is the amount the FSLIC would have to pay to an acquirer to immediately assume its liabilities. When the estimate was stated as a range, the midpoint of the range was charted. The estimates prior to 1988 do not include costs associated with FSLIC's provisions for future losses on assistance agreements or FSLIC's notes payable.

Dan Brumbaugh is an economist based in San Francisco, California. Brumbaugh arrives at his estimates by multiplying the assets of a predefined group of institutions by the FSLIC's average historical cost to resolve institutions during a recent period. Brumbaugh's December 1987 and January 1989 estimates include the costs of resolving solvent but troubled institutions. Brumbaugh's May 1985 and December 1986 estimates include only the costs of resolving insolvent institutions.

Bert Ely is a consultant based in Alexandria, Virginia. Ely's May 1988, September 1988, and January 1989 estimates are the simple average of the marked-down value of assets and the capitalized value of gross interest income. Estimates prior to May 1988 are based on the capitalized gross interest income stream. Ely's September 1987 estimate was stated as "at least 52 billion" and was based on March 1987 balance sheet data. Ely's September 1988 estimate was a range, $70–$75 billion, 20 to 25 percent of which was on the books of the FSLIC. Ely's January 1989 estimate was a range, $75–$80 billion, half of which was on the FSLIC's books. Ely's last two estimates were based on June 1988 financial data.

The General Accounting Office's January 1989 estimate was "at least $77 billion" of which $37 billion was for institutions that had already been resolved and $40 billion was for institutions that had not yet been resolved. The GAO's May 1988 estimate was a range, $26–$36 billion, and was based on the December 1987 financial audit. The GAO's estimates based on 1988 data were intended to include the costs of 1988 FSLIC actions to date that had been assumed by the FSLIC. The GAO's October 1988 estimate for the costs of resolving institutions that were insolvent at the end of September was a range, $45–$50 billion, to which $19.9 billion of FSLIC's provisions for losses and notes payable needs to be added. Thus, the October estimate ranged from $64.9–$69.9 billion. The GAO's March 1987 estimate is taken from its report to the Congress in which the GAO stated that given its "knowledge of the condition of the industry, we do not believe that $25 billion overstates the extent of the problem facing FSLIC."

The Federal Deposit Insurance Corporation's estimates include the costs of handling resolved institutions plus institutions that were unprofitable *and* insolvent. Institutions are insolvent for these estimates if the sum of tangible capital, loan loss reserves, and general valuation allowances is less than zero. The FDIC reduces the asset values at insolvent and unprofitable institutions by comparing the book value of these assets with corresponding book values of a related group of peer institutions. The liabilities of the insolvent and unprofitable institutions are then subtracted from the adjusted asset values to obtain a cost estimate for resolving these institutions. The FDIC's December 1987 estimate of $52.8 billion was based on 489 insolvent and unprofitable institutions holding assets of $209 billion. The FDIC's November 1988 estimate of $68.9 billion was based on 134 resolved institutions through October 20, 1988, and 396 institutions holding $167 billion in assets, yet to be resolved. The FDIC's November estimate was split between FLSIC's books, $24.8 billion, and the unresolved institutions.

The Bank Board's December 1985 estimate of $1.6 billion was a contingent liability for troubled institutions that the Bank Board believed would likely require financial assistance in the near term. This estimate was based on FSLIC's historical loss experience and an evaluation of the past and present financial condition of such institutions. This methodology focused on near term losses, and was not a projection of the cost of resolving all future problems in the savings and loan industry. The Bank Board's December 1986 estimate of $10.5 billion included only those institutions on the FSLIC case list as of December 31, 1986. This liability represented the present value of the estimated total cost to provide the most probable form of assistance in each case less any costs already recognized because of some currently provided FSLIC assistance. The Bank Board's December 1987 estimate of $22.7 billion or more included a contingent liability of $17.4 billion for future assistance to troubled (unresolved) institutions that was probable and estimable and the costs (at least $5.3 billion) to resolve the problems of the additional 300 GAAP-insolvent institutions. The contingent liability included bid prices received by the FSLIC and the estimable and probable resolution costs of the remaining thrifts in the FSLIC caseload, plus an additional allowance for institutions located in the Southwest that were not part of the FSLIC caseload as of December 31, 1987. The Bank Board's mid-year estimate of $30.9 billion revised the December 31, 1987, estimate upward by $8.2 billion for institutions in the Southwest based on an analysis of actual resolution costs on Southwest cases compared to year-end estimates. The Bank Board's October 1988 estimate was a range, $45–$50 billion, based on all unresolved institutions in FSLIC's caseload as of October 1, 1988, plus all other thrifts that were GAAP insolvent in June 1988 but not in FSLIC's caseload. Using its experience from resolving thrifts during the first three quarters of the year, the Bank Board estimated a range of costs for the resolution of future FSLIC cases, $24.9 to $29.9 billion. To this must be added the estimated $20 billion in FSLIC notes and guarantees under assistance agreements of previously resolved cases. The Bank Board's February 1989 estimate is a range, $75–80 billion.

Table 2.3   Estimated Cost of Resolving the Thrift Crisis

Source of Estimate	Estimated Cost ($ Billions)	Description
Ely (April 1990)	$125	Present-value estimate that includes $50 billion for pre-1989 resolutions.
Barth-Brumbaugh (April 1990)	$91–135	Present-value estimate that excludes pre-1989 resolutions. The estimate depends on the resolution costs per dollar of assets of resolved institutions.
Congressional Budget Office (March 1990)	$75–80	Cash-flow estimate based on the timing of working capital and expected return on assets. Limited to RTC-caseload.
Office of Management and Budget: OMB-1 (February 1989)	$158	The on budget resolution costs as measured by gross outlays from 1989 to 1999, including pre-1989 resolutions.
OMB-2 (February 1989)	$198	Gross on budget outlays and off budget costs from 1989 to 1999 for resolving failed thrifts and establishing SAIF, including those for pre-1989 resolutions.
General Accounting Office: GAO-1 (July 1989)	$257	Gross on budget outlays and off budget costs of restoring failed thrifts and establishing SAIF over a 33-year period, including those for pre-1989 resolutions.
GAO-2 (April 1990)	At least $325	Gross on budget outlays and off budget costs of restoring failed thrifts and establishing SAIF over a 40-year period, including those for pre-1989 resolutions.
GAO-3 (April 1990)	At least $140	Present-value estimate of GAO-2 stated by Bowser during questioning following testimony.

SOURCE: Office of Thrift Supervision and Congressional Budget Office.

two objectives. But it has not adequately protected taxpayers, despite the fact that "With deposit insurance . . . , the chief function of government supervision and examination . . . seems to be to prevent undue risk from falling upon the government and its agencies" (Jones, 1940, p. 192).

Chart 2.2 shows that when thrifts experienced huge losses and significant erosion in their capital in the early 1980s, the response of the Congress

Chart 2.2 FSLIC Insured Institutions, Capital-to-Asset Ratios: 1940–88

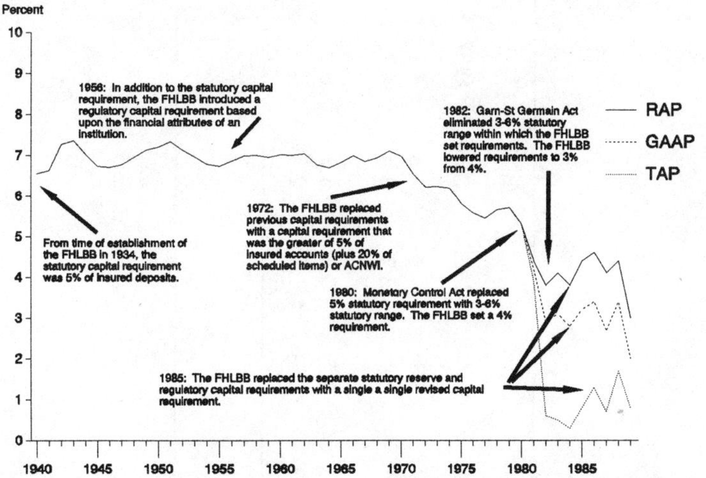

NOTE: RAP = Regulatory Accounting Practices, GAAP = Generally Accepted Accounting Principles, TAP = Tangible Capital.

SOURCE: Office of Thrift Supervision.

and the thrift regulator was to *lower* capital requirements and to broaden the measure of regulatory capital (RAP capital) relied on to close troubled institutions to include items not even counted under generally accepted accounting principles (GAAP). As a result, the divergence between alternative book-value measures of capital increased dramatically. In 1982, as Table 2.4 shows, the RAP capital-to-asset ratio was 3.8 percent, the GAAP capital-to-asset ratio was 2.9 percent, and the tangible capital-to-asset ratio was only 0.6 percent. Worse yet, all three measures actually overstated the financial condition of the thrift industry. For, as a former chairman of the Federal Home Loan Bank Board has recently testified, "By 1982, the real capital positions of all thrift institutions had been completely eroded, and virtually all thrift institutions had large negative net worths when their assets and liabilities were valued at actual market rates" (Pratt, 1988, p. 4). Indeed, when one adjusts for interest rate effects, the market value of thrift capital relative to assets was a *negative* 14.4 percent in 1982 (see Table 2.4). This means, as was pointed out in a major book on the thrift crisis in the early 1980s, "The evolution of the industry over the next few years has therefore been largely predetermined, and only the accounting rules that emphasize historical costs have prevented a widespread realization of this fact. It will become increasingly apparent that many firms cannot survive unassisted" (Carron, 1982, p. 84).

The important point about the increased divergence in the alternative measures of capital is that with the stroke of the regulatory pen many

Table 2.4   Alternative Capital-to-Asset Ratios for the Thrift Industry: 1980–88

	1980	1981	1982	1983	1984	1985	1986	1987	1988
Regulatory Capital (RAP)	5.3	4.4	3.8	4.1	3.8	4.4	4.6	4.1	4.4
Generally Accepted Accounting Principles Capital (GAAP)	5.3	4.2	2.9	3.1	2.8	3.2	3.4	2.7	3.4
Tangible Capital (TAP)	5.3	3.9	0.6	0.5	0.3	0.8	1.3	0.7	1.7
Market Value Capital (MVP)	(12.7)	(17.9)	(14.4)	(8.3)	(2.7)	1.5	2.3	0.3	1.7

NOTE: Last quarter of 1988 involved substantial FSLIC assistance.

SOURCE: Federal Home Loan Bank Board.

seriously troubled institutions were immediately restored to *regulatory* solvency rather than closed (that is, liquidated, sold, or stabilized). These are the very institutions that have little, if anything, to lose by raising their rates to attract more insured deposits with which to invest in those activities *promising* the highest returns. It is the "heads I win, tails federal insurer loses" scenario. Interestingly enough, even when the federal deposit insurance system was being established it was widely known that "The possibility of losing owners' capital is, without doubt, the strongest force in operation to prevent unsound banking" (Taggart and Jennings, 1934, pp. 514–15). Such a setting, moreover, was conducive to more fraud and abuse than would otherwise have occurred. As a current official of the Office of Thrift Supervision has recently stated: "With no money of their own at risk, the incentive to . . . engage in fraud proved compelling for many thrifts" (Black, 1989, p. 27).

A response on the part of the Congress and thrift regulator of capital leniency to trouble in the thrift industry was not unprecedented. As reported in an official publication of the Federal Home Loan Bank Board, "From 1961 to 1971, economic conditions were generally cited as the reason behind a number of liberalizing amendments [to the capital requirements]" (Rochester, 1979, p. 6). Not surprisingly, the economic conditions included narrowing yield spreads and volatile interest rates.

HOW DID THE GOVERNMENT RESPOND TO THE TURMOIL?

The government did indeed respond to the turmoil in the thrift industry. Prior to FIRREA, the Congress passed the Depository Institutions Deregulation and Monetary Control Act in 1980, the Garn-St Germain Depository Institutions Act in 1982, and the Competitive Equality Banking Act in 1987. But, as already noted, this legislation permitted the lowering of capital requirements. It also increased the availability of federal deposit insurance from $40,000 per account to $100,000. The legislation also provided thrift institutions with greater asset and liability powers and deregulated the rates that could be offered on deposits. Without *appropriate* risk-based premiums or risk-based capital requirements, however, the burden of curtailing risk or imposing discipline had to be borne almost entirely by the federal insurer. Although such discipline is admittedly extremely difficult to impose in an environment in which thousands of institutions are losing money and experiencing capital depletion, it is the very time discipline is most urgently needed.

The appropriate governmental response to deterioration in the financial condition of thrift institutions is to impose discipline on seriously troubled institutions, which includes closing such institutions in a timely and cost-effective manner. Yet this was not done to the degree required during the 1980s. As Tables 2.5 and 2.6 indicate, institutions resolved during the 1980s had been insolvent on a tangible (TAP) basis for quite lengthy periods of time before being closed. Indeed, in 1988 the 205 thrift institutions that were resolved at an estimated present-value cost of $31.8 billion had been insolvent on average for three and one-half years. This means that these institutions had no reported tangible capital as far back as 1984 or 1985. On the basis of market values, they were insolvent even years earlier. Only with federal deposit insurance could such seriously troubled institutions remain open for so long and obtain the funds with which to gamble for resurrection.

Troubled institutions that are left open have every incentive to bid up rates on deposits to attract funds to engage in excessively risky activities in an attempt to overcome their difficulties. Many troubled institutions pursued just such a strategy and not surprisingly only exacerbated an already serious situation. Broader asset powers, deposit rate deregulation, and greater deposit insurance coverage only gave these institutions more degrees of freedom in their endgame strategies. Even fraud and abuse were more likely to flourish in an environment in which institutions remained open while insolvent (see Table 2.7).

Tables 2.8 and 2.9 present selected information on the characteristics of the 205 thrift institutions that were closed in 1988. Cursory evidence indicates that the cost of resolution is directly related to the length of insolvency, the ownership form, and in the case of stock form, the dispersion of stock ownership. Lamar Savings Association, for example, was a closely held stock-type institution that grew at an average rate of 63 percent during the 1983–85 period. As it grew, it also increasingly shifted its portfolio toward high-risk investments. Although resolved in 1988, the state-chartered institution was insolvent on a tangible basis at least six years earlier.

Clearly, lenient regulatory capital requirements coupled with federal deposit insurance create not only a moral hazard problem, but also an adverse selection problem, whereby those most likely to impose costs upon the insurer seek the benefits of insurance. Unless the regulator intervenes in a timely manner (one institution was first insolvent 90 months prior to resolution), inadequately capitalized institutions can engage in excessively risky activities funded with insured deposits, almost always leading to even bigger costs being borne by the federal insurer when such institutions are eventually closed. The data in Tables 2.8 and 2.9 attest to this fact.

DOES FIRREA RESOLVE THE THRIFT CRISIS ONCE AND FOR ALL?

FIRREA mandates a number of changes in an attempt to resolve the thrift crisis and to ensure that a similar situation never again occurs (for more

Table 2.5 Comparison of Thrift Resolutions—U.S. and Texas: 1980–89

Year	Number of Resolutions		Total Assets of Resolutions ($ Billions)		Estimated Present Value Resolution Cost ($ Billions)		Average Number of Months of TAP-Insolvency	
	U.S.	Texas	U.S.	Texas	U.S.	Texas	U.S.	Texas
1980	11	0	1,458	—	167	—	5	—
1981	28	1	13,908	6	759	1	5	31
1982	63	8	17,662	1,031	806	78	8	11
1983	36	1	4,631	97	275	0	16	30
1984	22	2	5,080	348	743	164	23	16
1985	31	1	6,366	174	1,026	155	26	5
1986	46	2	12,455	1,080	3,065	493	31	14
1987	47	4	10,660	1,507	3,704	1,504	35	30
1988	205	81	101,242	35,978	31,790	19,491	42	38
1989	37	8	9,774	3,047	5,608	2,953	40	41

NOTE: Figures for 1989 may differ from previous years because of different methods of calculation by FSLIC and RTC. Resolution data for 1988 do not include 18 "stabilizations" that at year-end 1988 had assets of $7,463 million and tangible net worth of negative $3,348 million, and an estimated present-value resolution cost of $6,838 million. Resolution data for 1989 do not include two RTC cases reportedly resolved without cost to the RTC.

Table 2.6 Average Number of Months of TAP Insolvency of Thrift Resolutions by State: 1980–89

District	State	1980	1981	1982	1983	1984	1985	1986	1987	1988	1989
Boston	Massachusetts	0	0	7	0	0	0	0	0	0	0
	Rhode Island	19	0	0	0	33	0	0	0	0	0
New York	New Jersey	5	6	8	0	40	0	0	28	53	0
	New York	0	3	7	20	38	0	52	0	0	0
	Puerto Rico	0	5	7	0	40	0	0	0	0	0
Pittsburgh	Pennsylvania	0	0	8	14	0	0	0	0	0	49
	West Virginia	0	0	0	0	0	0	52	0	68	0
Atlanta	Alabama	0	0	0	24	0	0	0	41	78	63
	District of Columbia	0	24	0	0	0	38	0	0	0	0
	Florida	2	3	2	0	0	48	7	0	42	29
	Georgia	0	0	7	0	0	0	0	0	18	3
	Maryland	0	7	9	0	26	0	0	63	0	0
	North Carolina	0	1	0	0	0	0	0	60	14	15
	South Carolina	0	0	0	0	0	0	22	0	0	3
	Virginia	0	0	2	6	49	40	23	39	28	0
Cincinnati	Kentucky	0	0	10	0	0	29	54	0	44	0
	Ohio	3	0	0	11	24	40	41	38	58	0
	Tennessee	0	0	0	0	13	27	0	0	61	0
Indianapolis	Indiana	0	0	0	18	0	0	0	0	61	0
	Michigan	4	0	0	14	0	0	40	27	60	0
Chicago	Illinois	6	4	3	20	14	32	19	68	60	35
	Wisconsin	0	0	0	11	0	0	0	0	0	0

Des Moines	Iowa	4	0	0	18	0	24	0	17	42	20
	Minnesota	0	1	0	27	0	0	0	0	54	0
	Missouri	0	3	7	19	0	0	45	44	0	0
	North Dakota	0	3	6	0	27	0	0	0	0	0
	South Dakota	0	0	0	14	20	0	0	0	39	0
Dallas	Arkansas	0	0	0	0	0	3	72	15	39	49
	Louisiana	0	NA	20	16	16	22	33	36	17	65
	Mississippi	0	0	6	0	24	19	0	0	0	0
	New Mexico	5	0	8	23	0	52	51	0	16	0
	Texas	0	31	11	30	16	5	14	30	38	41
Topeka	Colorado	0	0	0	0	0	22	26	6	21	0
	Kansas	0	0	5	0	0	6	62	23	24	52
	Nebraska	0	0	0	0	0	0	0	7	0	87
	Oklahoma	0	0	0	0	0	0	25	67	27	0
San Francisco	California	0	0	18	0	18	12	19	37	36	30
	Nevada	0	0	0	0	0	0	4	0	0	0
Seattle	Alaska	0	5	0	0	0	0	5	6	0	0
	Hawaii	2	0	0	0	0	7	0	0	0	0
	Idaho	0	0	0	0	0	0	0	57	26	0
	Montana	0	0	2	0	0	26	0	0	66	0
	Oregon	0	0	0	0	0	42	25	30	57	0
	Utah	0	0	0	0	0	7	0	12	0	0
	Washington	0	0	0	0	0	21	24	30	34	0
	Wyoming	0	0	0	0	0	0	18	0	29	0

Table 2.7 Presence of Negligence and Fraud in 1988 Thrift Resolutions

All 205 Resolutions	Board Negligence	Bad Underwriting	Faulty Appraisals	Loans-To-One Borrower Violations	Professional Negligence	Self Dealing	Other Fraud
Yes	132	125	95	69	68	69	55
No	21	22	37	60	53	57	52
Too Early	50	56	71	74	82	77	96
No Claim	2	2	2	2	2	2	2

50 Costliest Resolutions	Board Negligence	Bad Underwriting	Faulty Appraisals	Loans-To-One Borrower Violations	Professional Negligence	Self Dealing	Other Fraud
Yes	35	36	29	25	26	25	21
No	1	1	2	6	5	8	6
Too Early	14	13	19	19	19	17	23
No Claim	0	0	0	0	0	0	0

Texas Resolutions (81 in 1988)	Board Negligence	Bad Underwriting	Faulty Appraisals	Loans-To-One Borrower Violations	Professional Negligence	Self Dealing	Other Fraud
Yes	48	45	35	31	21	31	19
No	3	4	6	11	33	8	8
Too Early	30	32	40	39	49	42	54
No Claim	0	0	0	0	0	0	0

All data collected and compiled during the period February 9–22, 1989.

NOTE: This information based on preliminary evaluations. If category was present, "Yes" was indicated. If category was not present, "No" was indicated. If it was too early to determine the presence of a category, then "Too Early" was indicated. In two cases, the FHLBB does not hold the D&O claim.

SOURCE: Federal Home Loan Bank Board.

Table 2.8 Facts about Four Selected 1988 Thrift Resolutions

	Lamar Savings Association	American Diversified Savings Bank	Bell Savings & Loan Association	Eureka Federal Savings & Loan Association
State Location	Texas	California	California	California
Charter at Time of GAAP Insolvency	State	State	State	Federal
Ownership Form	Stock	Stock	Stock	Mutual
Ownership Control	Closely Held	Closely Held	Widely Held	Not Applicable
Years of Ownership Change (If Any)	1980	1983	1982	Not Applicable
Assets at Time of Resolution ($ Millions)	1,940	510	953	1,744
Estimated Resolution Cost ($ Millions)	805	798	566	303
Estimated Liquidation Cost ($ Millions)	953	798	700	396
Month of Resolution	May 1988	June 1988	September 1988	May 1988
Resolution Action	Southwest Plan	Insurance Action	Assisted Merger	Assisted Merger
Years of TAAP Insolvency	6.25	2.5	2.5	3.75
Direct Investment to Assets (Industry Average = 0.5%)	15.8%	69.7%	2.6%	0.4%
Brokered Deposits to Assets (Industry Average = 1.8%)	3.2%	35.4%	5.2%	0.7%
Acquisition & Development Loans to Assets (Industry Average = 2.0%)	3.0%	0.1%	2.4%	0.4%
Real Estate Held to Assets (Industry Average = 1.8%)	9.2%	24.9%	1.7%	0.0%
Average Annual Growth Rate of Assets: 1983–85	63.1%	346.3%	48.0%	17.1%
Year Placed in MCP	Not Applicable	1986	1985	Not Applicable

SOURCE: Federal Home Loan Bank Board

Table 2.9 Selected Information on 1988 Thrift Resolutions

Name of Institution	State	Estimated Present Value Resolution Cost ($ Millions)	Months of Tangible Insolvency	Charter at Time of GAAP Insolvency (F=Fed, S=State)	Ownership at Time of GAAP Insolvency (M=Mutual, S=Stock)	Narrowness of Ownership	Average Annual Growth Rate 1983–5 (%)	Percentage of Liabilities in Residential Mortgages	Percentage of Liabilities in Brokered Deposits
First Texas SA	TX	2,601	27	S	S	Wide	16	24	5
American Savings	CA	1,699	66	S	S	Close	69	23	1
Gibraltar SA	TX	1,500	48	S	S	Close	11	21	4
Guaranty FSLA	TX	1,386	45	F	S	Close	NA	14	13
United SA of Texas	TX	1,374	15	S	S	Wide	37	22	21
Beverly Hills Savings, FSLA	CA	983	63	S	M	—	44	16	27
Beach FSLA	FL	978	45	S	M	—	NA	12	0
Commodore SA	TX	891	33	S	S	Close	90	10	27
Lamar SA	TX	805	74	S	S	Close	63	17	3
American Diversified SB	CA	798	30	S	S	Close	130	3	15
Pathway Financial, FA	IL	791	87	F	S	Close	136	33	0
State of Lubbock SA	TX	757	38	S	S	Wide	48	5	18
Stockton SA	TX	712	32	S	M	—	6	24	2
Champion	TX	602	24	S	M	—	NA	24	12
Bell SLA, FSLA	CA	566	30	S	S	Close	49	37	4
Franklin SA	TX	556	24	S	S	Close	35	16	25
City SLA	TX	524	83	S	S	Close	28	13	6
Creditbanc SA	TX	504	66	S	S	Close	16	10	15
Killeen SLA	TX	460	24	S	S	Wide	51	9	27
Charter SLA	TX	458	78	S	M	—	8	19	7
Southwest S LA	TX	421	28	S	M	—	NA	19	13
Cardinal FSB	OH	405	15	F	S	Close	87	38	2
Home SA	TX	390	39	S	M	—	NA	42	7

Lyons Savings, FSLA	IL	385	30	F	NA	NA	46	26	0
Height SA	TX	368	57	S	S	Close	30	30	6
Mercury SA of Texas	TX	333	32	S	M	—	17	10	13
Eureka FSLA	CA	303	44	S	M	—	100	45	1
Butterfield SLA, FSLA	CA	281	45	S	S	Wide	63	29	3
Banc Home SA	TX	272	67	S	S	Close	127	6	10
Peoples SLA	TX	235	33	S	S	Close	27	9	7
Ben Milam SLA	TX	229	32	S	S	Close	82	2	23
Mile High/Silverado	CO	228	9	S	S	Wide	24	13	17
Richardson SLA	TX	224	77	S	S	Close	67	37	12
Columbia FSLA	CO	221	15	F	S	Wide	24	21	5
Paris SLA	TX	210	23	S	S	Close	92	14	26
Home SLA	TX	203	69	S	M	—	0	12	10
Farmers Savings, A FSLA	CA	199	34	S	NA	NA	21	24	16
Delta SA of Texas	TX	196	72	S	M	—	10	13	6
American SB	IL	188	90	S	S	Close	88	46	0
First FSLA	TX	179	12	F	M	—	11	27	8
Twin City Savings, A FSA	LA	177	17	F	M	—	48	15	32
Tesoro SLA	TX	161	23	S	S	Close	47	12	32
Broward FSLA	FL	151	30	F	S	Wide	39	23	4
Lincoln FSLA	NJ	146	74	F	M	—	9	47	0
Petroplex SA	TX	143	49	S	M	—	NA	19	13
San Angelo SA	TX	143	31	S	S	Close	−5	19	2
Citizens SLA, A FSLA	OR	141	64	S	M	—	16	24	2
Majestic SA	TX	137	35	S	M	—	5	16	31
North America SLA, A FSLA	CA	133	21	S	M	—	3	32	0
Olney SA	TX	133	7	S	M	—	−1	35	8
Southern Fed Banc SLA	TX	132	42	S	M	—	5	9	10
Key SLA, FSLA	CO	131	32	S	M	—	7	17	1

Table 2.9 (*Continued*)

Name of Institution	State	Estimated Present Value Resolution Cost ($ Millions)	Months of Tangible Insolvency	Charter at Time of GAAP Insolvency (F=Fed, S=State)	Ownership at Time of GAAP Insolvency (M=Mutual, S=Stock)	Narrowness of Ownership	Average Annual Growth Rate 1983–5 (%)	Percentage of Liabilities in Residential Mortgages	Percentage of Liabilities in Brokered Deposits
Interwest SA	TX	120	75	S	S	Close	64	11	14
Columbus SLA	CA	115	33	S	S	Wide	78	55	0
Cal America SLA, FSLA	CA	113	30	S	NA	NA	60	22	5
American Home Savings, FSB	OR	113	66	F	M	—	46	83	0
The American FSLA	OK	112	49	F	M	—	20	20	4
Washington FSB	MN	108	71	F	NA	NA	17	18	0
Sentry SA	TX	99	27	F	M	—	7	13	31
Seguin SA	TX	99	54	F	S	Wide	1	17	12
Southern SLA	TX	99	52	S	NA	NA	35	34	14
Hi-Plains SLA, FSLA	TX	97	75	S	S	Wide	7	18	43
Northpark SA	TX	96	24	S	S	Wide	68	31	13
Cypress SA	FL	94	11	S	M	—	8	45	0
Pioneer FSLA	IA	94	80	F	M	—	17	48	0
United SB of Wyoming, FSB	WY	90	30	F	S	Wide	26	14	0
First SA of East Texas	TX	88	34	S	S	Wide	52	14	9
Irving SA	TX	86	56	S	S	Close	18	12	16
Alliance SLA	TX	84	35	S	M	—	78	33	0
First FSLA	TX	84	70	S	M	—	10	34	0
Security	TX	83	73	F	NA	NA	9	15	0
Montfort SA, FSA	TX	81	30	S	M	—	54	0	6
Liberty FSB	NM	80	16	F	M	—	NA	29	25

Ohio Valley SLA	OH	77	60	S	M	—	1	44	0
Ramona FSLA	CA	76	47	S	S	Wide	81	4	24
Briercroft SA	TX	75	11	S	NA	NA	18	25	3
Vista SA	TX	74	72	F	M	—	−12	17	15
First Federated SB	FL	73	21	F	S	Wide	93	28	11
First FSLA of Hammonton	NJ	72	56	F	NA	NA	10	45	0
American FSLA	IN	67	46	F	M	—	1	35	0
Mc Lean FSA	VA	66	15	S	M	—	39	60	26
First Financial SA	TX	66	66	S	S	Wide	52	23	4
First FSB	IA	66	48	F	NA	NA	−4	27	2
Midamerica	OK	65	18	F	M	—	−3	54	0
Bay City FSLA	TX	64	12	F	S	Wide	19	35	1
Mutual FSB	OK	64	63	S	M	—	22	28	0
Jackson County FSLA	OR	63	45	F	M	—	39	53	0
Bloomfield SLA, FA	MI	62	63	S	S	Close	122	42	0
Ranchers SA	TX	62	30	S	NA	NA	105	4	61
Longview SLA	TX	62	74	S	S	Close	57	35	0
Magnet Bank, FSB	WV	60	68	F	M	—	12	61	2
First Financial SB	IA	60	72	S	S	Wide	79	44	0
Shamrock FSLA	TX	58	16	F	S	Wide	519	21	0
Rocky Mountain FSLA	WY	57	27	F	M	—	6	37	0
First Dearborn, FA	MI	56	81	S	S	Wide	4	34	0
First FSLA	OK	56	22	F	M	—	20	36	3
Ultimate SB, FSB	VA	56	15	F	M	—	30	28	4
Community First Fed Savings	WA	54	81	F	M	—	15	55	0
Regency SB, FSB	MI	52	40	S	M	—	5	66	31
First FSLA	KY	52	18	F	M	—	5	42	0
Odessa SA	TX	50	22	S	S	Wide	9	27	0
Northwest FSLA of Spencer	IA	50	24	F	M	—	7	46	0

Table 2.9 (*Continued*)

Name of Institution	State	Estimated Present Value Resolution Cost ($ Millions)	Months of Tangible Insolvency	Charter at Time of GAAP Insolvency (F=Fed, S=State)	Ownership at Time of GAAP Insolvency (M=Mutual, S=Stock)	Narrowness of Ownership	Average Annual Growth Rate 1983–5 (%)	Percentage of Liabilities in Residential Mortgages	Percentage of Liabilities in Brokered Deposits
Greatwest Sav Banc	TX	49	21	S	S	Close	24	15	32
Allenpark FSLA	TX	47	36	S	S	Close	24	16	11
Mt Whitney SLA	CA	46	41	S	M	—	82	30	18
Territory SLA	OK	46	29	S	M	—	112	20	16
United Savings, A FSLA	OK	44	18	F	M	—	30	33	0
Security SLA	TX	42	11	S	S	Wide	1	33	3
First Western SLA	TX	42	9	S	S	Wide	20	14	35
Investors SLA, A FSLA	OK	41	18	F	S	Close	NA	31	0
Lee SA	TX	40	21	S	S	Wide	NA	19	18
Homestate SLA	CA	40	35	S	S	Wide	66	56	0
First FSLA	TX	39	33	F	M	—	8	16	14
First FSLA of Brainerd	MN	37	56	F	M	—	3	36	2
Universal SA, A FSLA	OK	36	37	F	S	Wide	132	18	14
Peoples FSB	OH	35	79	F	NA	NA	12	44	0
Cardinal SB, INC.	NC	34	14	S	S	Close	53	20	0
Tahoe SLA, FSLA	CA	34	45	S	M	—	73	42	0
Reliance SA	TX	33	54	S	S	Close	100	14	41
Independence SLA	TX	32	15	S	M	—	9	35	8
Arsenal, SA, FA	IN	32	75	F	M	—	8	50	0
First FSLA	TX	32	27	S	M	—	23	35	3
Heart o Texas SA	TX	31	22	F	S	Close	169	31	10
First FSLA of Grand Rapids	MN	30	35	F	S	Wide	−1	47	5

Freedom FSLA	OR	29	72	S	M	—	25	33	7
First FSLA	KY	25	61	F	M	—	3	28	0
Bayview FSA	TX	25	12	F	S	Wide	28	24	4
First FSB	AR	24	42	F	M	—	19	46	0
Flagship FSLA	CA	24	38	S	S	Wide	46	36	1
First Oklahoma	OK	24	18	F	M	—	72	577	1
First FSB of Indiana	IN	23	60	F	M	—	−1	73	0
Mutual SLA	IL	23	55	S	S	Wide	113	45	0
First FSLA of Hibbing	MN	22	56	F	S	Wide	19	21	0
Peoples FSLA	IA	22	12	F	S	Wide	41	63	0
Gulf Coast SA	TX	21	33	F	S	Close	40	44	0
Keystone SLA	TX	20	48	S	M	—	NA	41	4
Glen Ellyn SLA, FSLA	IL	20	39	S	M	—	12	47	0
Colorado County FSLA	TX	20	29	F	M	—	−2	42	0
Union SA	TX	20	24	S	NA	NA	61	12	1
First FSLA	FL	20	81	F	M	—	2	51	0
Rooks County FSA	KS	20	24	S	S	Close	19	29	0
American Banc SA	TX	19	47	S	S	Wide	NA	50	15
Republic Savings FSLA	IL	18	58	S	S	Wide	27	40	0
Brownfield SLA	TX	17	36	S	M	—	17	19	7
Peoria SLA	IL	17	69	S	M	—	6	27	0
Commerce FSB	TN	17	29	F	S	Wide	182	31	0
The Perpetual SLA	IA	17	45	S	S	Close	31	64	0
Capitol F S of America	IL	17	77	F	M	—	12	67	0
Tri-Cities SLA	WA	16	22	S	NA	NA	181	42	0
Peoples SLA	OR	16	39	S	S	Wide	10	22	3
First Security SB	CA	15	18	F	M	—	25	28	6
Metroplex FSA	TX	15	6	F	S	Wide	NA	37	21
Skyline SA	TX	15	8	S	S	Wide	39	31	0
First FSLA	WA	14	29	F	M	—	4	57	0
Gladwater FSLA	TX	14	71	F	M	—	3	20	1
Capital FSB	OK	14	6	S	S	Wide	1	120	1

Table 2.9 (*Continued*)

Name of Institution	State	Estimated Present Value Resolution Cost ($ Millions)	Months of Tangible Insolvency	Charter at Time of GAAP Insolvency (F=Fed, S=State)	Ownership at Time of GAAP Insolvency (M=Mutual, S=Stock)	Narrowness of Ownership	Average Annual Growth Rate 1983–5 (%)	Percentage of Liabilities in Residential Mortgages	Percentage of Liabilities in Brokered Deposits
Midamerica SB	IA	14	24	S	M	—	−1	60	0
First Border SB	OH	14	60	S	M	—	9	131	21
Virginia FSLA	VA	14	54	S	S	Close	41	36	0
Yoakum FSLA	TX	13	24	S	M	—	1	44	0
First FSLA of Freeport	IL	13	43	F	M	—	5	31	0
Coosa FSLA	AL	13	78	F	S	Wide	14	36	0
Reliance SLA	NJ	12	29	F	M	—	−5	43	0
Great Falls FSLA	MT	11	66	F	M	—	3	28	1
Mountain State FSLA	WV	11	80	F	M	—	2	71	0
Western FSLA	IA	11	53	S	M	—	−4	31	1
Southside SLA	OH	10	77	S	M	—	6	52	0
Traders FSLA	WV	10	56	F	M	—	5	55	2
Frontier FSB	TN	10	81	S	M	—	8	35	0
Bluebonnet SA of Texas	TX	9	50	S	M	—	53	19	0
Stanford SLA	CA	9	12	S	S	Wide	107	29	0
Home FSLA of Peoria	IL	9	61	F	M	—	13	47	0
South Florida Savings, FSLA	FL	9	39	S	S	Close	NA	30	0
United SA of Central Indiana	IN	8	63	S	S	Wide	52	66	0
Peoples SLA, FA	MN	8	53	F	S	Wide	4	38	0
United FSLA	SD	8	39	F	M	—	−2	67	1
Southland SA	TX	8	17	S	S	Close	NA	21	0
Mesquite SLA	TX	8	54	S	M	—	4	37	0

Valley FSLA	TN	7	73	F	M	—	36	54	0
Larue FSLA	KY	7	54	F	M	—	−3	23	0
Citizens SLA	IL	6	52	S	NA	NA	36	21	0
Lynnwood SLA	WA	6	24	S	M	—	47	6	0
Citizens FSLA of New Castle	IN	6	54	S	M	—	3	57	0
Capital FSLA	IN	5	75	S	S	Wide	34	52	0
Burnet SLA	TX	5	27	S	S	Wide	57	44	10
Home FSLA of Spencer	IA	5	33	S	S	Wide	3	32	0
Loves Park FSB	IL	5	48	F	S	Wide	30	54	0
First FSLA	GA	5	18	S	M	—	31	55	0
Mineral Wells SLA	TX	5	39	S	M	—	14	48	0
Commerce FSLA	TX	4	47	F	M	—	−7	42	0
Muskegon FSLA	MI	4	54	F	M	—	8	75	0
First FSLA	CO	4	27	S	M	—	13	59	0
Fidelity FSLA of Berwyn	IL	4	60	F	M	—	3	31	0
Central Arkansas SLA	AR	3	35	S	S	Wide	149	36	0
Adobe SB	CA	3	18	S	S	Close	44	32	1
Frankton FSLA	IN	3	57	S	M	—	9	68	0
First FSLA of Taylorville	IL	3	71	F	S	Wide	38	42	0
Northwest FSLA	ID	2	26	F	S	Wide	57	63	0
Galva FSLA	IL	2	55	S	M	—	4	75	0
Eastern Washington, SLA	WA	2	12	S	S	Close	346	30	15
First Federal Bank, FSB	IA	1	32	F	M	—	10	46	3
Lamesa FSLA	TX	1	9	S	M	—	18	64	2
Cameron County SA	TX	0	14	F	S	Wide	102	41	0
Victor SLA, A FSLA	OK	0	22	F	S	Wide	22	27	3
Citizens FSLA	FL	(1)	66	F	S	Wide	13	30	0

detail, see Barth, Benston, and Wiest, 1990). Among some of the important changes are the following:

- *Regulatory Structure.* The Office of Thrift Supervision (OTS) was created as a new bureau in the Department of Treasury to regulate, examine, and supervise all thrift institutions. Insurance for thrifts is provided by the Savings Association Insurance Fund (SAIF), while insurance for commercial banks is provided by the Bank Insurance Fund (BIF). Both are administered by the Federal Deposit Insurance Corporation (FDIC). The Resolution Trust Corporation (RTC) was created to resolve all insolvent thrifts turned over to it by the OTS after January 1, 1989, and for three years from the date of enactment of FIRREA. The RTC is overseen by the RTC Oversight Board which has five members, including the Treasury Secretary, Federal Reserve Chairman, HUD Secretary, and two independent members. The FSLIC Resolution Fund was created to handle all resolutions prior to January 1, 1989. The Federal Housing Finance Board was created as an independent agency to oversee the Federal Home Loan Banks.

- *Funding.* $50 billion is provided to resolve all insolvent thrift institutions. It is obtained from the insurance premiums paid by thrifts, the retained earnings from and assessments levied on Federal Home Loan Banks, and taxpayers.

- *Capital Requirements.* Thrift institutions are subject to new and more stringent capital requirements. A risk-based capital requirement may be imposed by OTS, but it must be no less stringent than the one applicable to national banks. There is a leverage ratio that requires core capital to be not less than 3 percent of assets, and a minimum tangible capital-to-assets ratio of 1.5 percent. Core capital may include supervisory goodwill, but it will be phased out by January 1, 1995.

- *Insurance Premiums.* Insurance premiums for thrifts and commercial banks are increased. Institutions insured by SAIF currently are assessed 0.208 percent of total deposits. This assessment will increase to 0.23 percent from January 1, 1991, through December 31, 1993, and then decrease to 0.18 from January 1, 1994, through December 31, 1997. The assessment rate will be 0.15 percent thereafter. BIF institutions are currently assessed at a rate of 0.12 percent of total domestic deposits. As of January 1, 1991, and beyond, this rate will increase to 0.15 percent. Under certain conditions, the premiums may be increased to a maximum assessment rate of 0.325 percent at a maximum year-to-year increase of 0.075 percent.

- *Enforcement.* Enforcement powers are considerably enhanced, including civil money penalties of up to $1,000,000 per day.

- *Qualified Thrift Lender Test.* Beginning July 1, 1991, all thrifts must meet a 70 percent qualified thrift lender test. Institutions failing the test lose their right to Federal Home Loan Bank advances and must either limit their new activities and new branches to those permitted a national bank or convert to a bank charter.

- *Asset and Liability Powers.* The asset and liability powers of thrifts are generally curtailed. Holdings of junk bonds by all institutions must be divested no later than July 1, 1994. All thrifts are also restricted to allocating only 15 rather than 100 percent of their capital to loans-to-one borrower. For federally chartered thrifts, commercial real estate loans may not exceed 400 percent of capital, whereas the previous limitation was 40 percent of assets. For state-chartered institutions, any institution that does not meet the fully phased-in capital requirement by January 1, 1990, will be limited to those activities authorized for federal thrift institutions. Furthermore, equity investments are prohibited unless authorized for federal institutions.

Overall, these and other provisions of FIRREA clearly lower the value of the thrift charter relative to those under which other depository institutions operate. The legislation means that the thrift industry will undergo major consolidation, shrinkage, and restructuring for several years. It may even disappear as a separately chartered and regulated industry. But the important questions that remain are: Does FIRREA provide sufficient funds to resolve all the thrift insolvencies? Will the resolutions be done in a timely and cost-effective manner? And most important, does FIRREA address the fundamental cause of thrift crisis? Or could a similar situation occur again?

To answer these questions, one must consider the following. First, the legislation acknowledges that taxpayers will be required to share in the losses to resolve troubled thrift institutions. Their share will be larger than anticipated as all cost estimates now exceed the $50 billion provided by FIRREA. Regardless of the eventual cost, sufficient funds are needed to make up the difference between the value of the assets at troubled institutions and the insured deposits. This is true whether troubled institutions are liquidated or sold. Beyond providing limited funds and acknowledging taxpayers will share in the losses, FIRREA is basically silent about how to resolve troubled thrift institutions in a timely and cost-effective manner.

Second, the new regulatory structure generated some confusion as questions arose as to which agency is responsible for which set of issues. Checks and balances are fine so long as one can still identify the exact agency that is accountable for specific actions. Of course, one can question whether there is any longer a need for OTS, especially in view of all the consolidation and shrinkage occurring in the thrift industry and, as Tables 2.10, 2.11, and 2.12 show, its comparatively high cost of operation. In any event, it is not yet clear who is ultimately responsible for being sure that troubled institutions will be reorganized or closed in a timely and cost-effective manner nor is it evident that FIRREA provides the incentives for the responsible party to engage in responsible behavior. Yet these are extremely important issues, for as was pointed out in the early 1930s, "If an insolvent bank is taken over promptly and its affairs administered by competent men, the loss to depositors may be greatly minimized. Otherwise, the yield from assets may be small and expenses large. There is considerable evidence of delays, inefficiency and political influence in this respect" (McCahan, 1931, p. 170).

Third, FIRREA does not correct the lack of diversification and maturity imbalance that has plagued the thrift industry. Indeed, the new and more stringent QTL test only compounds these problems. For as Carron and Brumbaugh (1990) have shown, traditional residential mortgage lending for thrift institutions has and is likely to remain unprofitable for the average institution.

Fourth, FIRREA does impose new and tougher capital requirements. However, as Chart 2.2 shows, these requirements are substantially lower than those in effect in 1980. Furthermore, they are based on book-value measures of capital. Yet, as one of many individuals has pointed out, "Unless financial regulators begin to monitor and control leverage on the basis of market values, the question of asset deregulation is not fundamental. An insured institution can engage in risk-taking by leverage as well as by taking on asset risk" (Pyle, 1985, p. 724). In the case of thrift insolvencies, moreover, it was empirically determined several years ago "that the book-value measures of net worth systematically understated the cost to the FSLIC of resolving the failures" (Barth, Brumbaugh, and Sauerhaft, 1986, p. 12). Even a Chairman of the Federal Home Loan Bank Board stated in the midst of the thrift crisis that "The management and accounting information now being generated within institutions and reported to the Federal Home Loan Bank Board and other supervisors is generally obsolete. Because historical generally accepted accounting principles (GAAP) fail to account for the real changes in the performance of financial institutions, it may lead to managerial behavior which seeks a certain historical cost accounting result but which actually damages both the institution, the insurance corporation, and the regulator" (Pratt, 1983, p. 4). For purposes of comparison, it should be noted that during the financial and economic collapse of the 1930s the first Chairman of the Federal Deposit Insurance Corporation, when asked about the informational content of the reports filed by banks, stated that "You take the old condensed statements gotten out by national banks and state banks for years; they did not show the market value of their bonds or the reasonable value of their loans" (Crowley, 1935, p. 97). Under such circumstances, is it surprising that depositors were unsure about the financial condition of banks and therefore engaged in widespread runs on them?

The important point is that appropriately measured capital is absolutely crucial for protecting taxpayers against losses. In this regard, it is instructive to note that, based on information available for banks, "Early in the 1800's the ratio of capital to total assets ranged around 60% and drifted down steadily thereafter. By the early 1900's this ratio had fallen to about 20% and the rapid expansion of bank assets during World War I and the 1920's pulled it down below 13%" (Lindow, 1963, p. 30). In an attempt to reverse this downward trend, "The 1939 Annual Report of the FDIC stated that the Corporation's policy with regard to capital would be to urge each bank to maintain a minimum capital account equal to at least 10% of the appraised value of its assets" (Ryon, 1969, p. 7). Both bank and thrift capital standards currently are not only less than 10 percent but also based on book rather than the appraised or market value of assets.

In sum, FIRREA does not adequately address the primary cause of the thrift crisis: the current structure of the federal deposit-insurance system. Admittedly, by mandating a study of the federal insurance system, FIRREA acknowledges this limitation, but this does not alter the fact that the focus of the legislation gives the impression that fraud and deregulation were the main causes of all the problems in the thrift industry. Available evidence suggests otherwise. These factors exacerbated the problems, but certainly were not the fundamental causes.

WHAT LESSONS CAN BE LEARNED FROM FOREIGN DEPOSIT-INSURANCE SYSTEMS?

The United States is not the only country that has a system of federal deposit insurance. At least 27 other countries guarantee deposits at financial institutions through a formal federal deposit-insurance system (see Bartholomew and Vanderhoff, 1990; Bartholomew, 1989b; McCarthy, 1980; Pecchioli, 1987; Talley and Mas, 1989; Woodward, 1989). All of the G-7 countries (Canada, France, Germany, Italy, Japan, the United Kingdom, and the United States) currently have a system of federal deposit insurance. Furthermore, all the signatory nations of the Basle Accord on uniform capital requirements (the G-7 countries and Belgium, the Netherlands, Luxembourg, Sweden, and Switzerland) except Luxembourg have a formal system of deposit insurance.

However, as may be seen in Table 2.13, the foreign insurance systems were established fairly recently. The United States has the oldest operating federal deposit insurance system. Czechoslovakia in 1924 was the first country to establish a national deposit-insurance system (see McCarthy,

Table 2.10 Staffing of Federal Depository Institution Regulatory Agencies (Fiscal Year, Permanent Full-Time Positions)

Agency	1970	1975	1980	1981	1982	1983	1984	1985	1986	1987	1988
Comptroller of the Currency	1,920	2,546	3,331	3,071	3,071	2,917	3,250	3,250	3,250	3,418	3,680
Federal Deposit Insurance Corporation	2,669	3,614	3,691	3,554	3,435	3,554	3,554	3,554	4,258	3,266	3,483
Federal Reserve System[a]											
Federal Reserve Banks	761	1,019	1,589	1,733	1,796	1,862	1,885	1,912	2,087	2,147	2,223
Board of Governors	188	298	330	355	344	359	404	440	352	413	429
	949	1,317	1,919	2,088	2,140	2,221	2,289	2,352	2,439	2,560	2,652
Federal Home Loan Bank System[b]											
Federal Home Loan Banks	NA	NA	NA	NA	NA	NA	NA	NA	NA	NA	NA
Federal Home Loan Bank Board	523	1,182	1,617	1,574	1,815	2,087	2,570	4,135	6,039	6,297	6,387
National Credit Union Administration	456	410	488	451	441	407	384	407	483	524	586
Total	6,517	9,069	11,046	10,738	10,902	11,186	12,047	13,698	16,469	16,065	16,788

Costs of Federal Depository Institution Regulatory Agencies (Fiscal Year, Millions of Dollars of "Obligations")

Agency	1970	1975	1980	1981	1982	1983	1984	1985	1986	1987	1988
Comptroller of the Currency	32	65	113	121	129	144	167	170	189	193	218
Federal Deposit Insurance Corporation	39	63	113	124	131	78	274	232	462	326	565
Federal Reserve System[a]											
Federal Reserve Banks	NA	NA	86	100	119	132	141	152	164	170	187
Board of Governors	5	11	20	21	22	25	26	28	29	24	25
	5	11	106	121	141	157	167	180	193	194	212
Federal Home Loan Bank System[b]											
Federal Home Loan Banks	10	39	55	77	91	116	144	198	317	385	420
Federal Home Loan Bank Board	3	6	9	11	12	13	15	13	10	9	11
	13	45	64	88	103	129	159	211	327	394	431
National Credit Union Administration	7	10	18	22	20	19	22	22	24	30	35
Total	96	194	414	476	524	527	789	815	1,195	1,137	1,461

a. Data for Federal Reserve System are on a calendar year basis.

b. Data for Federal Home Loan Bank System based on operating expense from Annual Reports.

SOURCES: Center for the Study of American Business, Washington University and Federal Home Loan Bank Board.

Table 2.11 Depository Institution Regulatory Resources: Staffing

Ratio	1970	1975	1980	1981	1982	1983	1984	1985	1986	1987	1988
Number of National Banks/OCC Staff	2.41	1.86	1.33	1.45	1.49	1.63	1.52	1.53	1.50	1.35	1.26
Number of FDIC-Insured Banks/FDIC Staff	5.19	4.07	4.15	4.32	4.49	4.15	4.16	4.17	3.45	4.35	3.91
Number of Member Banks/FRS Staff	1.21	0.79	0.52	0.49	0.49	0.47	0.46	0.46	0.45	0.43	0.43
Number of FDIC-Insured Banks/Bank Regulator Staff	2.50	1.97	1.71	1.76	1.78	1.70	1.63	1.62	1.48	1.54	1.39
Number of FSLIC-Insured Thrifts/FHLBS Staff	8.35	3.45	2.47	2.38	1.81	1.51	1.22	0.79	0.53	0.50	0.46
Number of NCUSIF-Insured Credit Unions/NCUA Staff	28.46	38.48	35.55	37.61	37.76	39.04	39.57	36.97	30.42	27.36	23.68
Total Number of Depositories/Depository Institution Regulatory Staff	4.78	3.81	3.32	3.36	3.24	3.02	2.75	2.42	1.98	1.97	1.81

($000)

Assets of National Banks/OCC Staff	178,447	219,070	NA	312,001	348,415	402,990	460,974	502,377	536,663	519,176	502,764
Assets of FDIC-Insured Banks/FDIC Staff	215,943	263,545	NA	516,942	591,841	618,487	756,626	826,140	746,351	999,007	980,503
Assets of Member Banks/FRS Staff	132,203	137,050	NA	137,970	154,250	151,705	199,702	210,721	219,073	206,770	201,455
Assets of FDIC-Insured Banks/Bank Regulator Staff	104,072	127,384	NA	210,859	235,135	252,888	295,727	320,675	319,490	352,959	347,946
Assets of FSLIC-Insured Thrifts/FHLBS Staff	326,281	279,407	373,531	406,607	377,961	390,034	380,545	258,767	192,747	184,850	182,245
Assets of NCUSIF-Insured Credit Unions/NCUA Staff	19,432	70,278	119,641	136,951	157,785	201,378	241,781	294,135	305,855	309,469	299,155
Assets of Depositories/Depository Institution Regulatory Staff	115,982	144,616	NA	236,448	255,784	276,602	312,102	301,198	272,615	285,647	283,202

NOTE: Staffing of regulators on fiscal year basis (except for Federal Reserve System), assets, and numbers of institutions on calendar year basis.

SOURCE: Federal Deposit Insurance Corporation, Federal Home Loan Bank Board, National Credit Union Administration, and Center for the Study of Business, Washington University.

Table 2.12 Depository Institution Regulatory Resources: Costs

Ratio	1970	1975	1980	1981	1982	1983	1984	1985	1986	1987	1988
OCC Costs/Number of National Banks	6,925	13,702	25,537	27,160	28,178	30,309	33,895	34,109	38,769	41,712	47,176
FDIC Costs/Number of FDIC-Insured Banks	2,818	4,282	7,371	8,076	8,500	5,283	18,530	15,666	31,469	22,946	41,450
FRS Costs/Number of Member Banks	4,359	10,516	106,319	118,627	135,577	149,240	156,955	167,442	176,095	177,007	184,830
Total Bank Regulator Costs/Number of FDIC-Insured Banks	5,491	9,447	21,657	23,836	26,019	25,672	41,117	39,300	57,489	50,187	72,995
FHLBS Costs/Number of FSLIC-Insured Thrifts	2,978	11,035	16,028	23,460	31,336	41,004	50,702	65,003	101,553	125,199	146,151
NCUA Costs/Number of NCUSIF-Insured Credit Unions	539	634	1,037	1,297	1,201	1,196	1,448	1,462	1,633	2,093	2,522
Depository Institution Regulatory Cost/Number of Depository Institutions	3,079	5,612	11,289	13,197	14,822	15,592	23,825	24,622	36,663	35,880	47,968

OCC Costs/Assets of National Banks	0.00009	0.00012	NA	0.00013	0.00012	0.00012	0.00011	0.00010	0.00011	0.00011	0.00012
FDIC Costs/Assets of FDIC-Insured Banks	0.00007	0.00007	NA	0.00007	0.00006	0.00004	0.00010	0.00008	0.00015	0.00010	0.00017
FRS Costs/Assets of Member Banks	0.00004	0.00006	NA	0.00042	0.00043	0.00047	0.00037	0.00036	0.00036	0.00037	0.00040
Bank Regulator Costs/Assets of FDIC-Insured Banks	0.00013	0.00015	NA	0.00020	0.00020	0.00017	0.00023	0.00020	0.00027	0.00022	0.00029
FHLBS Costs/Assets of FSLIC-Insured Thrifts	0.00008	0.00014	0.00011	0.00014	0.00015	0.00016	0.00016	0.00020	0.00028	0.00034	0.00037
NCUA Costs/Assets of NCUSIF-Insured Credit Unions	0.00079	0.00035	0.00031	0.00036	0.00029	0.00023	0.00024	0.00018	0.00016	0.00019	0.00020
Depository Institution Regulatory Cost/Assets of Depository Institutions	0.00013	0.00015	NA	0.00019	0.00019	0.00017	0.00021	0.00020	0.00027	0.00025	0.00031

NOTE: Expenditures of regulators on fiscal year basis (except for Federal Reserve System), assets and numbers of institutions on calendar year basis. For 1970 and 1975, Federal Reserve System costs understated because data on district bank expenditures unavailable.

SOURCE: Federal Deposit Insurance Corporation, Federal Home Loan Bank Board, National Credit Union Administration, and Center for the Study of Business, Washington University.

Table 2.13 Deposit-Insurance Systems

Country	Insuring Agency	Year Established	Membership	Administration
Argentina	Deposit Insurance Scheme (Central Bank)	1979	Voluntary	Officially Sponsored & Administered
Austria	Deposit Guarantee Fund	1987	Compulsory	Industry Arrangement
Belgium	Rediscount & Guarantee Institute	1985	Voluntary	Joint Administration
Canada	Canada Deposit Insurance Corporation	1967	Compulsory	Officially Sponsored & Administered
Chile	Superintendent of Banks & Financial Institutions	1986	Voluntary	Officially Sponsored & Administered
Colombia	Financial Institutions Guarantee Fund	1985	Compulsory	Joint Administration
Finland	Guarantee Fund	1969	Compulsory	Industry Arrangement
France	Deposit Guarantee Fund	1980	Voluntary	Industry Arrangement
Germany (Fed. Rep.)	Deposit Security Fund	1966	Voluntary	Industry Arrangement
	Savings Bank Security Fund	1969	Compulsory	Industry Arrangement
	Credit Cooperatives Security Scheme	1976	Compulsory	Industry Arrangement
India	Deposit Insurance & Credit Guarantee Corp.	1961	Compulsory	Industry Arrangement
Ireland	NA	1989	Compulsory	Officially Sponsored & Administered
Italy	Interbank Deposit Protection Fund	1987	Voluntary	Industry Arrangement
Japan	Deposit Insurance Corporation	1971	Compulsory	Industry Arrangement
Kenya	Deposit Protection Fund Board	1985	Compulsory	Officially Sponsored & Administered

Country	Scheme	Year	Membership	Administration
Netherlands	Collective Guarantee Scheme	1979	Compulsory	Joint Administration
Nigeria	Nigerian Deposit Insurance Corporation	1988	Compulsory	Officially Sponsored & Administered
Norway	Guarantee Fund	1961	Compulsory	Joint Administration
Pakistan	Bank Deposit Insurance Programme	1974	Compulsory	Officially Sponsored & Administered
Paraguay	Sistema Nacional de Ahorro Y Prestamo para la Vivienda	1971	Voluntary	Officially Sponsored & Administered
Philippines	Philippine Deposit Insurance Corporation	1963	Compulsory	Joint Administration
Spain	Deposit Guarantee Fund	1977	Voluntary	Officially Sponsored & Administered
Sweden	Deposit Insurance Fund	NA	NA	Industry Arrangement
Switzerland	Deposit Guarantee Scheme	1984	Voluntary	Offically Sponsored & Administered
Trinidad & Tobago	Deposit Insurance Corporation	1986	Compulsory	Industry Arrangement
Turkey	Turkish Deposit Insurance Fund	1983	Compulsory	Joint Administration
United Kingdom	Deposit Protection Fund	1982	Compulsory	Officially Sponsored & Administered
United States	Federal Deposit Insurance Corporation: Bank Ins. Fund	1933	Voluntary	Officially Sponsored & Administered
	FDIC: Savings Association Insurance Fund	1989	Voluntary	Officially Sponsored & Administered
	National Credit Union Share Insurance Fund	1970	Voluntary	Officially Sponsored & Administered
Venezuela	Bank Deposit Guarantee & Protection Fund	NA	NA	NA

SOURCE: Organization for Economic Co-Operation and Development, Federal Deposit Insurance Corporation, International Monetary Fund, World Bank, and annual reports of the Philippine Deposit Insurance Corporation, and the Deposit Insurance & Credit Guarantee Corporation of India.

1980), but it apparently ceased operations in 1938. The third country to establish federal deposit insurance was Cuba in 1952, a system designed to stem the flight of capital from Cuban banks to insured United States banks (see Talley and Mas, 1989). It is unclear what happened to this system after the revolution in 1958.

For the 32 separate insurance systems shown in Table 2.13 (Germany, like the United States, has separate funds for banks, thrifts, and credit unions), membership is strictly voluntary in nine countries. The remaining countries have compulsory membership for selected types of depositories, and in some cases permit other financial institutions to become members.

Deposit-insurance systems in the different countries are administered in one of three ways. Fourteen of the systems are officially sponsored and administered directly by the federal government. The exact structure varies from one system to another. Some insurers are subordinate to another government agency, such as the Ministry or Department of Finance or the central bank, while others are considered to be autonomous. Still other foreign deposit-insurance systems are either jointly administered through a public and private arrangement or administered through an industry arrangement.

Information on the coverage and premium structure of the foreign deposit-insurance systems is presented in Table 2.14 (Bartholomew and Vanderhoff, 1990). Although both of these aspects of foreign deposit-insurance systems vary considerably, some general observations may be made nonetheless. Most insurance systems have explicit limits on coverage, and only a few, albeit the more recent systems, have coinsurance. None of the systems has risk-based premiums, however. In fact, some of the systems do not even rely upon *ex ante* funding. Instead, they rely on *ex post* funding arrangements whereby assessments are made on members when losses are incurred. Some of the insurance systems with *ex ante* funding arrangements, moreover, have resorted to *ex post* assessments when the reserve fund was seriously encumbered (see, for example, Corrigan, 1990).

A comparison of the types of coverage provided by foreign deposit-insurance systems is presented in Table 2.15 (see Bartholomew and Vanderhoff, 1990). Unlike the United States, few countries extend coverage to interbank deposits. All countries for which information was available cover deposits held by nonresidents. However, only a few, including the United States, provide coverage of deposits denominated in foreign currencies. At least seven countries do not provide coverage for deposits in domestic branches of foreign banks, but the United States and nine other countries do provide such coverage. Most countries do not provide coverage to depositors of overseas branches of domestic banks.

One must be careful in drawing conclusions about deposit-insurance coverage. Many countries implicitly provide coverage of deposits either by not permitting some institutions to fail or by the method of resolving failed institutions. Indeed, some argue that the United States implicitly provides coverage of deposits in overseas branches and subsidiaries through a policy of too big to fail (see Congressional Budget Office, 1990, pp. 249–50).

The United States is not the only country that has had to deal with distressed financial institutions in recent years (see, for example, Cargill and Royama, 1988; Corrigan, 1990; Gilbody, Pecchioli, 1987; Woodward, 1989; and World Bank, 1989). Indeed, at least 25 countries have provided government assistance to distressed financial institutions in the past decade. Some of this assistance has been directly provided by a deposit-insurance system, and some has taken the form of central bank assistance, industry assistance, or direct and indirect government assistance.

The Canada Deposit Insurance Corporation is still C$851 million in deficit as of year-end 1989 as a result of resolving 21 trust and loan and mortgage loan companies and two small regional chartered banks. Canadian bank regulators have also resorted to supervisory mergers and financial assistance to resolve several other regional chartered banks. In 1973, the United Kingdom provided liquidity, through the Bank of England and clearing banks, to keep a number of relatively small, unregulated secondary banks open. This action was taken prior to the establishment of bank deposit insurance in 1982. In 1984, the Bank of England resolved Johnson Matthey by selling it to an Australian bank. Norway resorted to direct government intervention when depressed oil prices posed serious problems to some of its banks in the early 1980s.

Between 1978 and 1983, Spain rescued 51 depositories that held 20 percent of all deposits. In 1965, the Bank of Japan provided assistance to prevent the closure of Yamaichi Securities, one of the then four largest securities companies in the country. In 1974, German authorities closed a medium-sized bank, which led to losses for some large depositors. In 1983, the German central bank persuaded other banks to assist a medium-sized bank until it could be sold to another institution. In 1988, the French government arranged the resolution of a small bank with some losses incurred by insured domestic depositors, though foreign depositors were compensated in full. In 1988, the newly established Italian deposit-insurance fund resolved a large bank that the central bank had tried to rescue through capital injections.

There is relatively little evidence available thus far by which to evaluate the success of foreign deposit-insurance systems. Some have disappeared or been restructured. The Canadian insurance system may have contributed to the prevention of bank runs, but the response to an abnormal number of failures was a multiple-agency effort and included direct and indirect government assistance (see Bartholomew, 1989a). Apparently none of the foreign deposit-insurance systems has yet been required to deal with catastrophic losses. In this regard, the alternative structures of foreign insurance systems may be mainly interesting for their operating features. For example, the provision of coinsurance or an industry-funded arrangement may induce either depositors or other depositories to play a greater

Table 2.14 Insurance Coverage and Pricing Schemes of Deposit-Insurance Systems

Country	Insurance Coverage Limit (Domestic Currency)	U.S. $ Equivalent (as of 4/25/90)	Premium Pricing Scheme
Argentina	100% of deposits up to A$ 100,000,000, 90% above that amount	—	0.03% of total deposits
Austria	A$ 200,000	16,936	Unfunded Arrangement
Belgium	BF 500,000	14,445	0.02% of specified liabilities
Canada	C$ 60,000	51,690	0.1% of insured deposits
Chile	100% of demand deposits, 90% other deposits up to 120 UF	—	Unfunded Arrangement
Colombia	75% of Col$ 200,000	319	0.5% of required reserves on deposits
Finland	FM 500,000	126,040	Between 0.01% and 0.05% of total assets
France	FF 400,000	71,024	Collected as needed, assessments based on deposits
Germany [DSF]	30% of the "liable capital of bank concerned per depositor"	—	0.03% of total deposits
[SBSF]	100% of deposits and credits	—	0.03% of "claims on customers"
[CCSS]	100% of deposits and credits	—	Complex premiums and mutual guarantees
India	Rs 30,000	1,737	0.04% of total deposits
Ireland	80% of first IRP 5,000, 70% of next IRP 5,000, 50% of next IRP 5,000	15,925	0.2% of deposits
Italy	100% of first L 200,000,000, 90% of next L 800,000,000, 80% of next L 2,000,000,000	2,048,256	Unfunded Arrangement
Japan	Y 10,000,000	60,300	0.008% of covered deposit balance
Kenya	Kshs 100,000	NA	0.1% of deposits

Country			
Netherlands	G 35,000	18,533	Unfunded Arrangement
Nigeria	N. 50,000	NA	0.937% of deposits
Norway	Unlimited	—	0.015% of total assets
Pakistan	NA	NA	NA
Paraguay	G 5,000,000	NA	.25% of deposits
Philippines	P 15,000	675	0.0667% of total deposits
Spain	Pts 1,500,000	14,165	.2% of deposits
Sweden	NA	—	Fund at such a level that in recent years annual contributions considered to be unnecessary
Switzerland	SF 30,000	20,541	Unfunded Arrangement
Trinidad & Tobago	TT$ 50,000	NA	NA
Turkey	TL 3,000,000	1,206	0.3% of insured deposits
United Kingdom	75% of deposit balance up to L 10,000	12,281	Progressive levy with the effective rate not to exceed 0.3% of domestic sterling deposits
United States [BIF]	US$ 100,000	100,000	0.12% of deposits in 1990, 0.15% thereafter
[SAIF]	US$ 100,000	100,000	0.208% of deposits in 1990, 0.23% in 1991–93, 0.18% in 1994–97, 0.15% thereafter
[NCUSIF]	US$ 100,000	100,000	May assess 0.083% of insured shares; since 1984, assessed only to maintain level of 1% of insured shares
Venezuela	NA	NA	NA

SOURCE: Organization for Economic Co-Operation and Development, Federal Deposit Insurance Corporation, International Monetary Fund, Congressional Research Service, World Bank, and annual reports of the Philippine Deposit Insurance Corporation, and the Deposit Insurance & Credit Guarantee Corporation of India.

Table 2.15 **Selected Characteristics of Deposit-Insurance Systems**

Country	Coverage of Interbank Deposits	Coverage of Deposits Held By Nonresidents	Coverage of Deposits in Foreign Currency	Coverage of Deposits in Domestic Branches of Foreign Banks	Coverage of Deposits in Foreign Branches of Domestic Banks
Argentina	N	Y	N	—	—
Austria	N	Y	Y	N	N
Belgium	N	Y	N	N	N
Canada	Y	Y	N	—	N
Chile	N	Y	N	Y	N
Colombia	Y	Y	—	—	—
Finland	—	—	—	—	—
France	N	Y	N	Y	N
Germany [DSF]	N	Y	Y	Y	Y
[SBSF]	—	—	—	—	—
[CCSS]	—	—	—	—	—
India	N	Y	N	N	N
Ireland	—	—	P	—	—
Italy	N	—	Y	—	Y
Japan	N	Y	N	N	Y
Kenya	Y	Y	—	—	—

Netherlands	N	Y	Y	Y	N
Nigeria	Y	Y	Y	Y	N
Norway	Y	Y	Y	Y	Y
Pakistan	Y	Y	Y	Y	Y
Paraguay	N	Y	N	N	—
Philippines	N	—	Y	—	—
Spain	N	Y	N	—	N
Sweden	—	—	—	—	—
Switzerland	N	Y	Y	N	—
Trinidad & Tobago	Y	Y	Y	Y	N
Turkey	N	Y	Y	N	N
United Kingdom	N	Y	N	Y	N
United States	Y	Y	Y	Y	N
Venezuela	—	—	—	—	—

NOTE: N = No, Y = Yes, P = Provisionally, — = Information unavailable.

SOURCE: Federal Deposit Insurance Corporation and World Bank.

role in limiting risk. It is still too early to make such an assessment, however, because the experience with these systems is limited, particularly in view of the fact that the overall regulatory environments within which financial institutions operate vary from one to another.

HOW SHOULD THE FEDERAL DEPOSIT INSURANCE SYSTEM BE REFORMED?

More than 50 years ago, when federal deposit insurance was being established, it was stated that

> It [federal deposit insurance] will doubtless, as charged by its opponents, encourage unsound banking. The reckless banker will offer greater inducements to the public than the conservative banker, and as the public will realize that it is equally well protected in either institution, it will be attracted by the more liberal promises of the less sound bank. This will draw business away from the sound banks, and will increase the payments that the fund will be called on to make to reimburse depositors in failed banks. Careful, frequent and intelligent examinations and a vigilant and strict supervision of insured banks will keep down losses. But whether they can be maintained in this character and whether they can hold losses down to a point that makes the continuance of the guaranty possible can be told only by putting the plan in actual operation. (Malburn, 1934, p. 170)

The insurance plan for thrift institutions was put into operation in 1934 and the expected losses at insolvent institutions resolved during the 1980s and the 1990s exceed those incurred by depositors of thrifts during the Great Depression.

It has been argued here that the reason for the current thrift crisis is the structure of the federal deposit-insurance system. Before discussing how the system could be restructured, it may be instructive to recall that under the permanent deposit-insurance plan of the Banking Act of 1933, deposits were to be insured up to $10,000 in full, 75 percent of the next $40,000, and 50 percent of amounts over $50,000, and the funds for operating the plan were to be obtained by subscriptions to stock in the Federal Deposit Insurance Corporation by the Treasury, by the Federal Reserve System and by insured banks. Furthermore, repeated subscriptions to stock could be exacted from banks in times of stress. As has been noted, "The absence of any such reserve feature renders this a plan of mutual guaranty rather than insurance," a plan that was "attacked vigorously" by the bankers (Emerson, 1934, p. 235). However, this plan was scrapped in favor of simply providing for full insurance of deposits up to $5,000 and a flat insurance premium of one-twelfth of 1 percent per annum to generate operating funds. Interestingly enough, there are calls today for reforming federal deposit insurance by introducing coinsurance and putting the capital of institutions between the insured depositors and taxpayers in the form of a mutual or cross-guarantee system.

As regards the setting of the federal deposit-insurance premium at one-twelfth of 1 percent, it is interesting to note how this particular figure was arrived at (for more detail on the origin and evolution of the coverage and premium structures for both banks and thrift institutions, see Barth, Fied, Riedel, and Tunis, 1989). In testimony before the House Committee on Banking and Currency, the first Chairman of the Federal Deposit Insurance Corporation, Leo T. Crowley, stated that "a premium at the rate of one-third of 1 percent of total deposits would have been necessary to cover all losses to depositors during the past 70 years. A premium at the rate of one-eighth of 1 percent would have covered depositors' losses in all years except those of severe depression." He added that "It is one-tenth of 1 percent for the deposits of $5,000 and under." Then why was the premium set at one-twelfth of 1 percent? According to the Chairman, "we do not believe that one-twelfth of 1 percent will build large enough reserves for the Deposit Insurance Corporation for the future, but the earning capacity of the banks right now is very low" (Crowley, 1935, pp. 10, 49, and 48, respectively). But what was to be done during a period in which abnormal or catastrophic losses swamped the insurance fund? The question was left unanswered.

One final historical note is that the federal government did not provide federal insurance for the first time in the 1930s. In fact, it provided insurance for postal savings deposits in 1910. During the Great Depression, this system provided a place for depositors to run to with the funds they withdrew from banks and thrifts (see O'Hara and Easley, 1979). At the state level, moreover, several states established plans prior to the 1930s (see Calomiris, 1989 and Golembe, 1960).

In any event, it is time to return to the issue of reforming the structure of the federal deposit-insurance system. The need to reform is based on the view that although the insurance system protected the small depositor and prevented widespread runs in the 1980s it did not adequately protect the taxpayer. The cost of resolving insolvent thrift institutions escalated enormously when inadequately capitalized institutions were not closed in a timely and cost-effective manner. The rationale for reform is therefore based on the excessive costs imposed on taxpayers by the existing structure of the federal deposit-insurance system. By leaving this structure essentially intact, FIRREA does not ensure that such excessive costs will never again materialize.

The basic issues involved in deciding on the appropriate role for the federal government with respect to depository institutions center around the availability of accurate financial information, the ability and willingness to act appropriately on such information, and who shares in losses resulting from insolvencies. Without federal deposit insurance there is always the possibility that depositors will engage in widespread runs on banks, even solvent banks, and thereby disrupt the payments system and the credit process. The result will be not only insolvency losses, but excessive losses because even solvent banks will be driven into insolvency as they are forced to sell assets at fire-sale prices to meet the heavy deposit withdrawals. Of course, the losses would be shared by equity owners and depositors, not taxpayers. The fundamental problem is that inadequate information prevents depositors from distinguishing the solvent from the insolvent banks. And should widespread runs occur, taxpayers as well as bank owners and depositors would be seriously and adversely affected.

A lender of last resort, however, could supply liquidity to those banks that are solvent but nonetheless incurring heavy deposit withdrawals. Only the insolvent banks would then be forced to close by the heavy withdrawal of deposits. Yet, for the lender of last resort to function properly it, like a federal insurer, must have sufficient information to distinguish between solvent and insolvent banks and then the ability and willingness to act appropriately based on that information.

Federal deposit insurance removes the incentive for depositors to run on banks, whether solvent or insolvent. It protects small depositors and prevents runs, but simultaneously exposes taxpayers to losses resulting from risky actions taken by institutions induced by moral hazard and from inadequate preventive measures of the federal insurer. The federal insurer must close all insolvent banks in a timely and cost-effective manner or the losses from insolvencies will necessarily be excessive and therefore potentially shared by taxpayers.

One is clearly engaged in a balancing act when trying to structure federal deposit insurance properly. Information is crucial in this balancing act. *If* one can assess the market value of the assets and liabilities of a bank, then one can determine whether a depository institution is solvent or insolvent or, stated another way, adequately capitalized. To reduce the exposure of taxpayers to losses, one would simply assess the market value of an institution and then close the institution when the market value of the owner's contributed equity reaches zero (see Brumbaugh, 1988, and Benston and Kaufman, 1988).

Market values are not readily available for all assets and liabilities, however. This means that such values are necessarily estimates and hence imprecise. Despite this, one can require than an institution hold "adequate" capital relative to its assets to protect taxpayers as well as to provide an incentive for the institution to engage in less risky activities. The riskiest activities are likely to be undertaken by those institutions with inadequate capital and access to federal deposit insurance. The insurer could collect the best available market-value information, base capital requirements on this information, and then close or otherwise take appropriate action against an institution when its capital has been seriously dissipated or depleted. This clearly was not done by the federal insurer of thrifts during the 1980s, especially the early 1980s, or even during the 1960s and the 1970s when the thrift industry also encountered significant difficulties. Indeed, a case can be made that the *federal* laws and regulations governing thrift institutions since the Great Depression have failed to adapt rapidly enough to evolving market forces and have thereby increasingly exposed these institutions to greater risk which ironically enough was inadequately contained by the *federal* insurer. Would such a flawed institutional design have arisen in a free marketplace (see, for example, Barth and Regalia, 1988)?

The role for deposit-insurance premiums in a reformed system is to reflect the fair value of the deposit insurance to an institution. The riskier the activities in which an institution engages and the weaker its capital position, the greater the value of deposit insurance to that institution and therefore the higher the premium should be. But adjusting deposit premiums upward is no replacement for early intervention or for closing an institution when its owner's contributed equity has been depleted. In a recent paper, Barth, Page, and Brumbaugh (1992) show, using option-pricing techniques, that those thrift institutions that should have been assessed the highest premiums in the 1980s were actually operating without any owner-contributed equity whatsoever.

One could simply reform the federal deposit-insurance system by requiring that all deposits be backed or collateralized by highly marketable and essentially riskless assets. This would protect the payments system from widespread runs because depositors would know that the market value of the assets would essentially always equal the value of deposits. Thus limiting or narrowing the assets that could be acquired would convert the current commercial bank into a narrow bank (see Litan, 1987). The narrowness of the bank depends on the assets acquired with the insured deposits, such acquisition depending on the availability of accurate financial information regarding the market value of specific assets. Under this proposal, all remaining assets of the bank would be funded with uninsured liabilities and owner's contributed equity capital.

The narrow bank proposal accomplishes the following goals. First, it protects small depositors. Second, it prevents widespread bank runs by backing deposits with assets whose market value equals those deposits. Third, it protects taxpayers from losses arising from declines bringing asset values below the value of insured deposits plus uninsured liabilities plus owner's contributed equity capital because in essence there will be no such declines. Fourth, while the narrow or payments portion of the bank is fully protected against loss, the remaining or credit portion is not. Any losses associated with the credit portion are borne by the owners of the uninsured liabilities and capital, not by the taxpayers. Fifth, such a system actually makes deposit insurance redundant and the need for bank activity regulation irrelevant. This proposal seems to be based on the premise that market-value information for a broad range of assets is unavailable or too imprecise or that the insurer will not act on such information in a timely and cost-effective manner.

Another proposal is to retain federal deposit insurance but to impose more market discipline. This could be accomplished through coinsurance or by reducing the amount of deposit-insurance coverage, either per account or per depositor. Depositors will demand higher rates on their funds placed at banks engaged in relatively risky activities and with relatively little capital. This imposes discipline on banks operating in a competitive market. Moreover, the insurer can rely on the rates paid on uninsured deposits or any other uninsured liabilities to assess better the financial condition of an institution. However, the risk of a widespread run increases under this type of reform proposal as compared to the current federal insurance system.

Another proposal for reform also relies on market discipline, but in a different way. This is the proposal for cross-guarantees by banks themselves or self-insurance (see Ely, 1989). Banks would establish a fairly elaborate system under which the entire capital of the banking system would be available to cover losses from insolvencies. By charging appropriate premiums to one another, the banks themselves would provide the mechanism to induce banks to control their risk exposure through the types and degree of activities in which they engage or through a higher capital position. In the case of abnormal or catastrophic losses, the federal government or taxpayers would serve as a backstop to the banks. Two potential limitations of this proposal are that depositors may engage in widespread runs for fear that the combined capital of the banks is insufficient to protect them, and that the banks themselves will have an incentive to overstate any losses—the opposite of what troubled thrift institutions now have an incentive to do—to protect their capital from being depleted and thus put pressure on the federal government to step forward prematurely and share in the losses.

Finally, one could rely on a form of reinsurance in which the federal insurer would protect some relatively high percentage of all losses from insolvencies of depository institutions and the reinsurer the remaining percentage. The reinsurer would be responsible for assessing the overall riskiness of a depository institution and determining an appropriate insurance premium. The federal insurer could then, if it wished, apply this premium to all insured deposits. The merit of this particular proposal is that specialized private firms would be assessing the financial condition of insured depository institutions. In putting their own capital at risk, they would have every incentive to collect and assess the most appropriate financial information by which to set an appropriate deposit-insurance premium. More generally, such firms would establish contractual relationships with depository institutions that would provide market-based information to the federal insurer and the public, likely ensuring that inadequately capitalized institutions would be closed or reorganized in a timely and cost-effective manner. As Scott and Mayer said in a seminal paper on deposit insurance years ago, "This is probably the most promising solution. Part, if not all, of the pricing judgment could be transferred to the private sector. . . . The resulting demand would bring a new form of deposit insurance into existence and thereby create a large, independent set of risk judgments" (Scott and Mayer, 1971, p. 575).

In sum, all the proposals for reforming the structure of the federal deposit-insurance system involve the collection and assessment of market-based information, reliance on an adequate level of owner's equity capital, and the closure or reorganization of inadequately capitalized depository institutions in a timely and cost-effective manner. The disagreement is over who does these things or sees that they are done. If one cannot obtain good information for a broad range of assets, the narrow bank proposal or a modification thereof is quite attractive. If one can obtain enough information to both set appropriate insurance premiums and cancel insurance based on that information and still enable the firms paying and receiving the premiums to earn an acceptable profit, then the government and private firms, either independently or cooperatively, can operate an insurance plan. If the federal insurer will or cannot act upon the available information in an appropriate manner, then one would want heavy, if not exclusive, private sector involvement.

The basic question is: Who can collect and assess the best information to determine with substantial precision the financial condition of depository institutions? The depositors may not do so and may thus engage in widespread runs on *all* depository institutions. A narrow bank solves this problem by providing depositors with sufficient information so they will not run. Federal deposit insurance also provides depositors with enough information that they will not run. The information is that the federal government has sufficient capital or taxing power to make whole all insured deposits. But the federal insurer may not adequately protect taxpayers. It may either not collect and assess the best information to determine the financial condition of depository institutions or it may not act on such information in a timely and cost-effective manner. Hence, the private sector can be exposed to greater risk or asked to assume greater risk and to assist the federal insurer by collecting and assessing information and even setting deposit-insurance premiums that reflect the overall riskiness of the activities in which depository institutions are engaged, taking into account the owner's contributed equity capital. By putting more of its own capital at risk, the private sector will have every incentive to contain the riskiness of insured depository institutions. The greater the reliance on the private sector, however, the more concern there will be about sufficiency of capital to prevent depositors from engaging in widespread runs. To the extent that the federal government will always be in the picture, it may make the most sense to investigate more closely proposals involving reinsurance or private-firm risk-pricing schemes because of their information-signaling usefulness. The role of the federal government would then be more clearly defined and thus susceptible to more public scrutiny.

SUMMARY AND CONCLUSIONS

It has been argued here that the major culprit in the thrift crisis is the current structure of the federal deposit-insurance system. By failing to reform this system, FIRREA does not ensure that taxpayers will not again be called upon to share in excessive losses. But how should the deposit-insurance system be reformed? The easy answer is to rely more on the private marketplace. What this really means is subject to disagreement, however. The key is to restructure the federal deposit-insurance system to permit evolution in the depository institutions industry while simultaneously identifying, managing, and funding any troubled institutions in a timely and cost-effective manner. Furthermore, this task which is extremely complex and difficult, must not be considered in isolation. One must also consider the appropriate regulatory structure in any restructured insurance system as well as the overall effect on the long-run values of the charters for those depository institutions that will continue to function.

REFERENCES

Avery, Robert B., Gerald A. Hanweck, and Myron L. Kwast, "An Analysis of Risk-Based Deposit Insurance for Commercial Banks," *Bank Structure and Competition,* Federal Reserve Bank of Chicago, 1985.

Baer, Herbert, "Private Prices, Public Insurance: The Pricing of Federal Deposit Insurance," *Economic Perspectives,* Federal Reserve Bank of Chicago, September/October 1986, pp. 23–31.

Barth, James R., "Post FIRREA: The Need to Reform the Federal Deposit Insurance System," 26th Annual Conference on Bank Structure and Competition, Federal Reserve Bank of Chicago, May 9–11, 1990.

————, *The Great Savings and Loan Debacle,* American Enterprise Institute, University Press of America (Washington, D.C.), 1991.

Barth, James R., Philip F. Bartholomew, and Michael G. Bradley, "Reforming Federal Deposit Insurance: What Can Be Learned from Private Insurance Practices?" *Consumer Finance Law Quarterly Report,* Spring 1991.

Barth, James R., Philip F. Bartholomew, and Carol J. Labich, "Moral Hazard and the Thrift Crisis: An Analysis of 1988 Resolutions," *Bank Structure and Competition,* Federal Reserve Bank of Chicago, 1989.

Barth, James R., George J. Benston, and Philip R. Wiest, "The Financial Institutions Reform, Recovery, and Enforcement Act of 1989: Description, Effects, and Implications," *Issues in Bank Regulation,* vol. 13, Winter 1990.

Barth, James R., and R. Dan Brumbaugh, Jr., "The Continuing Bungling of the Savings and Loan Crisis: The Rough Road from FIRREA to the Reform of Deposit Insurance," *Stanford Law and Policy Review,* Spring 1990.

Barth, James R., R. Dan Brumbaugh, Jr., and Daniel Sauerhaft, "Failure Costs of Government-Regulated Financial Firms: The Case of Thrift Institutions," Research Working Paper No. 132, Office of Policy and Economic Research, Federal Home Loan Bank Board, (Washington, D.C.), October 1986.

Barth, James R., R. Dan Brumbaugh, Jr., Daniel Sauerhaft, and George H.K. Wang, "Insolvency and Risk-Taking in the Thrift Industry: Implications for the Future." *Contemporary Policy Issues,* Fall 1985, pp. 1–32.

Barth, James R., John J. Feid, Gabriel Riedel, and H. Hampton Tunis, "Alternative Federal Deposit Insurance Regimes," *Problems of the Federal Savings and Loan Insurance Corporation (FSLIC),* Hearings Before the Committee on Banking, Housing, and Urban Affairs, United States Senate, Part IV, 1989.

Barth, James R., and Martin A. Regalia, "The Evolving Role of Regulation in the Savings and Loan Industry," in *The Financial Services Revolution: Policy Directions for the Future,* eds. Catherine England and Thomas Huertas, Kluwer Academic Publishers (Norwell, Mass.), 1988.

Barth, James R., Daniel E. Page, and R. Dan Brumbaugh, Jr., "Pitfalls in Using Market Prices to Assess the Financial Condition of Depository Institutions," *Journal of Real Estate Finance and Economics,* forthcoming, 1992.

Bartholomew, Philip F., "Recent Developments for Canadian 'Near Banks'," *Housing Finance International,* vol. 4, no. 1, August 1989a, pp. 28–32.

————, "How Some Nations Regulate Depository Institutions," *Office of Thrift Supervision Journal,* vol. 19, no. 10, October 1989b, pp. 20–3.

Bartholomew, Philip F., and Vicki A. Vanderhoff, "Foreign Deposit Insurance Systems: A Comparison," *Consumer Finance Law Quarterly Report,* forthcoming.

Benston, George J., R. Dan Brumbaugh, Jr., Jack M. Guttentag, Richard J. Herring, George G. Kaufman, Robert E. Litan, and Kenneth E. Scott, *Blueprint for Restructuring America's Financial Institutions,* Washington, D.C.: The Brookings Institution, 1989.

Benston, George J., Robert A. Eisenbeis, Paul Horvitz, Edward J. Kane, and George G. Kaufman, *Perspectives on Safe and Sound Banking: Past, Present, and Future,* MIT Press (Cambridge, Mass.), 1986.

Benston, George J., and George A. Kaufman, "Risk and Solvency Regulation of Depository Institutions." Saloman Brothers Center for the Study of Financial Institutions, New York University, 1988.

Black, William K., Prepared Statement Before the Committee on Banking, Finance and Urban Affairs, U.S. House of Representatives Concerning Lincoln Savings and Loan Association, 1989.

Bremer, C. D., *American Bank Failures,* AMS Press, Inc. (New York), 1935.

Brumbaugh, R. Dan, Jr., *Thrifts Under Siege,* Ballinger Publishing Co. (Cambridge, Mass.) 1988.

Brumbaugh, R. Dan, Jr., and Andrew S. Carron, "Thrift Industry Crisis: Causes and Solutions," *Brookings Paper on Economic Activity,* 2: 1987, pp. 349–88.

Brumbaugh, R. Dan, Jr., and Robert E. Litan, "The S&L Crisis: How to Get Out and Stay Out," *The Brookings Review,* Spring 1989, pp. 3–13.

Calomiris, Charles W., "Deposit Insurance: Lessons from the Record," *Economic Perspectives,* Federal Reserve Bank of Chicago, May/June 1989, pp. 10–30.

Cargill, Thomas, and S. Royama, *The Transition of Finance in Japan and the United States: A Comparative Perspective,* Hoover Institution Press (Stanford, Cal.), 1988.

Carron, Andrew S., "Overseas Financial Sector Deregulation: Lessons from Australia and New Zealand," *Bank Structure and Competition,* Federal Reserve Bank of Chicago, May 1985, pp. 34–42.

———, "The Political Economy of Financial Regulation," in *The Political Economy of Deregulation,* eds. Roger G. Noll and Bruce Owen, American Enterprise Institute (Washington, D.C.), 1983.

———, *The Plight of the Thrift Institutions,* The Brookings Institution (Washington, D.C.), 1982.

Carron, Andrew S., and R. Dan Brumbaugh, Jr., "The Viability of the Thrift Industry," *Housing Policy Debate,* Federal National Mortgage Association, Summer 1990.

Congressional Budget Office, *Reducing the Deficit: Spending and Revenue Options,* A Report to the Senate and House Committees on the Budget—Part II, February 1990, pp. 249–50.

Corrigan, E. Gerald, "Statement Before the United States Senate Committee on Banking, Housing and Urban Affairs," May 3, 1990.

Crowley, Leo T., "Statement," *Banking Act of 1935,* Hearings Before the Committee on Banking and Currency, House of Representatives, 1935.

Ely, Bert, Presentation to the National Economists Club, June 27, 1989.

———, "Yes—Private Sector Deposit Insurance Is a Viable Alternative to Federal Deposit Insurance!" *Bank Structure and Competition,* Federal Reserve Bank of Chicago, 1985.

Emerson, Guy, "Guaranty of Deposits Under the Banking Act of 1933," *Quarterly Journal of Economics,* vol. 48, 1934, pp. 229–44.

England, Catherine, "Private Deposit Insurance: Stabilizing the Banking System," Policy Analysis, no. 54, Cato Institute (Washington, D.C.), 1985.

Federal Deposit Insurance Corporation, *The First Fifty Years: A History of the FDIC 1933–1983,* Washington, D.C., 1985.

Federal Deposit Insurance Corporation, *Deposit Insurance for the Nineties: Meeting the Challenge (Draft),* Washington, D.C., 1989.

Gilbody, John, *The UK Monetary & Financial System: An Introduction,* Routledge (London), 1988.

Golembe, C., "The Deposit Insurance Legislation of 1933: An Examination of Its Antecedents and Its Purposes," *Political Science Quarterly,* vol. 75, no. 2, June 1960, pp. 181–200.

Gup, Benton E., *Bank Fraud: Exposing the Hidden Threat to Financial Institutions,* Bank Administration Institute (Rolling Meadows, Ill.), 1990.

Horvitz, Paul M., "Capital is the Best Deposit Insurance Protector," *Outlook of the Federal Home Loan Bank System,* July/August 1987, pp. 32–4.

———, "The Case Against Risk-Related Deposit Insurance Premiums," *Housing Finance Review,* July 1983, pp. 253–63.

Jones, Homer, "An Appraisal of the Rules and Procedures of Bank Supervision, 1929–39," *Journal of Political Economy,* February–December, 1940, pp. 183–98.

———, "Some Problems of Bank Supervision," *Journal of the American Statistical Association,* vol. 33, no. 202, June 1938, pp. 334–40.

Kane, Edward J., "Dangers of Capital Forbearance: The Case of the FSLIC and Zombie S&Ls," *Contemporary Policy Issues,* vol. 5, no. 1, 1987, pp. 77–83.

———, *The S&L Insurance Mess: How Did It Happen?* The Brookings Institution (Washington, D.C.), 1987.

———, *The Gathering Crisis in Federal Deposit Insurance,* MIT Press (Cambridge, Mass.), 1985.

Lindow, Wesley, "Bank Capital and Risk Assets," *National Banking Review,* September 1963, pp. 29–46.

Litan, Robert E., *What Should Banks Do?* The Brookings Institution (Washington, D.C.), 1987.

Malburn, William P., *What Happened to Our Banks,* The Bobbs-Merrill Company (Indianapolis), 1934.

McCahan, David, "Failure of Bank Guaranty Plans," in *Federal Regulation of Banking,* compiled by James Goodwin Hodgson, The Reference Shelf, vol. 8, no. 6, The H. W. Wilson Company (New York), 1932.

McCarthy, Ian, "Deposit Insurance: Theory and Practice," *Staff Papers,* International Monetary Fund, vol. 27, no. 3, September 1980, pp. 579–82.

O'Connor, J. F. T., *Banking Act of 1935,* Hearings Before the Committee on Banking and Commerce, House of Representatives, 1935.

O'Hara, M., and D. Easley, "The U.S. Postal Savings System in the Depression," *Journal of Economic History,* vol. 39, no. 3, September 1979, pp. 741–53.

Pecchioli, R., *Prudential Supervision in Banking,* Organization for Economic Co-Operation and Development (Paris), 1987.

Pratt, Richard T., "Annual Report 1982," *Federal Home Loan Bank Board Journal,* April 1983.

———, Testimony Before the Committee on Banking, Housing and Urban Affairs, United States Senate, August 3, 1988.

Pyle, David H., "Comment on Bank Regulation and Monetary Policy," *Journal of Money, Credit and Banking,* November 1985, Part 2, pp. 722–4.

Rochester, David P., "Savings and Loan Reserve Requirements: An Analysis and Review," *Federal Home Loan Bank Board Journal,* October 1979, pp. 4–15.

Romer, Thomas, and Barry R. Weingast, "Political Foundations of the Thrift Debacle," presentation at the CEPR Conference on Reform of Deposit Insurance and the Regulation of Depository Institutions, Washington, D.C., May 18–19, 1990.

Ryon, Sandra L., "History of Bank Capital Adequacy Analysis," Working Paper No. 69-4, Division of Research, 1969.

Scott, Kenneth E., "Never Again: The S&L Bailout Bill," The 26th Annual Conference on Bank Structure and Competition, Federal Reserve Bank of Chicago, May 9–11, 1990.

Scott, Kenneth E., and Thomas Mayer, "Risk and Regulation in Banking: Some Proposals for Federal Deposit Insurance Reform," *Stanford Law Review,* May 1971, pp. 537–82.

Short, Eugenie D., and Gerald P. O'Driscoll, Jr., "Deregulation and Deposit Insurance," *Economic Review,* Federal Reserve Bank of Dallas, September 1983, pp. 11–22.

Smith, Fred L., Jr., and Melanie S. Tammen, "Plugging America's Financial Black Holes: Reforming the Federal Deposit Insurance System," *Consumer Finance Law Quarterly Report,* Winter 1989, pp. 44–8.

Strunk, N., and F. Case, *Where Deregulation Went Wrong: A Look at the Causes Behind Savings and Loan Failures in the 1980s,* U.S. League of Savings Institutions, Chicago, 1988.

Taggart, J. H., and L. D. Jennings, "The Insurance of Bank Deposits," *Journal of Political Economy,* February–December, 1934, pp. 508–16.

Talley, S., and I. Mas, "Deposit Insurance in Developing Countries," unpublished manuscript, World Bank, December 1989.

Warren, Melinda, and Kenneth Chilton, *The Regulatory Legacy of the Reagan Revolution: An Analysis of 1990 Federal Regulatory Budgets and Staffing,* Center for the Study of American Business, Washington University (St. Louis, Mo.), May 1989.

White, Lawrence J., "Problems of the FSLIC: A Former Policy Maker's View," *Contemporary Policy Issues,* vol. 8, no. 2, April 1990, pp. 62–81.

———, "Mark to Market Accounting is Vital to FSLIC and Valuable to Thrifts," *Outlook of the Federal Home Loan Bank System,* January/February 1988, pp. 20–4.

———, "The Reform of Federal Deposit Insurance," *Journal of Economic Perspectives,* November 1989.

———, "The Value of Market Value Accounting for the Deposit Insurance System," *Journal of Accounting, Auditing, and Finance,* April 1991.

Woodward, G. Thomas, "Deposit Guarantees in Other Countries," *Congressional Research Report for Congress,* Congressional Research Service, No. 89-637E, November 1989.

World Bank, *World Development Report 1989,* Oxford University Press (New York), 1989.

Appendix

ALL TANGIBLE INSOLVENT THRIFT INSTITUTIONS: TANGIBLE NET WORTH AND LENGTH OF INSOLVENCY, DECEMBER 31, 1989

Docket Number	Months Since First Insolvency	Months of Consistent Insolvency	Conservatorship Dummy Variable	Institution Name	City	St	Tangible Net Worth ($ mil)	GAAP Net Worth ($ mil)	GAAP Assets ($ mil)	Tangible Assets ($ mil)
3406	15	15	1	1st PS&LA of Estherville & Emmetsburg	Estherville	IA	−7.3	−7.3	47.8	47.8
2953	39	6	0	ABQ Bank, a Federal Savings Bank	Albuquerque	NM	−117.8	−93.7	2018.7	1994.6
8583	45	45	1	Alamo FSA of Texas	San Antonio	TX	−336.9	−336.9	528.9	528.9
3573	90	90	0	Albany First FS & LA	Albany	GA	−3.1	0.5	183.6	179.9
8641	18	18	1	Alpine Savings, A FS & LA	Steamboat Springs	CO	−8.7	−8.7	45.5	45.5
1398	84	84	0	American Bank, FSB	Sanford	ME	−6.4	0.7	51.8	44.6
4099	0	0	0	American Charter FS & LA	Lincoln	NE	−2.0	−2.0	1386.7	1386.7
1872	90	90	0	American Federal Bank, FSB	Greenville	SC	−12.7	36.0	1113.2	1064.5
6675	78	78	1	American FS & LA	Albuquerque	NM	−33.4	−33.4	142.1	142.1
7299	21	21	0	American FS & LA of Ada	Ada	OK	−1.4	4.9	108.2	101.9
3965	72	72	0	American FS & LA of Iowa	Des Moines	IA	−33.4	3.6	910.7	873.7
8675	3	3	1	American Home S & LA, FA	Edmond	OK	−4.2	−4.2	83.9	83.9
8595	9	9	1	American Interstate SA, FA	Los Angeles	CA	−1.9	−1.9	19.4	19.4
7796	9	9	0	American Pioneer Savings Bank	Orlando	FL	−7.1	45.2	1754.5	1702.2
6917	78	39	1	American S & LA of Brazoria	Lake Jackson	TX	−163.0	−163.0	189.4	189.4
8618	21	21	1	American S & LA, FA	New Orleans	LA	−15.0	−15.0	53.8	53.8

8670	12	12	1	American Savings of Colorado, A FS&LA	Colorado Springs	CO	−217.2	−217.2	681.5	681.5
8665	96	96	1	American Savings, A FS & LA	Salt Lake City	UT	−258.7	−258.7	1748.4	1748.4
104	63	18	1	American Security FS & LA	Chicago	IL	−5.9	−5.9	33.4	33.4
6743	69	66	1	Amerimac Savings Bank, FSB	Hillsboro	IL	−8.8	−8.8	17.3	17.3
6907	33	33	1	Ameriway Savings	Houston	TX	−147.1	−147.1	117.5	117.5
8632	84	30	1	Anchor FS & LA	Kansas City	KS	−76.7	−76.7	657.8	657.8
7814	96	96	0	Anchor Savings Bank, FSB	Northport	NY	−89.0	412.0	8928.1	8427.2
8710	90	90	1	Arlington Heights SA, FA	Arlington Heights	IL	−23.1	−23.1	509.8	509.8
8638	48	48	1	Arrowhead Pacific FSB	San Bernardino	CA	−33.8	−33.8	66.5	66.5
8694	18	18	1	Aspen Savings Bank, FSB	Aspen	CO	−21.7	−21.7	111.9	111.9
3546	0	0	0	Atlanta FS & LA	Atlanta	TX	−1.2	−1.2	94.6	94.6
2555	90	90	0	Atlantic Financial Federal	Bala Cynwyd	PA	−359.7	−359.7	5299.4	5299.4
8711	90	33	1	Atlantic Permanent FSB	Norfolk	VA	−17.9	−17.9	559.9	559.9
3009	78	3	0	Aurora FSB	Aurora	IL	−2.9	−2.9	320.0	320.0
8706	3	3	1	Austin FS & LA	Austin	TX	−1.3	−1.3	106.4	106.4
840	15	15	1	Baldwin County Federal Savings Bank	Robertsdale	AL	−10.3	−10.3	155.8	155.8
1718	90	90	1	Baltimore Federal Financial, FSA	Baltimore	MD	−265.4	−265.4	1183.8	1183.8
8680	12	12	1	Banc Iowa Federal Savings Bank	Cedar Rapids	IA	−20.1	−20.1	146.5	146.5
6433	51	51	1	Bancplus Savings Association	Pasadena	TX	−450.2	−450.2	489.2	489.2
7626	27	27	0	Bank USA SA	Silvis	IL	−0.4	0.7	22.7	21.7

Docket Number	Months Since First Insolvency	Months of Consistent Insolvency	Conservatorship Dummy Variable	Institution Name	City	St	Tangible Net Worth ($ mil)	GAAP Net Worth ($ mil)	GAAP Assets ($ mil)	Tangible Assets ($ mil)
17	63	63	1	Bankers S & LA	Galveston	TX	−18.0	−18.0	87.8	87.8
6228	3	0	0	Bannerbanc Savings Association	Garland	TX	−10.2	−10.2	54.2	54.2
6124	30	30	1	Bayshore SA	La Porte	TX	−29.6	−29.6	38.1	38.1
2810	84	84	0	Beacon Federal Savings Bank	Baldwin	NY	−5.7	5.1	476.0	465.2
8085	15	15	1	Bedford SA	Bedford	TX	−43.3	−43.3	71.9	71.9
8591	90	90	1	Benjamin Franklin FSA	Houston	TX	−412.2	−412.2	1838.0	1838.0
8289	12	12	1	Bexar Savings Association	San Antonio	TX	−402.1	−402.1	544.1	544.1
8633	6	6	1	Black Hawk S & LA, FA	Rock Island	IL	−1.4	−1.4	64.9	64.9
658	24	24	1	Blue Valley FS & LA	Kansas City	MO	−148.1	−148.1	680.7	680.7
7731	39	39	1	Brickellbanc SA	Miami	FL	−10.1	−10.1	35.3	35.3
6370	57	45	1	Bright Banc SA	Dallas	TX	−1219.9	−961.5	2832.1	2573.8
8639	78	36	1	Broadview Federal Savings Bank	Cleveland	OH	−71.9	−60.8	1383.1	1372.1
8705	63	3	1	Brookside FS & LA	Los Angeles	CA	−24.0	−24.0	551.8	551.8
8631	12	12	1	Cabrillo Federal Savings Bank	Hayward	CA	−2.3	−2.3	50.9	50.9
8615	12	12	1	Capital FS & LA	Little Rock	AR	−10.4	−10.4	77.6	77.6
759	84	84	0	Capital-Union Savings FA	Baton Rouge	LA	−51.1	−10.8	398.0	357.7
8608	90	15	1	Capitol City FSA	Austin	TX	−102.3	−102.3	408.6	408.6
1777	0	0	0	Capitol FS & LA of Denver	Aurora	CO	−49.4	−48.7	1077.7	1076.9
8624	51	9	1	Caprock FS & LA	Lubbock	TX	−228.5	−228.5	342.7	342.7
2769	78	78	1	Cass FS & LA of St. Louis	Florissant	MO	−14.7	−14.7	46.4	46.4

				Name	City	State				
8622	18	18	1	Centennial FS & LA	Greenville	TX	−24.2	−24.2	52.5	52.5
4153	96	96	0	Central Federal Savings FSB	Long Beach	NY	−66.9	−40.8	921.1	895.0
7514	84	33	1	Central S & LA	Jackson	MS	−24.8	−24.2	48.0	47.5
8605	72	72	1	Central S & LA, FA	New Orleans	LA	−21.8	−21.8	49.2	49.2
5347	78	78	1	Central Texas S & LA	Waco	TX	−63.9	−56.4	171.7	164.2
2745	72	12	0	Centrust Bank, A State Savings Bank	Miami	FL	−195.0	179.2	8217.6	7843.4
5242	60	60	0	Century Federal Savings Bank	Chicago	IL	−1.0	2.0	28.1	25.1
3946	63	12	1	Century Federal Savings Bank	Trenton	TN	−14.9	−14.9	58.4	58.4
4113	57	21	0	Certified SA	Georgetown	TX	−22.1	−16.9	118.9	113.6
4855	84	84	0	Champion FS & LA	Bloomington	IL	−17.7	89.6	2607.5	2500.3
360	90	90	0	Charter Federal Savings Bank	Bristol	VA	−15.9	33.7	1023.4	973.9
8009	0	0	0	Charter FS & LA	Stamford	CT	−0.0	−0.0	108.4	108.4
7608	15	15	0	Charter Savings Bank	Newport Beach	CA	−6.1	11.8	331.4	313.5
3416	60	60	1	Chilicothe FS & LA	Chillicothe	IL	−5.8	−5.8	39.6	39.6
8531	78	78	0	Citizens Federal Savings Bank	Out-of-District	IN	−6.0	2.9	80.0	71.1
8601	34	45	1	Citizens Homestead FSA	New Orleans	LA	−16.5	−16.5	99.0	99.0
5014	78	78	0	Citizens L & S Co	Lima	OH	−1.8	−1.8	120.5	120.5
6475	66	66	1	Citizens of Texas S & LA	Baytown	TX	−70.3	−70.3	60.1	60.1
8653	72	72	1	Citizens S & LA of Springfield FA	Springfield	IL	−4.7	−4.7	78.4	78.4
7347	72	72	1	City Federal S & LA	Oakland	CA	−10.9	−10.9	18.7	18.7
4939	54	54	1	City FS & LA	Birmingham	AL	−55.5	−55.5	492.4	492.4
7871	45	45	1	City SA	League City	TX	−17.0	−17.0	27.6	27.6
8734	90	3	1	City Savings Bank, FSB	Elizabeth	NJ	−805.1	−805.1	8582.5	8582.5
1981	78	78	1	Civic Savings Bank	Portsmouth	OH	−7.5	−6.3	74.5	73.3

Docket Number	Months Since First Insolvency	Months of Consistent Insolvency	Conservatorship Dummy Variable	Institution Name	City	St	Tangible Net Worth ($ mil)	GAAP Net Worth ($ mil)	GAAP Assets ($ mil)	Tangible Assets ($ mil)
3502	90	90	0	Clyde FS & LA	North Riverside	IL	−25.8	−11.1	574.7	560.0
8693	96	6	1	Colonial Federal Savings Association	Roselle Park	NJ	−48.5	−48.5	368.5	368.5
5147	90	90	0	Colonial FS & LA	Cape Girardeau	MO	−12.6	−12.6	171.5	171.5
6547	63	63	0	Colonial Savings, A FA	Prairie Village	KS	−14.7	−14.7	136.4	136.4
371	90	3	0	Colony Savings Bank, FSB	Monaca	PA	−13.6	−13.6	451.4	451.4
7623	15	15	1	Colorado S & LA	Englewood	CO	−17.4	−17.4	36.0	36.0
8669	15	15	1	Colorado Savings Bank, FSB	Sterling	CO	−1.5	−1.5	10.1	10.1
8679	24	24	1	Columbia Federal Hmstd Association	Metairie	LA	−9.3	−9.3	82.0	82.0
6927	45	45	1	Columbia Federal Savings Bank	Westport	CT	−28.5	−28.5	120.6	120.6
8700	3	3	1	Columbia FSA	Nassau Bay	TX	−1.3	−1.3	74.3	74.3
4071	63	63	0	Columbus FSB	Columbus	NE	−0.5	−0.5	101.7	101.7
6298	30	30	1	Commerce SA	San Antonio	TX	−301.6	−301.6	539.0	539.0
5198	30	30	0	Commercial FS & LA	Omaha	NE	−7.0	129.0	5937.0	5801.0
8612	12	12	1	Commercial S & LA, FA	Hammond	LA	−6.9	−6.9	68.6	68.6
8550	6		1	Commonwealth Federal SA	Houston	TX	−787.6	−787.6	1614.2	1614.2
8628	12	12	1	Commonwealth FS & LA	Margate	FL	−163.0	−163.0	1407.7	1407.7
7306	78	66	1	Commonwealth S & LA	Osceola	AR	−10.0	−10.0	29.7	29.7
8707	96	12	1	Community Federal Savings Association	Bridgeport	CT	−1.3	−1.3	55.0	55.0

7567	90	90	1	Community FS & LA	Newport News	VA	−1.4	−1.4	9.1	9.1
2403	84	84	0	Community FS & LA	St. Louis	MO	−464.0	−464.0	3003.5	3003.5
7163	54	54	1	Community FS & LA	Tampa	FL	−11.2	−11.2	6.4	6.4
2410	24	24	1	Community S & LA	Fond du Lac	WI	−19.7	−19.7	141.4	141.4
6338	69	66	0	Community Savings Bank	East Moline	IL	−4.5	−3.7	112.0	111.2
3366	90	90	1	Concordia Federal Bank for Savings	Lansing	IL	−70.3	−70.3	375.3	375.3
8604	15	15	1	Continental FS & LA, FA	Oklahoma City	OK	−107.0	−107.0	528.4	528.4
8532	30	30	1	Continental Savings, A FS & LA	Bellaire	TX	−461.4	−461.4	221.8	221.8
8584	9	9	1	Cornerstone FSA	Houston	TX	−16.1	−16.1	85.0	85.0
8697	0		1	Crest FS & LA	Kankakee	IL	0.2	0.2	126.4	126.4
8627	6	6	1	Cross Roads FS & LA, FA	Checotah	OK	−8.5	−8.5	13.8	13.8
1806	90	90	0	Custer FS & LA	Broken Bow	NE	−0.6	−0.6	52.8	52.8
7589	90	0	0	Cypress Bank, FSB	Pittsburg	TX	−0.2	0.3	31.5	31.1
7482	15	15	1	Deep East Texas SA	Jasper	TX	−8.2	−8.2	45.3	45.3
7538	39	39	1	Delta FS & LA	Drew	MS	−5.8	−5.8	6.1	6.1
8621	138	24	1	Delta FS & LA	Kenner	LA	−51.2	−51.2	133.9	133.9
8659	6	6	1	Denton FS & LA	Denton	TX	−16.1	−16.1	140.2	140.2
7876	3	3	0	Deposit Trust Savings Bank	Monroe	LA	−3.1	−3.1	98.0	98.0
8677	66	66	1	Deseret S & LA, FA	Salt Lake City	UT	−92.9	−92.9	130.1	130.1
3253	90	90	1	Durand FS & LA	Durand	WI	−38.9	−38.9	80.4	80.4
5731	84	84	0	Duval FS & LA	Jacksonville	FL	−54.9	−11.6	1016.3	973.0
8661	9	9	1	East Texas S & LA, FA	Tyler	TX	−33.3	−33.3	287.9	287.9
3671	96	96	0	Eastern FS&LA of Sayville	Sayville	NY	−10.3	−10.3	294.2	294.2
4087	69	0	0	Edgar County S & LA	Paris	IL	−0.1	−0.1	74.9	74.9
78	33	33	0	El Paso FS & LA	El Paso	TX	−20.4	21.8	482.9	440.7

Docket Number	Months Since First Insolvency	Months of Consistent Insolvency	Conservatorship Dummy Variable	Institution Name	City	St	Tangible Net Worth ($ mil)	GAAP Net Worth ($ mil)	GAAP Assets ($ mil)	Tangible Assets ($ mil)
7133	18	18	1	Elysian Federal Savings Bank	Hoboken	NJ	−15.4	−15.4	117.7	117.7
5160	90	90	0	Empire of America FSB	Buffalo	NY	−986.4	−949.4	8173.6	8136.6
2029	42	42	0	Emporia Federal Savings Bank	Emporia	VA	−0.1	−0.1	36.6	36.6
7966	84	84	0	Ensign Bank, FSB	New York	NY	−143.6	2.6	1889.0	1742.8
8053	0	0	0	Enterprise FS & LA	Clearwater	FL	−0.9	−0.9	65.5	65.5
3418	90	78	0	Enterprise Savings Bank, FA	Chicago	IL	−47.0	−15.3	531.2	499.4
4379	42	42	1	Equitable FSB	Fremont	NE	−23.7	−23.7	198.9	198.9
6728	78	78	0	Equitable S & LA, F.A.	Columbus	NE	−2.4	−2.4	73.2	73.2
5776	63	42	1	Equity FSB	Denver	CO	−1.4	−1.4	3.3	3.3
6222	18	18	1	Excel Banc Savings Association	Laredo	TX	−40.4	−40.4	104.5	104.5
1139	72	72	0	Fairmont FS & LA	Fairmont	MN	−2.3	−2.3	46.0	46.0
2289	84	3	0	Fairview FS & LA	Ellicott City	MD	−1.3	−1.3	121.8	121.8
7071	27	27	0	Falls FS & LA	International Fall	MN	−0.2	−0.2	8.5	8.5
2514	60	60	0	Family FS & LA	Dallas	OR	−4.9	−4.9	164.2	164.2
7804	108	15	1	Family FS & LA	Shreveport	LA	−6.7	−6.7	22.4	22.4
5251	54	6	0	Family S & LA	Los Angeles	CA	−0.6	−0.3	138.0	137.7
8676	15	15	1	Family Savings Bank, FSB	Sapulpa	OK	−2.4	−2.4	49.7	49.7
3091	90	90	0	Far West Federal Bank, S B	Portland	OR	−280.0	22.6	3672.8	3370.2
8614	57	57	1	Federal SA of The Southwest	Kilgore	TX	−7.2	−5.1	34.7	32.6

				Institution	City	State				
8698	84	84	1	Fidelity Federal Savings Association	Galesburg	IL	−34.6	−34.6	360.4	360.4
8683	84	21	1	Fidelity Federal Savings Association	Port Arthur	TX	−89.7	−89.7	207.5	207.5
8061	78	42	1	Fidelity FSB	Corinth	MS	−77.4	−77.4	74.6	74.6
650	96	96	0	Fidelity New York FSB	Floral Park	NY	−29.5	61.1	1937.3	1846.8
2441	54	12	0	Fidelity S & LA of Danville	Danville	IL	−0.6	−0.6	16.3	16.3
2485	51	51	1	Financial FS & LA	Joplin	MO	−47.7	−47.7	137.8	137.8
8164	15	3	0	Financial S & LA	Fresno	CA	−3.0	−3.0	31.2	31.2
8648	33	33	1	Financial Security FS & LA	Delray Beach	FL	−37.7	−37.7	104.9	104.9
668	84	84	0	First America Federal Savings Bank	Fort Smith	AR	−19.8	−10.1	476.4	466.7
3722	84	84	0	First American Savings Bank, F.S.B.	Greensboro	NC	−45.1	−3.9	920.2	882.6
1557	90	90	0	First Annapolis Savings Bank, FSB	Annapolis	MD	−52.3	6.9	750.1	691.1
292	90	90	0	First Atlantic S & LA	Plainfield	NJ	−19.2	16.3	1296.6	1260.6
5893	34	15	0	First Bankers Trust & SA	Midland	TX	−3.3	0.3	110.3	106.7
4604	9	9	0	First Central Bank, A FSB	Chariton	IA	−0.7	−0.7	112.8	112.8
6996	84	84	0	First Citizens FS & LA	Fort Pierce	FL	−16.0	−16.0	209.9	209.9
8600	24	24	1	First City FS & LA	Baton Rouge	LA	−5.0	−5.0	18.3	18.3
8635	39	39	1	First Equity Savings Association, FA	Tomball	TX	−64.9	−64.9	73.2	73.2
6020	24	24	1	First Federal Bank of Alaska, SB	Anchorage	AK	−105.2	−105.1	122.2	122.1
8725	66	0	1	First Federal Savings Bank	Diamondville	WY	−0.4	−0.4	21.1	21.1
3073	0	0	0	First Federal Savings Bank	Lubbock	TX	−0.0	−0.0	230.7	230.7

Docket Number	Months Since First Insolvency	Months of Consistent Insolvency	Conservatorship Dummy Variable	Institution Name	City	St	Tangible Net Worth ($ mil)	GAAP Net Worth ($ mil)	GAAP Assets ($ mil)	Tangible Assets ($ mil)
4592	84	84	0	First Federal Savings Bank	Wilmington	DE	−7.0	10.0	323.1	306.1
3975	84	84	0	First Federal Savings Bank of Hanover	Hanover	PA	−3.9	0.5	77.2	72.8
141	78	24	1	First FS & LA	Atlanta	GA	−30.1	−30.1	187.1	187.1
924	90	90	1	First FS & LA	Bakersfield	CA	−11.2	−11.2	117.6	117.6
6100	63	63	1	First FS & LA	Baton Rouge	LA	−21.2	−21.2	37.2	37.2
2549	54	48	0	First FS & LA	Belzoni	MS	−0.1	−0.1	5.1	5.1
7091	66	66	0	First FS & LA	Breaux Bridge	LA	−0.6	−0.6	20.7	20.7
7160	42	42	1	First FS & LA	Eunice	LA	−4.4	−4.4	14.5	14.5
5724	84	84	1	First FS & LA	Fayetteville	AR	−21.7	−18.9	107.2	104.3
6016	60	60	0	First FS & LA	Greenwood	MS	−2.1	−2.1	26.7	26.7
6596	84	84	1	First FS & LA	Largo	FL	−97.9	−97.9	272.8	272.8
3100	66	66	0	First FS & LA	Las Vegas	NM	−0.4	1.5	59.9	58.0
376	51	51	0	First FS & LA	Mt Vernon	OH	−0.9	−0.9	77.9	77.9
3281	9	9	0	First FS & LA	New Braunfels	TX	−4.1	−0.0	235.6	231.5
6345	21	21	1	First FS & LA	New Iberia	LA	−8.8	−8.8	56.5	56.5
25	90	90	1	First FS & LA	Shreveport	LA	−71.1	−71.1	174.7	174.7
6090	42	42	1	First FS & LA	Summerville	GA	−6.1	−6.1	27.5	27.5
6582	0	0	0	First FS & LA	Warner Robins	GA	−1.5	−1.5	157.5	157.5
3400	72	72	0	First FS & LA	Wichita Falls	TX	−3.9	−3.9	84.8	84.8
2941	72	72	0	First FS & LA	Winnfield	LA	−1.2	−1.2	56.8	56.8
2638	60	60	0	First FS & LA of Bismarck	Bismarck	ND	−6.9	−6.9	113.4	113.4
8668	12	12	1	First FS & LA of Brenham	Brenham	TX	−23.0	−23.0	128.3	128.3
6702	9	9	0	First FS & LA of Brookhaven	Brookhaven	MS	−2.1	−2.1	42.8	42.8
8704	63	63	1	First FS & LA of Central Indiana	Anderson	IN	−10.6	−10.6	183.9	183.9

				Name	City	State				
2424	15	15	1	First FS & LA of Colorado Springs	Colorado Springs	CO	−106.6	−106.6	254.1	254.1
2659	18	18	0	First FS & LA of Conroe	Conroe	TX	−2.7	−2.7	178.9	178.9
1186	72	72	1	First FS & LA of East Alton	East Alton	IL	−6.1	−6.1	39.4	39.4
1263	69	0	0	First FS & LA of Fargo	Fargo	ND	−1.2	−1.2	57.4	57.4
3251	33	33	1	First FS & LA of Hutchinson	Hutchinson	KS	−54.8	−54.8	154.9	154.9
5698	0	0	0	First FS & LA of Macon Co	Decatur	IL	−0.1	−0.1	64.4	64.4
3014	96	96	0	First FS & LA of Pittsburgh	Pittsburgh	PA	−107.9	91.5	3127.0	2927.5
2954	60	60	1	First FS & LA of Seminole	Seminole	OK	−4.4	−4.4	29.8	29.8
3421	84	60	0	First FS & LA of Seminole Co	Sanford	FL	−4.4	−4.4	215.4	215.4
259	78	78	1	First FS & LA of Southeast MO	Cape Girardeau	MO	−60.0	−60.0	274.2	274.2
5553	66	66	1	First FS & LA of The Florida Keys	Key West	FL	−56.8	−56.8	157.2	157.2
2817	63	12	0	First FS & LA of Thief River Falls	Thief River Falls	MN	−0.4	−0.4	56.7	56.7
6017	66	36	0	First FS & LA of York	York	NE	−2.4	−2.4	59.7	59.7
3187	78	78	1	First FSB of Kansas	Wellington	KS	−50.3	−50.3	125.0	125.0
7526	132	12	0	First FSB of New Orleans	Metairie	LA	−14.0	−13.0	167.0	166.0
392	69	0	0	First FSB of South Dakota	Rapid City	SD	−12.5	−9.0	344.1	340.6
8667	12	12	1	First Garland FS & LA	Garland	TX	−17.7	−17.7	109.5	109.5
7588	96	6	0	First Guaranty Bank for Savings	Hattiesburg	MS	−16.5	−14.6	241.0	239.0

Docket Number	Months Since First Insolvency	Months of Consistent Insolvency	Conservatorship Dummy Variable	Institution Name	City	St	Tangible Net Worth ($ mil)	GAAP Net Worth ($ mil)	GAAP Assets ($ mil)	Tangible Assets ($ mil)
7289	90	90	0	First Jackson Savings Bank, FSB	Jackson	MS	−5.1	3.3	124.2	115.7
8691	69	54	1	First Louisiana FSB, FA	Lafayette	LA	−25.8	−25.8	142.6	142.6
8284	69	66	0	First Minnesota Savings Bank, FSB	Minneapolis	MN	−5.7	50.0	3151.0	3095.4
7974	27	0	0	First Network Savings Bank	Los Angeles	CA	−2.5	−0.4	416.5	414.4
8626	27	27	1	First of Kansas Savings, A FS & LA	Hays	KS	−5.1	−5.1	40.7	40.7
1339	51	51	0	First S & L Co	Massillon	OH	−7.2	−3.2	167.9	163.9
5327	63	63	0	First S & LA	Borger	TX	−5.1	−5.1	65.5	65.5
8599	15	15	1	First S & LA, FA	Waco	TX	−65.9	−65.9	342.5	342.5
7486	39	39	1	First Savings Assn of Southeast Texas	Silsbee	TX	−8.4	−8.4	50.0	50.0
5230	84	84	0	First Savings Bank of Zion	Zion	IL	−1.7	1.4	82.8	79.7
1243	51	0	0	First Savings Bank & Trust, FSB	Kansas City	MO	−1.9	−1.5	26.1	25.6
8582	57	39	1	First Savings of Americus, A FS & LA	Americus	GA	−4.5	−4.5	50.8	50.8
8643	84	84	1	First Savings of Arkansas, FA	Little Rock	AR	−679.4	−679.4	1007.5	1007.5
8666	72	9	1	First Savings of Laredo, FA	Laredo	TX	−13.7	−13.7	168.3	168.3
5647	36	36	1	First South SA	Port Neches	TX	−318.7	−318.7	237.0	237.0
5476	84	84	0	First Standard Savings FA	Fairmont	WV	−5.0	1.7	77.6	70.9
8585	69	36	1	First State FSA	San Antonio	TX	−205.8	−205.8	173.4	173.4

6401	45	45	1	First State Savings Bank, FSB	Mountain Home	AR	−42.3	−42.3	83.1	83.1
7829	45	45	1	First Venice S & LA	Venice	FL	−6.2	−6.2	51.5	51.5
7674	126		0	First Western Federal Savings Bank	Rapid City	SD	−0.1	1.3	19.0	17.6
1943	0	0	0	Florida Federal Savings Bank	St Petersburg	FL	−30.8	18.1	4657.8	4608.9
7747	114	30	1	Fontainebleau Federal Savings Bank	Slidell	LA	−17.0	−17.0	31.3	31.3
8724	24	24	1	Fortune Financial FS & LA	Copperas Cove	TX	−6.9	−6.9	87.7	87.7
8634	84	84	1	Founders FS & LA	Los Angeles	CA	−45.4	−45.4	111.5	111.5
3375	96	96	0	Franklin Federal Savings Bank	Morristown	TN	−3.3	4.9	105.6	97.5
385	84	84	0	Freedom FS & LA	Columbus	OH	−25.6	−17.9	360.4	352.7
8404	48	42	1	French Market Homestead, FSA	Metaire	LA	−57.0	−57.0	181.0	181.0
241	72	72	0	Frontier Financial	Belleville	IL	−2.5	−2.5	45.3	45.3
2322	84	84	0	Fulton Federal Savings Bank	Atlanta	GA	−54.8	20.9	2310.0	2234.8
422	84	84	0	Future Federal Savings Bank	Louisville	KY	−15.6	4.6	479.9	459.8
8640	60	60	1	Gateway Federal Savings Bank	San Francisco	CA	−68.8	−68.8	67.1	67.1
2442	78	78	0	Gem City S & LA	Quincy	IL	−15.0	−3.7	290.4	279.1
2968	84	84	0	Gem SA	Dayton	OH	−45.5	−11.5	1452.6	1418.6
8695	108		1	General Federal Savings Bank	Miami	FL	2.6	2.6	345.9	345.9
7469	12	12	1	General SA	Henderson	TX	−12.1	−12.1	40.5	40.5
5217	0	0	0	Germaniabank, A FSB	Alton	IL	−1.4	2.3	809.1	805.3
7562	9	9	1	Germantown Trust Savings Bank	Germantown	TN	−14.4	−14.4	110.2	110.2

Docket Number	Months Since First Insolvency	Months of Consistent Insolvency	Conservatorship Dummy Variable	Institution Name	City	St	Tangible Net Worth ($ mil)	GAAP Net Worth ($ mil)	GAAP Assets ($ mil)	Tangible Assets ($ mil)
8610	45		1	Gibraltar S & LA, FA	Annapolis	MD	−5.9	−5.9	29.9	29.9
8688	48	27	1	Gibraltar Savings Bank, FSB	Seattle	WA	−3.7	−3.7	1474.2	1474.2
8687	9	9	1	Gibraltar Savings, FA	Simi Valley	CA	−47.0	−47.0	7147.9	7147.9
7082	36	36	1	Gill SA	Hondo	TX	−1045.4	−1045.4	920.0	920.0
8020	66	18	1	Golden Circle SA, FSB	Corsicana	TX	−1.3	−1.3	14.9	14.9
7460	63	63	1	Golden Triangle S & LA	Bridge City	TX	−44.9	−44.9	19.6	19.6
6482	84	84	0	Goldome Savings Assn	St Petersburg	FL	−142.2	31.8	1678.7	1504.6
7700	54	54	0	Grand Prairie S & LA	Stuttgart	AR	−0.4	0.9	31.5	30.1
2605	84	21	0	Great American FS & LA	Oak Park	IL	−23.3	14.0	1013.2	975.9
8689	9	9	1	Great Plains Savings Association, FA	Weatherford	OK	−13.5	−13.5	93.6	93.6
8586	84	51	1	Great Southern FS & LA	Savannah	GA	−123.9	−123.9	570.3	570.3
8476	42	42	0	Great West SB, F.S.B.	Craig	CO	−2.4	−0.4	37.0	34.9
8657	66	18	1	Guadalupe S & LA, FA	Kerrville	TX	−0.9	−0.9	25.4	25.4
284	36		0	Guaranty Federal Savings Bank	Fayetteville	NC	−2.1	−2.1	60.3	60.3
7852	90	42	0	Guaranty Federal Savings Bank	Warner Robins	GA	−1.4	1.4	33.3	30.6
4439	90	90	1	Guaranty FS & LA	Birmingham	AL	−61.8	−61.8	294.2	294.2
8597	57	12	1	Hallmark S & LA, FA	Plano	TX	−70.0	−68.8	124.8	123.6
8060	0	0	0	Hansen Savings Bank	Palm Beach Gardens	FL	−0.0	4.4	86.1	81.6
6268	57	57	0	Hansen Savings Bank, SLA	East Brunswick	NJ	−1.1	14.2	613.3	598.0

8497	72	45	0	Haven FS & LA	Winter Haven	FL	−17.5	1.4	172.4	153.5
8649	9	9	1	Hearne B & LA, FA	Hearne	TX	−1.0	−1.0	25.2	25.2
3242	90	90	0	Heartland FS & LA	Mattoon	IL	−3.1	5.6	152.0	143.3
538	9	9	0	Henderson Home FS & LA	Henderson	KY	−2.0	−2.0	50.4	50.4
5634	90	90	1	Heritage FS & LA	Monroe	NC	−57.9	−57.9	214.0	214.0
3273	90	90	0	Heritage FSB	Omaha	NE	−5.6	−0.4	225.0	219.8
5134	0	0	0	Heritage S & LA	Lamar	CO	−1.9	−1.9	48.8	48.8
7649	84	84	0	Heritage SA	Lancaster	PA	−1.1	−1.1	55.1	55.1
8658	18	18	1	Heritage Savings Association, F.A.	Jerseyville	IL	−0.8	−0.8	29.3	29.3
7103	84	84	0	Heritage Savings Bank, FSB	Richmond	VA	−6.5	2.8	837.0	827.7
6761	78	78	1	Heritagebanc SA	Duncanville	TX	−59.1	−59.1	131.7	131.7
5269	39	39	0	Home Federal Savings Bank	Worcester	MA	−29.6	−7.5	235.5	213.4
664	84	84	1	Home FS & LA	Memphis	TN	−26.5	−26.5	192.4	192.4
3745	84	84	0	Home FS & LA	Rome	GA	−3.3	−3.3	174.3	174.3
2193	60	60	1	Home FS & LA of Centralia	Centralia	IL	−4.2	−4.2	36.7	36.7
3696	84	0	0	Home Owners Savings Bank F.S.B.	Boston	MA	−23.7	43.1	3622.8	3556.1
4104	12	12	0	Home Plan S & LA	Johnston	IA	−0.7	−0.7	33.3	33.3
2645	57	57	0	Home S & LA	Defiance	OH	−2.3	−2.3	209.5	209.5
8623	12	12	1	Home S & LA, FA	New Orleans	LA	−2.9	−2.9	33.5	33.5
439	0		0	Home SA	Bellevue	PA	−0.1	−0.1	7.8	7.8
2882	27	0	0	Home SA of Kansas City, FA	Kansas City	MO	−26.3	−6.1	3264.0	3243.8
8647	24	24	1	Home Savings Bank, F.S.B.	Anchorage	AK	−41.8	−41.8	54.7	54.7
8654	84	84	1	Home Savings, A FS & LA	Joliet	IL	−17.7	−17.7	126.3	126.3
2521	90	12	0	Home Unity S & LA	Lafayette Hill	PA	−12.3	1.4	884.5	870.8

Docket Number	Months Since First Insolvency	Months of Consistent Insolvency	Conservatorship Dummy Variable	Institution Name	City	St	Tangible Net Worth ($ mil)	GAAP Net Worth ($ mil)	GAAP Assets ($ mil)	Tangible Assets ($ mil)
2211	84	48	0	Hometown Federal Savings Bank	Delphi	IN	−4.3	1.3	68.6	63.0
5150	72	72	0	Hometown S&LA, FA	Winfield	IL	−2.4	0.6	47.5	44.5
687	78	78	0	Homewood FS & LA	Homewood	IL	−8.7	9.5	230.3	212.1
4124	33	33	0	Honfed Bank, A FSB	Honolulu	HI	−24.5	46.6	3166.2	3095.1
2651	84	84	0	Horizon Federal Savings Bank	Wilmette	IL	−112.3	−11.8	1223.7	1123.2
4159	96	96	1	Horizon Financial, FA	Southampton	PA	−313.2	−313.2	1931.8	1931.8
8299	63	63	1	Horizon FS & LA	Metairie	LA	−134.3	−134.3	361.5	361.5
7846	27	0	0	Huntington S & LA	Huntington Beach	CA	−0.6	−0.6	120.4	120.4
5560	84	84	0	Illini FS & LA	Fairview Heights	IL	−5.7	7.5	501.8	488.6
6798	84	15	1	Illinois Savings Bank, FA	Peoria	IL	−6.6	−5.2	44.3	42.9
1761	0	0	0	Imperial Savings Association	San Diego	CA	−89.0	−23.1	9581.6	9515.7
7255	96	96	1	Independence FS & LA	Batesville	AR	−249.4	−226.0	171.7	148.3
7634	42	3	0	Investment S & LA	Woodland Hills	CA	−8.5	−8.5	247.8	247.8
7556	66	3	0	Investor Federal Savings Bank	Nashville	TN	−1.3	−1.3	81.1	81.1
4825	63	63	0	Irving S&LA	Paterson	NJ	−12.3	−11.4	257.2	256.3
3190	72	72	1	Jasper FS & LA	Jasper	TX	−37.6	−36.8	117.2	116.5
6882	48	48	1	Jefferson S & LA	Beaumont	TX	−51.7	−51.7	103.0	103.0
2959	6	6	0	Jennings FS & LA	Jennings	LA	−2.2	−2.2	54.5	54.5
5020	84	84	0	Jersey Shore S & LA	Toms River	NJ	−8.2	18.3	665.5	639.0
7018	30	30	0	Karnes County S & LA	Karnes City	TX	−10.5	−10.5	53.1	53.1
7670	63	39	1	La Hacienda Savings Association	San Antonio	TX	−83.3	−81.6	57.9	56.2
8611	138	12	1	Lafayette S & LA, FA	Gretna	LA	−1.4	−1.4	24.3	24.3

2979	84	3	0	Lakeland Federal Savings Bank	Detroit Lakes	MN	−6.0	−6.0	79.6	79.6
3115	48	48	1	Landmark Savings Bank, FSB	Hot Springs	AR	−58.3	−58.3	115.5	115.5
3094	24	24	1	Liberty County FS & LA	Liberty	TX	−5.5	−5.5	41.8	41.8
3966	10		0	Liberty Federal Savings Bank	Randallstown	MD	−4.4	−4.2	49.5	46.2
54	39	39	0	Liberty Savings Association	Houston	TX	−1.9	3.6	98.2	87.7
72	39	24	1	Libertyville FS & LA	Libertyville	IL	−15.0	−15.0	77.4	77.4
8674	30	30	1	Lincoln FS & LA	Miami	FL	−43.5	−43.5	170.4	170.4
7549	30	30	1	Lincoln FS & LA	Mt Carmel	TN	−10.3	−10.3	56.7	56.7
8619	69	12	1	Lincoln S & LA, FA	Los Angeles	CA	−1289.9	−1285.6	2906.3	2902.0
6686	52	9	0	Lincoln-Way Federal Savings Bank	New Lenox	IL	−1.6	3.5	76.0	70.9
8741	24	24	1	Louisiana Savings Association, FA	Lake Charles	LA	−43.2	−43.2	416.4	416.4
238	69	30	1	Madison County FS & LA	Granite City	IL	−12.8	−12.8	109.9	109.9
7601	30	30	1	Madison Guaranty S & LA	Augusta	AR	−26.7	−26.7	111.1	111.1
5608	72	0	0	Marion County Mutual L & BA	Hannibal	MO	−0.0	−0.0	63.1	63.1
3493	84	12	0	Marshall FS & LA	Marshall	TX	−3.0	−3.0	62.0	62.0
6877	84	12	0	Merabank, A Federal Savings Bank	Phoenix	AZ	−498.5	−158.0	6381.9	6041.5
126	66	66	0	Merchants and Mechanics FS & LA	Springfield	OH	−12.2	−11.1	271.9	270.9
6649	96	0	0	Mercury S & LA	Huntington Beach	CA	−33.2	−0.1	2158.8	2125.7
7784	63	48	1	Meridian Savings Association	Arlington	TX	−469.2	−469.2	29.5	29.5
5907	54	54	1	Meritbanc Savings Association	Houston	TX	−162.3	−156.7	200.7	195.1

Docket Number	Months Since First Insolvency	Months of Consistent Insolvency	Conservatorship Dummy Variable	Institution Name	City	St	Tangible Net Worth ($ mil)	GAAP Net Worth ($ mil)	GAAP Assets ($ mil)	Tangible Assets ($ mil)
1421	30	30	1	Mesa FS & LA of Colorado	Grand Junction	CO	−2.8	−2.8	104.3	104.3
8660	6	6	1	Metropolitan Financial FS & LA	Dallas	TX	−78.9	−78.9	779.8	779.8
5248	72	72	1	Metropolitan FS & LA	Denville	NJ	−8.4	−8.4	156.7	156.7
7363	63	63	1	Miami Savings Bank	Miami	FL	−38.5	−25.8	114.9	102.1
8685	78	45	1	Mid Kansas S & LA, FA	Wichita	KS	−32.1	−32.1	693.0	693.0
8589	60	60	1	Mid Missouri S & LA, FA	Boonville	MO	−13.5	−13.5	55.2	55.2
2359	78	78	0	Mid-America FS & LA	Columbus	OH	−60.5	11.8	1275.1	1202.8
985	33	33	1	Mid-America FS & LA	Parsons	KS	−9.6	−9.6	69.0	69.0
8655	27	27	1	Midland-Buckeye Savings, A FS & LA	Alliance	OH	−29.0	−29.0	177.1	177.1
546	84	84	0	Midwest Federal Savings Bank	Minot	ND	−99.2	−99.2	955.0	955.0
2998	69	66	1	Midwest FS & LA	Nebraska City	NE	−29.6	−29.6	112.7	112.7
168	69	66	1	Midwest Home FSB	Belleville	IL	−14.2	−14.2	92.6	92.6
8574	69	66	1	Midwest Savings Association, FA	Minneapolis	MN	−788.1	−788.1	2245.3	2245.3
354	90	90	1	Midwestern SA	Macomb	IL	−20.3	−13.6	89.8	83.1
7309	24	24	1	Mission SA of Texas	San Antonio	TX	−49.2	−49.2	50.6	50.6
8588	18	18	1	Missouri Savings Association, FA	Clayton	MO	−49.7	−49.7	537.3	537.3
2337	42	42	1	Modern FS & LA	Grand Junction	CO	−3.7	−3.7	56.0	56.0
5304	84	84	0	Morton FS & LA	Morton	IL	−5.6	1.1	163.1	156.4
490	63	63	0	Moultrie Federal Savings Bank	Moultrie	GA	−0.3	−0.3	68.1	68.1
8537	72	72	1	Mountainwest S & LA, A FS&LA	Ogden	UT	−53.4	−53.4	171.2	171.2

				Institution	City	State				
8580	27	27	1	Murray FS&LA	Dallas	TX	−346.5	−346.5	961.9	961.9
4809	78	0	0	Mutual Aid S & LA	Manasquan	NJ	−3.0	−3.0	104.4	104.4
2482	6	6	0	Mutual B & LA	Weatherford	TX	−1.1	−1.1	104.8	104.8
3688	84	84	0	Mutual FSB, A Stock Corporation	Zanesville	OH	−4.4	0.6	309.9	305.0
2947	78	78	0	Nassau FS & LA	Brooklyn	NY	−39.9	−9.2	296.8	266.1
5931	9	9	0	Nassau S & LA	Princeton	NJ	−10.4	−9.0	313.1	311.6
64	6	0	0	New Age FS & LA of St Louis	St Louis	MO	−0.1	−0.1	10.1	10.1
6489	66	66	0	New Athens S & LA	New Athens	IL	−0.9	−0.9	30.4	30.4
8607	51	42	1	New Braunfels S & LA, FA	New Braunfels	TX	−34.1	−34.1	49.0	49.0
8598	84	63	1	New Guaranty FS & LA	Taylor	MI	−14.5	−14.5	193.7	193.7
8331	84	45	0	New Metropolitan FS & LA	Hialeah	FL	−18.7	−18.7	26.0	26.0
8616	78	66	1	New Mexico FSA	Albuquerque	NM	−25.9	−25.9	197.4	197.4
8594	72	72	1	North American FSA	San Antonio	TX	−26.2	−26.2	68.6	68.6
7414	84	3	0	North Carolina FS & LA	Charlotte	NC	−22.1	−10.8	628.1	616.9
4636	96	96	1	North Jersey S&LA	Passaic	NJ	−104.3	−104.3	250.6	250.6
2363	63	63	0	North Texas FS & LA	Wichita Falls	TX	−4.2	−4.2	98.7	98.7
7484	90	0	0	Nowlin SA	North Richland Hill	TX	−18.6	−18.6	200.5	200.5
2264	66	66	0	Nutley Savings Bank, SLA	Nutley	NJ	−3.4	−3.4	224.6	224.6
8603	27	27	1	Occidental Nebraska Savings Bank, FSB	Omaha	NE	−132.9	−132.9	552.5	552.5
5679	90	6	0	Old Borough S&LA	Trenton	NJ	−2.6	−2.6	149.9	149.9
982	90	90	0	Olympic Federal S & LA	Berwyn	IL	−92.7	23.5	1145.6	1029.4
948	12	12	1	Otero Savings, A FS & LA	Colorado Springs	CO	−163.5	−163.5	395.7	395.7
7272	138	36	1	Padre FS & LA	Corpus Christi	TX	−15.0	−15.0	15.4	15.4

Docket Number	Months Since First Insolvency	Months of Consistent Insolvency	Conservatorship Dummy Variable	Institution Name	City	St	Tangible Net Worth ($ mil)	GAAP Net Worth ($ mil)	GAAP Assets ($ mil)	Tangible Assets ($ mil)
4545	84	84	0	Palisade Savings Bank, SLA	Ridgefield Park	NJ	−8.6	24.3	266.3	233.4
7840	15	15	0	Palo Duro S & LA	Amarillo	TX	−4.6	−4.6	65.0	65.0
8617	120	12	1	Parish FS & LA	Denham Springs	LA	−1.6	−1.6	12.4	12.4
1195	90	90	0	Park View FS & LA	Cleveland	OH	−1.8	−1.8	252.0	252.0
3584	84	84	0	Pelican Hmstd & SA	Metairie	LA	−225.3	−147.7	1687.3	1609.6
322	57	48	1	Peoples Savings Association, FA	St Joseph	MI	−11.4	−11.4	73.2	73.2
6249	9	9	0	Peoples B & LA of Oblong	Oblong	IL	−0.0	−0.0	9.3	9.3
7508	90	36	1	Peoples FS & LA of Thibodaux	Thibodaux	LA	−3.2	−3.2	18.4	18.4
8648	9	9	1	Peoples Heritage Savings, A FS&LA	Salina	KS	−388.2	−388.2	1248.6	1248.6
8684	60	30	1	People's Hmstd Savings Bank, FSB	Monroe	LA	−43.6	−43.6	254.2	254.2
424	39	39	1	Peoples S & LA	Parsons	KS	−12.2	−12.2	51.3	51.3
1470	9	9	1	Peoples S & LA FA	Hampton	VA	−1.2	−1.2	22.2	22.2
8609	48	6	1	Peoples S & LA, FA	Streator	IL	−12.9	−12.9	33.0	33.0
1278	84	84	0	Peoples Savings Bank	Ashtabula	OH	−3.4	8.5	297.4	285.5
6408	27	21	1	Permian S & LA	Kermit	TX	−1.9	−1.9	8.0	8.0
8439	36	36	1	Phenix FS & LA, FA	Phenix City	AL	−60.2	−60.2	118.8	118.8
5762	90	0	0	Pima S & LA	Tucson	AZ	−12.7	26.8	2734.1	2694.6
5942	90	90	0	Pioneer Savings Bank	Clearwater	FL	−95.3	−4.8	1935.7	1845.2
8629	84	84	1	Pioneer Savings, FA	Plymouth	IN	−12.3	−12.3	73.9	73.9
8662	12	12	1	Plano S & LA, FA	Plano	TX	−36.3	−36.3	247.1	247.1
8632	42	42	1	Platte Valley Savings, A FS & LA	Gering	NE	−126.7	−126.7	240.9	240.9
3154	0	0	0	Progressive Federal Savings Bank	Natchitoches	LA	−1.3	−1.3	58.0	58.0
1344	18	18	0	Provident FS & LA	Casper	WY	−3.3	−3.3	244.9	244.9

8740	138	42	1	Red River FS & LA	Coushata	LA	−0.1	−0.1	10.4	10.4
249	78	78	0	Regency Savings Bank, A FSB	Naperville	IL	−6.5	−6.5	336.3	336.3
7387	69	15	0	Remington SA	Elgin	TX	−2.6	3.4	174.2	168.2
7152	72	27	1	Republic Bank for Savings, FA	Jackson	MS	−61.8	−61.8	29.0	29.0
33	24	24	1	Resource SA	Denison	TX	−134.9	−129.6	387.2	382.0
7782	30	30	1	Rocky Mountain Savings, A FSB	Woodland Park	CO	−5.8	−5.8	13.5	13.5
1999	57	57	0	Royal Oak FS & LA	Randallstown	MD	−1.6	−1.6	30.2	30.2
7886	69	15	1	Royal Oak S & LA	Manteca	CA	−2.6	−2.6	24.3	24.3
8602	15	15	1	Royal Palm FS & LA	West Palm Beach	FL	−126.2	−126.2	420.3	420.3
2813	69	33	1	Rusk FS & LA	Rusk	TX	−17.0	−17.0	30.3	30.3
6371	33	33	1	Sabine Valley S & LA	Center	TX	−6.3	−5.5	29.5	28.7
8702	3	3	1	Salamanca Federal Savings Association	Salamanca	NY	−0.4	−0.4	29.2	29.2
8596	12	12	1	San Antonio Savings Association, FA	San Antonio	TX	−479.1	−479.1	2208.7	2208.7
6321	90	0	0	San Jacinto SA	Bellaire	TX	−19.8	16.4	3319.9	3283.6
8646	66	66	1	Sandia Federal Savings Association	Albuquerque	NM	−753.2	−691.7	612.9	551.4
2079	63	0	0	Santa Barbara S & LA	Santa Barbara	CA	−25.8	−25.8	4677.0	4677.0
7928	0		1	Saratoga S & LA	San Jose	CA	4.8	4.8	104.6	104.6
8673	39	39	1	Savers Savings Association, FSA	Little Rock	AR	−428.4	−428.4	565.6	565.6
7456	78	78	1	Savings of Texas Association	Jacksonville	TX	−44.3	−44.3	49.8	49.8
8686	69	30	1	Seasons Federal Savings Bank	Richmond	VA	−29.5	−29.5	206.2	206.2
8671	42	42	1	Security Federal Savings Association	Texarkana	TX	−403.0	−403.0	163.0	163.0
8709	84	84	1	Security Federal Savings, FSB	Columbia	SC	−47.7	−46.2	711.5	709.9
3121	84	84	0	Security First FS & LA	Daytona Beach	FL	−27.8	21.2	1115.1	1066.1

Docket Number	Months Since First Insolvency	Months of Consistent Insolvency	Conservatorship Dummy Variable	Institution Name	City	St	Tangible Net Worth ($ mil)	GAAP Net Worth ($ mil)	GAAP Assets ($ mil)	Tangible Assets ($ mil)
8644	78	78	1	Security FS & LA	Peoria	IL	−27.3	−27.3	234.4	234.4
5854	90	90	0	Security FS & LA	Richmond	VA	−27.3	−2.1	341.6	316.4
8708	72	66	1	Security FSA	Garden Grove	CA	−4.6	−4.6	69.4	69.4
8606	72	72	1	Security Homestead FSA	New Orleans	LA	−64.5	−64.5	513.0	513.0
6875	84	84	1	Security S & LA	Scottsdale	AZ	−570.8	−570.8	521.3	521.3
6957	57	36	0	Security Savings Bank, FSB	Carlsbad	NM	−8.2	−8.2	27.8	27.8
8065	0	0	0	Sentinel S & LA	Phoenix	AZ	−1.7	−1.7	174.9	174.9
4613	78	78	0	Shadow Lawn Savings Bank, SLA	Long Branch	NJ	−16.1	5.7	695.5	673.7
2485	57	57	1	Shawnee FS & LA	Topeka	KS	−11.9	−11.9	223.4	223.4
8613	9	9	1	Sierra S & LA, FA	Beverly Hills	CA	−2.6	−2.6	34.6	34.6
8699	6	0	1	Silver Savings Association, FA	Silver City	NM	−0.3	−0.3	30.8	30.8
6137	15	15	1	Skokie FS & LA	Skokie	IL	−98.4	−98.4	678.7	678.7
8690	3	3	1	Sooner Federal Savings Association	Tulsa	OK	−89.3	−89.3	1429.7	1429.7
8620	36	36	1	South S & LA, FA	Slidell	LA	−31.4	−31.4	235.6	235.6
6632	45	45	1	Southeast Texas S & LA	Woodville	TX	−2.2	−2.2	28.6	28.6
7593	42	42	1	Southeastern SA	Dayton	TX	−52.5	−52.5	65.1	65.1
6865	42	42	1	Southmost S & LA	Brownsville	TX	−43.8	−43.8	84.5	84.5
8651	15	15	1	Southside FS & LA	Austin	TX	−3.0	−3.0	46.6	46.6
8678	60	21	1	Southwest FS & LA	Los Angeles	CA	−99.0	−99.0	605.2	605.2
8636	96	96	1	Southwest S & LA, FA	Phoenix	AZ	−374.7	−374.7	1749.8	1749.8
5603	84	84	0	Southwest SA	Dallas	TX	−271.4	−246.5	5514.1	5489.2
8703	72	6	1	Southwestern FSA	El Paso	TX	−10.4	−10.4	120.5	120.5
8656	33	33	1	Spindletop Savings Association, FA	Beaumont	TX	−195.7	−195.7	152.4	152.4

6139	84	72	1	Spring Branch S & LA	Houston	TX	−85.8	−85.8	83.9	83.9
1497	66	66	0	St Anthony FS & LA	Cicero	IL	−1.2	−1.2	36.7	36.7
1006	63	63	0	St Charles S & LA	St Charles	IL	−8.9	−8.9	146.5	146.5
3308	0	0	0	St Louis County FS & LA	Duluth	MN	−0.0	−0.0	234.2	234.2
2637	72	72	0	St Louis County FS & LA of Ferguson	Ferguson	MO	−4.8	−4.8	85.8	85.8
6314	24	24	0	Standard SA	Houston	TX	−1.6	−1.6	13.5	13.5
1228	57	57	0	State FS & LA	Tulsa	OK	−40.2	4.4	526.3	481.7
309	84	84	0	State Home SA	Bowling Green	OH	−3.7	13.0	323.3	306.6
6614	188	90	1	State Mutual FS & LA	Jackson	MS	−2.0	−2.0	7.7	7.7
8482	60	12	0	Statesman Bank for Savings, FSB	Waterloo	IA	−2.7	20.0	615.0	592.2
7918	72	72	0	Sterling Savings Assn	Spokane	WA	−9.9	11.0	708.2	687.2
7557	12	12	1	Suburban SA	San Antonio	TX	−17.5	−17.5	36.5	36.5
2779	78	78	0	Summit First FS & LA	Summit	IL	−1.5	−1.5	60.5	60.5
7749	84	84	1	Sun Country SB of New Mexico, FSB	Albuquerque	NM	−40.9	−39.5	58.6	57.2
3651	12	12	1	Sun S & LA	Parker	CO	−115.9	−115.9	191.2	191.2
7162	48	3	0	Sun Savings Bank	Fort Dodge	IA	−0.2	0.4	24.2	23.8
2172	33	33	1	Sun SA, F. A.	Kansas City	KS	−50.4	−50.4	135.5	135.5
8590	12	12	1	Sun State S & LA, FSA	Phoenix	AZ	−216.1	−216.1	825.8	825.8
8513	66	12	0	Sunbelt Savings FSB	Dallas	TX	−7.9	1.0	9108.1	9099.2
2688	90	90	0	Superior Federal Bank, FSB	Fort Smith	AR	−16.4	16.4	764.5	731.7
6077	84	84	0	Superior Federal Savings Bank	Nacogdoches	TX	−6.1	2.4	82.9	74.4
8681	12	12	1	Surety Federal Savings Association	El Paso	TX	−21.1	−21.1	287.4	287.4
8459	72	72	0	Surety FS & LA, FSA	Morganton	NC	−3.0	5.9	226.1	217.2
3557	0	0	0	Sweetwater FS & LA	Rock Springs	WY	−0.2	−0.2	12.4	12.4
8650	9	9	1	Taylorbanc FS & LA	Taylor	TX	−15.6	−15.6	129.6	129.6
6673	90	90	0	TCF Banc Savings Association	Houston	TX	−7.8	5.5	23.6	10.4

Docket Number	Months Since First Insolvency	Months of Consistent Insolvency	Conservatorship Dummy Variable	Institution Name	City	St	Tangible Net Worth ($ mil)	GAAP Net Worth ($ mil)	GAAP Assets ($ mil)	Tangible Assets ($ mil)
8625	84	72	1	Terrebonne S & LA, FA	Houma	LA	−4.2	−4.2	24.7	24.7
5140	0	0	0	Texas S & LA	San Antonio	TX	−0.7	−0.7	59.0	59.0
8692	90	90	1	Texas Western FSA	Out-of-District-CI	OK	−11.0	−11.0	98.0	98.0
7314	72	3	0	Texasbanc Savings, FSB	Conroe	TX	−148.1	−147.4	248.8	248.1
178	21	21	1	The Barber County S & LA	Medicine Lodge	KS	−8.9	−8.9	40.3	40.3
1165	84	84	0	The Benj. Franklin FS & LA	Portland	OR	−127.5	155.2	4968.1	4685.4
4585	12	12	1	The Duncan S & LA	Duncan	OK	−8.3	−8.8	138.2	138.2
2314	84	9	0	The First Federal Association	Orlando	FL	−2.0	49.8	1247.8	1196.5
3582	9	9	1	The Garnett S & LA	Garnett	KS	−0.1	−0.1	17.5	17.5
7896	46	9	1	The Guardian FS & LA	Bakersfield	CA	−13.5	−13.5	17.0	17.0
2171	60	0	0	The Hiawatha S & LA	Hiawatha	KS	−7.2	−6.1	49.2	48.1
2811	96	96	0	The Long Island S/B of Centerface FSB	Centerface	NY	−239.7	248.8	2752.0	2263.5
6439	66	15	0	The Savings Banc, A S & LA	Arlington	TX	−2.0	3.1	142.7	137.6
1223	90	90	0	The Talman Home FS & LA of Illinois	Chicago	IL	−209.8	331.6	6072.7	5531.3
7534	0	0	0	The Tennessee Savings Bank	Cookeville	TN	−0.5	0.5	42.8	41.9
5	84	0	0	The United S&LA of Trenton NJ	Trenton	NJ	−8.3	−8.3	294.7	294.7
7591	36	36	1	Timberland SA	Nacogdoches	TX	−7.8	−7.8	43.7	43.7
8447	39	39	1	Topeka Savings, A FS & LA	Topeka	KS	−46.1	−46.1	73.4	73.4

				Institution	City	State				
8637	84	84	1	Unifirst Bank for Savings, A FS & LA	Jackson	MS	−123.7	−123.7	635.8	635.8
7617	51	51	1	Unipoint Federal Savings Bank	Trumann	AR	−16.1	−16.1	13.1	13.1
3058	78	78	0	United Federal Savings Bank	Windom	MN	−9.3	−5.4	169.3	165.4
3228	60	0	0	United Federal Savings Bank of Iowa	Des Moines	IA	−6.3	2.8	999.7	990.6
6997	63	0	0	United FS & LA	New Orleans	LA	−0.4	−0.4	53.6	53.6
6650	84	0	0	United FS & LA	Smyrna	GA	−0.2	4.7	149.1	144.2
7512	60	60	1	United Guaranty Federal Savings Bank	Tullahoma	TN	−2.1	−2.1	7.0	7.0
3412	72	72	0	United Home Federal	Toledo	OH	−9.6	−0.5	505.3	496.3
636	84	84	0	United Savings of America	Chicago	IL	−57.8	60.5	1347.4	1229.1
8493	18	18	1	Universal S & LA, A FS & LA	Scottsdale	AZ	−21.9	−20.7	71.7	70.6
7213	36	36	1	Universal SA	Houston	TX	−203.7	−203.7	115.5	115.5
7722	3	3	0	Uvalde S & LA	Uvalde	TX	−2.9	−2.9	13.3	13.3
8682	6	6	1	Valley Federal Savings Association	McAllen	TX	−107.4	−107.4	482.8	482.8
8642	54	54	1	Valley FS & LA	Grand Junction	CO	−77.2	−77.2	57.9	57.9
7443	0	0	0	Valley FS & LA	Van Nuys	CA	−28.1	−28.1	3015.4	3015.4
8645	45	45	1	Valley Savings Banks, FSB	Roswell	NM	−128.5	−128.5	132.6	132.6
8652	39	39	1	Valley Savings, A FS & LA	Hutchinson	KS	−56.2	−56.2	164.8	164.8
3474	84	84	0	Vanguard Federal Savings Bank	Vandergrift	PA	−7.1	0.7	176.9	169.1
4177	84	84	0	Vermont FS & LA	Timonium	MD	−33.9	−17.7	334.9	318.7
8587	84	18	1	Victoria Savings Association FSA	Victoria	TX	−239.8	−239.8	742.9	742.9
7830	102	6	0	Viking Savings Association, FA	Alexandria	MN	−0.9	−0.3	20.7	20.1

Docket Number	Months Since First Insolvency	Months of Consistent Insolvency	Conservatorship Dummy Variable	Institution Name	City	St	Tangible Net Worth ($ mil)	GAAP Net Worth ($ mil)	GAAP Assets ($ mil)	Tangible Assets ($ mil)
7592	27	27	1	Vision Banc Savings Association	Kingsville	TX	−45.8	−45.8	65.2	65.2
7835	18	18	1	Washington S & LA	Stockton	CA	−3.9	−3.8	69.4	69.2
6859	6	6	0	Washington Shores Savings Bank, FSB	Orlando	FL	−0.2	−0.2	9.2	9.2
845	69	66	0	Watadga S & LA	Boone	NC	−2.0	−2.0	113.4	113.4
1737	57	57	1	Westco Savings Bank, FSB	Wilmington	CA	−23.1	−14.3	139.3	130.5
8249	0	0	0	Westcoast S & LA	Pacific Palisades	CA	−0.6	1.5	59.3	57.1
7853	24	0	0	Western Empire S & LA	Yorba Linda	CA	−8.6	0.1	406.6	397.9
7489	48	48	1	Western Gulf S & LA	Bay City	TX	−164.6	−164.6	143.6	143.6
8579	12	12	1	Western S & LA, FA	Phoenix	AZ	−1412.6	−1412.6	4221.3	4221.3
7663	60	0	0	Westport Savings Bank	Hanford	CA	−4.8	−4.8	169.6	169.6
7611	48	48	1	Westwood S & LA	Los Angeles	CA	−247.8	−247.8	271.1	271.1
4925	90	90	0	Whitestone Savings, FA	Whitestone	NY	−34.9	−34.9	396.9	396.9
7367	78	0	0	Williamsburg Savings Bank	Salt Lake City	UT	−21.4	−15.8	310.5	304.9
7979	69	0	0	Wilshire S & LA	Los Angeles	CA	−0.4	−0.4	78.1	78.1
1709	63	33	0	Yankton S & LA	Yankton	SD	−0.3	−0.3	35.8	35.8
8701	90	90	1	Yorkridge-Calvert FSA	Baltimore	MD	−14.9	−14.9	539.5	539.5
5279	84	84	0	Yorkwood S&LA	Maplewood	NJ	−10.7	−10.7	205.3	205.3

SOURCE: Office of Thrift Supervision

A Critique of the Financial Institutions Recovery, Reform and Enforcement Act (FIRREA) of 1989 and the Financial Strength of the Commercial Banks

R. Dan Brumbaugh, Jr.

Senior Research Scholar, Center for Economic Policy Research, Stanford University

and

Robert E. Litan

Senior Fellow, The Brookings Institution, and Visiting Lecturer in Banking Law, Yale University

At first glance the title of this paper may seem to combine two generally unrelated topics. The Financial Institutions Recovery, Reform and Enforcement Act (FIRREA) of 1989, after all, was primarily designed and is thoroughly perceived as being the fourth major piece of legislation in the 1980s to address the savings and loan crisis. Why then combine a critique of FIRREA with an assessment of the financial strength of commercial banks? Part of the reason is that the commercial banks are bifurcated with a large and growing segment of market-value insolvent banks whose negative net worth could easily exceed the reserves of the bank insurer. These issues were completely ignored by FIRREA. We have contended for some time that if it were not for the gargantuan difficulties of the savings and loans, the difficulties of the commercial banks and concern over the solvency of the banks' insurance fund would be an urgent national priority. The exclusion of banks as a focus of FIRREA is, therefore, a noteworthy limitation of FIRREA.

In addition, the cause of the savings and loans' and the commercial banks' deterioration is the same: deposit insurance and the regulatory system required by deposit insurance. Deposit insurance creates moral hazard which has not been controlled either by deposit-insurance practices per se or by regulation. Even fraud in the savings and loans, currently an almost tabloid-like topic in descriptions of the savings and loan crisis, reflects the moral hazard created by deposit insurance. If all savings and loans had been closed when they initially became insolvent as deposit insurance was designed to accomplish, the subsequent systemwide fraud that developed would have been avoided. Whether FIRREA should have addressed some aspects of deposit-insurance reform directly is an appropriate issue.

This paper first addresses the condition of the commercial banking industry and the Bank Insurance Fund (BIF). A summary and critique of FIRREA follows.

THE STRENGTH OF COMMERCIAL BANKS

The Bifurcation of the Condition of Commercial Banks

Between 1980 and 1982 virtually all thrift institutions were insolvent due to the effect of substantial and unexpected increases in interest rates on largely homogeneous portfolios dominated by unhedged, fixed-rate, long-term mortgage assets and shorter-term liabilities (see Carron, 1982 and 1983). A former chairman of the Federal Home Loan Bank Board recently testified, for example, that "By 1982, the real capital positions of all thrift institutions had been completely eroded, and virtually all thrift institutions had large negative net worths when their assets and liabilities were valued at actual market rates" (see Pratt, 1988, as quoted in Barth, 1990).

After the unexpected interest rate decline in late 1982, the thrift industry was bifurcated with one large set of thrifts insolvent and troubled primarily by growing defaults on commercial real-estate assets. The other set was comprised of a majority of thrifts that regained solvency as interest rates fell (see Barth 1991, Brumbaugh 1988, and Kane 1985 and 1989b, for detailed analyses of the ongoing thrift decline). The thrift-industry bifurcation continues today with hundreds of open and insolvent thrifts. The bifurcation of commercial banks is a newer phenomenon which appears to have developed between December 1986 and December 1987 when there was a substantial increase in insolvent and weakly capitalized banks.

Declining Net Worth of a Distinctly Weak, Large Segment of Banks

In 1988 we estimated the newly adopted risk-based capital of commercial banks with more than $50 million in assets and found that between 1986 and 1987 the number of insolvent banks grew from 2 to 15 with assets growing from approximately $200 million to more than $5 billion (see Brumbaugh and Litan, 1989). Table 3.1 presents these data. During the same period, the number of banks with estimated risk-based capital between zero and 3 percent grew from 20 to 42 with assets growing from approximately $9 billion to $89 billion (for a growing literature on bank weaknesses, see Barth, Brumbaugh, and Litan, 1992; Brumbaugh, Carron, and Litan, 1989; Brumbaugh and Litan, 1988/89, 1989, 1990; Eisenbeis, 1990; Ferguson, 1989, 1990; Kaufman, 1990; Kane, 1989; and Shadow Financial Regulatory Committee, 1988).

The commercial banks as a whole, however, appeared relatively prosperous. As shown in Table 3.2, between 1986 and 1987 the ratio of reported industrywide total capital to average assets grew. Although industrywide net income fell dramatically in 1987, the decline was due almost entirely to money-center bank additions to reserves for losses on loans to lesser developed countries (LDCs). By 1988 net income rebounded to a level that provided a return on average equity of 14.5 percent, just above the high previously set in 1979.

This pattern persisted through 1989. As Table 3.3 shows there has been general growth in the number and assets of banks reporting equity capital at or below 3 percent. As with the ratios reported in Table 3.1, the number and assets of banks with this level of capitalization began to grow significantly after 1986. Although the number of banks in the 0–3 percent net-worth category remained relatively stable between 1988 and 1989, their assets grew substantially from $52.9 billion to $136.2 billion.

The capital levels in Tables 3.1 and 3.3 are not directly comparable. The numerator for the capital ratios in Table 3.1 includes common and preferred stock, retained earnings, and subordinated debt. Subordinated debt is excluded in Table 3.3. The denominator in Table 3.1 includes off balance-sheet items and adjusts for the risk weights of assets. Off balance-sheet items are excluded in Table 3.3 and the table makes no adjustment for risk weights. Table 3.3 includes data for all banks. Both the risk-adjusted capital for the subset of banks and the equity capital for all banks, however, show the same general pattern of decline.

Another pattern has been consistent throughout the savings and loan debacle and with the closure of commercial banks. When closure occurs when historical cost or book-value net worth reaches zero, market-value net worth has always been negative (see Barth, Bartholomew, and Labich, 1989; Barth, Brumbaugh, and Sauerhaft, 1986; Barth, Brumbaugh, Sauerhaft, and Wang 1985, 1986; Benston, 1985; Benston and Kaufman,

Table 3.1   Risk-Adjusted Capital Ratios for Commercial Banks with Assets of $50 Million or More, Selected Periods, 1986–88[a]

Ratio of Risk-Adjusted Capital to Total Assets (Percent)	September 1988		June 1988		March 1988		December 1987		December 1986	
	Banks	Assets	Banks	Assets	Banks	Assets	Banks	Assets	Banks	Assets
Less than 0	28	22.5	18	26.7	24	33.1	15	5.1	2	0.2
Between 0 and 3	48	43.4	47	22.5	44	31.4	42	89.4	20	8.8
Between 3 and 6	150	926.0	168	959.2	154	959.4	166	914.0	116	896.9
Greater than 6	5,094	1,894.5	5,139	1,839.0	5,144	1,784.0	5,229	1,771.8	5,239	1,762.3
Total	5,320	2,886.4	5,372	2,847.4	5,376	2,807.8	5,452	2,780.3	5,377	2,668.2

a. Risk-adjusted capital = equity capital + perpetual preferred stock + subordinated debt & limited preferred stock − investments in unconsolidated subsidiaries.

NOTE: Billions of dollars except as noted.

SOURCE: Authors' calculations based on data and assistance from Drexel Burnham Lambert, Inc., MBS Institutional Databank.

1988; James, 1989; and Kane, 1985). Moreover, as institutions near book-value insolvency, accounting techniques are used to bolster net worth. The most widely cited technique is to sell selected assets at a gain and book the gain as income while leaving at book value assets whose market value has fallen (for studies that emphasize the dangers of book-value accounting for depositories, see Barth, et al. 1989; Brumbaugh, 1988; Benston and Kaufman, 1988; Kane, 1985, 1989, 1989b; and White, 1990). As a result, those institutions with equity to assets at or below 3 percent in Table 3.3 almost certainly have market-value net worth substantially below the reported levels and many, perhaps most, may be market-value insolvent.

It is important to point out, moreover, that $1.7 trillion or 49.1 percent of commercial-bank assets shown in Table 3.3 are in banks whose net worth is at or below 6 percent. Even if book values were accurate reflections of market value, they are substantially below the 10 percent range that prevailed immediately following the creation of federal deposit insurance and far below the range that existed before deposit insurance (see Spellman, 1982, and Landow, 1963, as quoted in Barth and Bartholomew in their paper presented at this conference). Many economists consider a depository weakly capitalized if market-value capital is between 6 and 8 percent (see Benston, Brumbaugh, Guttentag, Herring, Kaufman, Litan, and Scott, 1989).

Persistent Negative Income for an Overlapping but Somewhat Distinct Group of Banks

In demonstrating the magnitude of the troubled portion of commercial banks, it is helpful to evaluate income as well as capital. Net operating income—for commercial banks essentially the difference between net interest income and noninterest expense—is particularly helpful because it reflects the profitability of the core lending business. It is also more difficult than net worth to fudge through the use of accounting techniques. Table 3.4 presents data on commercial banks that had negative net operating income in 1986 through 1989. Income is defined here as operating income before securities gains, extraordinary items, and income taxes. Table 3.4 reveals the following important findings.

- In 1989 there were $42.1 billion in assets in 479 banks which had negative net income in each of the four years since 1986.

- From 1986 to 1989 these banks grew approximately $6 billion or 17 percent.

- The negative net income rose in each year from negative $119.7 million in 1986 to negative $1.3 billion in 1989.

- For these banks equity capital fell from 7.35 percent in 1986 to 3.35 percent in 1989 (equity capital includes common and preferred stock and retained earnings).

Table 3.2   Selected Financial Data for All Open Commercial Banks, 1986–89

	1986	1987	1988	1989
Balance Sheet:[a]				
Total Assets	2,654,548,577	2,783,219,339	3,035,120,903	3,303,308,975
% Change in Assets	16.36%	4.85%	9.05%	8.84%
Securities—Book Value	442,443,659	489,873,348	521,832,390	559,190,567
Securities—Market Value	455,924,541	485,963,746	514,087,571	562,733,147
Domestic Loans & Leases	1,403,371,635	1,524,701,706	1,717,381,471	1,910,204,168
Domestic Deposits	1,745,965,675	1,830,263,142	2,044,303,556	2,236,498,529
Foreign Loans & Leases	193,477,580	183,009,928	167,362,606	163,454,942
Foreign Deposits	302,869,747	332,375,885	309,019,497	311,755,483
Capital:[a]				
Equity Capital	166,027,030	170,181,513	193,113,785	205,868,794
Primary Capital	195,299,392	219,967,660	241,502,016	261,948,615
Total Capital	210,828,528	236,160,737	258,341,516	282,865,820
Preferred Dividends Declared	61,226	81,082	103,075	126,251
Common Dividends Declared	8,256,572	9,961,590	12,828,813	13,922,349
Equity Capital/Average Assets	6.78%	6.37%	6.64%	6.55%
Primary Capital/Adj Avg Assets	7.91%	8.11%	8.19%	8.21%
Total Capital/Adj Avg Assets	8.54%	8.71%	8.76%	8.86%
Equity—Capital/Total Capital	78.75%	72.06%	74.75%	72.78%
Dividends Declared/Net Income	46.51%	198.58%	48.68%	86.59%

Profitability:[a]

Net Income (Loss)	17,883,207	5,057,320	26,567,631	16,224,351
Return on Average Assets	0.73%	0.19%	0.91%	0.52%
Return on Average Equity Cap	11.33%	2.99%	14.51%	8.10%
Net Interest Margin	3.95%	3.91%	3.99%	3.97%
Net Interest Income/Avg Assets	3.50%	3.50%	3.59%	3.57%
Noninterest Income/Avg Assets	1.35%	1.47%	1.50%	1.64%
Noninterest Expense/Avg Assets	3.31%	3.38%	3.36%	3.45%

Asset Quality:[b]

Nonaccrual Loans/Total Loans	2.08	2.74	2.37	2.55
Nonaccrual Loans/Primary Cap	16.88	21.11	18.36	20.07
Nonaccrual Loans/Loan Loss Res	130.32	102.56	100.00	98.74
ORE/Total Assets	0.26	0.28	0.30	0.42
90+ Day Del Loans/Total Loans	0.53	0.45	0.45	0.47
Loan Loss Reserves/Total Loans	1.60	2.67	2.37	2.59
Net Charge-offs/Average Loans	0.96	0.89	0.97	1.18
Earnings Coverage/Net Chg-offs	2.71	2.98	2.94	2.43

Liquidity:[b]

Brokered Dep/Total Dom Dep	1.59	1.93	2.57	2.88
$100M+ Time Dep/Total Dom Dep	14.92	16.90	17.86	17.83
Int Earn Assets/Int Bear Liab	121.36	120.04	118.53	117.55
Pledged Sec/Total Sec	40.89	42.66	42.56	44.32
Market Val/Book Val Securities	103.05	99.20	98.52	100.63

a. Thousands of dollars.

b. Percent.

Table 3.3 Ratio of Total Equity to Total Assets, All Commercial Banks, Selected Periods, 1986–89

	Ratio < 0%		0% < Ratio < 3%		3% < Ratio < 6%		> 6% Ratio	
	Banks	Assets[a]	Banks	Assets[a]	Banks	Assets[a]	Banks	Assets[a]
12/89	76	12.4[b]	177	123.8	1290	1604.3	11,653	1804.6
9/89	N/A	10.5	171	77.0	1142	1552.1	11,901	1798.1
6/89	73	4.2	188	46.7	1158	1611.2	11,964	1747.4
3/89	71	3.3	196	39.6	1220	1645.7	11,957	1684.4
12/88	77	3.6	240	71.1	1380	1722.2	11,793	1541.9
12/87	63	3.6	250	117.0	1587	1638.0	12,172	1423.6
12/86	46	1.3	199	22.0	1969	1769.2	11,888	1138.6

a. In billions of dollars.

b. Not clear how many of these banks already have been "reserved for" by the FDIC.

NOTE: Figures for 12/88 and later exclude MCorp Bridge Bank and Texas American banks in Texas for which the FDIC reports it established loss reserves in 1988.

SOURCE: *Bank Source,* W.C. Ferguson & Co., Irving, Texas.

- Total capital fell from 8.46 percent to 6.13 percent and equity capital as a proportion of total capital fell from 86 percent to 53.1 percent (total capital adds subordinated debt, loan loss reserves, and other minor items to equity capital).

- These banks declared preferred and common dividends in each of the four years totaling $239.2 million and

- Nonaccrual loans represented 4.42 percent of the banks' total loans in 1986 and 5.86 percent in 1989 (the comparable percentages for all open banks are 2.08 percent and 2.55 percent).

The data in table 3.4 through the third quarter of 1989 were presented by Furgeson in 1989 in testimony before the House Subcommittee on Financial Institutions Supervision, Regulation and Insurance. He pointed out that if the earnings trends for these banks continued, the banks would run out of capital before the end of 1990.

Table 3.5 presents additional data on another segment of troubled banks.

- In 1989 there were $30.9 billion in assets in 244 banks that earned negative net income in 1988 and 1989 but positive income in 1986 and 1987.

- Between 1986 and 1988 these banks grew approximately $6.5 billion or 25 percent.

- The negative net income grew from a negative $201 million to negative $464 million from 1988 to 1989.

- Equity capital fell from 8.2 percent to 5.23 percent from 1986 to 1989.

- Total capital fell from 8.96 percent to 6.91 percent over that period with equity capital as a percent of total capital falling from 90.9 percent to 74.6 percent.

- Dividends were declared in each year since 1986 with $89.3 million declared in 1988 and 1989 and

- Nonaccrual loans grew from 1.57 percent of total loans in 1986 to 4.48 percent in 1989.

The bifurcation between these two groups of low-income banks and all open banks is striking. As shown in Table 3.2, net income for all open banks fluctuated, with the drop in 1987, but remained relatively substantial over the 1986–89 period. Equity and total capital ratios also remained stable and relatively substantial. Equity capital as a percent of total capital did decline, however, and nonaccrual loans as a percent of total loans did increase as well for all open banks.

Brokered Deposits as a Barometer of Bank Strength

Tables 3.4 and 3.5 provide a glimpse of how the market perceives the banks that have had losses consistently in recent years. For those banks with losses since 1986, brokered deposits as a portion of total deposits have fallen from 2.08 percent in 1986 to 0.55 percent in 1989. For the banks with losses since 1988, the ratio declined from a high of 1.97 percent in 1987 to 0.55 percent in 1989. These brokered deposits are almost exclusively from institutional investors. As Table 3.2 shows, brokered deposits in all banks rose from 1.59 percent in 1986 to 2.88 percent in 1989. For the largest banks in 1989 with assets over $10 billion brokered deposits were 4.47 percent. For banks with assets ranging from $1 to $10 billion, the ratio was 4.32 percent in 1989. These data suggest that institutional investors have been pulling away from the weak banks as their condition deteriorates.

Problem and Failed Banks

Problem and failed banks show a pattern somewhat similar to that of the net worth and income data for troubled banks, and reveal additional worrisome aspects of the banks' difficulties. Problem banks are banks with examination ratings of four or five where ratings are based on a scale of one to five. Both problem and failed banks increased throughout the 1980s, as shown in Table 3.6, though there was a decline in problem banks in 1988 and 1989. Problem banks nonetheless numbered 1,093 in 1989. Before the high in 1987 the peak number of problem banks was 385, recorded in 1976 (see FDIC, 1988). The number of failed banks increased throughout the decade beginning with 10 in 1980 and ending with 206 in 1989. Between 1987 and 1988, the increase in the assets of failed banks substantially outpaced the increase in the number of failed banks.

Table 3.4 Selected Financial Data for Commercial Banks Reporting Net Operating Losses for 1986–89

	1986	1987	1988	1989
Balance Sheet:[a]				
Total Assets	36,307,660	36,896,142	42,722,637	42,107,825
% Change in Assets	1.93%	1.62%	15.79%	(1.44%)
Securities—Book Value	6,335,416	6,726,661	7,661,851	6,946,648
Securities—Market Value	6,436,729	6,566,049	7,423,556	6,919,012
Domestic Loans & Leases	21,267,240	22,520,085	26,002,192	24,344,275
Domestic Deposits	29,354,158	29,617,798	36,546,571	36,868,426
Foreign Loans & Leases	112,187	143,794	59,953	53,010
Foreign Deposits	335,509	320,795	285,173	239,203
Capital:[a]				
Equity Capital	2,522,922	2,124,472	2,025,352	1,392,681
Primary Capital	2,902,656	2,897,103	2,896,163	2,594,986
Total Capital	2,934,486	2,932,859	2,928,887	2,620,880
Preferred Dividends Declared	840	1,025	518	0
Common Dividends Declared	94,374	116,886	23,852	1,665
Equity Capital/Average Assets	7.35%	5.77%	5.05%	3.35%
Primary Capital/Adj Avg Assets	8.37%	7.71%	7.07%	6.07%
Total Capital/Adj Avg Assets	8.46%	7.80%	7.15%	6.13%
Equity Capital/Total Capital	85.97%	72.44%	69.15%	53.14%
Dividends Declared/Net Income	(79.54%)	(15.04%)	(2.49%)	(0.13%)

Profitability:[a]

Net Income (Loss)	(119,702)	(784,122)	(980,487)	(1,308,811)
Return on Average Assets	(0.35%)	(2.13%)	(2.45%)	(3.15%)
Return on Average Equity Cap	(4.67%)	(32.69%)	(47.25%)	(76.58%)
Net Interest Margin	3.69%	3.51%	3.63%	3.37%
Net Interest Income/Avg Assets	3.28%	3.10%	3.19%	2.95%
Noninterest Income/Avg Assets	0.98%	1.11%	1.28%	1.22%
Noninterest Expense/Avg Assets	3.67%	4.14%	4.94%	5.06%

Asset Quality:[b]

Nonaccrual Loans/Total Loans	4.42	6.86	6.38	5.86
Nonaccrual Loans/Primary Cap	32.27	53.24	56.85	54.65
Nonaccrual Loans/Loan Loss Res	210.77	189.94	181.07	115.73
ORE/Total Assets	1.15	2.29	2.51	2.86
90+ Day Del Loans/Total Loans	1.37	1.17	0.93	0.75
Loan Loss Reserves/Total Loans	2.10	3.61	3.52	5.06
Net Charge-offs/Average Loans	2.09	2.98	3.92	3.34
Earnings Coverage/Net Chg-offs	0.45	0.04	(0.20)	(0.44)

Liquidity:[b]

Brokered Dep/Total Dom Dep	2.08	1.09	0.62	0.55
$100M+ Time Dep/Total Dom Dep	28.28	24.22	20.68	16.63
Int Earn Assets/Int Bear Liab	115.55	114.29	113.49	111.74
Pledged Sec/Total Sec	56.34	62.08	55.33	54.59
Market Val/Book Val Securities	101.60	97.61	96.89	99.60

a. Thousands of dollars.

b. Percent.

Table 3.5   Selected Financial Data for Commercial Banks Reporting Net Operating Losses for 1988, 1989

	1986	1987	1988	1989
Balance Sheet:[a]				
Total Assets	26,304,758	28,443,409	32,831,991	30,851,882
% Change in Assets	11.23%	8.13%	15.43%	(6.03%)
Securities—Book Value	4,361,797	5,139,255	5,577,527	5,119,720
Securities—Market Value	4,444,656	5,063,423	5,450,904	5,117,027
Domestic Loans & Leases	16,687,174	18,143,290	21,587,895	19,370,594
Domestic Deposits	21,836,420	23,198,844	26,829,756	25,827,726
Foreign Loans & Leases	177,454	209,712	227,576	150,164
Foreign Deposits	82,518	184,859	207,948	77,148
Capital:[a]				
Equity Capital	1,924,918	2,102,535	2,073,140	1,655,909
Primary Capital	2,100,097	2,327,851	2,411,274	2,137,035
Total Capital	2,118,883	2,344,120	2,441,632	2,218,593
Preferred Dividends Declared	2,904	3,919	1,242	0
Common Dividends Declared	90,809	83,392	66,720	21,381
Equity Capital/Average Assets	8.20%	7.89%	6.76%	5.23%
Primary Capital/Adj Avg Assets	8.88%	8.66%	7.78%	6.66%
Total Capital/Adj Avg Assets	8.96%	8.72%	7.88%	6.91%
Equity Capital/Total Capital	90.85%	89.69%	84.91%	74.64%
Dividends Declared/Net Income	71.30%	56.60%	(33.85%)	(4.61%)

Profitability:[a]

Net Income (Loss)	131,438	154,258	(200,747)	(464,021)
Return on Average Assets	0.56%	0.58%	(0.65%)	(1.47%)
Return on Average Equity Cap	7.42%	7.62%	(9.61%)	(24.89%)
Net Interest Margin	4.80%	4.58%	4.31%	4.02%
Net Interest Income/Avg Assets	4.27%	4.10%	3.87%	3.62%
Noninterest Income/Avg Assets	0.98%	1.13%	1.14%	1.23%
Noninterest Expense/Avg Assets	3.89%	3.77%	4.07%	4.46%

Asset Quality:[b]

Nonaccrual Loans/Total Loans	1.57	2.25	3.91	4.48
Nonaccrual Loans/Primary Cap	12.44	17.56	35.12	40.65
Nonaccrual Loans/Loan Loss Res	112.97	142.34	183.33	142.01
ORE/Total Assets	0.63	0.98	1.40	1.84
90+ Day Del Loans/Total Loans	1.05	1.01	1.32	1.32
Loan Loss Reserves/Total Loans	1.39	1.58	2.13	3.16
Net Charge-offs/Average Loans	1.10	1.03	2.18	2.95
Earnings Coverage/Net Chg-offs	1.92	2.22	0.67	0.20

Liquidity:[b]

Brokered Dep/Total Dom Dep	1.18	1.97	1.81	0.55
$100M+ Time Dep/Total Dom Dep	21.76	23.95	20.70	14.02
Int Earn Assets/Int Bear Liab	120.00	117.57	114.25	114.11
Pledged Sec/Total Sec	58.84	61.46	54.52	55.65
Market Val/Book Val Securities	101.90	98.52	97.73	99.95

a. Thousands of dollars.

b. Percent.

Copyright 1988, 1989, 1990, W.C. Ferguson & Company, Irving, TX 75039.

Table 3.6 Problem and Failed Commercial Banks, 1980–89

	Problem Banks	Deposits ($Millions)	Failed Banks	Deposits ($Millions)
1989	1,093[a]	N.A.	206[a]	N.A.
1988	1,495	287,914	200	24,931
1987	1,575	282,450	184	6,282
1986	1,484	271,320	138	6,471
1985	1,140	197,127	120	8,059
1984	848	186,109	79	2,883
1983	642	129,081	48	5,442
1982	369	57,338	42	9,908
1981	223	42,564	10	3,826
1980	217	21,644	10	216

a. From Quarterly Banking Profile, FDIC Fourth Quarter, 1989.
SOURCE: FDIC 1988 Annual Report and FDIC Problem Bank List.

The increase in problem banks through 1985, and in particular its magnitude, suggest that they were a reliable leading indicator of the net worth decline that occurred between 1986 and 1987. The continued large number of problem banks is consistent with the continued deterioration of both net worth and income of a significant number of banks between 1986 and 1989. The decline in the number of problem banks was accompanied in 1988 by an increase in the assets of problem banks. This indicates smaller banks may be improving and may also reflect the increased number of closures.

INDICATIONS OF BANK REGULATORY LENIENCY AND FORBEARANCE

"Too Large to Fail" Issues

Whether the problem-bank list has ever included money-center banks is unclear, although the average size would indicate that it is unlikely. In 1989 we estimated the risk-based capital of the money-center banks for 1987 or 1988 (depending on which data were available) and adjusted their LDC debt reserves to reflect reasonable approximations to market levels, making appropriate adjustments for inadequacies of the secondary LDC debt market (see Brumbaugh, Carron, and Litan, 1989). We found that three banks, Bank of America, Chemical Bank, and Manufacturers Hanover, had risk-adjusted capital levels below 2 percent. They were above 2 percent after adjustments for taxes. If these banks with $198.6 billion in assets were not on the problem list, it suggests the possibility of regulatory forbearance and a possible manifestation that some banks are "too large to fail" in regulators' minds.

At the end of 1989 one money-center bank, Bankers Trust Company with assets of $51 billion, and one super regional bank, Bank of New England with assets of $14 billion, fell into the 0 to 3 percent net-worth category with equity-to-capital ratios of 2.49 percent and 1.48 percent. As we have pointed out elsewhere (see Brumbaugh and Litan, 1990, p. 7) deterioration can be abrupt and dramatic. We found 16 banks that went from the 0 to 3 percent category to insolvency, in some cases deep insolvency, between September 1988 and March 1989. Of the 242 banks reporting 0 to 3 percent net worth at year-end 1988, 120 were insolvent by yearend 1989, 65 were unchanged, 48 rose to the 3 to 6 percent category, and 9 were above 6 percent. Thus, about half declined and a quarter improved. In this context, the decline of Bankers Trust and Bank of New England, which were probably not on the problem-bank list, is troubling.

Closure Rule: Banks Open but Apparently Insolvent

Tables 3.1 and 3.3 indicate that throughout the post-1986 period some banks have been open and operating while insolvent based even on accounting techniques. The failed-bank data also suggest regulatory forbearance in closure. The number of failed banks jumped between 1984 and 1985 as shown in Table 3.6. The data in the table show that the average annual assets for problem banks for the three years before the jump in failed banks was $124 billion and was $250 billion for the three years after the jump, a 50 percent increase. The average annual assets for failed banks, however, rose from $6.1 billion to $6.8 billion for the same period, an increase of only 13 percent. Given the relatively large number of failed banks, the FDIC was closing a larger number of smaller banks.

Closing a larger number of smaller banks at a time of significant deterioration of the largest banks and among other larger banks, suggests that the FDIC was trying to meter out closure costs in order to maintain the level of reported FDIC reserves. Closing small banks reduces the exposure of the reported reserves and obscures the scope of the threat to the FDIC fund. If this is the strategy, larger insolvent banks benefit from forbearance and have an incentive to take great risks in order to resurrect themselves. In such a strategy the FDIC is betting on unexpected beneficial economic developments to improve the insolvent banks and on the ability of the examination and supervisory process to contain risk-taking. This was essentially the strategy followed by the FSLIC before 1987 (for a description of this phenomenon in the context of the savings and loan crisis, see Brumbaugh, chapter 2, 1988).

Additional Capital Forbearance

There are several other examples of capital forbearance. The Competitive Equality Banking Act (CEBA) of 1987 allowed a bank to operate temporarily with a capital ratio as low as 0.5 percent. Original eligibility for this forbearance was limited to banks heavily involved in agricultural and energy lending but was expanded to include any bank with difficulties attributable primarily to "economic problems beyond management control." The FDIC extended forbearance to 135 banks under this program in 1988 (see FDIC 1988, p.7). Second, the FDIC established a "bridge bank" program for selected insolvent banks allowed to remain open under directors appointed by the FDIC. Third, the FDIC, the Federal Reserve Board, and the Comptroller of the Currency in 1987 allowed small agricultural banks to amortize farm-related losses over seven years instead of recognizing the losses immediately and to count the unamortized portions in primary capital.

Additional practices allow troubled assets to be overstated. Banks, for example, may not report the value of troubled real estate at an amount exceeding the present value of expected cash flows—the "net realized value." But this value may be calculated at a 0 percent discount rate. Finally, notwithstanding significant additions to reserves and net charge-offs for LDC debt, some money-center banks—most notably Citibank— remained relatively substantially underreserved.

Weak Bank Dividending: Eroding the Buffer between the BIF and Future Losses

From 1980 through 1987 cash dividends for all commercial banks grew steadily and additions to retained earnings fell steadily. This pattern persisted despite the precipitous increase in loan loss provisions that occurred in and continued after 1981 (see Brumbaugh, Carron, and Litan, 1989). In 1987 when major banks significantly added to reserves for LDC debt, regulators did not require any of the banks to suspend dividends and many of the banks paid dividends out of shareholder equity. Allowing banks to pay increasing dividends, in some cases out of shareholder equity, at a time of persistent increases in loan loss provisions, reduces the buffer between the insurance fund and potential losses.

As Table 3.4 shows, the 479 banks with losses from 1986 through 1989 have declared dividends in every year although the magnitude dropped significantly in 1988 and 1989. The 244 banks with losses in 1988 and 1989 also paid dividends throughout the period, as shown in Table 3.5. The prolonged and significant decline of these banks indicates that many of the banks were declaring dividends when they were at or near market-value insolvency after years of operating losses. This is an example of regulatory forbearance that has directly reduced the buffer between the BIF and future losses.

THE THREAT TO THE BANK INSURANCE FUND
Reported FDIC and BIF Reserves

Table 3.7 presents the reported reserves of the FDIC fund through 1988. As the table shows, reported reserves rose between 1980 and 1987 and fell precipitously in 1988. The FDIC announced recently that the reported reserves fell in 1989 to $13.2 billion (see Duke and Thomas, 1990). The reported reserves as a percentage of insured deposits in the BIF fell in 1989 to 0.7 percent, substantially below the targeted range of approximately 1.25 percent roughly maintained earlier in the decade.

Actual reserves may differ substantially from reported reserves if there are significant assets in insolvent but open banks and if closure of the banks will cost considerably. Given the ability of accounting techniques to raise book values above market values, many of the 177 banks shown in Table 3.3 reporting net worth between 0 and 3 percent with $123.8 billion in assets are probably market-value insolvent. Reserves have not been established for all of the 76 banks with $12.4 billion in assets that are reporting insolvency. Some of the 479 banks with $42 billion in assets that have had negative operating income since 1986 (and will deplete reported net worth

Table 3.7   Federal Deposit Insurance Corporation Fund Reserves, 1970–88

Year	Reserves
1970	4.38
1971	4.74
1972	5.16
1973	5.62
1974	6.12
1975	6.72
1976	7.27
1977	7.99
1978	8.80
1979	9.79
1980	11.02
1981	12.25
1982	13.77
1983	15.43
1984	16.53
1985	17.96
1986	18.25
1987	18.30
1988	14.06

NOTE: In billions of dollars.

SOURCE: FDIC 1988 Annual Report.

this year if their earnings continue) are not included in the 177 banks because their net worth exceeds 3 percent. The same is true for the 244 banks with $31 billion in assets that reported losses for 1988 and 1989.

Expected Losses and Actual BIF Reserves

These data strongly suggest that the reported reserves of the BIF are substantially exaggerated because expected future losses in currently insolvent but open banks will be large. What the actual future losses will be is extremely uncertain. Losses depend on how many banks are market-value insolvent, how large the banks are, and how soon banks are closed after market-value insolvency is reached. Given the current closure rule, closures invariably occur after market-value insolvency has been reached. In general, market-value insolvency is greater for banks reporting accounting insolvency than for those which are market-value insolvent but reporting low net worth.

The FDIC's loss experience in the 1980s (through 1987) averaged approximately 26 percent of assets in insolvent banks, ranging as high as 75 percent in 1982 and 1984 and as low as 10 percent in 1981 and 1985. If all 253 banks reporting net worth at or below 3 percent with $142 billion in assets are ultimately closed, it would only take a loss ratio of 9.3 percent to eliminate the BIF's reported reserves of $13.2 billion. As Furgeson has pointed out, a loss ratio of 25 percent applied to the 479 banks with losses since 1986 would cost the BIF $10.5 billion and would cost another $7.8 billion if applied to the 244 banks reporting losses in 1988 and 1989. These estimates, even with their admitted limitations, suggest that future losses on currently insolvent banks could easily equal or exceed the BIF's reported reserves.

A CRITIQUE OF FIRREA

FIRREA is comprised of essentially five parts:

1. Providing for funding of the closure of savings and loans
2. Reorganizing the regulatory agencies responsible for savings and loans and deposit insurance
3. Establishing new minimum capital levels
4. Restricting allowable assets
5. Providing additional enforcement authority to combat fraud in savings and loans

See Arnold and Porter, et al. (1989) for a comprehensive and readable summary of FIRREA's provisions. The law does not in any meaningful sense address reform, recovery, and enforcement beyond the savings and loans and the portion of the law's title referring to "financial institutions" is a misnomer. Most important, the law addresses directly none of the banks' difficulties we have described.

A critique of FIRREA, therefore, should analyze the law's adequacy in dealing with savings and loans and whether, under the circumstances, it should have dealt directly with broader issues or with savings and loans in the broader context of deposit-insurance reform (for other critiques, see Barth, Benston, and Wiest, 1990; Barth and Brumbaugh, 1990; and Scott, 1990). The issue of funding the closure of savings and loans has been dealt with by James Barth and Philip Bartholomew in their paper at this conference so we will address the remaining four parts of the bill regarding savings and loans.

Savings and Loan Regulatory and Deposit-Insurance Reorganization

FIRREA abolished the Federal Home Loan Bank Board, the independent federal savings and loan regulator and head of the FSLIC. The FSLIC was also abolished. The Bank Board's regulatory functions were shifted to the Office of Thrift Supervision (OTS), a new agency much like the Office of the Comptroller of the Currency, placed within the Treasury Department. The FSLIC insurance functions were placed in the Savings Association Insurance Fund (SAIF). The insurance function of the FDIC was placed within BIF with the FDIC overseeing both the SAIF and BIF. The FSLIC's responsibilities for the disposition of closed savings and loans were transferred to the Resolution Trust Corporation (RTC) administered essentially by the FDIC but directed by an oversight board on which the chair of the FDIC is a member.

What improvement this reorganization made in the regulation, examination, and supervision of savings and loans is unclear but appears meager (for an alternative approach, see Carron, 1984). The new organizational structure is not materially simpler than its predecessor. Lines of authority are rearranged giving the Executive, and especially the Treasury Department, more direct authority over savings and loan regulation and disposition of closed savings and loans. The Executive, however, had substantial control before, primarily through appointments to the Bank Board. Congressional oversight is reduced, though the OTS director is appointed with Senate confirmation, because the OTS now reports directly to the Treasury.

The benefits of the transfer of the savings and loan insurance functions to the FDIC are also unclear. The conflict of interest between being regulator and insurer is somewhat muted by the separation of the OTS from the SAIF but remains substantial. Because the Bank Board was appointed by the President with Senate confirmation, transferring responsibility to the chair of the FDIC who is similarly appointed and confirmed, did not materially improve oversight controls. At least temporarily offsetting whatever gains were accomplished for both regulation and insurance are the disruptions caused by the organizational reshuffling. The diversion of a significant number of bank insurance personnel to savings and loan issues especially burdened FDIC staff already struggling with increased bank difficulties.

Though organizational and reporting improvements are thus meager, other goals may have motivated the changes. Pervasive discontent with the Bank Board peaked within Congress and the Administration at the beginning of 1989 following several acquisitions of closed savings and loans in which tax benefits and government guarantees were used instead of cash. Derision about the competency of the Bank Board was rampant. The chairman of the Bank Board, however, was the former staff director of the Senate Banking Committee and close aide of the former committee chairman and then ranking minority member of the Committee. The organizational structure that evolved increased Executive control and shifted major responsibilities to bank regulators without having to dismiss the Bank Board chairman, though his authority was diminished significantly.

In contrast to this approach, the President could have replaced the Bank Board chairman with an individual whose task it could have been to make Bank Board regulatory and insurance policies more consistent with Administration and congressional goals. An overhauling of the existing agency structure could have been effected more quickly and just as thoroughly as the organization that resulted. This would have left the FDIC alone to handle its problems. Ironically, the chairman of the FDIC breeched traditional interagency etiquette by vociferously criticizing the Bank Board. The effect in part was to distract attention from growing bank difficulties and, by making the FDIC appear strong by comparison, to lobby implicitly for the acquisition of FSLIC's authorities.

New Minimum Capital Standards for Savings and Loans

Under FIRREA, savings and loans must meet three capital requirements simultaneously: a leverage ratio that requires core capital (generally equity plus allowable goodwill) to be not less than 3 percent of assets, a minimum tangible capital ratio of not less than 1.5 percent, and a risk-based capital requirement imposed by the OTS but which cannot be less stringent than the requirement for banks.

Although the new capital requirements are higher than those that prevailed immediately before them, they are substantially below the levels that have been historically required. As recently as 1980, the minimum capital requirement for savings and loans was 5 percent based on generally accepted accounting principles. Because there was essentially no goodwill the standard was equal to a tangible new worth requirement.

In this context the new standards are a form of regulatory forbearance. As mentioned earlier, we and many other economists believe that savings and loans and banks with capital between 6 and 8 percent are weakly capitalized.

Moreover, legislation was not required to raise the minimum capital requirements. They were lowered by the Bank Board in several stages during the 1980s and could have been raised under the same authority. The development of three different types and levels of capital requirements has no economic basis and is needlessly cumbersome. The risk-based requirements are among the most perplexing. Risk for a financial institution is a measure of the entire portfolio, reflecting the variability of individual assets and the covariability of all the assets. The risk-based capital requirements rely solely on perceived variability of some assets. They are not based on any study of the actual variability of assets in savings and loan portfolios and they do not address covariability.

Other problems exist with the risk-based requirements. Unsecuritized mortgage loans held by savings and loans and banks require $4 of capital for each $100 of assets, for example, in contrast to mortgage securities guaranteed by the Federal National Mortgage Association and the Federal Home Loan Mortgage Corporation which require $1.60 in capital. Because the mortgage securities carry an agency guarantee, the basis for the $1.60 requirement is unclear. Furthermore, it is estimated that FNMA and FHLMC hold less than $1.75 in capital for each $100 in exposure. Since they hold unsecuritized mortgage loans, the differential between their capital per $100 in exposure and the $4 per $100 for savings and loans is also unclear (see Carron and Brumbaugh, 1990). This inconsistency can be important and is a shortcoming of FIRREA.

NEW ASSET RESTRICTIONS FOR SAVINGS AND LOANS

Junk Bonds

The law restricts allowable assets in three major ways. FIRREA lowers the percentage of certain nonresidential mortgage assets that a savings and loan can hold, a reduction from levels set primarily by the Garn-St Germain Act of 1982. It prohibits the acquisition of below-investment-grade "junk" bonds and requires the sale of existing junk bonds "as quickly as prudently can be done" but no later than July 1, 1994. Finally, the law raises from 60 percent to 70 percent in 1991 the minimum percentage of assets that a savings and loan must hold in housing finance and related activities in order to pass the Qualified Thrift Lender (QTL) test. Failure to pass the test means sacrifice of certain benefits and imposition of certain penalties which can be relatively severe.

In 1988 the total percentage of junk bonds in savings and loans was

1.1 percent and represented 0.8 percent of assets in savings and loans closed that year (see Barth, 1988; Barth and Bradley, 1989; and Barth, Bartholomew, and Labich, 1990, for analyses and data on junk bonds in savings and loan portfolios). Of the $14.5 billion in junk bonds at their peak, approximately $4.5 billion, 31 percent, were in one savings and loan. Most of the junk bonds were in a handful of savings and loans. Only 149 savings and loans ever held junk bonds. Savings and loans holding junk bonds held 47.9 percent of their assets in one- to four-family residential mortgages or mortgage-backed securities compared to 57.6 percent for those holding no junk bonds. Regardless of the role junk bonds would have played in the difficulties of savings and loans, the total volume of junk bonds and their distribution are too small to justify the attention paid to them by FIRREA.

The divestiture requirement is also difficult to justify. The requirement was perceived by the market as a dumping of junk bonds and depressed their price. According to Arnold and Porter, et al., the Conference Report states that the conferees did not intend the divestiture requirement to lead to "held for sale" status and subject the bonds to mark to market. Due primarily to accounting interpretations, mark to market occurred nonetheless and interacted with the lower prices caused by the divestiture requirement to compound the problem.

We believe that savings and loans and banks should report market values to regulatory authorities on all assets and liabilities for the purpose of assisting the regulators in determining overall solvency and whether closure or supervisory action is appropriate. This is substantially different from requiring directly or indirectly the marking to market of some assets and not others. This practice can lead to distortions that decrease the value of savings and loan and bank portfolios.

The Qualified Thrift Lender Test

The tightening of the QTL test and the rollback of the deregulated assets in the Garn-St Germain Act primarily reflect a backlash against the perceived dangers of nonhousing financial assets. After 1982 the portfolios of closed savings and loans contained substantial portions of nonhousing related assets, primarily commercial real estate. The perception within Congress appears to be that these assets are riskier than housing related assets and that they caused the deterioration of the savings and loans. The perception also appears to be that a return to housing related assets will be less risky and provide more stable income.

The major complicating phenomenon is that most of the savings and loans that were closed and exposed the insurer to losses through nontraditional assets were open and operating while insolvent for years. These savings and loans had an incentive to take excessive risks and may have done so with nontraditional assets. Others diversified before 1982 when their portfolios of fixed-rate, long-term mortgages were imposing substantial losses. Their diversification may have reflected a desire to minimize risk but may have gone awry due to inexperience. Several studies indicate that the effect of insolvency, not assets per se, caused the problems associated with nontraditional assets (see Barth, Bartholomew, and Bradley, 1990; Barth, Brumbaugh, and Sauerhaft, 1986; Barth, Brumbaugh, Sauerhaft, and Wang, 1985, 1989; Benston, 1985; and Benston and Brumbaugh, 1988).

Another important issue is whether savings and loans can earn positive income from holding mortgages in their portfolios. In particular, without taking interest-rate risk by lending long and borrowing short, can matched funded mortgage interest payments more than cover the all-in costs of funding mortgages? This is essentially what is required for savings and loans to earn positive income from most of the assets in the QTL test. The major complicating issue is the option that the borrower has to prepay the mortgage. This option has the effect of lowering the expected stream of income from the mortgage. Carron and Brumbaugh (1990) calculated the option-adjusted return on mortgages in savings and loan portfolios and found that with brief exceptions since 1984 savings and loans on average have had negative income holding fixed-rate mortgages in portfolio and meager and declining income from adjustable-rate mortgages.

Savings and loans can earn a profit from fees from origination and servicing of mortgages, the two other major components of mortgage-lending income. On average, however, the one aspect of housing finance lending required by the QTL test imposes losses on savings and loans. Because diversification is so difficult to manage adequately, the alternatives are risky (for a treatment of diversification risks in banks see Litan, 1987), but the current requirement is worse because it imposes losses.

ENFORCEMENT AND FRAUD IN THE SAVINGS AND LOAN CRISIS

FIRREA provides additional enforcement authority for all relevant agencies, increases penalties, and broadens offenses. It also provides the Justice Department with $50 million to increase its efforts to combat fraud in savings and loans. The director of the Federal Bureau of Investigation has said that the FBI currently has seven thousand case referrals and has allocated approximately 450 agents from the white collar crime staff of 1800 to such cases (statement made on the MacNeil/Lehrer NewsHour, April 12, 1990).

Evaluating fraud in the savings and loan crisis involves the following questions: In how many closed savings and loans did fraud occur? In how many was fraud a material cause of the closure? Finally, what component of the cost to the insurer was due to fraud? Barth, Bartholomew, and

Labich (1990) tested econometrically for fraud the 205 closures that took place in 1988. Since then there have been only 60 closures. According to the enforcement officials at the Bank Board at the time, fraud was a material problem in 30 to 40 percent of the closures. The study then estimated what percentage of the losses expected by the FSLIC were due to fraud and found the percentage to be 10 percent.

The FSLIC has estimated that its losses through 1988 on savings and loans closed since 1980 have been approximately $90 billion. One of us has estimated that the present value of future losses will range between $100–140 billion (see Barth and Brumbaugh, 1990). Other estimates range higher. If, for example, the total present value of losses is $200 billion, the study cited above indicates that the cost due to fraud will be $20 billion. The FBI director said that bank robberies the year he became director in 1987 amounted to $34 million. Twenty billion dollars represents 588 years of bank robberies.

Two conclusions strike us. First, even if the percentage of cost due to fraud is small the cost is enormous because the overall losses are so great. Second, even if the percentage due to losses is double or triple what the Barth study indicates, fraud is still a relatively modest component of the overall savings and loan debacle.

At the moment fraud is being emphasized by the Attorney General, the FBI director, the FDIC chairman, and the chairman of the Securities and Exchange Commission in the context of junk bonds and the Michael Milken settlement. In addition, the newly appointed OTS director is an attorney with an enforcement background and no prior experience with savings and loans. The cost estimates above and almost all studies of the savings and loan debacle suggest that the major policy issues in the savings and loan crisis and the developing crisis in commercial banks do not involve fraud. The primary issues involve the incentives caused by deposit insurance and the regulatory apparatus required by deposit insurance.

One of the ironies of the emphasis on fraud is that the resources allocated to combat it seem extremely small. This suggests that the official emphasis on fraud is not connected to a strong program to confront fraud but rather may be designed to divert attention from the need to deal with the larger issues of deposit insurance and regulation. Despite the current public relations attention on fraud, the absence of funds and personnel to confront fraud means that the government's attempts to deal with it will likely flounder.

CONCLUSIONS

In this paper we have tried to demonstrate the bifurcation of the commercial banks into two groups, one relatively healthy and one extremely weak. The weak are characterized by low and declining reported net worth and substantial and sustained negative operating income. Because of the widespread use of accounting conventions to conceal balance-sheet weakness, the number and assets of market-value insolvent banks cannot be known with certainty. Our data and interpretation suggest that the number of market insolvent banks is large and raise the possibility that the losses associated with them could deplete the reserves of the BIF.

Our critique of FIRREA highlights the fact that the law does not address the condition of the banks or the banks' insurance funds and did not address the major issues of deposit-insurance reform or the regulation demanded by deposit isurance (see Flannery, 1982, on how deposit insurance creates the need for regulation). In light of the bank deterioration that we have emphasized and and that has been relatively widely discussed, these are serious omissions. Our critique also points out serious flaws in FIRREA's approach to regulatory reorganization, savings and loan capital requirements, asset restrictions, and enforcement. The inadequacies that we have discussed, combined with the well-known flaws in funding and organizing the closure of insolvent savings and loans, point out the need for a major congressional evaluation of all the issues. A sense of emergency seems in order.

REFERENCES

Arnold & Porter, The Secura Group, and Arthur Andersen & Co., *Understanding FIRREA: A Practical Guide to Planning and Compliance,* Prentice Hall Law & Business (Englewood Cliffs), 1989.

Barth, James R., *Post-FIRREA: The Need to Reform the Federal Deposit Insurance System,* presentation at the 26th Annual Conference on Bank Structure and Competition, Federal Reserve Bank of Chicago, May 9–11, 1990.

———, comments prepared for a conference on Financial-Economic Perspectives on the High-Yield Debt Market, December 8–9, 1988.

———, *The Great Savings and Loan Debacle,* American Enterprise Institute, University Press of America (Washington, D.C.), 1991.

Barth, James R., Philip F. Bartholomew, and Michael G. Bradley, "The Determinants of Thrift-Institution Resolution Costs," *Journal of Finance,* July 1990, vol. 45, pp. 731–54.

Barth, James R., Philip F. Bartholomew, and Carol Labich, "Moral Hazard and the Thrift Crisis: An Empirical Analysis," *Consumer Finance Law Quarterly Report,* 44(1) 1990, pp. 22–34.

Barth, James R., and Michael Bradley, "Thrift Deregulation and Federal Deposit Insurance," *Journal of Financial Services Research,* vol. 2, no. 3, 1989, pp. 231–59.

Barth, James R., George J. Benston, and Philip Wiest, "The Financial Institutions Reform, Recovery and Enforcement Act of 1989: Description, Effects and Implications," *Issues in Bank Regulation,* vol. 13, Winter 1990, pp. 3–11.

Barth, James R., and R. Dan Brumbaugh, Jr., "The Continuing Bungling of the Savings and Loan Crisis: The Rough Road from FIRREA to the Reform of Deposit Insurance," *The Stanford Law and Policy Review,* Stanford University (Palo Alto), vol. 2, May 1990, pp. 58–67.

Barth, James R., R. Dan Brumbaugh, Jr., and Daniel Sauerhaft, "Failure Costs of Government-Regulated Firms: The Case of Thrift Institutions," Research working paper no. 123, Federal Home Loan Bank Board, Washington, D.C., October 1986.

Barth, James R., R. Dan Brumbaugh, Jr., and Robert E. Litan, *The Future of American Banking,* M. E. Sharpe, Inc. (Armonk, N.Y.), 1992.

Barth, James R., R. Dan Brumbaugh, Jr., Daniel Sauerhaft, and George H. K. Wang, "Thrift Institution Failures: Causes and Policy Issues," in *Proceedings of a Conference on Bank Structure and Competition,* Federal Reserve Bank of Chicago, 1985, pp. 184–216.

Barth, James R., R. Dan Brumbaugh, Jr., Daniel Sauerhaft, and George H. K. Wang, "Thrift-Institution Failures: Estimating the Regulator's Closure Rule," in *Research in Financial Services,* ed. George G. Kaufman, vol. 1, pp. 1–23, JAI Press Inc. (Greenwich), 1989.

Barth, Mary, William Beaver, and Chris Stinson, "Supplemental Data and the Structure of Thrift Share Data," *Accounting Review,* vol. 66, January 1991, pp. 56–66.

Benston, George J. *An Analysis of the Causes of Savings and Loan Association Failures,* Monograph Series in Finance and Economics, Monograph 1985–45. Salomon Brothers Center for the Study of Financial Institutions, New York University, 1985.

Benston, George J., and R. Dan Brumbaugh, Jr., "On the Controversy Over Asset Restrictions for Thrift Institutions," *Housing Finance Review,* Fall/Winter 1988, vol. 7, nos. 4 & 5, pp. 361–69.

Benston, George J., R. Dan Brumbaugh, Jr., Jack M. Guttentag, Richard J. Herring, George G. Kaufman, Robert E. Litan, and Kenneth E. Scott. *Blueprint for Restructuring America's Financial Institutions*, The Brookings Institution (Washington, D.C.), 1989.

Benston, George J., and George G. Kaufman, *Risk and Solvency Regulation of Depository Institutions,* Salomon Brothers Center for the Study of Financial Institutions, New York University, 1988.

Brumbaugh, R. Dan, Jr., *Thrifts Under Siege: Restoring Order to American Banking,* The Ballinger Publishing Co. (Cambridge), 1988.

Brumbaugh, R. Dan, Jr., Andrew S. Carron, and Robert E. Litan, "Cleaning Up the Depository Institutions Mess," *Brookings Papers on Economic Activity,* 1:1989, pp. 243–95.

Brumbaugh, R. Dan, Jr., and Robert E. Litan, "Insuring the Insurers: The Banks Are in Big Trouble, Too," *The New York Times,* August 21, 1988, sec. 3, p. 3.

Brumbaugh, R. Dan, Jr., and Robert E. Litan, "Facing Up to the Crisis in American Banking," *The Brookings Review,* Winter 1988/89, pp. 36, 37.

Brumbaugh, R. Dan, Jr., and Robert E. Litan, Joint Testimony before the Subcommittee on Financial Institutions Supervision, Regulation and Insurance of the House Committee on Banking, Finance and Urban Affairs, September 19, 1989, and before the Senate Committee on Banking, Housing and Urban Affairs, October 5, 1989.

Brumbaugh, R. Dan, Jr., and Robert E. Litan, "The Banks Are Worse Off Than You Think," *Challenge,* vol. 33, no. 1, January/February 1990, pp. 4–12.

Carron, Andrew S., *The Plight of the Thrift Institutions,* The Brookings Institution (Washington, D.C.), 1982.

————, *The Rescue of the Thrift Industry,* The Brookings Institution (Washington, D.C.), 1983.

————, *Reforming the Bank Regulatory Structure,* The Brookings Institution (Washington, D.C.), 1984.

Carron, Andrew S., and R. Dan Brumbaugh, Jr., "The Viability of the Thrift Industry," *Housing Policy Debate,* Federal National Mortgage Association, Summer 1990.

Duke, Paul, Jr., and Paulette Thomas, "Bank-Failure Rate Has Slowed Sharply This Year, Chairman of the FDIC Says," *Wall Street Journal,* May 10, 1990, p. A2.

Eisenbeis, Robert A., "Restructuring Banking," *Challenge,* vol. 33, no. 1, January/February 1990, pp. 18–21.

Federal Deposit Insurance Corporation, *Annual Report* (Washington, D.C.), 1988, 1989, and 1990.

Flannery, Mark J., "Deposit Insurance Creates a Need for Bank Regulation," *Business Review* (Federal Reserve Bank of Philadelphia), January/February, 1982.

James, Christopher, *The Costs of Resolving Bank Failures,* unpublished mimeograph, December 1989.

Kane, Edward J., "The Need for Timely and Accurate Measures of Federal Deposit Insurers' Net Reserve Position," statement before the Subcommittee on Financial Institutions Supervision, Regulation and Insurance, September 20, 1989.

————, *The S&L Insurance Mess: How Did It Happen?* The Urban Institute (Washington, D.C.), 1989b.

————, *The Gathering Crisis in Federal Deposit Insurance,* MIT Press (Cambridge, Mass.), 1985.

Kaufman, George G., "Make FDIC Insurance Redundant," *Challenge,* vol. 33, no. 1, January/February 1990, pp. 13–17.

Lindow, Wesley, "Bank Capital and Risk Assets," *National Banking Review,* September 1963.

Litan, Robert E., *What Should Banks Do?* The Brookings Institution (Washington, D.C.), 1987.

Pratt, Richard T., Testimony before the Committee on Banking, Housing, and Urban Affairs, United States Senate, August 3, 1988.

Scott, Kenneth E., *Never Again: The S & L Bailout Bill,* the 26th Annual Conference on Bank Structure and Competition, Federal Reserve Bank of Chicago, May 9–11, 1990.

Spellman, Lewis J., *The Depository Firm and Industry: Theory, History and Regulation,* Academic Press (New York), 1982.

Statement of the Shadow Financial Regulatory Committee, "The Need to Estimate the True Economic Condition of the FDIC," December 5, 1988.

White, Lawrence J., "The Value of Market Value Accounting for the Deposit Insurance System," *Journal of Accounting, Auditing, and Finance,* 6 (April 1991).

CHAPTER 4

The Incentive Incompatibility of Government-Sponsored Deposit-Insurance Funds

Edward J. Kane

Reese Professor of Banking and Monetary Economics,
Ohio State University

Government-sponsored deposit insurance has a long and checkered history. Before federal insurance emerged in 1933, 14 states had experimented with bank-obligation insurance schemes. As Table 4.1 shows, these state systems were established in two waves: 1829–58 and 1910–17. Although several nineteenth-century systems enjoyed at least a "moderate degree of success" [Federal Deposit Insurance Corporation (FDIC), 1952, p. 60], pre-1933 state schemes survived only about 17.5 years on average, with a standard deviation of just over 10 years.

More recent testimony to the difficulty of keeping a deposit-insurance fund whole is provided by the 1989 demise of the Federal Savings and Loan Insurance Corporation (FSLIC), secular deterioration in the FDIC's net reserve position (Kane, 1989b; Brumbaugh and Litan, 1989), and the hard times experienced by 13 post-1930 state-sponsored funds set up to guarantee deposits at state-chartered thrift institutions. As recently as late 1984, 11 state-based guarantee funds underwrote deposit insurance for about 650 state-chartered institutions. Since then, as Table 4.2 indicates, state-based funds have shrunk greatly in importance. Four have been declared insolvent, two no longer have any thrift clients, and two others wound down

Table 4.1 State Insurance Systems for the Protection of Bank Creditors Prior to 1933

State	Date of Passage of Law	Period of Operation[a]	Years of Existence
Adopted from 1829 to 1858			
New York	April 2, 1829	1829–1866	37
Vermont	November 9, 1831	1831–1866	35
Indiana	January 28, 1834[b]	1834–1866	32
Michigan	March 28, 1836	1836–1842	6
Ohio	February 24, 1845[c]	1845–1866	21
Iowa	March 20, 1858	1858–1865	7
Adopted from 1907 to 1917			
Oklahoma	December 17, 1907	1908–1921	13
Kansas	March 6, 1909	1909–1926	17
Nebraska	March 26, 1909[d]	1911–1930	19
Texas	May 12, 1909	1910–1925	15
Mississippi	March 9, 1914	1914–1930	16
South Dakota	March 5, 1915	1915–1925	10
North Dakota	March 10, 1917	1917–1929	12
Washington	March 10, 1917	1917–1921	4

a. In a number of cases the law was repealed subsequent to the terminal date shown here. In some of the first six states closing dates may have preceded the date shown by one year.

b. Indiana's insurance system was included in the act establishing the State Bank of Indiana, the charter of which expired January 1, 1857. The same insurance system was included in the March 8, 1855 act establishing the successor institution, the Bank of the State of Indiana.

c. An insurance system was provided for in an act of March 7, 1842; however, no banks were organized under the law and it was repealed in 1845.

d. A permanent injunction preventing the state banking board from putting the law into operation was not dissolved until January 3, 1911, when the United States Supreme Court ruled the Oklahoma, Kansas, and Nebraska laws constitutional.

SOURCE: FDIC, 1952, p. 61.

their operations. The remaining three funds decided to limit sharply the business they underwrite.

This paper argues that these funds' problems and pre-1984 insolvencies of deposit-insurance funds in Mississippi (1976) and Nebraska (1983) trace to systematic incentives to misregulate. The fundamental difficulty is that deposit insurers have hidden or unacknowledged objectives that conflict sharply with their ostensible long-run goals of protecting depositors of modest means and curtailing in a cost-efficient manner the threat of destructive runs.

Golembe (1960) argues that bank deposit-insurance schemes were adopted primarily "to restore to the community, as quickly as possible, circulating medium destroyed or made unavailable as a consequence of

Table 4.2   State Based Entities Offering Deposit Insurance to Thrift Institutions in Late 1984

	Now Technically Insolvent	
Fund Name (Year Incorporated)	**Crisis Date**	**Rough Estimate of Deficiency**
Industrial Bank Savings Guaranty Corporation (Colorado, 1973)	Sept. 1987	$35 million
Maryland Savings-Share Insurance Corporation (1962)	May 1985	$350 million
Ohio Deposit Guarantee Fund (1956)	March 1985	$15 million
Utah Industrial Loan Guaranty Corporation (1975)	July 1986	$34 million

Fully Divested Now of Thrift Clients

Georgia Credit Union Insurance Corporation (1979)	All 11 S & L members sought and obtained federal insurance after the Ohio and Maryland crises.
Financial Institutions Corporation (North Carolina, 1967)	Divestment was FIAC Assurance management response to Ohio and Maryland crisis. The fund's last thrift client qualified for federal insurance on December 2, 1988.

Wound Down Operations

California Thrift Guaranty Corporation (1971)	April 1984 failure of Western Community Money Center led to a July 1985 state law that required members to obtain federal insurance by June 30, 1989.
Iowa Thrift Guaranty Corporation (1981)	1986 state law phased out insurance as existing CDs matured.

Operations or Coverages Now Limited

Pennsylvania Savings Association Insurance Corporation (1979)	After Ohio and Maryland crises, PSAIC board placed a $5 million cap on size of firm it would insure. In September 1987, cap was raised to $20 million and a 7-percent net-worth requirement instituted. In September 1989, a plan was adopted to raise PSAIC's net-worth requirement in steps to 10 percent by 1995. On

---

Table 4.2 (*Continued*)

	October 31, 1989, PSAIC's 52 members had $126 million in deposits.
Massachusetts Cooperative Central Fund (1932)	Now limits members' deposit coverage to balances in excess of federal coverage ceiling.
Massachusetts Mutual Savings Central Fund (1932)	Now limits members' deposit coverage to balances in excess of federal coverage ceiling.

SOURCE: Adapted from Saulsbury (1987) by telephone calls to authorities in particular states.

---

bank failures" (p. 189), particularly to overcome delays in repayment associated with the failed-bank liquidation process. Such benefits are, of course, predominantly once-over or transitional. An at least equally important goal, whose benefits are both transitional and continuing, has been to extend hidden (that is, off budget) subsidies to economically weak and/or politically strong deposit institutions. White (1981) develops evidence that the state schemes founded in 1910–17 were intended primarily to assist small country banks to compete with well capitalized and better diversified large banks. Marvell (1969, p. 28) plainly lists among the chief reasons for creating FSLIC that it "would help the savings and loan associations attract funds."

This paper seeks to explain and document the tendency for political processes to transform any ongoing government-sponsored deposit-insurance scheme's wealth-redistribution goal into its de facto paramount purpose. This is why, looked at as strictly *economic* enterprises, deposit-insurance funds tend to be operated in ways that are incompatible with the interests of the deliberately underinformed taxpayers who serve as guarantors of last resort.

The limited life observed for government-sponsored funds is less a matter of bad economic luck or specific "mistakes" in regulatory management than of generic principal–agent problems that support structural imbalances in their information, monitoring, enforcement, and incentive systems (Kane, 1987). Large losses develop because informational, statutory, and political restraints make it technically difficult and personally painful for fund managers to rein in risk-taking by aggressive or undercapitalized deposit-institution clients. Bureaucratic restraints and managers' career interests create a preference for accounting systems that can be used to conceal readily appraisable losses and for deferring resolution of these losses in ways that set the stage for even more severe losses in the longer run.

The willingness of authorities to tolerate a high economic cost for rapidly resolving a perceived short-run threat to their stabilization mission may well be absolute, at least as long as they believe that the cost to taxpayers can be deferred and hidden for a long while. To justify what in the wake of the Continental Illinois and Franklin National bail-outs has been characterized as the too big to fail doctrine, politicians and regulators repeatedly sound the following theme:

> Allowing a major bank to default could destabilize the total financial system. . . . *[N]obody really knows what might happen if a major bank were allowed to default* (author's emphasis), and the opportunity to find out is not likely to be appealing to those in authority, or to the public. (Siedman, 1988)

PRINCIPAL–AGENT PROBLEMS AND INCENTIVE INCOMPATIBILITY IN DEPOSIT INSURANCE

In a representative democracy, the polity may be conceived as taxpayer principals who delegate a set of tasks to elected and appointed government agents. Ideally, every principal would like its agents to perform the delegated activities exactly as the principal would do them if the principal had the time, talent, or information available to the agent. Every agent, however, faces temptations to promote its own welfare at the expense of his or her principal. Conflicts between the interests of taxpayers as a whole and the specific interests of government bureaus and individual officials abound in real-world systems of deposit insurance. Politicians and deposit-insurance managers face strong political and economic pressures to tolerate and even to promote client gambles that impose unfunded long-run losses on the insurance fund.

Direct and indirect incentive incompatibility exists between taxpayers and all other contracting parties: politicians, insurance-fund managers, and the stockholders, managers, and creditors of insured deposit institutions. This incentive incompatibility manifests itself in pricing, client-monitoring, and risk-management procedures that lead these other parties to pursue risks that undermine fund reserves.

Incentives supporting innovative forms of risk-taking are particularly defective. The aggregate size of these incentives increases with the volatility of the financial environment, with opportunities for degrading the flow of information to regulators or taxpayers, and with the extent to which regulators count on exacting implicit post-government compensation (that is, an *ex post* settling up) for their term of regulatory service (Kane, 1989a).

Information asymmetries and other principal–agent problems make government-based deposit insurers slow to see the extent to which clients' reliance on innovative financial instruments and activities threatens the solvency of the funds they administer or protect. Even when fund administrators finally see the dangers inherent in client innovations, absence of takeover discipline makes them slow to control their funds' exposure to these risks. These two lags permit aggressive clients to extract unfunded subsidies to risk-taking. If and when risks taken by these clients produce hidden losses that loom large relative to fund size, the political pressure and short horizons under which the administrators operate make it advantageous for officials to temporize and to tolerate massive endgame gambles by failing clients. Opportunities for effecting a reputationally clean getaway to a better job encourage regulators to provide relief from capital requirements precisely when the continued solvency of associated insurance funds most strongly demands that such requirements be enforced.

IMPERFECTLY INFORMATIVE ACCOUNTING SCHEMES AND DEPOSITOR RUNS

What finally forces the demise of an insolvent deposit-insurance fund is the development of a stubborn systemwide depositor run. An individual deposit institution is said to undergo a run when it experiences a sudden wave of depositor requests for withdrawal. Systemwide runs occur when depositors lose confidence in an insurance fund's economic solvency, that is, its capacity to back up its clients' liabilities.

Economic insolvency occurs when the market value of an organization's nonownership liabilities exceeds the market value of its assets. Economic insolvency differs from both legal and accounting insolvency. It looks at all items in a firm's expanded balance sheet, recognizing every explicit and implicit source of value to the firm and all explicit and implicit nonownership claims against it.

Accountants employ valuation and itemization principles different from those of economists. In valuing a deposit institution, accountants typically substitute book values (which often embody adjusted or unadjusted historical costs) for market values and typically relegate a number of potentially important categories of assets and liabilities to an "off balance sheet" status. Rules that indicate what substitutions and omissions are permitted are termed "generally accepted accounting principles" (GAAP).

United States deposit-institution regulators' closure decisions turn on neither accounting insolvency nor economic insolvency but on an inherently more discretionary concept of legal insolvency. If regulators choose, they may selectively and asymmetrically recognize sources of income or capital gains and defer losses or capitalized expense that GAAP would treat more conservatively. In practice, regulators tend to focus primarily on a troubled institution's liquidity: its capacity to cover its debts as they come due or accrue. Since (except in the most extreme cases of economic insolvency) collateralized last-resort lending from an institution's district

Federal Reserve Bank or Federal Home Loan Bank can maintain the firm's capacity to service its debts, using a liquidity criterion leaves the legal solvency of deeply troubled firms largely at the discretion of federal and state officials.

Because of information asymmetries, a depositor run may be rational or irrational. An irrational run occurs when, in response to false rumors, a substantial percentage of depositors tries at the same time to remove their deposits from an economically solvent deposit institution. Such a run can be stopped by a credible flow of accurate information. Customers waste resources in an irrational run, because by definition they would never have engaged in panicky withdrawals if they had been reliably informed about the institution's true condition.

In the face of concealed insolvencies, however, runs may be based rationally on accumulated learning or quick-breaking information, rather than on inaccurate rumors. In a rational run, a depositor's time and trouble waiting on a long queue are not wasted. They represent an investment in preserving wealth. This is because anyone who manages to withdraw his or her deposits before an insolvency has been officially declared is certain to escape whole. Absent government bail-outs, depositors of record as of the instant an institution is closed have to absorb whatever net insufficiencies exist in its and its guarantors' resources.

If the economic solvency of every deposit institution and deposit-insurance fund could be regularly and costlessly verified, irrational runs would never occur. The threat of rational runs would create strong incentives for institutions and fund managers to keep themselves adequately capitalized.

It is important to recognize that weaknesses in insurers' information systems are design defects and not acts of God. The willingness of authorities to keep themselves underinformed about an insurance fund's implicit (that is, unbooked) losses is consistent with an intention to be able to deny adequate knowledge of its problems in the event a meltdown ensues. Suppressing information on deposit-insurance losses shields elected politicians from timely criticism for poor monitoring and regulatory performance. It increases the credibility of politicians' attempts to deny responsibility for any mistakes that do emerge and leaves them asymmetrically free to bring forward information on whatever regulatory successes their regulatory agents may have achieved. In effect, restricting the flow of relevant information lessens market pressure on politicians and regulators and creates rents for them to share.

This analysis tells us not to regard the recognition and action lags featured in the profession's standard model of dynamic policy making (Kareken and Solow, 1963) as exogenous variables. For those charged with operating an incentive-incompatible deposit-insurance scheme, the recognition lag is lengthened by psychological propensities to deny painful facts and by natural as well as artificial blockages in the flow of information about the extent and consequences of client riskiness. A further danger is that, by the time the need for corrective action is recognized, the implicit losses the insurer has experienced may have become large relative to its reserves. The larger a fund's hidden economic insolvency, the more a public acknowledgment of this insolvency threatens to damage the careers of incumbent politicians and regulators. Large insolvencies dispose officials to adopt "best case planning." This means they elect to postpone effective action until the occurrence of an unrealistically "convenient" event which would have the capacity to replenish fund and client resources.

The idea that regulators' and politicians' careers would be damaged merely by alerting taxpayers to the insolvency is enshrined in the ancient practice of killing the messenger who brings bad news. The length of the odds against having their deception revealed by an exogenous meltdown during their watch tempts regulators and politicians to gamble on making a clean getaway. However, the probability that officials' getaways will be aborted—as well as the size of the hidden economic losses experienced by the insurance fund—increases geometrically the longer the coverup is kept in place. Because transactions costs that decapitalized institutions incur in making the endgame financial plays that exploit an incentive-incompatible insurance fund are small, the speed with which hidden losses develop is subject to an acceleration absent from incentive-incompatible bureaucratic arrangements in the real sector. Whereas neglected physical capital (such as priceless marble monuments) decays at a fairly slow and steady pace, a benignly neglected deposit-insurance insolvency may accelerate rapidly.

SOURCES OF EMPIRICAL EVIDENCE OF REGULATORY GAMBLING

This paper draws primarily on a variety of court and legislative documents to show empirically that a principal–agent model of recognition and action lags and that joint regulator–client gambling accounts for the downfall of the Ohio Deposit Guarantee Fund (ODGF) and the Maryland Savings-Share Insurance Corporation (MSSIC) in 1985 and of FSLIC in 1989. Evidence is developed to show that the recurrence of deposit-insurance scandals and crises supports the theory that government officials are tempted to defer needed regulatory adjustments and to suppress unfavorable information about the consequences of these and other short-sighted decisions.

The key step in the evidentiary chain is to show that, until confronted with a potentially ruinous depositor run, in all three cases regulators and politicians repeatedly temporized. They were not simply blindsided by the expanding cost of deposit-insurance subsidies, but engaged actively in buying time. Moreover, in each case, they used the time they bought predominantly to roll the problem forward and conceal for long periods information relevant for evaluating the effects and quality of their performance.

It would be rash to dismiss the evidence assembled here as merely anecdotal. There is no reason to suppose that the three bureaus whose deterioration this paper analyzes do not form an at least partly representative sample from the population of modern government-sponsored deposit-insurance funds. The model under test is a special case of rational behavior, but one whose subjects are likely to conceal their motives or misrepresent them even to themselves. This renders straightforward survey research unreliable and leads one to look for admissions of lapses in regulatory behavior in legal proceedings, legislative hearings, official investigations, and public debates. In such forums, officials can be pressed by the weight of collateral evidence and by penalties that can be imposed for making false statements to give damaging testimony both against themselves and against one another.

To confirm the model empirically, data are assembled from these sources to establish two common findings. First, insurance-fund managers engaged in systematic strategies of coverup and regulatory forbearance. Second, at least some elected and appointed officials were aware of the disastrous long-run consequences of these strategies. Other responsible authorities were at least culpably ignorant in the lack of awareness on which they may now insist. In all three cases, the evidence indicates that, when a substantial amount of unfunded but appraisable losses and loss exposures developed, this fact was systematically hidden from public view. Moreover, the coverup left top regulators more concerned with avoiding a bad press than with delivering a best-efforts regulatory performance to their taxpayer principals. Staff proposals for bringing insolvent clients' risk-taking under administrative control were regularly rejected on the grounds that the publicity they would generate might undermine public confidence in the insurance fund.

Psychologists might say that Ohio, Maryland, and FSLIC regulators' short-sighted strategies received an unfortunate amount and scheduling of misleading reinforcement. The slow and hidden pattern of losses to each fund prior to the onset of their death throes might be described as neither sharp enough nor steady enough to overcome the immediate and inertial benefits of politicians' and regulators' deluding themselves into thinking that they were doing a good job.

EMPIRICAL EVIDENCE OF INFORMATION COVERUP AND REGULATORY TEMPORIZATION

Evidence from the Ohio Case

The ODGF's demise was occasioned by a rational depositor run on its largest and politically most influential client, Home State Savings. In turn, the bulk of Home State's $150 million capital shortage came from losses suffered in the fraudulent March 4, 1985 default of a single customer, E.S.M. Securities of Fort Lauderdale, Florida (ESM).

Evidence of Foreknowledge.   Kane (1989a) explains that ESM's fraud consisted of reselling without replacement securities that Home State had pledged as collateral for reverse repurchase agreements with ESM. Although Home State could have required this collateral to be held in trust by a third party, ESM persuaded Home State to let ESM itself hold the securities.

The responsibility for examining Home State for the ODGF, and indeed for regulating the ODGF, lay with what is now the Ohio Division of Savings and Loan Associations (ODSL). In response to ODSL criticism of Home State's severely overcollateralized repo position with ESM, on March 2, 1982, a top Home State executive offered this potentially disturbing justification:

> With the large equity ratio that we pledge, we have the opportunity to have repos at a rate far below the industry average. This has enabled Home State . . . to obtain returns far in excess of the industry average. These repos have been for fixed periods, usually for one year, so as not to adversely affect the profitability of the transaction, should there be volatile swings in the interest rate.
>
> We disagree with the philosophy that a repo is borrowed money, as the Federal Home Loan Bank Manual describes repos as "like borrowed money." If, in fact, they felt like it was borrowed money, they would not refer to it as *like* borrowed money. In August 1981, Home State paid off its borrowed money at the banks and at that time, our repos were 47.6% of the withdrawable accounts. At December 31st, we were 34%.

Home State's pettifogging insistence that proceeds from reverse repos do not constitute borrowed money, the concessionary financing rate EMS proferred on these contracts, and the unremitting success of a series of day trades ESM claimed to be executing for Home State (returns that at one point were reported to be 42.5 percent per annum) were recognized as signals of a need for ODSL and ODGF officials to understand and regulate the risks that Home State's repo position posed for the ODGF. These risks were of two kinds: exposure of the market value of Home State's short-funded securities position to loss from interest-rate increases, and the possibility that ESM would not return the securities when the repurchase contract matured.

In the wake of ODSL's June 1981 examination, in the first two months of 1982 Home State's dangerous concentration of business with ESM surfaced as a regulatory problem at both ODSL and ODGF. Although ODGF officials claim ignorance of pre-1985 chicanery by ESM, evidence of fraudulent activity by ESM had been uncovered by the U.S. Comptroller of the Currency in 1976 and by the Federal Home Loan Bank (FHLB) of Chicago in 1981. ODSL examiners learned of the Chicago FHLB's experience in an August 24–28, 1981 training seminar. Follow-up meetings called between ESM managers and ODSL officials reinforced concerns about ESM trustworthiness. These developments help to explain why Home State's repos were characterized eventually as a "ticking time bomb" in examiner Sylvester Hentschel's draft of Home State's examination report for July 1982 (see addendum to Table 4.3). This report assigned Home State the ODSL's lowest rating. According to the ODSL *Manual of Examinations,* "This rating is reserved for institutions with major and serious problems which management appears to be unable or unwilling to correct."

Evidence of Official Temporizating.   Table 4.3 is pieced together from sometimes-incomplete data from Home State Examination reports made public by the Ohio legislature's Joint Select Committee on Savings and Loans (OJSC). The purpose of the table is to clarify that Ohio regulators possessed information sufficient to indicate that Home State had imbedded (but unbooked) losses in its securities and mortgage portfolios that rendered it economically insolvent by at least mid-1981, even neglecting the possibility that ESM might default on its repos. Corporate-finance theory predicts that economically insolvent firms are attracted to go-for-broke risk-taking. That Home State's economic insolvency continued to grow after interest rates turned around in mid-1982 was evidenced by further increases observed in scheduled items and in imbedded securities losses at later dates. These unbooked losses disturbed ODSL and ODGF management (who professed to believe Home State could "grow out of this problem") less than the continued growth of the firm's speculative repo position with ESM. From 1982 until Home State's closure in March 1985, ODGF and ODSL regulatory pressure focused on informally persuading Home State both to reduce its repo position with ESM and to lessen the degree to which the position was overcollateralized.

Even in the face of blatant Home State disregard of Ohio regulators' polite requests, ODGF never adopted a regulation setting limits on reverse repos and neither ODGF nor ODSL used its formal disciplinary powers to put teeth into its requests for restructuring. Throughout the period, ODGF never exercised its right to withhold approval for dividends, mergers, branch-office purchases, and related-party transactions. Nor did it use its powers to subject a member to fine, expulsion, or a cease-and-desist order. In deposition testimony, ODGF officials have not precisely explained the absence of formal action in 1982–85. However, ODSL Superintendents Wideman and Huddleston have tried explicitly to justify their own temporizing behavior.

ODSL examiners recognized the possibility that ESM would eventually default on its repos to Home State and the dangers to the ODGF posed by Home State's unwillingness to scale back its position with ESM. They saw Home State as pursuing a business strategy designed to cure its insolvency at the risk of bankrupting its supporting deposit-insurance fund. The examiners are on record as recommending repeatedly that ODSL superintendents deny regulatory permissions and subject Home State to tough formal action. Ex-superintendents claim that it was necessary to reject these recommendations because of the danger that the bad publicity attached to news of a formal disciplinary action against Home State might subject the firm to a ruinous run that would be interpreted by the public (and future employers) as evidence of poor regulatory performance. Implicit acceptance of this strategy by the politicians is indicated by Superintendent Huddleston (who took office in 1983), who acknowledges seeking guidance through channels from the governor on what to do about Home State's losses. As their terms wore on, both superintendents saw how badly Home State's attempts to grow out of its problems were proceeding and how unpersuasively its managers were seeking to excuse their failure to keep various promises to ODGF and ODSL officials about safely restructuring their position with ESM. The toughest official action taken proved eventually to be the basis of the state's criminal prosecution of owner M. Warner for "unauthorized acts." This was to require Home State's board of directors to pass a resolution in the early spring of 1983 to require management to correct the situation.

Perhaps the clearest evidence of regulatory gambling is shown by the wimpy way in which top ODGF and ODSL officials dealt with the clear circumvention (if not actual violation) of the board's resolution that the reported June 1983 increase in borrowed money constitutes. Given this resolution, it was hard not to recognize that the expansion of the repo position could be construed as an "unauthorized act" for which individual Home State managers could be removed and prosecuted.

Almost day by day, the long-run interests of Ohio taxpayers and other member firms of ODGF would have been better served by directing Home State's owners to recapitalize or else. The element in the Ohio regulatory system that most facilitated the coverup and the temporizing let-things-ride policy also complicated the resolution of the ODGF insolvency. This is the system's reliance on historical-cost accounting. Although some S & L spokespersons want to blame all industry ills on federal "deregulation," post-1980 federal deregulation of deposit rates could have had only a secondary effect on the net worth of nonfederally regulated institutions. These institutions—which had never been subject to federal deposit-rate ceilings—paid market rates of explicit interest throughout the 1970s and 1980s.

If a system of market-value reporting had been in place and examiner ratings were public information, other fund members (whose contributions

Table 4.3   Reported Status of Home State Savings, at Selected Dates during 1979–85

Date	Total Assets	Scheduled Items	Net Worth	Imbedded Losses on Selected Govt. & Agency Securities	Other Borrowed Money
6-30-79	286		11.7		65.1[a]
12-31-79	279	5.2	12.5		39.8
6-30-80	535.1	17.1	13.0		232.4
12-31-80	548.1	7.0	13.7		209.5
6-30-81	579.3	11.5	14.2	22.1	198.5
12-31-81	617.7	10.3	13.1		148.3
6-30-82	560.2	12.9	11.9	31.1	83.8
12-31-82	562.1	14.1	16.3		86.0
6-30-83	1,101.2	19.6	17.0		607.3
9-30-83	1,146.2		16.3	46.5 (some hedging)	614.9
12-31-83	1,146.9		15.8		610.0
3-31-84	1,148.4		16.2		589.0
6-30-84	1,101.2		17.2		561.2
9-30-84	1,420.2		20.1		755.3
12-31-84	1,438		19.7		713.2
2-28-85	1,424.5		20.5		685.7
4-30-85	626		6.2		

a. This amount is in excess of allowable "additional borrowing" underregulations in effect at this time.

NOTE: In millions of dollars.

NOTE: The statutory net worth requirement was 3 percent either of current deposits or of the five-year average of deposits.

SOURCE: 1979 through 6-30-83 figures and embedded losses for 9-30-83 taken from ODSL examination reports, given in Appendix to OJSC testimony of Sylvester Hentschel. Later figures come from Monthly Reports filed with the ODSL.

Addendum
Ticking Time Bomb Memo Filed on Home State Savings
by ODSL Examiner in Early 1983

I have deliberately retained the working copy of this examination report several days past the mandatory five-day deadline because it is my understanding that the new Superintendent will not formally assume his duties in the office until the end of the second week in February.

I respectfully submit that the new Superintendent should be alerted to the veritable time-bomb that is ticking away in this association. Briefly stated, the problems can be summarized in the following two sentences. In June 1982 the

---

Table 4.3 (*Continued*)

association borrowed $84 million for one year from a small investment firm called E.S.M. Government Securities, Inc. located in Fort Lauderdale, Florida. As collateral for this borrowed money, the association assigned to E.S.M.'s control various types of securities which the association had bought for $209 million.

As stated in my examination report of July 10, 1982, should E.S.M. be unable for any reason to redeliver the securities in June 1983, the association will be confronted with a loss of $125 million. If that happens, the association's savings depositors will be required to bear a considerable portion of the loss. The association's net worth is less than $12 million and the total assets of the Ohio Deposit Guarantee Fund, of which the association is a member, are only about $65 million. The association does not have FSLIC insurance.

An association's loss exposure in transactions of this type should never exceed its net worth.

In view of former Superintendent Wideman's perfunctory letter transmitting this report to the association, I would appreciate receiving a copy of the board of directors' response when it is received.

February 8, 1983   Sylvester F. Hentschel

---

to ODGF counted in their net worths) would have felt strong economic pressure to help with the prefailure monitoring and discipline of troubled clients. State officials' career and other reputational interests would have been more clearly aligned with determining quickly and simply which ODGF member institutions were receiving unreasonable amounts of credit support from Ohio taxpayers. The determination would have been simpler because the primary task of examiners would have become to detect the presence or absence of securities in ESM's vaults (proof of which ESM's accountant was falsifying) and of fraudulent or flawed appraisals of property, loan, and security values. These conditions could have been established by closely checking each firm's records on a sampling basis.

As late as December 1984, the ODSL's monthly report, *Rapid Regulatory Review,* claimed that "the statutory and regulatory shortcomings that permitted the failure of the California and Nebraska funds do not exist here in Ohio where the legislature has provided more authority to the regulatory structure." In the absence of state-connected guarantees, Home State would have had to release on a regular basis information sufficient to convince potential depositors of their continuing solvency. By assigning to state employees the task of examining in secret ODGF institutions for insolvency, state officials reduced the natural interest of depositors and other members of the state-connected insurance pool in receiving timely information on the financial condition and investment strategies of Home

State and other insured firms. This effectively relieved high-flying deposit-institution managers of responsibility for communicating accurate information to their customers and cross-guarantors, and increased the conflict between Ohio regulators' career interests and the long-run interests of Ohio taxpayers.

Possibility of Political and Corrupt Influences on ODSL Superintendents. Ex-ODSL Superintendent C. Wideman (September 1978 to January 1983) was appointed by Republican Governor Rhodes, and his successor C. L. Huddleston (February 1983 to January 1985) was appointed by Democratic Governor Celeste. Evidence exists that Home State had political ties to both parties. First, its president B. Bongard had made substantial campaign contributions to the Republicans and its owner M. Warner was a much more generous giver to the Democrats. Second, a late-1985 indictment brought against Mr. Bongard characterized a handful of loans made to former leaders of the two parties as a "willful misapplication" of funds. Finally, analysis of Governor Celeste's schedule shows that he met with owner Warner on 32 different dates between November 1982 and February 1985.

Although no evidence of explicit influence has emerged, ODSL superintendents could not fail to recognize the existence of implicit political pressure to be lenient toward Home State. Explaining why he had felt the need in March 1983 to alert his superiors of ODSL's concerns about Home State, Mr. Huddleston said in a November 4, 1986 deposition: "[It] was politically important because the Governor was—Mr. Warner was a supporter of the Governor's and that it was sensitive enough with respect to the adminstration that it was important that they know" (p. 54).

Huddleston's predecessor, C. Wideman had to address intimations that he approved several Home State requests for branch offices over staff objections in return for promises of post-government consulting work. At the least, he showed questionable judgment in allowing himself to be hired as a consultant by Home State three weeks after he left office and in involving himself (without pay) in negotiations between Huddleston and Home State over restructuring the firm's deals with ESM.

Evidence from the Maryland Case

The Maryland Savings Share Insurance Corporation began operations in 1962. Events leading up to its May 14, 1985 meltdown parallel the ODGF debacle in at least three respects. First, as in Ohio, examination of insured firms was conducted by a State Division of Savings and Loan Associations (MDSL), with supervision conducted jointly by MDSL and the insurance fund. Second, economically insolvent clients known to be operating in an unsafe and unsound manner had for years received kid-glove regulatory

treatment. As in Ohio, regulators proved too willing to favor the pleas and excuses of high-flying managements over the well reasoned recommendations of state examiners. Finally, the first open runs on insolvent MSSIC thrifts were rational ones that were occasioned by losses two of them were known to have sustained in a well publicized repurchase-agreement default at a failed securities firm. These runs, which affected MSSIC's second-largest institution, $839-million Old Court Savings and Loan, and $370-million Merritt Commercial Loan, followed closely upon the April 8, 1985 failure of Bevil, Bresler, and Shulman Asset Management Corp. However, a silent run on MSSIC institutions by so-called "smart money" began in the wake of the ODGF crisis and had cumulated to $375 million by mid-April (Preston, 1986, p. 21).

In contrast to the Ohio case, the root cause of these and four other large MSSIC firms' legal insolvencies was speculative lending and an astonishing pattern of insider theft and misappropriation. The most spectacular felon in the lot proved to be Jeffrey A. Levitt of Old Court S & L. This is evidenced by his receiving a 30-year sentence for theft and misappropriation in Maryland and a further one-to-three-year sentence for securities fraud in New York.

Unwillingness to Enforce MSSIC and MDSL Regulations.   Levitt's behavior (along with that of Allan Pearlstein) first surfaced as a regulatory problem in 1978. MSSIC issued a May 25, 1978 temporary cease-and-desist order to First Progressive Savings and Loan Association of Westminster, Maryland. This document asserted that, as an officer of that S & L, Levitt had diverted association funds to his own use. Three state examiners

> unanimously concluded that the people who are currently operating First Progressive Savings and Loan Association should not be permitted to operate a savings and loan association.
>
> Management has demonstrated a total disregard for state statutes and regulations which establish lending limitations and procedures. . . . [P]ervasive self-dealing . . . is discussed in the report of examination. (Preston, 1986, pp. 149–50)

Instead of heeding the examiners' advice, MSSIC officials settled for assurances that the problems would be corrected. Not only did 1979 and 1981 examinations document further irregularities, but a Maryland court suspended Levitt from the practice of law for most of 1980 for dishonest behavior (Preston, 1986, pp. 153–4 and 159–60). Although a capital deficiency forced First Progressive to operate under a December 31, 1981 letter of agreement ("insurance agreement") requiring prior MSSIC approval for most significant transactions, control of the firm was allowed to pass during 1982 to Levitt and Pearlstein. In fall 1982, MDSL and MSSIC approved $2.2 million in loans from First Progressive, which Levitt and Pearlstein used to buy 82 percent of the stock of Old Court S & L (Preston, 1986, pp. 163–5). Old Court was itself operating under a July 1981 insurance agreement triggered by capital deficiency.

Soon thereafter, Old Court and Progressive embarked on an aggressive strategy of growth, which Preston characterizes as operating "as commercial real estate corporations fueled by depositors' money" (Preston, 1986, p. 14). Although the high rates of asset growth and deposit interest these firms recorded might have been warning enough, MDSL examiners also reported numerous and potentially criminal irregularities and violations of MDSL and MSSIC rules in their lending programs during their 1983 and 1984 examinations. Notwithstanding this disturbing evidence, MSSIC allowed its insurance agreement with Old Court to be terminated on April 23, 1984.

At the May 1984 meeting of the MSSIC Board, the significant financial deterioration of First Progressive was discussed and Old Court held to be "responsible at least in part." A preliminary examination by MDSL revealed "very weak operational standards" at both institutions. In August, the MSSIC Board noted that Old Court was growing rapidly by writing primarily large construction loans funded by jumbo CDs and exceeding MSSIC guidelines on the proportion of assets invested in such loans. The Board failed to adopt its staff recommendation that Old Court be directed by letter to cease and desist from further construction and land loan commitments. Moreover, on November 1, 1984, First Progressive was allowed to be merged into Old Court.

The issue of a cease-and-desist order to Old Court resurfaced at a December 12, 1984 meeting of the MSSIC membership committee, which unanimously recommended this action. Two and a half months later (on February 27, 1985), MSSIC's Board finally resolved to subject Old Court to a cease-and-desist order and to require it to enter into a restrictive operating agreement. However, the cease-and-desist order was not issued until March 22 and the operating agreement was not signed until April 23, 1985.

In several of MSSIC's other problem institutions, the fine corrupting hand of Old Court was also detected well in advance of the fund's crisis. At Security and Sharon S & Ls, examiners cited sweetheart loans to Levitt and Pearlstein partnerships, while at Friendship S & L they uncovered a fraudulent loan swap with Old Court.

Another "habitual violator" of MDSL and MSSIC rules was Merritt S & L, which was run by Gerald Klein. Evidence of insider lending abuse and other serious irregularities emerged in the firm's December 31, 1981 examination and was reinforced by the results of its January 31, 1984 examination (Preston, 1986, pp. 237–54). As with Old Court and Progressive, MSSIC officials bent over backward to keep from accepting and reacting to ample evidence of wrongdoing. Not until February 13, 1985 did MSSIC's membership committee recommend a cease-and-desist order, but the crisis occurred before the order ever came to be issued.

MSSIC and MDSL officials explain their failure to enforce rules and regulations in almost the same words that the ex-ODSL superintendents used. One Maryland official attributed his agency's paralysis to the fear that regulatory sanctions against any major client firm "would result in publicity that would denude the industry he felt bound to protect" (Preston, 1986, p. 13).

Preston concludes that MDSL and MSSIC officials were "afraid to institute conservatorship or receivership proceedings or issue violation orders because of a fear that a run would start in the savings and loan industry, even as far in the past as 1981" (Preston, 1986, p. 136). The refusal of MDSL and MSSIC to discipline fiduciary and regulatory violators proved so thoroughgoing and consistent that in one case Levitt offered Maryland regulators' toleration of his behavior as a legal defense. He pictured himself as having "relied upon and trusted" MSSIC to monitor and police his actions. He argued that MSSIC's failure to discipline his dishonest and opportunistic activities could be interpreted as tacit approval of them.

Possibility of Political and Corrupt Influences on Maryland Regulators. The official investigation of the MSSIC failure makes no mention of campaign contributions, political gifts, or influence-peddling by state politicians. In contrast with the Ohio case, MSSIC and MDSL officials appear to have kept higher authorities in the dark up to the bitter end. In private and public, Maryland regulators steadfastly maintained, even after the ODGF crisis and as late as six weeks before the meltdown, that they had the situation "under control" (Preston, 1986, pp. 398, 411, 413, and 440). On March 16, 1985, MSSIC officials persuaded administration officials to force withdrawal of General Assembly House Bill 1609, which would have required all 102 MSSIC institutions to state in their ads that they were not backed by the full faith and credit of the state. On March 25, the head of MSSIC circulated a reassuring memo to MSSIC's membership about the adequacy of MSSIC's reaction to the Ohio crisis.

The possibility exists, however, that the law firm that advised MSSIC on its regulatory powers and responsibilities had been corrupted by Levitt. Although it specifically denied any wrongdoing, this firm (Venable, Baetjer, and Howard) settled in May 1987 a malpractice lawsuit brought by the state for $27 million. The Preston Report notes that lawyers from this firm had on several occasions rendered questionable advice or service to MSSIC and allowed a disturbing conflict of interest to develop. The conflict flowed from the firm's simultaneously having as clients MSSIC and individuals such as Levitt and Pearlstein whose interests could be seen to be directly and antithetically affected by the decisions on which MSSIC was seeking the firm's legal advice.

Evidence from the FSLIC Case

A comprehensive official investigation into FSLIC decision making has yet to be undertaken. So far official examinations have focused on documenting the role of specific members of Congress in pressing FHLB System regulators for favorable supervisory treatment of a few well connected owners of economically insolvent thrifts.

Evidence of Foreknowledge and Misregulation.   Academic research by Merton (1977), Sharpe (1978), and Kareken and Wallace (1978) established an insightful framework for understanding how mispriced deposit insurance provides a subsidy to risk-taking for insured firms. Buser, Chen, and Kane (1981) clarified that regulations imposed on institutions as a condition for being insured (particularly net-worth requirements) could be interpreted instructively as a risk-sensitive implicit premium. Applying this analysis to thrift institutions in the 1965–80 era, Kane (1981, p. 89) notes that FSLIC was not enforcing the implicit premiums this interpretation supposed:

> [T]he political clout of S & Ls . . . has allowed them, in the face of threatened insolvencies, to pressure FLSIC officials into not exercising their options to close underwater institutions unless they allow the book value of their [accounting] net worth to deteriorate or show evidence of dishonest management or overly aggressive risk-taking.

This same source calculates that by 1980 aggregate unbooked mortgage losses were two to three times the size of the industry's accounting net worth. It also explains that S & L stock prices were not devastated by these losses because, once an institution's enterprise-contributed capital is exhausted, FSLIC forbearance shifts the onus from stockholders to FSLIC to cover these losses in the event of liquidation. For decapitalized or "zombie" firms, the value of deposit-insurance guarantees increases in an offsetting manner as new losses accrue.

The losses that were accruing were papered over by accounting gimmicks, many of which were invented by FHLB System regulators for precisely this purpose (Kane, 1989a). Zombie thrifts' liquidity was supported by increasing deposit-insurance coverage to $100,000 per account name in 1980 and by maintaining opportunities for insured thrifts to borrow in collateralized form from district FHLBs and other nondeposit creditors.

For two decades, FHLB System accountants and General Accounting Office auditors ignored the value of the claims that capital forbearance implicitly levied against FSLIC reserves. Not until yearend 1986 was FSLIC's net reserve position first officially acknowledged to be negative.

With at least tacit congressional approval, the bureaucracy running

FSLIC adopted a strategy of denying FSLIC's growing underfunding, suppressing critical information, granting regulatory breaks, and extending new powers to troubled thrifts. Comments made by two former FHLBB chairmen at a December 1988 conference (FHLB of San Francisco, 1989, pp. 61–8) provide the clearest evidence that coverup and forbearance were explicitly chosen as ways to help troubled thrifts to grow out of their problems. One acknowledges in line with calculations made by outside economists that his estimates of "the depth of the thrift problem at that time [1982] were about $100 billion" (p. 62), that "Congress played a major role in forbearance" (p. 63), and that "there was a consensus of those in power that constrained the parameters within which the regulator could operate" (p. 65).

Possibility of Political and Corrupt Influences on FHLB System Regulators

Circumstantial evidence suggests that congressional interest in restraining FHLB regulators was at least partly rooted in a desire to sustain or repay campaign contributions. First, key members of congressional banking committees received a substantial flow of campaign funds and other favors from S & L interests. Kane (1989a, p. 53) documents the pattern of PAC giving. Former House Banking Committee Chairman Fernand St Germain's carrying a credit card issued in the name of a U.S. League of Savings Association lobbyist illustrates the extent to which other kinds of donations could be garnered. Second, contributors were fully aware that such donations built political clout that they could use to battle efforts to subject them to regulatory discipline. Charles Keating of the once-giant ($5.5 billion) Lincoln S & L of Irvine, California, made this crystal clear in an April 1989 press conference. Asked whether his financial support had influenced political figures to intervene with FHLB System regulators on behalf of his troubled firm, Keating quipped "I want to say in the most forceful way I can: I certainly hope so."

The record of undue political intervention into FSLIC's affairs during the 1970s and 1980s is still being developed. The most disturbing single piece of evidence is Congress's continuing failure to expressly define the term "undue influence." Members of Congress prefer not to establish enforceable limits on what a member may do to assist a troubled constituent. The report of the Special Outside Counsel appointed by the House Ethics Committee to investigate Speaker James Wright's dealings with the FHLB Board concluded that "Wright's communications with the Bank Board resulted in four violations of House Rule XLIII, clause 1, as interpreted by Advisory Opinion No. 1" (Phelan, 1989, p. 277). Almost one-third of Phelan's report is devoted to clearly documenting the egregious nature of these violations. Nevertheless, the House Ethics Committee chose not to endorse these charges.

Because Phelan's report develops evidence of clearly understood threats, it makes the November 1989 testimony before the House Banking Committee about senatorial influence seem tame. This testimony focuses on four points. First, it establishes that five senators (Cranston, DeConcini, McCain, Riegle, and Glenn) met with FHLB Chairman Wall in 1987 to express concern over allegations of unfair regulatory treatment. At that time, regulators from the FHLB of San Francisco were moving to close Mr. Keating's high-flying and economically insolvent S & L. It is hard to argue that the extraordinary nature of such a meeting would not have generated at least implicit pressure on Wall to ease Lincoln's plight. Second, testimony shows that soon after this meeting Mr. Wall pulled the San Francisco FHLB examiners out of Lincoln and replaced them with another team of examiners. This new team had to begin its examination more or less from scratch. Third, the additional time granted to Lincoln by restarting the examination process delayed its closure to April 1989 at great expense to federal taxpayers (perhaps $1 billion). Fourth, testimony documents other forms of pressure brought by Keating against accountants, SEC officials, and former FHLB Board members. This testimony even forced Alan Greenspan to defend a representation filed in February 1985 before he became Federal Reserve Chairman attesting that Lincoln was "financially strong" and "presents no foreseeable risk to the Federal Savings and Loan Insurance Corporation."

IMPLICATIONS FOR DEPOSIT-INSURANCE REFORM

Suppressing information on the weakening condition of insured deposit institutions lessens market pressure on politicians and top regulators and creates rents for them to share. Given officials' sensitivity to media criticism, the most important regulatory reform is to increase accountability. To lessen officials' temptation to exploit them, taxpayers need two things: a timely flow of accurate information on regulator performance, and to constrain the capacity of elected officials and regulatory bureaus to generate unfunded deposit-insurance subsidies and insurance-fund losses.

The Financial Institutions Reform, Recovery, and Enforcement Act of 1989 does not make authorities more accountable for the effects their actions have on the present value of government deposit-insurance enterprises. Each insurer's unfunded losses still need not be calculated explicitly, let alone be communicated openly to Congress to be incorporated and financed in the annual federal budget. Moreover, the insurer's ability to demand timely and adequate recapitalization from failing clients was further restricted by congressionally imposed grace periods and loopholes in the definition of what constitutes capital for regulatory purposes.

At least three steps are needed (Kane, 1989a). First, politicians and regulators must surrender the accounting discretion that permits them not to budget officially for changes in the size of appraisable financial commitments. Second, limits on the ways in which members of Congress can pressure regulators into giving troubled firms a break must be defined explicitly and enforced by means of an express framework for reporting and evaluating this activity. Third, conformance with these requirements must be tested regularly by requiring government insurers to reinsure at least some of their coverages and to compete at least in part with one another and with private suppliers of deposit insurance.

REFERENCES

Brumbaugh, R. Dan, Jr., and Robert Litan, "Testimony," U.S. Congress, House of Representatives, Subcommittee on Financial Institutions Supervision, Regulation and Insurance, Committee on Banking, Finance and Urban Affairs, *Hearings on the State of the Bank and Credit Union Insurance Funds,* September 20, 1989.

Buser, Stephen, Edward Kane, and Andrew Chen, "Federal Deposit Insurance, Regulatory Policy, and Optimal Bank Capital," *Journal of Finance,* 35, March 1981, pp. 51–60.

Federal Deposit Insurance Corporation, *Annual Report* (Washington, D.C.), 1952.

Federal Home Loan Bank of San Francisco, *The Future of the Thrift Industry: Proceedings of the Fourteenth Annual Conference,* 1989.

Federal Reserve Bank of Cleveland, *1985 Annual Report,* 1985.

Golembe, Carter H., "The Deposit Insurance Legislation of 1933: An Examination of Its Antecedents and Its Purposes," *Political Science Quarterly,* 75, June 1960, pp. 181–200.

Kane, Edward J., "Reregulation, Savings and Loan Diversification, and the Flow of Housing Finance," in *Savings and Loan Asset Management Under Deregulation,* Federal Home Loan Bank (San Francisco), 1981.

————, "No Room for Weak Links in the Chain of Deposit-Insurance Reform," *Journal of Financial Services Research,* 1, September 1987, pp. 77–111.

————, "How Incentive-Incompatible Deposit-Insurance Funds Fail," Prochnow Report No. PR-014., The Prochnow Educational Foundation (Madison, Wis.), 1988.

————, *The S&L Insurance Mess: How Did It Happen?,* The Urban Institute Press (Washington, D.C.), 1989a.

————, "The Need for Timely and Accurate Measures of Federal Deposit Insurers' Net Reserve Position," U.S. Congress, House of Representatives, Subcommittee on Financial Institutions Supervision, Regulation and Insurance, Committee on Banking, Finance and Urban Affairs, *Hearings on the State of the Bank and Credit Union Insurance Funds,* September 20, 1989.

Kareken, John, and Robert M. Solow, "Lags in Monetary Policy," in *Stabilization Policies,* prepared for the Commission on Money and Credit (Englewood Cliffs), 1963, pp. 14–96.

Kareken, John, and Neil Wallace, "Deposit Insurance and Bank Regulation: A Partial Equilibrium Exposition," *Journal of Business,* 51, July 1978, pp. 413–38.

Marvell, Thomas B., *The Federal Home Loan Bank Board,* Frederick Praeger, Publishers (New York, Washington, and London), 1969.

Merton, Robert C., "An Analytic Derivation of the Cost of Deposit Insurance Loan Guarantees: An Application of Modern Option Pricing Theory," *Journal of Banking and Finance,* 1, June 1977, pp. 3–11.

Ohio Joint Select Committee on Savings and Loans, *Hearings* and *Report,* the 116th Ohio General Assembly, 1985.

Phelan, Richard J., *Report of the Special Outside Counsel in the Matter of Speaker James C. Wright,* U.S. Congress, House of Representatives, Committee on Standards of Official Conduct, U.S. Government Printing Office (Washington, D.C.), 1989.

Preston, Wilbur D., Jr., *Report of the Special Counsel on the Savings and Loan Crisis,* State of Maryland, Executive Department (Baltimore, Md.), 1986.

Saulsbury, Victor L., "The Current Status of Private Insurance Funds and Their Membership," *Regulatory Review,* September/October 1987, pp. 21–4.

Seidman, L. William, "Remarks before the Garn Institute Insurance Forum," November 14, 1988.

Sharpe, William F., "Bank Capital Adequacy, Deposit Insurance and Security Values," *Journal of Financial and Quantitative Analysis,* 13, November 1978, pp. 701–18.

White, Eugene Nelson, "State-Sponsored Insurance of Bank Deposits in the United States," *Journal of Economic History,* 41, September 1981, pp. 537–57.

CHAPTER 5

Political Foundations of the Thrift Debacle*

Thomas Romer

Woodrow Wilson School of Public and International
Affairs, Princeton University

and

Barry R. Weingast

Hoover Institution,
Stanford University

INTRODUCTION

The collapse of the U.S. savings and loan industry is one of the major
economic developments of the 1980s. [1] Current official estimates of the cost

*This paper was commissioned by NBER as part of a series surveying "Politics and
Economics in the Eighties." This draft was prepared for presentation at an NBER
conference in Cambridge, Massachusetts, on May 14–15, 1990, and at the CEPR
Conference on Reform of Deposit Insurance and the Regulation of Depository Institu-
tions, Washington, D.C., May 18–19, 1990. The authors thank James Barth, Philip
Bartholomew, Dan Brumbaugh, Dennis Epple, Allan Meltzer, and Kenneth Scott for
helpful conversations or comments on an earlier draft. We are especially grateful to
James Barth and Philip Bartholomew for their assistance in obtaining some data. Keith
("General Crunch") Poole gave unstintingly of his time and expertise. Mike Caldwell,
Paul Joyce, and Michael Loomis provided able research assistance. Partial research
support was provided by the Center for the Study of Public Policy at Carnegie-Mellon
University (Romer) and the National Science Foundation (Weingast).

1. We will sacrifice some precision and use the terms "savings and loans" and "thrifts"
interchangeably to mean federally insured thrift institutions (which include both S &
Ls and some mutual savings banks).

to American taxpayers of resolving failed thrift institutions exceed $300 billion over the coming decade. Some knowledgeable observers contend that even that figure is optimistically low.[2]

There has been a torrent of analysis of the thrift debacle. Much of this work has focused on the debacle's economic underpinnings. These economic factors include the adverse interest rate environment facing savings and loan institutions at the beginning of the decade, particularly when coupled with the imbalance in maturities of S & L assets and liabilities. In mid-decade, the collapse of real estate markets in the oil patch and hard times in the farm belt had a devastating impact on S & Ls in those areas. Federal deposit insurance provided what has amounted to a government-backed guarantee that encouraged many thrift institutions to hold increasingly risky assets as their net worth declined. Low capital requirements further encouraged a type of risk-taking behavior that has been characterized as "gambling for resurrection." In a number of spectacular cases, outright fraud and theft have occurred.

The American thrift industry, like the financial services sector generally, has been highly regulated for the last half century. The events of the 1980s have called into question the effectiveness of regulatory structure and performance. Many of those who have explored the economic aspects of the S & L crisis have at least alluded to regulatory failures. Though some have noted links to the political process generally and to congressional politics in particular,[3] there has been no systematic treatment of the political underpinnings of the crisis.

In this essay, we are concerned with documenting these political aspects of the thrift debacle, focusing on the role of elected officials. We contend that, although the industry did face severe economic shocks during the decade, political action—and inaction—played an important role in shaping the environment in which thrift institutions and regulators operated. The regulatory structure in place at the beginning of the decade was itself a political creation. Its key elements—such as deposit insurance, portfolio restrictions, capital requirements, resources available to regulators—were politically determined. Any changes in these elements in response to changing economic environments would also be subject to political forces.

Other writers have detailed the escalating costs associated with delay and regulatory forbearance in the face of mounting problems in the thrift

---

2. The *Wall Street Journal* reported on April 6, 1990, that Congressional Budget Office and General Accounting Office projections of spending through the 1990s will be between $300 billion and $350 billion, "*before* factoring in increased net losses from an unexpectedly greater number of [thrift] insolvencies" (emphasis in original). The article quotes an estimate by James Barth, a close observer of the industry, that the likely 10-year cost will exceed $400 billion.

3. See especially Kane (1989a,b,c).

industry during the second half of the decade.[4] We argue that Congress was the major source of regulatory forbearance during the crucial period 1985–87.

Our analytical perspective centers on the institutional structure of congressional decision making and on incentives faced by individual congressmen. These incentives led to intervention by some legislators on behalf of constituents (individuals and thrift institutions) to urge regulatory relief. Systemwide, they also resulted in delay in recognizing the magnitude of the problems facing the Federal Savings and Loan Insurance Corporation (FSLIC). Conflicting interests across key committees of the House and Senate—under different party control during the first six years of the decade—also militated against timely, corrective legislation.

In 1981, 85 percent of the approximately 3,750 thrift institutions insured by the FSLIC had negative earnings (Barth and Bradley, 1988). This was the worst of a series of increasingly unprofitable years for the industry. More significantly, the 1979–81 surge in interest rates had wiped out the industry's net worth, as measured by current market value.[5] Even by the more lenient standards of generally accepted accounting principles (GAAP), there was a marked deterioration in the financial health of thrift institutions.[6] The FSLIC was faced by a record number of problem thrifts. The regulatory response was to merge or liquidate only some of the worst cases, and to allow many insolvent thrifts to remain open.

The pattern of easing up on regulatory enforcement was codified in the Garn-St Germain Depository Institutions Act passed by Congress in late 1982. This legislation had as its primary goal the partial deregulation of the financial sector. It expanded the scope of activities permitted to thrift institutions, and broadened the types of assets that they could hold. It also relaxed regulatory accounting standards for thrifts.[7] Over the next two years, as interest rates declined, it appeared to many observers that the

---

4. See, for example, Brumbaugh and Carron, 1987; Brumbaugh, 1988; Barth and Bradley, 1988; Brumbaugh et al., 1989; Kane, 1989a,b,c; Scott, 1989a.

5. By 1981, market-value net worth of federally insured thrifts had fallen to −17.3 percent of total assets (Brumbaugh, 1988, Table 2–7, p. 50).

6. In 1982, nearly 10 percent of FSLIC-insured thrifts were insolvent by GAAP standards, more than in any prior year (Brumbaugh, 1988, Fig. 2–1, p. 37).

7. Prior to the Garn-St Germain Act, the FHLBB had eased some accounting rules to help ailing thrifts, by lengthening the list of items that could be excluded as liabilities and those included as assets, in computing net worth. Under Garn-St Germain, "well managed" thrifts with net worth between 0.5 and 3 percent of assets could issue "net worth certificates" that could be exchanged for FSLIC promissory notes and counted as assets. In this way a thrift institution could convert what was, in effect, a liability into an asset. Moreover, once FSLIC agreed to buy such certificates from an institution, it was committed to continue buying them, as long as the institution was deemed to be "well managed."

crisis was over.[8] The number of thrifts that received direct or indirect FSLIC assistance fell (see Table 5.1).

As is now well known, 1983 through early 1985 was just the calm before the storm. By late 1985, Edwin Gray, chairman of the Federal Home Loan Bank Board (FHLBB), testified before Congress that FSLIC would require $14–15 billion in additional funds to handle newly emerging problems. When Congress passed legislation nearly two years later, the magnitude of the thrift solvency crisis had grown to an estimated $50 billion. Yet the 1987 legislation provided only $10.8 billion in additional FSLIC funding, less than regulators had requested in 1985. The problems of the thrift industry continued to mushroom; by the time new legislation was once again considered in 1989, the scope of the liabilities facing FSLIC and American taxpayers had exploded to $200 billion.

In this essay, we focus on the issue of how the thrift problem of the mid-1980s exploded. It is widely recognized that a major factor in the magnitude of the problem has been the behavior of insolvent thrifts. The structure of deposit insurance gave insolvent but open thrifts (what Edward Kane has called "zombie" institutions) strong incentives to undertake high-risk investments. If the investments turned sour (as many of them did), thrift owners had little or nothing to lose—the institution was already insolvent anyway. The additional losses would eventually have to be covered by FSLIC, whose ultimate guarantors were the taxpayers. If, on the other hand, the investment paid off, the thrift might be able to lift itself out of insolvency, with the positive returns going to the thrift's owners. This systematic "gambling for resurrection" has meant that, except in the extremely unlikely event that most of the gambles were to pay off, the cost of the eventual resolution of the debacle would grow dramatically.

Table 5.1   Attrition among FSLIC-Insured Thrifts, 1980–84

	FSLIC-Assisted		FSLIC Supervisory Mergers	Voluntary Mergers	Total
	Liquidations	Mergers[a]			
1980	0	11	24	82	117
1981	1	27	53	206	287
1982	1	69	182	262	514
1983	6	47	49	107	209
1984	9	18	14	33	79

a. Includes other types of assistance cases.

SOURCE: Brumbaugh, 1988, Table 3–2.

---

8. A typical report, carried in the August 13, 1983, issue of *National Journal,* proclaimed that Garn-St Germain had "rescued" the thrift industry, and that thrift executives were optimistic about their new options.

Gambling for resurrection may well have been largely responsible for the explosive growth of the thrift problem. But why was such gambling allowed? Why did regulators not stop it? Given the rapid growth in the problem, why was Congress so slow to respond? Why was the 1987 legislation too little, too late?

Several hypotheses have emerged to address these questions. Some argue that the regulators were incompetent and failed to do their job. Had the FHLBB only been more attentive to what was going on in the industry, for example, it could have abated the crisis when it was much smaller. A second argument suggests that fraud by greedy thrifts hid the problem from view. A third explanation suggests that the thrifts, through intense lobbying and large campaign expenditures, were able to sway key congressmen to violate "ethical practices" by intervening in the regulatory process on behalf of the thrifts.[9]

Although each of these hypotheses is partially correct, they all miss the key element in the foundations of the thrift debacle. Massive gambling for resurrection was allowed to proceed because Congress intervened in the regulatory process to establish and enforce a policy of *forbearance*. This policy, initiated at the start of the decade, was later expanded in two ways. First, by delaying FSLIC recapitalization (partly by design, and partly for other reasons discussed below) and by keeping recapitalization to low levels, Congress ensured that regulators could force only some insolvent S & Ls to close or reorganize. Second, the FHLBB was generally on the side of forbearance. When regulators did propose to embark on a tougher policy, Congress intervened to prevent enforcement of existing rules and, through new legislation, relaxed many regulatory provisions. Moreover, in many respects, *congressional behavior with respect to the thrift industry should be seen as fairly routine politics, rather than as an outrageous deviation.*

Our thesis, then, is that the way Congress handled the emerging thrift crisis fits into a more general pattern of the way Congress responds to constituencies and to regulatory developments. Relatively routine behavior during 1985–87 generated both delay in legislation and the reinforcement of forbearance that allowed thrifts to gamble for resurrection.

To establish this thesis, we begin by summarizing a framework that encompasses the relationship between a regulatory agency and Congress, and by delineating how bureaucratic policy choice comes systematically under congressional influence. We then shift to a more specific discussion of the regulatory environment of the thrift industry circa 1985. This sets the stage for a somewhat detailed narrative of legislative responses to the changing economic environment and the regulators' proposals to deal with

---

9. Kane (1989b) provides a good overview of the first and third of these hypotheses. Explanations that lean heavily on fraud and skulduggery are presented in a spate of "inside story" books, for example, Adams, 1989; Pizzo et al., 1989; Pilzer and Dietz, 1989. Movie versions cannot be far behind.

it. This narrative not only tells an intriguing story, but also is useful because it shows how legislative response fits into the framework we have outlined. As part of the discussion of the 1986–87 legislation, we provide some econometric evidence about the connection of constituent interests to congressional behavior. We then summarize our findings and draw some lessons we think are applicable to other potential debacles.

CONGRESS AND THE REGULATORY BUREAUCRACY

Because many of the strongest effects of politicians are brought about through indirect mechanisms that are not easily observed, the relationship between Congress and the ongoing process of regulatory decision making is often misunderstood. In this section, we present a framework for the analysis of regulatory policy making, focusing on the role of Congress. [10]

We begin with the premise that congressmen are motivated in large part to seek reelection—certainly other goals such as implementing good policy require reelection. This motivation forces congressmen to respond to the interests in their districts. But this does not mean that constituents' interests are weighed in a uniform way. Rather, weights accorded different interests reflect the degree to which particular interests within the district attend and respond to the actions of a congressman. Since most individuals have only the vaguest notion of their congressman, the main challenge to a congressman is to break through the information barrier. According to Mayhew (1979, p. 74), "A successful congressman builds what amounts to a brand name," and empirical studies repeatedly show that name recognition is valuable on election day. [11]

The problem of building sufficient recognition to succeed on election day leads congressmen to focus on two types of activities: constituency service and national policy issues (Fiorina, 1989). Constituency service includes a wide range of activities, which can be grouped into two categories. First, this service entails the congressman's securing for his district its share of governmental expenditures—highway funds, a new post office, urban development grants, sewage treatment facilities, and so on. Also in this category is direct service to individuals and groups, ranging from helping individuals find their lost social security checks to intervening in regulatory proceedings on behalf of prominent district interests. Congressmen serve as ombudsmen on behalf of their constituents before a host of

---

10. Our discussion is based on a large and growing literature on this topic: Fiorina, 1981; Fiorina and Noll, 1978; Ferejohn and Shipan, 1989; McCubbins and Schwartz, 1984; Kiewiet and McCubbins, 1990; McCubbins et al., 1989; Moe, 1985, 1989; Weingast, 1984; and Weingast and Moran, 1983. For a survey of some of this work, see Romer and Rosenthal, 1987.

11. On recognition, see Jacobson, 1987.

regulatory agencies. The large presence of the federal government in the economy ensures that the opportunities to play this role are numerous, and this activity typically consumes a major portion of a congressman's workday. Moreover, the federal system of regulation is designed to be open to the influence of congressmen, [12] as we will discuss below.

The second form of activity in which every member of Congress engages in order to develop a favorable reputation involves specialization in the policy making process. This is most effectively done through the work of congressional committees. The committee system divides the large set of national public issues into jurisdictions and assigns policy areas by jurisdiction to specific committees. This affords congressmen the opportunity to obtain membership on committees with policy jurisdictions important to their constituencies. Few congressmen can credibly claim a key role in major new legislation, but with the committee system many members can specialize and build a reputation for expertise and influence in a specific area.

The Role of Congressional Institutions

The literature on congressional institutions demonstrates that they play an important role in determining the specific form of policy outcomes. Recent work has aimed at formalizing the relationship between institutional structure and policy. [13] For our purposes, what is most relevant is that these institutions set up *multiple veto points*, that is, positions within the institution that can readily delay or prevent legislation on a specific topic from becoming law. A major implication of veto power is that it endows relevant legislators with the ability to protect the interests they represent. Attention to the key veto points goes a long way toward understanding policy choice. [14]

Committees are by far the most important veto points because each committee plays a strong role in shaping policy within its jurisdiction. Part of a committee's power arises from gatekeeping—the ability to keep legislation from coming to a vote by the full House or Senate. Exercising such veto power usually requires the support of the committee chairman and a majority of the committee. Put another way, opening the gates typically requires that the committee chairman and a majority of committee members expect to benefit from the legislation. If the legislation will only make them worse off, then the veto power will be exercised. Committees rarely

---

12. Fiorina, 1981; McCubbins and Schwartz, 1984; McCubbins et al., 1989.

13. This line of work has provided insights into equilibrium and comparative statics, applied in a variety of settings. See, for example, Romer and Rosenthal, 1978; Weingast and Moran, 1983; Ferejohn, 1986; Ferejohn and Shipan, 1989; and Kiewiet and McCubbins, 1990.

14. As emphasized in Gilligan et al., 1989.

bring their bills before the entire chamber unless they have the support of a majority. Hence most bills succeed once they get to the floor, that is, once they come up for a vote. In summary, then, committees are powerful because they have a fundamental role in shaping the legislative *agenda* as well as the *substantive content* of legislative proposals.

If committees are the most important veto points within Congress, they are hardly the only ones. The bicameral structure of Congress implies that any legislation must attain majority support in both the House and the Senate. While obvious, this condition can be hard to satisfy when the houses are dominated by different parties, as in 1981–86, when the Democrats held a majority in the House and the Republicans a majority in the Senate. Additionally, in each chamber there are players other than committee members who may be relevant for particular issues. In the House, in the 1980s, the leadership played a strong role in scheduling and passing legislation. [15] In the Senate, individuals may hold up legislation by filibustering at strategic moments.

Constituency interests represented by congressmen at key veto points are advantaged in the policy process. Veto power usually assures these interests that legislation will not make them worse off (otherwise it will never make it past the veto point). Though floor majorities, the leadership, and other well placed individuals such as the President often play important roles, an understanding of committees and their leaders remains central to the analysis of policy formation.

Congressmen and Their Constituents

In order to understand the legislative preferences of congressmen, we need to know the types of constituencies they face (Moe, 1989). The relationship between congressmen and their constituents can be divided into several politically relevant subcategories. The first is a congressman's entire district, his "legal constituency." More relevant, however, are a congressman's supporters within the district who provide resources and votes. These include organized interests such as environmentalists, labor unions, firms, and trade associations. Congressmen are especially attentive to the active interests within their districts, and this attention provides the basis for the commonly observed geographically based dispersion of interests in Congress (representatives from farm states are advocates of farm benefits; those from cities are advocates of funds for local highways, urban redevelopment). Another subgroup consists of those with a potential interest in some policy, but who not only lack an organization, but are nearly completely inattentive and can be mobilized only with great difficulty. A good example are individuals who, because of dairy price supports, pay too high a price for milk. Were they politically active, they might counterbalance

---

15. On the role of the House leadership in the 1980s, see Sinclair, 1989.

the influence of milk producers over policy to maintain prices. Taxpayers rarely organize to oppose a specific increase in revenue or a new loophole or for some political purpose. Only on occasion can such a politically latent group play a major role in politics.

A final set of relevant constituents comes from outside the congressional district. These constituencies usually have interests that fall within the jurisdiction of a committee on which the congressman serves, but congressmen rarely favor organized interests outside their districts over active interests within the district. The typical pattern is for a congressman to receive money and support from groups whose interests are compatible with those in his or her district or concerning which the district is inactive or indifferent (Denzau and Munger, 1986).

In what follows we use the terms constituents and constituency to refer to those active interests (whether organized or diffuse, inside the district or out) that play a role in a congressman's support coalition. Hence we exclude those interests within the district that are either latent or not represented by the congressman's group of supporters. For any given issue area, legislative preferences of relevant congressmen, especially those positioned at key veto points, must be assessed. This requires focusing on their constituency pressures, typically by examining the various active and potentially active constituencies likely to be interested in the issue.

The Relationship of Regulatory Agencies to the Political System

Because regulatory agencies affect a broad range of interests, it would be surprising to find politicians without the means to influence their decisions. Although direct attention through hearings, investigations, and policy pronouncements is relatively sporadic, there are many other, often more effective, devices for political influence. These include a complex incentive system that rewards agencies that follow political intentions and punishes those that do not. The routine process of regulatory oversight does not involve much direct congressional intervention. A regulatory agency attuned to congressional interests (particularly those represented on relevant committees) will rarely deviate in such a way as to incur congressional ire. Such deviations, when they occur, can damage an agency and its leaders— resulting, for example, in the removal of an issue from an agency's jurisdiction, cutting off funds, or ruining a regulator's political career. Because of such costs, agencies tend to be attentive to the relevant congressional constituents. Direct intervention, then, is episodic and relatively unusual, not because congressional influence is weak, but because direct congressional attention and participation are required only when agencies go astray.[16]

The structure of congressional institutions assures that committees

---

16. McCubbins and Schwartz, 1984; Weingast, 1984.

with jurisdiction over a regulatory agency's policy area play a major role in the agency's fate. These committees handle new legislation concerning the agency and respond to problems with its performance. Two types of changes in the regulatory environment tend to attract considerable attention by the relevant congressional committees: a change in the economic environment that threatens the regulated industry and an attempt by an agency to alter the regulatory status quo. In the case of the thrift industry both these changes took place.

Implications for Regulatory Policy Making

The implications of this view of regulatory politics are as follows.

First, congressmen on the relevant committees play important roles for ongoing policy decisions within a regulatory bureaucracy. Even though congressmen may not be attentive, members of their active support constituency are. Because congressmen collaborate with these constituents to intervene when regulatory agencies seek to deviate from the constituents' interests, regulators pay close attention to these interests. Intervention by politicians usually means trouble for bureaucrats and it is widely agreed that agencies seek to avoid it. If an agency presses on in spite of congressional opposition, congressional intervention usually follows. The main lesson for regulatory policy making is that in a confrontation between a congressional committee (that is, a committee chair and a supportive committee majority) and an agency, the committee usually prevails.

Second, politicians have a variety of strategies available to them for influencing agencies. Actual legislation is usually not necessary for Congress to get the agency to change course. [17] Thus congressmen can play the role of ombudsman on behalf of their constituents in a way not particularly visible to outsiders. Faced with a conflict between regulators and constituents, congressmen nearly always side with their constituents.

Third, when examining a particular regulatory policy initiative, we should distinguish between the actors *implementing* policy and the *political forces* that led to the policy. Too often, students of regulation presume that because a regulatory agency initiates a policy without explicit instructions from politicians, the agency—and not the politicians—must be responsible for the policy change. By the framework we outlined above, this inference is incorrect because it ignores the political forces working on the agency.

One can frequently find good evidence of congressional influence by comparing agency proposals with what actually happens, whether through legislation or an agency's implementing a revised proposal. An example is useful here. In studying the 1960s policy initiatives of the Securities and Exchange Commission (SEC), many scholars provided explanations in

---

17. See Kiewiet and McCubbins' (1990) discussion of delegation, and Ferejohn and Shipan (1989) on the legislative threats of intervention in agency decisions.

terms of the agency itself, focusing especially on the preferences of new SEC leaders. [18] Weingast (1984) showed that, in fact, the SEC had proposed these apparently new policies as early as the 1940s, but they had fallen on deaf congressional ears and went nowhere. Only when a set of interests newly represented on the relevant Senate committee began to favor these initiatives were they actually implemented. [19]

Fourth, the lineup of constituency interests facing congressmen on the relevant committee is an important foundation for regulatory policy choice. When only one interest is active, it tends to dominate policy choice, often at the expense of a much larger group of inactive individuals. When several constituencies are relevant, policy tends to be a compromise among them, but again, often at the expense of inactive interests.

Fifth, when policy initiatives backfire, congressmen often blame bureaucrats. This rhetoric is part of the system itself. Because the influence of Congress on the bureaucracy is subtle and not readily known, Congress can rail against the very bureaucracy it created (Fiorina, 1981). Since the public holds regulators responsible for a host of policy problems, the bureaucracy becomes a convenient whipping boy.

We have concentrated on the congressional influence on regulation, and have paid little attention to the President or his Administration. This is not to deny that the President is always a potential participant in most policy areas, requiring that his influence be taken into account. Presidents, however, have finite resources and must husband them for policy concerns of high priority. For a variety of reasons during the mid-1980s, the Reagan White House remained absent from the day-to-day political activity on the emerging thrift issue. Most important, aggressively pursuing a plan to resolve the thrift crisis conflicted with the president's other goals, especially deregulation and containment of spending and taxes. As we shall see, White House involvement did play a role in engineering the compromise legislation of 1987, but during the previous two years, members of Congress held center stage.

THE THRIFT PROBLEM AND THE RELEVANT CONSTITUENCY INTERESTS

Background of the Regulatory Environment

To put the events of the eighties in proper perspective, a brief sketch of the political setting of the thrift industry is useful. Many thrift institu-

---

18. See Weingast, 1984, for a review of the literature and evidence for this claim.

19. Other examples are provided by Ferejohn and Shipan's (1989) study of Federal Communications Commission policies after the AT&T divestiture and Weingast and Moran's (1983) work on the Federal Trade Commission.

tions were formed between the World Wars by real estate, construction, and development companies, as a natural adjunct to their other activities. The regional Federal Home Loan Bank (FHLB) system was established in 1932 to provide for thrift institutions the services that commercial banks obtained through the Federal Reserve system. The Federal Savings and Loan Insurance Corporation was established in 1934, as part of a political compromise to gain the support of thrift institutions for Roosevelt's National Housing Act.[20] The FSLIC was placed under the supervision of the FHLB Board.[21]

The linkage between the housing industry and the thrift industry was a politically potent force in the decades following World War II. Much of the argument for the special status of thrifts was based on the premise that a strong housing industry required strong thrift institutions, and that these institutions, in turn, required favorable treatment to assure a healthy market for residential mortgages.[22]

The geographic dispersion of the thrift industry—with firms in nearly every congressional district—has meant that when the industry required congressional attention, it could usually get it. Through the 1970s, the industry was quite homogeneous in its interests. Consequently, its trade association, the U.S. League of Savings Associations (later renamed the U.S. League of Savings Institutions), was able to marshal considerable agreement on policy matters, and to "speak with one voice" to regulators and politicians. Indeed, the U.S. League was so effective in making its views known that its name was nearly always accompanied in newspaper accounts by the adjectives "powerful" and "influential."

The relative homogeneity of the industry also worked to its direct advantage with the relevant congressional committees and hence with the industry's chief federal regulator, the Federal Home Loan Bank Board. Forces tending toward "capture" of a regulatory agency by the industries it regulates are magnified when the regulated interests are themselves not in conflict. The absence of conflict among constituents led to an FHLBB that in many ways has looked like the paradigmatic captured agency: responsive for the most part to thrift industry interests, promulgating regulations that would increase industry rents, staving off competition from unwelcome poachers from commercial banking. Congress supported

---

20. Thrifts had objected to the federal mortgage insurance provisions of the Housing Act, fearing that it would increase the ability of commercial banks and insurance companies to compete in the mortgage market. On this, and other details of the history of the thrift industry, see Woerheide, 1984.

21. This arrangement differs from the case of the FDIC, which is an agency independent of the Federal Reserve Board.

22. The economic argument for subsidies to mortgage lenders as a way to encourage demand for housing is a weak one, and had been frequently challenged, by economists, if not by developers and thrift institutions. See, for example, Meltzer, 1981, and Weicher, 1988.

these policies both with active legislation, and—more generally—simply by not opposing them.

As a response to the straitened economic circumstances faced by the industry at the beginning of the 1980s, the Garn-St Germain Act of 1982 loosened restrictions on thrifts' activities. This helped to provide the industry with greater scope to make investments and compete for deposits. As the adverse interest-rate environment of the early 1980s receded, the apparent health of the industry improved. Encouraged by spokesmen for the thrift industry, most members of Congress were ready to believe that legislation in 1982, coupled with regulatory actions from then on, had succeeded in handling the problems that had surfaced at the beginning of the decade.

During this time, there is little evidence that the FHLBB disagreed with the policy of forbearance. Indeed, a case can be made that warning signs about the looming losses imbedded in many thrift balance sheets were systematically downplayed, both by industry groups and by the regulators.[23] The accounting rules adopted by FHLBB pursuant to the guidelines of the Garn-St Germain Act made this possible. The gambles of insolvent thrifts, made with at least tacit regulatory approval, were backed by congressional mandate.

The Administration and the Emerging Thrift Crisis

The Administration's domestic policy emphasized reduction of the scope of government activity. As far as the thrift industry was concerned, this meant strong support for the deregulatory components of the 1982 legislation. It also meant looking at thrift regulators with a somewhat jaundiced eye, at least when it came to the question of bank examination and supervision. A minority voice within the Administration recognized the problems inherent in the system of deposit insurance in a deregulated environment. The 1984 *Economic Report of the President* contained a recommendation by the Council of Economic Advisers (CEA) that the deposit-insurance system be reformed because of the adverse incentives it created. The 1986 *Report,* published in February, devoted a chapter to "The Federal Role in Credit Markets," which gave a succinct explanation of the thrift problem as of late 1985, including the risks posed by "gambling for resurrection." The CEA also sounded a warning that the FSLIC's problems could turn into a potential liability for taxpayers, and again called for deposit-insurance reform.

The economists' position was not reflected in the Administration's

---

23. Since the early days of deposit insurance, economists had pointed to the perverse incentives for bank risk-taking that it created. Barth and Bradley (1988) quote observers from 1931 and 1936 on this point. By the early 1980s, some FHLBB economists were warning about the riskiness of allowing zombie thrifts to operate, and those outside the industry were calling attention to this problem as well (Kane, 1985, 1989b).

policy. The President continued to support further deregulation of financial markets, but there were no initiatives to deal specifically with the problems of the thrifts. [24] Action by the Office of Management and Budget (OMB) to limit FHLBB budget requests (see below) was consistent with this stance. The Administration did not introduce any legislation to deal with the deposit-insurance question.

Regulators and the Emerging Crisis

As the scope of thrifts' lending activities—and hence their asset risk exposure—increased, the resources devoted to monitoring their health stayed constant or actually declined. Table 5.2 shows that FHLB examination and thrift supervisory budgets were roughly constant from 1982 through 1984, whether measured in numbers of people or dollars. Yet during this time, industry assets grew by 50 percent. Arguing that the growth in the industry required greater regulatory resources, the FHLBB requested a significantly increased budget for 1985. This request was rejected by the Office of Management and Budget as unjustified, given the administration's overall stance on regulation as well as its desire to limit government spending.

Table 5.2 FHLB Regulatory Resources and Thrift Industry Assets

	Examination & Supervision Resources		Assets of FSLIC-Insured Thrifts ($ Billions)
	Staff[a]	Budget[b] ($ Millions)	
1979	1,282	$ 41.0	$ 568.1
1980	1,308	49.8	620.6
1981	1,385	52.8	658.5
1982	1,379	57.3	686.2
1983	1,368	62.5	813.8
1984	1,337	67.0	977.5
1985	1,990	108.8	1,070.0
1986	2,986	168.5	1,163.8
1987	3,258	297.6	1,250.8

a. Staffing figures are based on full-time-equivalent personnel engaged in examination or supervision at both the Bank Board and the district Home Loan Banks.

b. Budget figures are budget or actual expenditures, as available, on examination or supervision at both the Bank Board and the district Home Loan Banks.

SOURCE: Barth and Bradley, 1988, Table 8.

---

24. In the 1986 *Economic Report,* for example, in the President's report itself (as distinct from that of the CEA), the message was that continued deregulation of financial institutions should proceed apace. The thrifts were not mentioned.

Even peering through the distorting lenses of regulatory accounting practices, the regulatory agency was beginning to realize in 1985 that the gambles of many insolvent thrifts would probably result in heavy losses for FSLIC.[25] Having been rebuffed by OMB, the agency decided in mid-1985 to decentralize its examination activities by shifting personnel to the district Home Loan Banks. This ploy allowed the FHLB budget to increase, since the district Banks' budgets were not subject to OMB review. The last three years' entries in Table 5.2 reflect this administrative shift by the agency.

This shift and Edwin Gray's announcement in October 1985 that FSLIC needed about $15 billion in new capital to handle insolvent thrifts provided a clear signal of a change in regulatory position. Through much of 1984, the agency had not been sending out distress signals. Gray's position in 1985 was driven to a large extent by knowledge within the agency that disaster was impending—FSLIC was clearly going broke. If nothing were done, Gray and the agency would be blamed. Blame might be avoided if the problem were brought to urgent public attention. The FHLBB chairman testified to Congress that were the Board to resolve all insolvent savings and loans immediately, the deposit-insurance fund would run out of money within a year.

Congressional Response

In looking at congressional response to these developments, two elements should be emphasized. First, it is not unusual for an agency to cry "wolf "—a crisis is emerging—and claim that if its budget is not increased dramatically, life as we know it cannot go on. Why, in a given instance, would congressmen believe the alarm? For the case of the S & Ls, had not the 1982 legislation fixed the problem? In what sense was there a new problem? Even congressmen without a special interest axe to grind might well rationally react with skepticism to the new tune being sung by regulators.

The second element relevant to the emerging crisis was the fiscal austerity of the mid-1980s. In times of budgetary constraint, nearly all congressmen had to face, without the political wherewithal for added revenues, constituents who wanted funds for existing programs increased. To the extent that new resources for the FSLIC or the FHLBB were to come in the form of newly funded budget authority, these resources would probably have to come at the expense of competing programs. To refuse valued, long-term constituents while creating a large new program would be politically difficult. Congressmen (and the President) would thus be

---

25. Some FHLBB economists had been warning about the gambling-for-resurrection problem throughout this period. See, for example, Barth et al., 1985a, b, and Brumbaugh and Hemmel, 1984.

reluctant to address any problem with big fiscal requirements unless there were large political rewards to be gained. Since the nature and potential proportions of the problem were not well known, these rewards were likely to be perceived as small.

To understand the nature of the political costs and benefits associated with new legislation, we turn to the lineup of interests on this issue.

The Thrift Industry.   A key feature of the economic developments in the thrift industry over the 1981–87 period is the growing disparity between the healthy thrifts and those that were not doing well. Table 5.3 shows that the gap between the worst performing institutions (those in the 5th and 10th percentiles of the industry, as measured by after-tax income) and the ones doing best (those in the 90th and 95th percentiles) widened hugely from 1983 to 1987.

As Figures 5.1 and 5.2 show, there was also a geographical segmentation of the industry, with some regions having particularly heavy concentrations of insolvent thrifts.[26] By 1986, concern about the thrift industry would be more relevant generally, but perhaps more important, Figure 5.2 reveals that the immediacy of the concern would be manifest more clearly to legislators in the southwest and parts of the farm belt than to those in other parts of the country.

These effects eventually led to a divergence of interests within the industry, but in a way that had both segments of the industry supporting only limited help for FSLIC.

Troubled Thrifts. Troubled S & Ls would seem to be the most likely source of active support for legislation to resolve the problems in the

Table 5.3   Net After-Tax Income of FSLIC-Insured Thrifts[a]

	5th Percentile	10th Percentile	Industry Median	90th Percentile	95th Percentile
1979	0.0%	0.2%	0.7%	1.1%	1.2%
1981	−1.9	−1.4	−0.5	0.4	0.7
1982	−2.1	−1.6	−0.5	0.6	1.1
1983	−1.1	−0.8	0.3	1.1	1.6
1984	−1.1	−0.7	0.4	1.0	1.4
1985	−1.7	−0.8	0.7	1.4	1.6
1986	−3.7	−1.3	0.8	1.6	1.9
1987	−7.8	−2.7	0.5	1.2	1.6

a. Annualized, percent of average assets.
SOURCE: Barth and Bradley, 1988, Chart 3.

---

26. Figures 5.1 and 5.2 are based on yearend data, using GAAP definitions.

Figure 5.1   Percent of Thrifts Insolvent in 1981

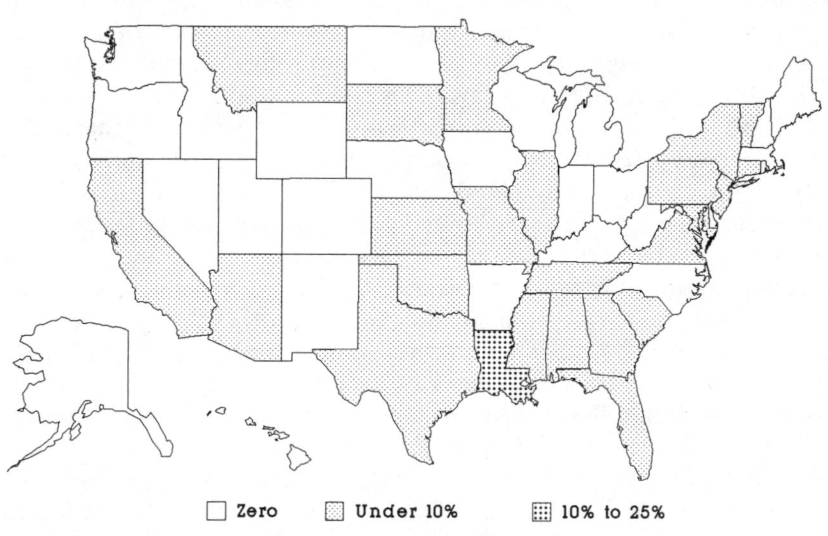

Figure 5.2   Percent of Thrifts Insolvent in 1986

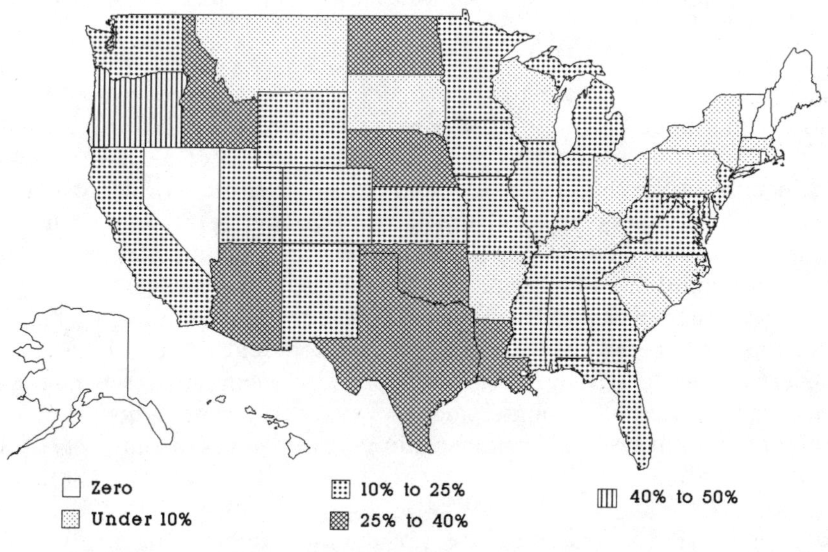

industry. There was indeed active support—but not for increased regulatory activity. Instead, these thrifts, and especially the U.S. League of Savings Institutions, argued for continued forbearance, so that weak and insolvent thrifts could grow out of their current problems, much as they were claimed to have done in 1983. They were opposed to increasing deposit-insurance levies to generate more funds for the FSLIC. Generally, they supported a limited recapitalization for FSLIC. This would provide the insurance fund with some resources to handle the worst cases, but not allow it to move aggressively against many insolvent institutions.

Healthy thrifts. Healthy firms recognized that allowing FSLIC to fail would create depositor uncertainty that would harm even the healthy thrifts, so they preferred some recapitalization over doing nothing. Healthy thrifts would obviously have liked to shift to taxpayers as much of the cost of resolving failed institutions as possible.[27] But they also recognized that to expect a totally taxpayer-financed recapitalization was unrealistic. At least initially, increases in FSLIC capital would have to be financed in large measure by increased assessments on the industry. If the sick thrifts did not get better, these assessments would have to be borne by the segment of the industry that had a positive cash flow. The larger the FSLIC recapitalization, the larger the cost to the currently healthy firms—except in the highly unlikely event that many of the zombies were indeed resurrected. A recapitalization large enough to cover all likely losses by zombie thrifts, if borne by the healthy members of the industry, would wipe out most of their profits and a substantial portion of their net worth. So, from the healthy thrifts' viewpoint, a large recapitalization, drawing mostly on in-dustry funds, was not necessarily better than doing nothing. This group was therefore inclined to support a modest recapitalization on the order of $5 billion.

Depositors.   The clear preference of account holders was to ensure that the various guarantee schemes—thrifts backed by FSLIC, and FSLIC backed by the government—work as promised. This system of pledges removed the incentives for this group to monitor the institutions that held their deposits. Although depositors were likely to react quite strenuously if these pledges were threatened, they were unlikely to play an active role in the choice among different alternatives for honoring the pledges.

Where there were relatively heavy concentrations of failing thrifts, the immediacy of the problem would be more apparent to depositors whose concerns could be strong enough to register on the political seismograph. This effect would pull a congressman's preferences toward a higher FSLIC capitalization, providing a countervailing force against the interests of the troubled thrifts.

Taxpayers.   Taxpayers, of course, are the most diffuse constituency. Be-cause of this diffusion, only a few issues ever become sufficiently salient to play a role in the mass politics of taxation. In the short run, this group simply prefers lower taxes. Although in principle it may have an interest

---

27.   Their position, as described by banking consultant Bert Ely, was: "After all, Ford and GM didn't bail out Chrysler. Boeing didn't bail out Lockheed." *Wall Street Journal,* July 22, 1987.

in spending more money today to avoid spending much more money tomorrow, in practice politicians can act on this principle only if they can credibly claim credit for actually having saved the money tomorrow. Such claims typically look like rationalizations for boondoggles for some other group, and are usually avoided by politicians. Before the crisis became common knowledge, therefore, it was unlikely that politicians would claim credit for saving future taxes by big appropriations today.

There is a clear overlap between depositors and taxpayers but their interests are not identical. Not all taxpayers have significant deposits at thrift institutions. Because depositors are a subset of all taxpayers, they prefer policies that secure their deposits while spreading the costs over the much larger group of taxpayers. For depositors, especially large ones, the benefits in more secure deposits outweight their share of the increase in taxes.

This discussion suggests that, outside of a small group of experts, there was little initial support for developing a legislative solution that covered the full scope of the thrift problem. The problem was big enough in late 1985 to demand some attention, but it was not considered large enough to generate sufficient public attention to gain large political rewards from a major new, expensive policy. A recapitalization that would have given FSLIC sufficient resources to resolve all current and expected insolvencies would, by late 1986, have required a $50-billion program, a level of funding totally outside the scope of anything that could be financed from assessments on the industry. It would have meant a significant commitment of taxpayer resources. [28]

It must be emphasized that while regulators and a small group of experts were warning of dire things to come, no significant group was mobilized to support a large-scale recapitalization. Congressmen were faced with a situation in which the lineup of interests was largely against the high levels of recapitalization called for by some regulators. In such a situation, congressmen did not need elaborate rationalizations to follow their legislative preferences and side with their constituents.

Committee Jurisdictions and Other Interests

In the Senate, the jurisdiction over thrifts is assigned to the committee on Banking, Housing, and Urban Affairs, while in the House the committee on Banking, Finance, and Urban Affairs deals with these matters. As their

---

28. Given the economic status of the thrifts, even a $15-billion recapitalization would have required assessments of over $1 billion per year and would have cut severely into the income of the segment of the industry that was healthy in 1986. By 1987, tangible net worth (GAAP net worth minus certain items such as goodwill) of the industry had shrunk to $9 billion. Thrifts with GAAP capital-to-asset ratio above 3 percent had tangible net worth of $34 billion. Tangible net worth of the rest of the industry was *negative* $25 billion (Barth et al., 1990, Table 1).

names suggest, the domain of these committees is extensive, and includes a large variety of issues beyond the S & L industry. Not only are other financial markets and regulatory agencies within their realms, but so too are such diverse policies as housing and even some aspects of international development. A common occurrence in the legislative process is that members of committees with legislative interests in one policy area must negotiate with other members of the committee whose interests lie elsewhere, often in policy issues logically unrelated except that they come under the purview of the same committee. This *politically induced interdependence* among issues may have a strong effect on legislation aimed at a particular problem because the fate of one policy may be tied to political circumstances involving other, possibly unrelated, issues.

An ongoing concern for both these committees throughout the 1980s was the question of deregulation of commercial banks. A particularly contentious issue involved the entry into banking of nonbanking institutions, such as Sears and American Express. The regulation of such "nonbank banks" did not directly involve most of the problems confronting the thrift industry, but in a larger sense, a case could be made that the health of the thrift industry was linked to the overall competitive environment of the banking sector. In any event, over the 1986–87 period, these issues became linked in the political process.

THE POLITICS OF LEGISLATIVE DELAY AND FORBEARANCE, 1986–87

In this section we examine the legislative consideration of a response to the regulators' signal that all was not well, and that a major change in policy would be needed. The conjunction of constituent interests and the institutional structure of congressional decision making provides a road map through the events of the two years following Gray's October 1985 testimony. The trail to follow in this narrative is the one laid out by our framework: attention to players at key veto points and their role in structuring the legislative agenda.

The 1986 Stalemate

The reaction by the two committee chairmen to the emergence of a new thrift problem differed in ways that foretold conflict: St Germain (D-RI, chairman of the House committee) called for extension of the 1982 legislation and opposed further financial deregulation. In contrast, Garn (R-UT, chairman of the Senate committee) announced that he was "vitally committed" to broad financial deregulation. He planned to use a yet undrafted bill to strengthen the FSLIC system as a vehicle for banking deregulation. As will become clear, Garn was not alone in this sentiment. Thus, St Germain, at least initially, sought a bill that focused on the thrift problem whereas Garn's interest focused on deregulation of the financial system, using the legislation on the thrifts as a potential vehicle.

In the early spring of 1986, a plan emerged to finance the recapitalization of FSLIC. The FHLBB proposed to tighten regulations concerning thrift investments and accounting standards, arguing that half a decade of permissiveness had done much harm. Among other things, the new rules would require thrifts to double their capitalization to 6 percent of assets in six years and to replace the current accounting conventions that, according to the Board, had obscured the emerging problems. By early May, the proposed plan would raise sufficient funds to cover deposits in the (then) estimated 216 failing thrifts.

Proceedings in the Senate began when Garn introduced an omnibus banking bill that included provisions for dealing with thrifts and other problems. Shortly thereafter, however, he dropped the additional provisions as his committee passed a bill with FSLIC provisions nearly identical to those in the House. Nonetheless, William Proxmire (D-WI), ranking minority member of the committee, threatened to filibuster unless other, unrelated aspects of bank regulation—especially the issue of the nonbank banks—were dealt with at the same time. In late September, the House committee, hoping to use the FSLIC recapitalization as a vehicle to move other legislation, joined this measure with political alternatives of its own, especially additional authorization for some housing programs.

Before a vote could be taken on the House floor, however, majority leader Jim Wright of Texas (who would soon succeed Tip O'Neill as Speaker) removed the bill from the House calendar. Texas bankers and real estate developers had complained to Wright that regulators were restricting real estate loans and refusing to restructure bad loans. The bill was not rescheduled until Edwin Gray met with Wright and assured him that regulators would cooperate with ailing thrifts in Texas. By holding hostage the legislation sought by regulators, this intervention compelled an agreement by the regulators not to enforce their own rules against ailing thrifts—assuring an expanded de facto policy of forbearance, at least for politically favored institutions.

Shortly thereafter (October 1986), the House passed its measure. The House bill created a new financing corporation with the authority to borrow up to $15 billion over three years, to be used to fund the FSLIC. Only a limited amount of new FSLIC resources would come from extra assessments on thrifts. Like the regulators, legislators also proposed changes in the regulatory restrictions, but instead of *increasing* the stringency with which insolvent thrifts were regulated, legislators *weakened* the position of regulators vis-à-vis the zombies. Regulators were given expanded powers, not to force failing banks to close, but to keep them open until new owners could be found or the hoped-for resurrection took place.

On the Senate side, the final bill called for only $3 billion in FSLIC recapitalization, and did not include housing provisions that St Germain strongly favored. St Germain had earlier indicated that he would not accept any compromise that excluded the housing issues. At this point a stalemate occurred. None of the policies preferred by House members at key veto points (that is, policies calling for funds for FSLIC and housing, but *without* provisions dealing with commercial bank regulation) were acceptable to key veto players in the Senate (who supported lower FSLIC recapitalization *without* the housing provisions but *with* the commercial banking matters)—and vice versa. With the congressional session ending before the 1986 elections, there was insufficient time to resolve the differences between the Senate and House versions. Both bills died.

The end-of-the-session rush combined with strategies by several politicians to link the thrift issue to other issues. Even a partial resolution of the growing thrift problem was thereby delayed for nearly a year. Part of the explanation for the intransigence of the relevant committee members in both chambers is that those with strong constituency interests were inclined toward lax regulation. Since, for the most part, thrifts were arguing for forbearance, delay would ensure greater laxity by forcing the regulators to wait for needed funds. Committee members with relatively few weak thrifts in their state (such as Proxmire of Wisconsin) did not have a compelling interest in raising substantial revenues for FSLIC, but were interested in other banking issues. Finally, there was the general unwillingness by many congressmen to find the FHLBB warnings of impending doom credible, given the long-standing appearance (buttressed by regulatory accounting practices and the claims of the thrift constituency) that the thrift problem was at worst a temporary and regional one.[29]

A year of legislative deadlock was not without its legacy. Though no legislation had passed, the direct interaction of regulators with Wright and other members of Congress from states with many problem thrifts (especially Texas, California, Louisiana, Nebraska, and Oklahoma) made it clear that any future attempts to deal with the thrift problem would involve large doses of forbearance.

Legislation in the 100th Congress (1987)

With the Democrats' recapture of a majority of Senate seats in the 1986 elections, the chairmanship of the Senate committee passed to Proxmire. Within a month of the elections, he announced support for a plan drafted by the Administration that would have permitted up to $15 billion in borrowing authority for an FSLIC recapitalization. He intended, however, to include this in an omnibus bill (S 790) that also placed a moratorium on the creation of new nonbank banks.

The U.S. Savings League lobbied aggressively against the $15 billion

---

29. Kane (1989b) provides a good discussion of the extent to which accounting numbers systematically provided rosy pictures of the thrift situation.

recapitalization.[30] They argued against its cost, and supported a much weaker proposal that would have allowed for a temporary $5 billion funding authority. This proposal would also have continued and even extended regulatory forbearance toward insolvent thrifts in "economically distressed" areas. The League proposal thus combined the forbearance measures sought by the sick thrifts and the limited funding that the healthy thrifts preferred.

As approved by the Senate Banking committee, S 790 limited FSLIC borrowing to $7.5 billion over two years, with no more than $3.75 billion to be spent in either year.[31] The bill also included forbearance provisions for thrifts in economically depressed areas. Attempts to increase the borrowing limit were rejected by the committee. Most of the debate in the committee focused on issues relating to the nonbank bank matter and other financial sector regulatory questions, such as the entry of commercial banks into the securities industry.

The Senate approved S 790 79 to 11 without significant change in the FSLIC financing provisions. An attempt by Garn to strike the non-FSLIC-related matters from the bill to provide a "clean" recapitalization bill failed by a vote of 35 to 54. The committee bill had also contained a provision that would have exempted bank regulatory agencies (including the FHLBB) from any automatic Gramm-Rudman-Hollings cuts. Approving by a voice vote an amendment by Gramm (R-TX), the Senate stripped this provision from the committee bill, making clear that additional funds for FSLIC would be subject to the general fiscal restraints of the time.

On the House side, St Germain had signaled early on that he would refuse to permit a bill to reach the House floor with the nonbank bank provision, and his committee prepared its own version of the legislation (HR 27). As to the message that the bill would send to regulators, Speaker Wright had met with committee Democrats, and according to news reports, "Mr. Wright in effect said, no forbearance, no bill."[32]

As it appeared in the markup session of the Financial Institutions Supervision, Regulation and Insurance subcommittee of the House Banking committee, HR 27 was essentially the bill supported by the U.S. League. The major issue of debate was the level of recapitalization. By a 23 to 20 vote, the subcommittee approved an amendment to raise FSLIC's borrowing limit from $5 billion over two years to $15 billion over five years,

---

30. The aggressive lobbying and campaign financing activities of thrift industry groups and individual thrifts on this issue have been well documented. See, for example, Jackson, 1988.

31. Although we refer to FSLIC borrowing, under all the plans discussed here, the actual borrowing was to be done by a newly created financing corporation (FICO). The principal on the borrowed amounts would be secured by zero-coupon bonds issued by the Treasury. Interest on FICO borrowing would be paid by FSLIC-insured thrifts.

32. *New York Times,* February 9, 1987.

with a limit of $3.5 billion on borrowing in any given year. The next day (April 1) the full committee reversed this action, and approved, 25 to 24, an amendment sponsored by Neal (D-NC) to return to the $5 billion, two-year plan. Amendments to increase the recapitalization to $12 billion over four years or $10.5 billion over three years were rejected. The committee then voted 45 to 5 to report HR 27, with the two-year $5 billion plan, and including many forbearance provisions.

FHLBB chairman Gray attacked the committee bill because, in contrast to the measure the committee had passed in 1986, it included many new forbearance provisions. He noted that these were pushed by "some of the worst-managed thrifts" in order to "hamstring" regulators. Proponents of HR 27 explicitly argued that its main goal was indeed to put regulators "on a short leash." [33]

The St Germain Amendment

As the FSLIC's cash woes mounted, Speaker Wright made the surprise announcement toward the end of April that he would favor increasing the capitalization to $15 billion, though with the forbearance provisions of the committee bill left intact. Speculation about Wright's motives included his increasing concern about adverse media coverage of his connection with some spectacular Texas thrift failures, and indications that the $5-billion package would fail on the House floor. [34] St Germain joined Wright in this reversal, and announced that he would sponsor an amendment to raise the FSLIC borrowing limit to $15 billion—but retain the forbearance provisions—when HR 27 came to a House vote.

The U.S. League lobbied vigorously against St Germain's proposed amendment. Healthy thrifts were particularly concerned about the additional assessments that the higher borrowing limit would impose on them. When the St Germain amendment came to a vote in the House (May 5), it lost by a resounding 153 to 258. [35] The leader of the floor fight against the amendment was Representative Stephen Neal (D-NC) who put the issue in the following terms: "The argument is between more money and less oversight [of the regulators by Congress] and less money and more oversight." [36]

---

33. *Washington Post,* April 29, 1987.

34. The day before Wright's announcement of his support for the $15 billion limit, the FHLBB "filed a $350 million lawsuit against seven former officers of the Vernon Savings and Loan Association of Dallas charging them with looting the organization of hundreds of millions of dollars. Vernon was one of the thrift institutions for which Mr. Wright had sought leniency." *New York Times,* April 29, 1987.

35. The St Germain amendment is CQ Roll Call 83. Democrats voted 81 Yea and 160 Nay; Republicans voted 72 Yea and 98 Nay.

36. *Wall Street Journal,* May 6, 1987.

The authors conducted a simple econometric analysis of voting on the St Germain amendment to examine our hypothesis that the opposition of healthy thrifts played an important role in defeating the amendment. We obtained data on the number of FSLIC-insured thrift institutions falling into each of five GAAP capital/asset ratio categories in each state.[37] We constructed two variables, WEAK and STRONG. The former is the number of thrifts in the state with negative GAAP net worth, the latter the number of those with GAAP net worth above 3 percent of GAAP assets. Both variables were measured as of yearend 1986.[38] We then divided each variable by the number of congressional districts in the state, to get an admittedly crude measure of the constituency pressure on each member. (Ideally, we would have liked these data by congressional district, but they were not available in time for this conference.) The resulting variables are WEAKDIS and STRONGDIS, respectively.

As another thrift constituency variable, we constructed PACMONEY, which measures the campaign contributions received (in thousands of dollars) by each congressman from the largest thrift industry PACs in the 1983–84 and 1985–86 election cycles.[39]

To capture purely partisan effects, we used party affiliation (a dummy variable PARTY, which equals 1 for Democrats and 0 for Republicans). Another variable, IDEOL, is intended to capture a congressman's general legislative preference with respect to government intervention. IDEOL is computed from scaling of the roll calls and legislators in the 100th House using the NOMINATE procedure of Poole and Rosenthal. This variable ranges from approximately $+1.3$ to approximately -1.3, with high values corresponding to "liberal" positions and low ones to "conservative" positions.[40] Including IDEOL allows for within-party variation according to individual constituency or representative characteristics that are not cap-

---

37. The categories are: (GAAP net worth/GAAP assets) less than 0; between 0 and 1.5 percent; between 1.5 percent and 3 percent; between 3 percent and 6 percent; and over 6 percent.

38. Using yearend 1987 data instead did not affect our qualitative results, nor did defining WEAK as thrifts with GAAP net worth less that 1.5 percent of GAAP assets or STRONG as those with GAAP net worth above 6 percent.

39. The PACs are those affiliated with the U.S. League and with the National Council of Savings Institutions (Thriftpac). These were the only two thrift PACs among the 500 largest (in terms of campaign contributions) PACs in 1985–86. The totals do not include "soft money" or honoraria received by congressmen from thrift industry groups.

40. We thank Keith Poole for the data. The IDEOL variable for each congressman equals the coordinate of the first dimension estimated from running two-dimensional NOMINATE on the 100th House. The IDEOL variable correlates highly (over 0.9) with the more familiar ADA score, but is based on a much wider set of roll calls. For details, see Poole and Rosenthal, 1991.

tured in our economic variables. Finally, we allowed for the possibility that members of the committee behaved differently than nonmembers by including COM, which equals 1 for committee members and 0 otherwise.

We estimated the probability of observing a Yea vote on the St Germain amendment. Using probit analysis, we estimated

$$P \equiv \text{Prob (Yea vote)} = F(Z) \tag{1}$$

where $F(\cdot)$ is the standard normal cumulative distribution. Our specification of Z is given by:

$$Z = \beta_0 + \beta_1 \text{ PARTY} + \beta_2 \text{ IDEOL} + \beta_3 \text{ COM} \\ + \beta_4 \text{ PACMONEY} + \beta_5 \text{ STRONGDIS} + \beta_6 \text{ WEAKDIS} \tag{2}$$

Based on our earlier discussions, we expect β_5 to be negative. To the extent that a "liberal" overall legislative preference is also "proregulation," we expect $\beta_2 > 0$. Since the St Germain amendment was supported by the Administration, Republicans would be more likely to be in favor of it, so we expect $\beta_1 < 0$.

The committee had, of course, reported the $5-billion package, but this amount had been approved in committee by a one-vote margin. The committee chairman was now sponsoring an amendment to raise the recapitalization level—a switch from the way he voted in committee. This does not imply any clear prediction about β_3, but if committee members tend to support the chairman's position on the floor (as part of an implicit bargain in a continuing relationship), then we should see $\beta_3 > 0$.

The predicted sign of β_6 is negative if WEAKDIS is primarily a measure of constituent pressure from insolvent thrifts. But, as we noted in our earlier discussion, having a larger number of insolvent thrifts in one's district also heightens depositors' concerns in the district. This may lead to increasing willingness to vote for a larger recapitalization.[41] The net effect on β_6 is unclear.

As to β_4, it would be natural to suppose that higher contributions from the thrift PACs would be associated with a lower probability to vote for the amendment, but studies of the relationship of campaign contributions to voting on individual roll calls have shown no clear indication of such direct association.

Table 5.4 presents our probit estimates. As expected, Republicans were more likely to vote for the amendment than Democrats—and liberal Democrats (there are no Republicans with high IDEOL values) were more likely to vote Yea than their more conservative brethren. Committee mem-

---

41. This could be more directly tested with a variable that measured the number of depositors with accounts at insolvent thrifts in the district. We did not have such a variable at our disposal.

Table 5.4   Voting on the St Germain Amendment to HR 27 Probit Estimates

	1	2	3	4	5
CONSTANT	0.287	0.014	−0.130	0.081	−0.134
	(0.199)	(0.182)	(0.168)	(0.142)	(0.164)
PARTY	−1.225	−0.250		−1.164	
	(0.303)	(0.130)		(0.291)	
IDEOL	0.819		−0.011	0.778	
	(0.228)		(0.099)	(0.217)	
COM	0.728	0.675	0.679	0.756	0.680
	(0.227)	(0.224)	(0.223)	(0.200)	(0.222)
PACMONEY	0.037	0.042	0.038		0.038
	(0.040)	(0.040)	(0.040)		(0.040)
STRONGDIS	−0.072	−0.078	−0.077		−0.077
	(0.029)	(0.029)	(0.029)		(0.029)
WEAKDIS	0.130	0.060	0.060		0.061
	(0.071)	(0.068)	(0.069)		(0.068)
Ln Likelihood	−251.45	−258.04	−259.87	−255.92	−259.88

$N = 411$.

Estimated asymptotic standard errors in parentheses.

bers were more likely to favor the amendment, *ceteris paribus,* than non-members (indeed, committee members voted 30 to 18 in favor[42]). Money from PACs does not appear to have had a significant, independent association with voting Yea.[43]

We see that the coefficient on STRONGDIS is negative and quite precisely estimated in all the specifications. Both the estimated coefficient and its standard error are insensitive to which of the political variables are included in the specification. We can say with some confidence, therefore, that the probability of voting *against* raising the FSLIC borrowing limit was significantly higher, *ceteris paribus,* for members from states where the average number of healthy thrifts in a district was higher. The effect of the presence of sick thrifts is somewhat ambiguous; though the estimate of β_6 is positive, it is much less precisely estimated than β_5.

To get a sense of the importance of the thrift constituency variables, we used the specification in column one of Table 5.4 to compute the

42. That this may have involved strategic voting by at least some committee members has not escaped our attention. All members who, in committee, had voted to keep the borrowing limit at $15 billion, voted for the St Germain amendment on the floor. Five members (including St Germain) who had voted to reduce the limit from $15 billion to $5 billion in committee, switched their position and voted for the St Germain amendment on the floor.

43. It should be recalled that PACMONEY is an imprecise and almost certainly understated measure of actual contributions (see footnote 39). It is not clear how the "true" measure and our measure would be correlated.

probability of voting Yea on the amendment[44] for two types of hypothetical congressmen not on the House Banking committee. One is a Democrat whose IDEOL has the median value for all Democrats (0.745); the other is a Republican at the median of Republican IDEOL (-0.394). For each of these congressmen, Table 5.5 shows P, the estimated probability of voting Yea, as the value of WEAKDIS or STRONGDIS varies.

Not surprisingly, P is generally below 0.5, reflecting the fact that the amendment lost by a two-to-one majority among noncommittee members. As noted in column one of Table 5.5, for our hypothetical Democrat, P = 0.305 when PACMONEY, STRONGDIS, and WEAKDIS are at their sample mean values (for the Republican, P = 0.394). Moving from the mean value of STRONGDIS ($\approx$ 5) to its lowest value in the sample (= 1), increases the probability of a Yea vote by about 33 percent, to P = 0.414. On the other hand, a change from column one to a STRONGDIS = 10 (a change of about two standard deviations from the mean), reduces P by

Table 5.5   Probability of Yea Vote on St Germain Amendment to HR 27

	1 Means	2 Low STRONGDIS	3 High STRONGDIS	4 Low WEAKDIS	5 High WEAKDIS
Democrat at median Democrat IDEOL	0.305	0.414	0.192	0.258	0.397
Republican at median Republican IDEOL	0.394	0.510	0.265	0.341	0.492

Computations are based on estimates in column one of Table 4.

NOTES:

For all computations, COM = 0.

Median IDEOL for Democrats = 0.745.

Median IDEOL for Republicans = -0.456.

Maximum value of IDEOL = 1.34; minimum value of IDEOL = -1.41.

Column 1: Economic variables at their means:

    PACMONEY = 1.112;

    STRONGDIS = 5.032;

    WEAKDIS = 1.087.

Column 2: STRONGDIS = 1 and PACMONEY and WEAKDIS at their means.

Column 3: STRONGDIS = 10 and PACMONEY and WEAKDIS at their means.

Column 4: WEAKDIS = 0 and PACMONEY and STRONGDIS at their means.

Column 5: WEAKDIS = 3 and PACMONEY and STRONGDIS at their means.

---

44. Column one is the specification that follows directly from our discussion. Likelihood ratio tests of comparisons with the results of the other columns also argue in favor of the column one specification.

about one-third, to $P = 0.192$. Changes for the Republican are similar, though less pronounced. The table displays similar calculations for changes in WEAKDIS, which go in the opposite direction.

To summarize, the condition of thrifts in the congressman's state was clearly related to his legislative preferences in voting on the key amendment in the recapitalization debate. Because the number of healthy thrifts exceeded that of weak thrifts in most states (by more than a factor of two in many cases), the effect of STRONGDIS predominated for most congressmen. The net effect, by our estimates, was to reduce the probability of a Yea vote in nearly all districts.

There were no comparable roll calls in the Senate. Presuming that similar forces operated in that chamber, our findings are consistent with Proxmire's willingness effectively to veto legislation in 1986, and with his intransigence throughout the FSLIC debate. In a state with only healthy thrifts, any constituency pressure he faced on the issue would be in the direction of delaying recapitalization or reducing its level.

After the defeat of the St Germain amendment, HR 27 was adopted by the House, 402 to 6. There were no other controversial amendments to the bill reported by the committee. The Senate had also approved its committee's bill (S 790) with only minor changes. This lack of controversy on the floor provides additional evidence for our thesis that there was not a significant constituency for confronting the full magnitude of the thrift problem or to curtail—rather than extend—forbearance. Even a small group of dissenters can require roll call votes, forcing their opponents to go on record against a position, while the dissenters signify their concern on the issue. The virtual absence of roll call votes on the thrift issue in 1986–87 is like Sherlock Holmes's dog that did not bark in the night. It is mute testimony to the fact that members of Congress did not believe there was an audience to whom it was worth sending stronger signals about the thrift problem.[45]

Compromise in Conference: The Competitive Equality Banking Act

As the House and Senate conference committees prepared to meet to resolve differences between the two bills, Administration spokesmen indicated that the President was seriously considering a veto of any bill that did not raise the recapitalization limit or—more important—relax the restraints on nonbank banks. As to raising the FSLIC limit, Proxmire "told an industry group . . . that the Treasury Department and the bank

---

45. In 1986 there was one roll call vote dealing with thrifts in the House; there were none in the Senate. In 1987, aside from final passage, there were two roll call votes on HR 27 in the House and two on S 790 in the Senate.

board are exaggerating the urgency of the FSLIC's problem and that he would not be pressed into quick action."[46]

By the end of July, as conferees were meeting, the General Accounting Office was reporting that FSLIC was $6 billion in the red and was confronting future claims up to $50 billion. In an agreement with the Administration, leaders of the conference committees agreed to raise the FSLIC borrowing limit to $10.8 billion, with not more than $3.75 billion to be raised in any one year. The forbearance provisions were left intact. In early August, both chambers passed the conference report (the House by 382 to 12 and the Senate by 96 to 2).[47] The President signed the Competitive Equality Banking Act on August 10, 1987.

The final legislation reinforced continued forbearance by allowing thrifts in farm and oil-patch states to continue to use lenient regulatory accounting practices adopted in 1982. Thrifts in these areas (and other areas deemed economically depressed) would also be allowed to stay open with a ½ percent capital-asset ratio, instead of the 3 percent required by existing law. The Act also explicitly reaffirmed the commitment that the "full faith and credit" of the U.S. government stands behind the FSLIC. Given the limited amount of new FSLIC funding relative to the magnitude of the thrift insolvency problem, the Act ensured that many failing thrifts would have considerably more time to gamble for resurrection. The crisis would grow.

The Thrift Debacle and Beyond.   The policy of forbearance did not, of course, lead to the resurrection of the zombie thrifts. Instead, as many economists had warned, the losses incurred by thrifts gambling for resurrection continued to escalate. The net income of the thrift industry for 1988 was − $12.0 billion, down from − $7.8 billion in 1987. Barth et al. (1989) report that the estimated cost of the 205 thrift resolutions begun in 1988 is $31.8 billion. Over half of these thrifts had been GAAP-insolvent for more than three years before they were closed or merged. At year-end 1988, there were 364 thrifts that were insolvent but still open. Many of these thrifts had been insolvent for a long time—some for as long as ten years (Barth et al., 1990)!

---

46. *New York Times,* May 5, 1987.

47. At first, the U.S. Savings League announced that it would oppose the compromise, saying that the borrowing limit was excessive. Given the GAO report, however, it was unlikely that many congressmen would have been willing to reopen the issue for a major floor fight. Final passage of the bill in the House did require a parliamentary maneuver. "Because the conference report broke new ground, beyond the scope of either the House or Senate's original bills, it was vulnerable to a point of order on the House floor. St Germain appealed to the Rules Committee for a waiver of this and other procedural points that might have deterred final passage. In the end, the Rules Committee granted the waivers on a voice vote" (*Congressional Quarterly,* 1988, p. 636).

Congress did not return to the thrift problem in 1988. By the time the woes of FSLIC reappeared on the legislative agenda after the 1988 elections (in which they played little or no role), the costs of delay and forbearance were increasingly evident to nearly everyone. The 1989 "bail-out" (Financial Institutions Reform, Recovery, and Enforcement Act or FIRREA) was enacted in the context of predictions that the liabilities facing FSLIC were expected to exceed $200 billion. [48] FIRREA and its legislative history are beyond the scope of this paper. But its enactment was necessitated by the legislative failures of the previous five years.

It is now widely recognized that a policy of forbearance under the existing structure of deposit insurance has been a prime contributor to the escalation of the thrift debacle, but the political foundations for this behavior are not so widely appreciated. This paper has pointed to these foundations as being rooted in the logic of the connections between elected officials and regulatory policy. By this view, regulatory agencies are viewed not as autonomous decision makers, but as closely tied to the political system. Constituency pressures work on regulators through the (often implicit) connections with politicians.

The legislative response to the problems of the thrift industry in the 1980s is an excellent example of how this process works. In summary, we note the following:

1. The political process provides at least tacit support for regulatory policy when the policy is consistent with the preferences of active constituent groups. This characterized policy toward thrifts until the late 1970s.

2. Significant changes in the economic environment typically lead to constituency pressures for regulatory change. This change may be initiated by the regulatory agency, but to be sustainable, it must meet congressional approval. The 1982 legislative response to the erosion of thrift profitability—deregulation coupled with forbearance for sick thrifts—can be seen in this light.

3. Regulatory change resisted by active constituencies and not supported by other active constituencies rarely succeeds. In 1985 the FHLBB appeared to be deviating from its earlier course. The 1986 stalemate in refinancing FSLIC, and the 1987 legislation worked—through delay, direct intervention, and explicit limitation on FSLIC resources—to rein in the FHLBB.

4. The emergence of constituencies for whom an issue becomes more salient can alter legislative preferences. As the scale of insolvencies grew,

---

48. Some observers have noted that FIRREA does not address many of the fundamental problems facing the industry. See, for example, Barth and Brumbaugh, 1990; Scott, 1989b.

depositor concern over FSLIC solvency also mounted. By late 1988, the policy preferences of the insolvent thrifts (in favor of continued forbearance) were more strongly opposed by concerns about the viability of deposit-insurance guarantees. As our empirical results on the St Germain amendment suggest, this would lead to an increase in support for larger levels of FSLIC capitalization. Moreover, once the required funding exceeded an amount that could be covered mostly by assessments on the industry (around $15–$20 billion over five years), healthy thrifts would no longer oppose *additional* amounts. The financing costs of such increments would come from general revenues; deposit guarantees financed in this way would benefit healthy thrifts.

Information and Policy Choice

It is sobering to note that the political behavior surrounding the thrift debacle is absolutely ordinary. Through 1988, congressmen behaved as they do in ordinary circumstances: paying solicitous attention to active, well organized interests, provided that the readily apparent costs to their other constituents were not noticeably high.

It is an intriguing question whether congressmen would have acted differently had they "really known" in 1986 that delay, forbearance, and intervention would lead to a $400-billion (or more) debacle. If by "really known," we mean that there was a widely shared consensus held by broad constituencies, then the answer to the question would probably be "Yes." But this was not the situation. It is no doubt correct to say that any economist who thought seriously about the situation would have seen that the combination of forbearance and deposit insurance was a recipe for disaster. Some economists actually said so, within the regulatory agency and outside it.

But the more widespread belief, reinforced by constituency pressures, was that—as in 1982–84—the problem would abate, rather than explode. To a large extent, of course, this perception was created by the very process of forbearance the politically endorsed policies made possible. Accounting procedures and regulatory reporting effectively minimized the magnitude of the losses. This put most congressmen in the position of "not knowing" the consequences of forbearance. The lack of an active constituency against forbearance (together with knowledge that agencies often cry "wolf") allowed congressmen to act in standard ways, that is, intervening in the regulatory process on behalf of their constituents. Thus, even in the face of the GAO predictions that FSLIC was facing a $50-billion problem in 1987 nothing near this level of recapitalization was ever on the political agenda in that year. Nor was there any consideration of restructuring the guarantees under deposit insurance.

Beyond the Thrift Debacle

Given the nature of incentives facing politicians, it is extremely difficult for Congress to deal at a sufficiently early stage with emerging policy problems that may turn into catastrophes if left unattended. Unless they can claim credit today for actions to stem the crisis, congressmen face great difficulties in bucking the current set of interest group forces. Perversely, even when congressmen know that policy crises are emerging, they may have to wait for the crisis to occur before they can take and be rewarded for remedial actions. Part of the foundation for this tendency is that individual legislators are not seen by their voters as playing a role in the problem. They are not penalized for letting the problem grow.

These considerations are particularly relevant because many aspects of the thrift debacle appear now to be replicated in several other financial problems that loom on the congressional horizon—the solvency of commercial banks, farm-loan guarantee programs, and various government-guaranteed pension systems.[49] If the wrong lessons are drawn from the thrift debacle, similar crises may reappear in new settings.

It is tempting to explain the thrift debacle as a story about greed, fraud, and criminal behavior. Surely that *is* part of the story. It is also tempting to argue that this was a case of regulators in bed with the industry they were supposed to oversee. This certainly also played a role. But underlying these factors is the essential component: Congress sanctioned regulatory forbearance and actively intervened against it when regulators sought a new, more restrictive path.

To argue that the next potential crisis will unfold differently, one would need to demonstrate that the structure or incentives have changed. It is possible that, in commercial banking, for example, healthy firms will behave differently than such firms did in the thrift industry. They may perceive that early action to deal effectively with insolvencies is in the long-run interest of the rest of the industry, but it is also possible that, in each case, the regulated interests will remain major constituents of politicians and will argue against forceful regulators.[50] Will politicians be more wary? The answer to this depends on the degree to which currently diffuse interests—generally, taxpayers as a group—see their representatives as having played a major role in the crisis. Moving the focus to shifty opera-

---

49. Commercial banks are the most directly related concern. See Starobin, 1989, and Brumbaugh et al., 1989.

50. As of this writing, congressmen from New England have called bank regulators to task for being too vigorous in dealing with commercial banks with weak balance sheets (*Wall Street Journal,* April 12, 1990). While gratifyingly consistent with our thesis, such a development hardly bodes well for taxpayers in the 1990s.

tors in the industry or blaming incompetent or biased regulators, obscures the political source of the crisis.

REFERENCES

Adams, James Ring, *The Big Fix: Inside the S&L Scandal,* Wiley (New York), 1989.

Barth, James R., Philip F. Bartholomew, and Michael G. Bradley, "The Determinants of Thrift Institution Resolution Costs," *Journal of Finance,* vol. 45, July 1990, pp. 731–54.

Barth, James R., Philip F. Bartholomew, and Carol J. Labich, "Moral Hazard and the Thrift Crisis: An Empirical Analysis," *Consumer Finance Law Quarterly Report,* 44(1), 1990, 22–34.

Barth, James R., and Michael G. Bradley, "Thrift Deregulation and Federal Deposit Insurance," *Journal of Financial Services Research,* vol. 2, September 1989, pp. 231-59.

Barth, James R., and R. Dan Brumbaugh, Jr., "The Continuing Bungling of the Savings and Loan Crisis: The Rough Road from the Legislation of 1989 to the Reform of Deposit Insurance," *Stanford Law & Policy Review,* vol. 2, May 1990, pp. 58–67.

Barth, James R., R. Dan Brumbaugh, Jr., Daniel Sauerhaft, and George H. K. Wang, "Insolvency and Risk-Taking in the Thrift Industry: Implications for the Future," *Contemporary Policy Issues,* Fall, 1985a:1–32.

Barth, James R., R. Dan Brumbaugh, Jr., Daniel Sauerhaft, and George H. K. Wang, "Thrift Institution Failures: Causes and Policy Issues," in *Proceedings of a Conference on Bank Structure and Competition,* Federal Reserve Bank of Chicago (Chicago), 1985b, pp. 184–216.

Barth, James R., and James L. Freund, *The Evolving Financial Services Sector, 1970–1988.* Office of Thrift Supervision (Washington, D.C.), 1989.

Benston, George J., et al., *Blueprint for Restructuring America's Financial Institutions,* Brookings Institution (Washington, D.C.), 1989.

Brumbaugh, R. Dan, Jr., *Thrifts Under Siege: Restoring Order to American Banking,* Ballinger (Cambridge, Mass.), 1988.

Brumbaugh, R. Dan, Jr., and Andrew S. Carron, "The Thrift Industry Crisis: Causes and Solutions," *Brookings Papers on Economic Activity,* 1987, pp. 349–88.

Brumbaugh, R. Dan, Jr., Andrew S. Carron, and Robert E. Litan, "Cleaning Up the Depository Institutions Mess," *Brookings Papers on Economic Activity,* 1989, pp. 243–95.

Brumbaugh, R. Dan, Jr., and Eric I. Hemmel, *Federal Deposit Insurance as a Call Option: Implications for Depository Institutions,* Office of Policy and Economic Research, Federal Home Loan Bank Board (Washington, D.C.), October, 1984.

Carron, Andrew S., and R. Dan Brumbaugh, Jr., "The Viability of the Thrift Industry," *Housing Policy Debate,* vol. 2, Issue 1, 1991, pp. 1-24.

Congressional Quarterly, 1987 CQ Almanac, CQ Press (Washington, D.C.), 1988.

Denzau, Arthur T., and Michael C. Munger, "Legislators and Interest Groups: How Unorganized Interests Get Represented," *American Political Science Review,* 80, 1986, 89–106.

Ferejohn, John A., "Logrolling in an Institutional Context: A Case Study of Food Stamp Legislation," in *Congress and Policy Change,* G. C. Wright, L. N. Rieselbach, and L. C. Dodd, eds., Agathon Press (New York), 1986, 223–53.

Ferejohn, John A., and Charles R. Shipan, "Congressional Influence on Administrative Agencies: A Case Study of Telecommunications Policy," in *Congress Reconsidered,* Lawrence C. Dodd and Bruce I. Oppenheimer, eds., C.Q. Press, 4th edition (Washington, D.C.), 1989.

Fiorina, Morris P., "Congressional Control of the Bureaucracy: A Mismatch of Incentives and Capabilities," in *Congress Reconsidered,* Lawrence C. Dodd and Bruce I. Oppenheimer, eds., C.Q. Press, 2d edition (Washington, D.C.), 1981.

———, *Congress: Keystone of the Washington Establishment.* Yale University Press, 2d edition (New Haven), 1989.

Fiorina, Morris P., and Roger G. Noll, "Voters, Bureaucrats and Legislators: A Rational Choice Perspective on the Growth of Bureaucracy," *Journal of Public Economics,* 9, 1978, 239–54.

Gilligan, Thomas W., William J. Marshall, and Barry R. Weingast, "Regulation and the Theory of Legislative Choice: The Interstate Commerce Act of 1887," *Journal of Law and Economics,* 32, 1989, 35–62.

Jackson, Brooks, *Honest Graft.* Knopf (New York), 1988.

Jacobson, Gary C., "Running Scared: Elections and Congressional Politics in the 1980s," in *Congress: Structure and Policy,* Mathew D. McCubbins and Terry Sullivan, eds., Cambridge University Press (Cambridge), 1987.

Kane, Edward J., *The Gathering Crisis in Federal Deposit Insurance,* MIT Press (Cambridge, Mass), 1985.

———, "The High Cost of Incompletely Funding the FSLIC's Shortage of Explicit Capital," *Journal of Economic Perspectives,* 3, 1989a, 31–47.

———, *The S&L Insurance Mess: How Did It Happen?* Urban Institute Press (Washington, D.C.), 1989b.

———, "The Unending Deposit Insurance Mess," *Science,* 27, 1989c, 451–6.

Kiewiet, D. Roderick, and Mathew D. McCubbins, The Logic of Delegation: *Congress and The Spending Power,* University of Chicago Press, 1991.

Mayhew, David, *Congress: The Electoral Connection,* Yale University Press (New Haven), 1974.

McCubbins, Mathew D., and Thomas Schwartz, "Congressional Oversight Overlooked: Police Patrols vs. Fire Alarms," *American Journal of Political Science,* 28, 1984, 165–79.

McCubbins, Mathew D., Roger G. Noll, and Barry R. Weingast, "Structure and Process, Politics and Policy: Administrative Arrangements and the Political Control of Agencies," *Virginia Law Review,* 75, 1989, 431–82.

Meltzer, Allan, "Major Issues in the Regulation of Financial Institutions," *Journal of Political Economy,* 75 (supplement), 1967, 482–501.

———, "The Thrift Industry in the Reagan Era," in *Managing Interest Rate Risk in the Thrift Industry: Proceedings of the Seventh Annual Conference,* Federal Home Loan Banks (San Francisco), 1981, pp. 5–13.

Moe, Terry M., "Control and Feedback in Economic Regulation: The Case of the NLRB," *American Political Science Review,* 1985, 1094–116.

————, "The Politics of Bureaucratic Structure," in *Can the Government Govern?* John E. Chubb and Paul E. Peterson, eds., Brookings Institution (Washington, D.C.), 1989.

Pilzer, Paul Zane, with Robert Dietz, *Other People's Money: The Inside Story of the S&L Mess,* Simon and Schuster (New York), 1989.

Pizzo, Stephen P., Mary Fricker, and Paul Muolo, *Inside Job: The Looting of America's Savings and Loans,* McGraw-Hill (New York), 1989.

Poole, Keith T., and Howard Rosenthal, "Patterns of Congressional Voting," *American Journal of Political Science,* vol. 35, February 1991, pp. 228–78.

Romer, Thomas, and Howard Rosenthal, "Political Resource Allocation, Controlled Agendas, and the Status Quo," *Public Choice,* 33(4), 1978, 27–43.

Romer, Thomas, and Howard Rosenthal, "Modern Political Economy and the Study of Regulation," in *Public Regulation: New Perspectives on Institutions and Policies,* E. E. Bailey, ed., MIT Press (Cambridge, Mass.), 1987, 73–116.

Scott, Kenneth E., "Deposit Insurance and Bank Regulation," *Business Lawyer,* 44, 1989a, 907.

————, "Never Again: The S&L Bailout Bill," manuscript, 1989b.

Sinclair, Barbara, "House Majority Leadership in the Late 1980s," in *Congress Reconsidered,* Lawrence C. Dodd and Bruce I. Oppenheimer, eds., C.Q. Press (Washington, D.C.) 4th edition, 1989.

Starobin, Paul, "Will the Banks Be Next?" *National Journal,* December 30, 1989.

Weicher, John C., "The Future of the Housing Finance System," in *Restructuring Banking & Financial Services in America,* William S. Haraf and Rose Marie Kushmeider, eds., American Enterprise Institute (Washington, D.C.), 1988, pp. 296–342.

Weingast, Barry R., "The Congressional-Bureaucratic System: A Principal-Agent Perspective (with Applications to the SEC)," *Public Choice,* 44, 1984, 147–91.

Weingast, Barry R., and Mark J. Moran, "Bureaucratic Discretion or Congressional Control? Regulatory Policymaking by the Federal Trade Commission," *Journal of Political Economy,* 91, 1983, 765–800.

White, Lawrence J., "The Reform of Federal Deposit Insurance," *Journal of Economic Perspectives,* 3, 1989, 11–29.

Woerheide, Walter J., *The Savings and Loan Industry,* Quorom Books (Westport, Conn.), 1984.

CHAPTER 6

Financial Innovation and the Provision of Liquidity Services

Gary Gorton

Finance Department,
The Wharton School,
University of Pennsylvania

and

George Pennacchi

Department of Finance,
University of Illinois

Historically, banks jointly produced two types of services, credit services (loan making) and liquidity services (transactions). There have been some economies of scope in the provision of credit and liquidity, but combining them has also been problematic. Financing nonmarketable bank loans with demandable liabilities exposes banks to panics and has led to government intervention in the form of deposit insurance and bank regulation. In this essay, we offer reasons why credit and liquidity services were jointly produced. Then we provide a variety of evidence which suggests that technological change and competition, and the associated creation of new markets and institutions, are leading to a natural splitting up of these two services. The private provision of liquidity can occur via mechanisms other than banks and, what is important, may require very little government intervention. We conclude that bank regulation should not attempt to keep credit and liquidity services bound together.

INTRODUCTION

Must banks forever be regulated? Should they be regulated in essentially the same manner as in the past, perhaps with some minor modifications? Surely the world's financial system is much different now than when the basic public policies toward banks were created in the 1930s. The debate about reform and redesign of these policies, however, often fails to recognize such changes. Instead, discussions usually presume that the economy's credit and liquidity services are being performed, and will continue to be performed, by banks as they have been historically.

The traditional view considers banks to be flawed institutions. The problem is that banks finance nonmarketable bank loans with short-maturity debt (demand deposits). In the absence of government deposit insurance, this can lead to banking panics. Given that this combination of nonmarketable assets and demandable liabilities is necessary, yet problematic, then the reform of deposit insurance and bank regulation should be confined to minor modifications of the existing system. In this essay we argue that such a viewpoint may well be misguided. Technological change in the production and transmission of information, and associated new markets and contracts, are leading to a separation of nonmarketable assets and demandable liabilities. Commercial banking, as it has been traditionally viewed, is becoming a significantly smaller component of our financial system. This paper discusses evidence of fundamental change in the provision of credit and liquidity services and considers the implications for bank regulation.

In designing bank regulations some understanding of the effects of technological change would seem to be important. If there are forces which are naturally leading to a split between the activities of creating loans and issuing demandable liabilities, then bank regulations which prevent such a separation are likely to be inefficient and counterproductive. The rationale for traditional bank regulation may no longer exist. Regulations which are inappropriate for the current technological setting can lead to worse outcomes than those which the regulations were designed to prevent. In fact, the demise of the FSLIC and the declining competitiveness of U.S. commercial banks forcefully suggest that the costs of regulatory mistakes can, minimally, be of the same order of magnitude as the historical costs of banking panics.

We first briefly review some recent theoretical work on the economic functions of banks, as a basis for understanding why banks historically combined nonmarketable assets with demandable debt liabilities. The basic point is that investors can rely on a bank to provide credit-enhancing services if the bank holds a diversified portfolio of loans financed by senior debt claims (bank debt held by investors). Because the risk of these senior claims is less than the risk of the typical loan that backs them, they are natural candidate securities to be used for transactions. The risk of these senior claims can be lowered even further, that is, they can be made even more liquid, if their maturity is the shortest possible (demandable). To the extent that these senior claims cannot be made completely riskless, government deposit insurance can further increase liquidity creation.

We next illustrate that banks which issue demandable debt are not the only way that credit and liquidity services can be privately produced. Technological change and deregulation have generated a growing number of institutional arrangements that provide these same services. We argue that this represents a fundamental movement away from the joint production of credit and liquidity services traditionally performed solely by banks. Furthermore, unlike banks making loans financed by demandable debt, these new arrangements separate the production of credit and liquidity services in a way that resolves the problem of banking panics. A by-product of these arrangements is the creation of money market instruments.

We then examine the feasibility of introducing a payments system in which checkable liabilities are provided by Money Market Mutual Funds (MMMFs), rather than by insured bank deposits. Examining the current economy, we adduce a variety of evidence to suggest that this is possible. We consider evidence about what the economy would look like under this new system. In particular, we ask whether the economy could privately produce more marketable securities which could be used to back MMMF shares. That is, we study the potential endogenous supply response if the economy demanded more liquidity. We also consider possible government policies that could augment liquidity creation.

WHAT SERVICES DO BANKS PERFORM?

Loans held by banks are generally considered nonmarketable, or illiquid, assets, meaning that they are difficult to value and hence difficult to trade. Banks finance these loans mainly with short-maturity debt that is often used for transactions purposes (for example, demand deposits). The combination of these two sets of activities, loan making (or credit enhancement) and the provision of transactions media (or liquidity creation), has been the source of problems. Without deposit insurance, bank debt holders may en masse demand redemption of their deposits in cash, as happened during the banking panics of the 1930s. Banks, holding nonmarketable loans, often could not satisfy these demands and became insolvent.[1]

The problems associated with financing nonmarketable assets with short-maturity debt led to the introduction of deposit insurance and bank regulation as solutions. To understand current banking issues, a logical starting point is to consider why these two banking activities have, histori-

---

1. For a background discussion of the history of panics in the United States, together with a survey of theories of panics, see Calomiris and Gorton, 1990.

cally, been combined. We will then consider what forces are currently driving them apart. We start by briefly reviewing some recent research on banks.

Bank Credit Services

Empirical evidence suggests that banks, in making loans to particular firms, provide a fundamentally different service than when firms issue debt or equity directly to capital market investors. In other words, for many firms, borrowing $10 million in the form of a bank loan is not a perfect substitute for borrowing $10 million by issuing a corporate bond. It appears that many firms benefit from borrowing from a bank rather than issuing bonds or stock even though banks are often handicapped by regulations which raise the cost of their funds.[2]

The consensus among academics appears to be that banks provide two main credit services. The first is the production of information about the borrower's credit risk. A brief summary of the argument is as follows. The risk of individual borrowers must be determined in order to be priced correctly, but determining this risk is costly. In a market setting it may be very difficult for investors to recover the costs of producing information about firms because other investors can take advantage of their research. For example, in order for an investor to profit from obtaining costly information about an undervalued firm, the investor would need to purchase the undervalued firm's securities at a "low" price, but in a market context it is difficult to keep information secret. This would signal to other investors that the firm is undervalued and they could "free ride" on the original investor's information production. The price of the firm's securities will be bid up and will no longer be undervalued; hence the return to information production will be negative, implying that no investor would engage in the activity. Even without the free riding problem, there would be a costly duplication of effort if many investors produced the same information.

---

2. Such evidence is provided by James (1987) and Fama (1985). James finds that there is a pronounced difference in the market reaction to the announcement of bank loans and public traded corporate liabilities. The stock market reaction (that is, abnormal return) is negative on the announcement of offerings of common stock, preferred stock, convertible preferred stock, convertible bonds, and straight bonds (though the reaction is not always statistically significant). In the case of bank debt, however, James shows that there is a significant *positive* market reaction. Another point made by both Fama and James is that bank borrowers, not depositors, appear to bear the cost of bank reserve requirements. This is demonstrated by comparing the yield spreads between bank CDs, which are subject to required reserves, and other money market securities. When reserve requirements were changed, there was no statistically significant change in the spreads, implying bank CD holders do not bear the cost of reserve requirements.

A bank can solve the problems of costly duplication of effort and of free riding by coordinating information production about credit risk. Instead of acting individually to produce information, the many investors purchase bank liabilities. Then the bank can act as the sole information producer.[3]

The second credit service that banks provide is monitoring firm managements. Bank loan contracts contain a large number of covenants which restrict the activities of firm managements. As with information production, enforcement of these restrictions is costly. Individual debt holders would free ride on each other's enforcement of the covenants and, as with information production, they would duplicate each other's efforts if they did monitor. But again, a bank, by coordinating the activities of many investors can effectively monitor firm managements.[4]

If banks produce information about firms and monitor firm managements, how do the investors who supply banks with funding produce information about banks and monitor bank managements? First, consider the case in which investors can observe a borrower's loan payment to the bank, which would be the case if the economy had well developed accounting and information systems. Then if the bank management (owners) issued to investors a senior (debt) claim on the loan while retaining a junior (equity) claim, the bank managers would retain a disproportionately large share of the credit risk of the borrower's loan. It then follows that the bank managers would also retain a disproportionately large share of the gains from producing information on and monitoring the borrower, thus giving the bank's management the incentive to efficiently provide credit services even though those services cannot be directly verified by the outside investors.

Now consider the case in which investors could not directly observe a borrower's loan payment to the bank, which would tend to be a realistic assumption for economies with less well developed accounting and information systems. Again suppose that the bank managers (owners) retain a junior (equity) claim while issuing a senior (debt) claim to the outside investors. But now assume that these claims are not claims on a single loan but claims on a well diversified portfolio of loans originated by the bank. If bank managers efficiently performed credit services, the debt claims on the bank's diversified portfolio of loans would not be very risky (aside from aggregate risk which everyone can observe). Debt holders would know that the bank had performed its functions if the bank debt was honored at par. If it was not, then it could only be due to the bank's failure to perform its functions (aside from aggregate risk). Hence bank debt holders could

---

3. These arguments are due to Campbell and Kracaw (1980) and Boyd and Prescott (1986).

4. See Diamond, 1984, and Gorton and Haubrich, 1987.

indirectly verify whether banks were efficiently performing these tasks and could take punitive action if they did not.[5]

To summarize, the production of credit services requires that a bank retain a significant share of the credit risk of borrowing firms. One way for a bank to do this is by issuing to outside investors (senior) debt claims while retaining a (junior) equity claim on the borrowers. This may explain why banks are relatively highly levered firms. But why should bank debt be of rather short maturity, for example, demand deposits? Financing non-marketable assets with demandable liabilities would appear to be a very undesirable combination since it exposes the bank to depositor runs. The following section offers a solution to this puzzle.

Bank Liquidity Services

In modern economies individuals and firms find it desirable to hold liquid assets for the purpose of transferring wealth. Some of these liquid assets are produced by the government, such as currency and Treasury bills, but liquid assets can also be privately created. Banks can play a role in this private creation of liquidity. They provide transactions services by creating liquid securities from illiquid assets. Let us consider the nature of these transactions services.

A transaction is an exchange between two parties. There is often some urgency to the transaction when, for example, one party experiences an unexpected need to consume some good or service quickly. This party, call him the "consumer," may encounter a problem when the transaction is made with another agent who has better information about the value of the asset being offered in exchange for consumption goods. This better informed agent or "insider" can take advantage of the urgency with which the consumer wants to trade. The consumer does not have time to determine the true value of the asset, so the insider can exchange an "unfair" number of consumption units for the asset, unbeknownst to the consumer.[6]

A situation in which some traders have superior information often leads to the absence of a market because the less well informed agents understand that they will experience trading losses at the hands of the better informed agents and refuse to trade with them.[7] Refusal is not always possible, however, if there are pressing needs to trade, say for consumption purposes. These less well informed agents would, therefore, have an incentive to design institutions and securities which can overcome the problem of trading losses to insiders.

---

5. This argument is due to Diamond, 1984.

6. The formal arguments are provided by Gorton and Pennacchi, 1990a, b.

7. This is the notion of a "lemons market" that was first introduced by Akerlof (1970) in reference to the failure of the market for used cars.

How could consumers prevent trading losses? A security whose value was always known would be very useful to consumers because they would suffer no information disadvantage. Such a security could then always be traded at this fair value. An asset with the property that it is easily valued would be a riskless security. We refer to the provision of liquidity as the creation of securities that are relatively easy to value and hence, are demanded for trading purposes. Assets which are idiosyncratic, such as rare paintings, are very illiquid because their value is difficult to determine and consequently better informed traders can earn more at the expense of uninformed traders.

Banks can create liquidity by producing riskless, or relatively riskless, securities. Two characteristics of banks' investment and financial structure that are optimal for the provision of credit services are coincidentally beneficial for the provision of liquidity services. First, as mentioned earlier, banks find it optimal to issue debt, as well as bank equity. Bank debt, or deposits, is a senior claim on the bank's assets, and hence possesses less rate-of-return risk than the bank's portfolio of assets. (Equity possesses more rate-of-return risk than the bank's portfolio of assets.) Second, banks find it optimal to hold fairly diversified portfolios of assets; thus a claim on the portfolio will have less risk than a claim on a single asset within the portfolio. Hence, because the provision of credit services requires banks to issue senior (debt) claims on diversified portfolios of loans, banks are in a much better position than most other firms to create a low-risk security. In other words, historically, there have been strong economies of scope between the creation of bank loans and the private production of liquid securities (bank debt). This explains why banks choose to provide transactions services while firms like General Motors might not.

Thus far we have argued that a bank which issues debt on a diversified portfolio of loans is an efficient mechanism for providing both credit and liquidity services, but we have not determined the bank's choice of debt maturity. It is clear, however, that the shorter the maturity of the debt, the smaller is its (default) risk.[8] Hence, bank debt can be made even more "liquid" if its maturity is made as short as possible. Although financing nonmarketable assets with demandable liabilities is problematic in that it exposes the bank to depositor runs, from the viewpoint of creating liquidity, demand deposits are the lowest-risk security that banks can issue. To resolve the problem of depositor runs, governments have chosen to intervene by insuring deposits. Note that federal insurance, by making deposits riskless, further augments the creation of liquidity. Thus, deposit insurance is similar to the government issuing Treasury bills, as it involves government creation of a riskless asset.

To summarize, the private creation of liquid securities requires that

---

8. Merton (1974) obtains this result using a contingent claims framework to value a firm's debt.

claims on baskets or portfolios of assets be produced such that these claims are relatively easy to value. Debt claims on highly diversified loan portfolios result in securities that are relatively riskless and hence satisfy the necessary requirements for a highly liquid security. From this point of view the combination of nonmarketable bank loans and demand deposits is clearly not an historical accident. The economies of scope between the two sets of bank activities will exist if the economy lacks alternative ways to produce sufficient amounts of liquidity. We now consider some alternative mechanisms of private liquidity creation.

TECHNOLOGY, COMPETITION, AND THE SEPARATION OF CREDIT AND LIQUIDITY

Our discussion of bank credit services concluded that for a bank to have an incentive to efficiently produce information on and monitor a borrower, it needed to retain a significant share of the borrower's credit risk. Traditionally, a bank did this, and combined it with the provision of liquidity services by issuing demandable debt claims to outside investors (bank depositors) on a portfolio of loans, with the bank retaining a junior claim in the form of bank equity. However, in this section we show that there are other contracts between a bank, a borrower, and investors that can result in the efficient production of credit services. What is important, these other contracts do not combine the direct creation of liquidity services with the creation of loans. By not using demandable liabilities to finance nonmarketable assets, these alternative contracts largely reduce the problems associated with bank panics that arise from banks' issuance of demand deposits.

We will show, however, that these alternative contracts do result in the creation of money market instruments. By holding a diversified portfolio of these money market securities, liquidity can be indirectly created by Money Market Mutual Funds (MMMFs) which issue demandable equity liabilities. This section describes these alternative contracts and offers explanations for their recent development. The order in which we describe these contracts corresponds to a progressively increasing separation of credit and liquidity services by banks.

Bank Certificates of Deposit

A close substitute to their traditional joint production of credit and liquidity services is for banks to provide credit services but stop short of the direct provision of liquidity by not issuing demandable debt but rather Certificates of Deposit (CDs).[9] CDs are issued by U.S. domestic banks as

____

9. It may be argued that banks that issue (uninsured) large CDs might still be subject to "panics." However, the impact of such a bank run (perhaps better referred to as a

well as by off-shore banks; in the latter case they are referred to as Euro-CDs. Large denomination CDs were first issued domestically in 1961 by Citibank. Volume grew rapidly throughout most of the 1960s as large CDs allowed banks to raise funds from good sized institutions and corporations. However, during periods when market interest rates rose above Regulation Q ceilings (for example, in 1969), the volume of outstanding domestic CDs declined (though the market for Euro-CDs expanded). Responding to the greater deposit market competition from unregulated intermediaries, such as MMMFs, interest rate ceilings on CDs were lifted in 1973 and their rapid growth resumed. Growth slowed again during the 1980s as banks and corporations increasingly found other sources of financing, such as loan sales and commercial paper. However, by yearend 1989, the Federal Reserve reported that large denomination time deposits in all U.S. banks exceeded $554 billion. Relative to domestic CDs, Euro-CDs are often a lower cost source of funding because they are free from the 3 percent reserve requirement imposed on nonpersonal domestic CDs.

Since CDs are generally not payable on demand, CD dealers make an over-the-counter secondary market in large denomination CDs. Approximately 35 dealers quote bid and ask prices on domestic CDs with the typical bid-ask spread being 5 basis points. At yearend 1985, daily transactions volume was about $1.5 billion in the domestic CD market and $2 billion in the Euro-CD market. [10] Undoubtedly, advances in computer and telecommunications technology that have reduced the costs of processing and transmitting information have helped make these secondary markets feasible. One reflection of the lower cost of producing information might well be the existence of a number of companies which rate bank CDs: Duff & Phelps, Inc.; McCarthy, Crisanti, & Maffei, Inc.; Moody's Investor Service, Inc.; and Standard & Poor's Corp.

Although large CDs do not offer the same high level of liquidity offered by checkable bank deposits, the emergence of an organized secondary market allows them to be easily valued since quoted prices can be continuously observed. Because CDs are easily valued, they are natural assets to be held by MMMFs, who can then issue demandable claims against these assets. Figure 6.1 shows that domestic and Euro-CDs make up almost 16 percent of the assets of MMMFs. Thus, MMMFs provide a vehicle for the creation of liquidity (checkable accounts) rather than banks directly creating liquidity via demand deposits. In a sense, MMMFs provide even greater (privately created) liquidity than a single demand-deposit-issuing

---

"bank walk") would surely be less disruptive, and is highly unlikely to have any monetary consequences. (We cannot believe that large CD holders would withdraw their funds at maturity and increase the demand for currency. More likely, their wealth would be transferred into another financial asset.) We view bank CDs as being similar to commercial paper (see the following discussion of finance companies). In any case, the arguments we will make for banking reform do not hinge on this point.

10. These figures are from Willemse, 1986.

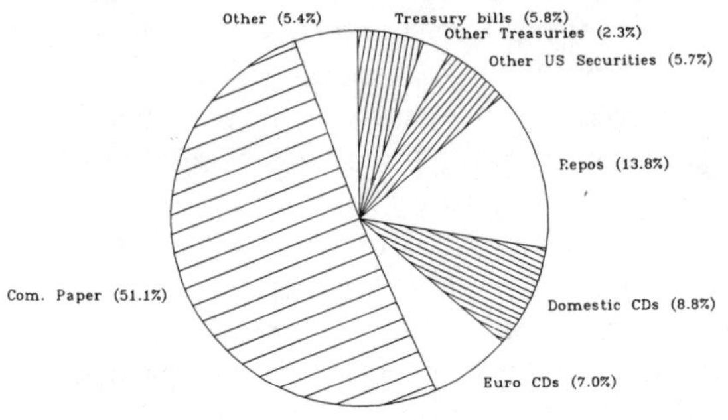

Figure 6.1　Composition of MMMF Assets, March 1990

Total assets of all Money Market Mutual Funds equaled $386,456 million.

SOURCE: "Trends in Mutual Fund Activity," The Investment Company Institute.

bank. Because MMMFs can hold a diversified portfolio of bank CDs, as well as other money market instruments, a MMMF equity claim will have less risk than the typical bank liability in the MMMF's portfolio.

Finance Companies

A finance company that makes loans financed by debt, such as commercial paper, is closely related to a commercial bank that makes loans financed by CDs. Broadly defined, the types of loans that banks and finance companies make are fairly similar. Categorizing loans into three types, business (including government), consumer, and residential, one finds that, as a whole, finance companies make a higher proportion of business loans than commercial banks (56 percent versus 40 percent), as well as a higher proportion of consumer loans (33 percent versus 20 percent), but a lower proportion of real estate loans (11 percent versus 40 percent).[11] Figure 6.2 shows the composition of finance companies' liabilities. Similar to commercial banks, they are highly levered, having an equity to asset ratio of 8.6 percent. Commercial paper accounts for approximately one third of their liabilities. Of course, this commercial paper is often held by MMMFs, representing the separate provision of liquidity services.

In terms of providing credit services, the main difference between finance companies and banks is the type of regulation to which they are subject. In one sense, finance companies illustrate the operation of banks

---

11. These figures reflect third quarter 1989 flow of funds data compiled by the Board of Governors of the Federal Reserve System.

Figure 6.2   Liabilities of Finance Companies, Third Quarter 1989

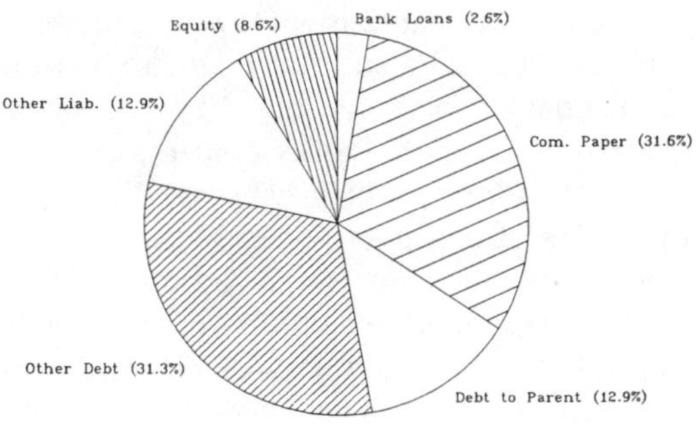

SOURCE: Board of Governors of the Federal Reserve System.

in which credit services, but not liquidity services, are permitted. [12] Operating costs at finance companies, especially the smaller ones, tend to be greater than those of commercial banks or thrifts, which is consistent with the notion that they tend to originate riskier loans requiring relatively greater information production and monitoring. This would seem to dispel the idea that demand deposits are somehow necessary or beneficial for the intensive provision of credit services. It is consistent with the idea that the provision of credit services facilitates the private creation of demandable liabilities (liquidity), but that the creation of demandable liabilities does not benefit the production of credit services. Finance companies give us a clear example of how banks' lending operations would be carried out under a system where the joint production of credit and insured liquidity services was disallowed.

Because finance companies are generally not permitted to issue insured deposits, they have been subject to less regulation in interstate branching and the types of loans and assets they may hold. Bank holding companies own approximately one quarter of finance companies and often use them to originate loans that may be costly or impossible for their bank subsidiaries to make. Finance companies are involved in numerous types of lending and raise funds from a variety of sources, as indicated in Figure 6.2. As of February 1990, total finance company assets equaled $464 billion, compared to $64 billion in 1970 and $202 billion in 1980. [13]

---

12. In 20 states, finance companies can be chartered as "industrial banks," in which case they may accept deposits. In aggregate, deposit liabilities account for less than 2 percent of all finance companies' liabilities, so we can safely ignore them in our discussion.

13. Board of Governors of the Federal Reserve System flow of funds data.

Commercial Paper Backed by Bank Credit Lines or Letters of Credit

A firm that issues commercial paper is somewhat different from our previous two examples. Investors who supply them funds do not usually have a claim on a bank or finance company, but they do have a direct claim on a firm issuing commercial paper. Banks continue to play a role in this market, however, by providing credit services in the form of loan commitments or standby letters of credit.

Firms that find it advantageous to issue commercial paper are generally larger, better known, and more creditworthy than firms depending primarily on bank loans for financing. One could argue that many of these firms could issue securities whose risk is known by investors to be low even without information production and monitoring by banks. Due in great part to technological change which has lowered the cost of acquiring information, a large amount of information about these firms is publicly available. As in the CD market, there are a number of companies which rate the credit risk of commercial paper issues, such as Duff & Phelps, Fitch Investors Service, McCarthy Crisanti & Maffei, Moody's Investor Service, and Standard and Poor's.

Almost all commercial paper is issued, however, with some type of assistance from banks. This assistance usually takes the form of a bank line of credit (loan commitment) extending to the date when the borrower is due to repay its commercial paper. In principle, if the company experiences trouble in repaying, it can then draw down its line of credit to pay the commercial paper holders. Under this scenario, the bank issuing the credit line is providing the commercial paper holders a guarantee against default by the borrowing firm. Since the bank is exposed to the borrowing firm's credit risk, it has the incentive to efficiently provide information on or monitor the borrower.

In practice, it is unclear how strong a guarantee is given when banks provide credit lines backing commercial paper. Bank loan commitment contracts usually contain a clause allowing the bank to legally withdraw its credit line if there is a "materially adverse change" in the condition of the borrowing firm. A bank provides a stronger guarantee when it issues an irrevocable standby letter of credit backing the firm's commercial paper. Approximately 8 percent of the amount of commercial paper outstanding is backed in this manner.[14] Under this type of contract the bank explicitly guarantees to pay back the commercial paper holders if the borrowing firm does not. As evidence of the greater credit service thus provided, commercial paper rating agencies assign the bank's credit rating to the commercial paper when it is backed by a letter of credit but assign the borrowing firm's credit rating when it is backed by a line of credit. Not surprisingly, less

---

14. See Rowe, 1986, for additional details regarding the commercial paper market.

creditworthy firms (those needing more of a bank's credit services) tend to back their commercial paper with standby letters of credit. It is interesting to note that insurance companies, as well as banks, provide letter-of-credit guarantees backing commercial paper. This indicates that the essence of bank credit services involves extending a guarantee or insurance to outside investors. The provision of funding is not really an essential function of banks.

Although the commercial paper market can be traced back to the early nineteenth century, only recently did it begin to be a major source of corporate financing. Greater deposit market competition, followed by the breakdown of Regulation Q (which set interest rates on bank deposits), increased banks' cost of funds and contributed to the growth of the commercial paper market. For banks which must pay market interest rates on deposits and are further burdened by the regulatory costs of required reserves and capital, the overall cost of funds make them uneconomical sources of funding. Funds provided by commercial paper investors avoid these regulatory costs, making this market attractive to firms that can gain access by virtue of their higher credit quality.

Figure 6.1 shows that commercial paper accounts for over half the assets held by MMMFs. Although the secondary market is not so active as with bank CDs, most primary commercial paper dealers stand ready to buy back their issues. Its short maturity, low risk, and publicly available credit ratings allow commercial paper to be easily valued, making it an attractive asset for MMMFs. The amount of commercial paper outstanding now exceeds $300 billion, making it the second largest U.S. money market, exceeded only by the Treasury bill market. Figure 6.3 shows the growth of commercial paper relative to commercial and industrial (C & I) bank loans. [15] Prior to the 1960s the ratio of commercial paper to C & I loans was less than 10 percent, whereas it currently exceeds 70 percent. This clearly represents a fundamental shift in corporate short-term financing, and a significant new source of liquidity.

Loan Sales

Our last example of the separation of credit and liquidity services is the loan sales market. This market can be divided into two categories: loans sold in pools, such as mortgages and consumer receivables, and loans sold individually, such as C & I loans. In both cases, banks originate these loans but funding is provided primarily by the investors who buy the loans or who buy shares in pools of the loans.

With the exception of pools of government guaranteed residential mortgages (for example, GNMA pools), pools of mortgages and consumer

---

15. Commercial paper issued by commercial banks or thrift holding companies is excluded from this comparison.

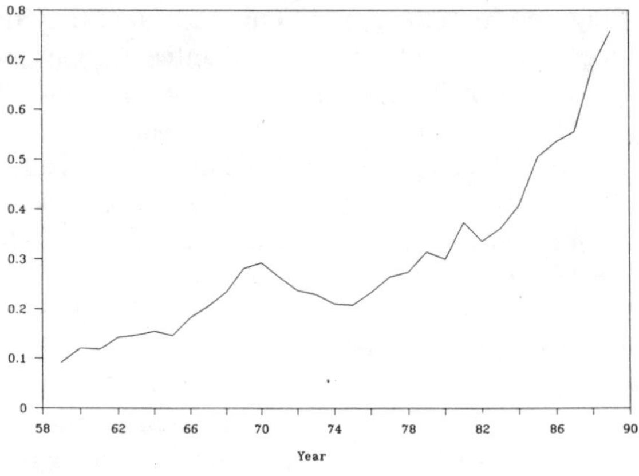

Figure 6.3   Ratio of Commercial Paper to C & I Loans

Commercial paper excludes bank-related issues.
SOURCE: Board of Governors of the Federal Reserve System.

receivables are sold with either a bank or an insurance company bearing a signficant share of the loans' default risk. This usually entails the originating bank retaining a junior (equity) share in the pool of loans and/or having a bank or insurance company issue a standby letter of credit backing the pool. Of course this practice comes as no surprise, since the retention of credit risk is a necessary feature of an incentive-efficient credit service contract.[16]

A bank faces more restrictive regulation in selling individual C & I loans. In order legally to remove a loan from its balance sheet, so the funds raised from loan buyers are not subject to required reserves and capital, the bank must sell the loan without recourse. This means that the bank cannot sell a senior share of the loan to loan buyers or provide a guarantee, such as a letter of credit. However, the bank can retain a limited portion of the loan's credit risk by selling only a portion of the loan, so that both the bank and loan buyers are given equity shares. In an analysis of C&I loan sales by a major money center bank, Gorton and Pennacchi (1989) found that, on average, the bank retained a 24 percent share of the loans it sold. Based on inferences from the loans' yields, they found that the bank retained a greater share of its riskier loans, as theory would predict.

The amount of C & I loan sales outstanding has grown from $26.7 billion in the second quarter of 1983 to $236.3 billion in the first quarter

16. For a formal derivation of this result, see Pennacchi, 1988.

of 1988. As with the commercial paper market, the growth in the loan sales market can be explained by increased competition in the deposit markets of certain banks. This increased competition, along with costly regulation, makes deposit funding unprofitable for many banks. [17] Banks are likely to produce some credit services for most loan sales, but the liquidity of loans sold is uncertain. Banks that sell loans will usually agree to buy them back if necessary, but the lack of explicit credit ratings on loans sold make them less attractive than commercial paper as an asset for MMMFs to hold.

IS A PAYMENTS SYSTEM BASED ON MONEY MARKET MUTUAL FUNDS FEASIBLE?

The previous section described a number of ways in which credit and liquidity services are currently being separated. In these examples, liquidity was created without resort to directly financing nonmarketable assets with demandable liabilities, as occurs when banks issue demand deposits. Rather, by-products of banks' credit services were money market securities that could then be packaged together as backing for MMMF shares. If these money market securities were available in sufficient quantities, then, in principle, an MMMF-based payments system would be preferable to our current system based on bank demand deposits. This is because bank provision of liquidity results either in occasional banking panics or in the necessity for government intervention in the form of deposit insurance and regulation. We can dispense with almost all bank regulation if financing via demand deposits is disallowed.

The key question then, in our view, concerns whether or not significant amounts of liquidity might be produced through mechanisms other than banking. Substituting an MMMF-based payments system for the current insured deposit-based system will, of course, lead to an increase in money funds' demand for money market instruments. A potential worry is that increased demand could lead to a large fall in short-term interest rates, possibly disrupting the financial system and the economy. Is this fear valid? The effect of the increased demand on the economy will depend on the equilibrium supply of money market instruments from corporations, in both domestic and foreign security markets. In addition, possible changes in the supply of money market instruments from federal, state, and local governments can have an effect on the resulting financial market equilibrium. The nature of these endogenous supply responses is the focus of this section of the paper. But first, let us examine the recent history of nonbank liquidity creation, as it may shed light on the nature of the supply of these instruments.

---

17. This explanation is given in Pennacchi, 1988. See Flannery, 1989, and James, 1988, for additional incentives for loan sales.

The Current Supply of Money Market Instruments

One potential indicator of nonbank liquidity is the volume of MMMF shares. Figure 6.4 gives a rough comparison of the evolution of MMMF shares versus bank liquidity, where bank liquidity is proxied by the volume of checkable deposits. The amount of these deposits surged in the early 1980s due to legislation allowing interest to be paid on these accounts and expanding thrifts' freedom to offer checking services. This rapid growth has leveled off in the last few years, however, whereas the growth of MMMFs seems to be returning to its explosive rate of the late 1970s. The rapid expansion of MMMF shares was interrupted only momentarily in the early 1980s as banks gained greater freedom to compete for funds. In general, the movements in these two series point to the growing relative importance of MMMF shares.

As mentioned previously, liquidity is generated by the government when it creates riskless securities. This is done in two ways, by the federal insurance of bank deposits and by the issuance of its own short-term default-free debt. If we wish to consider government created money market instruments as a potential security for backing MMMF shares, then it may be of interest to compare government insured bank liquidity with government and privately produced money market instruments. This is done in Figure 6.5. Assuming that all checkable bank deposits are officially or de facto insured by federal deposit insurance allows us to again proxy short-term insured bank liquidity by checkable deposits. Also shown in Figure

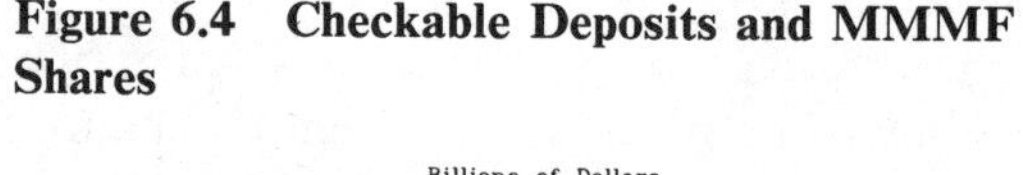

Figure 6.4   Checkable Deposits and MMMF Shares

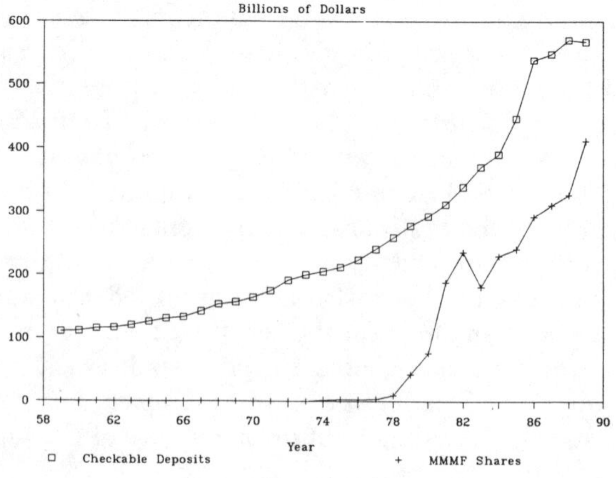

SOURCE: Board of Governors of the Federal Reserve System.

Figure 6.5   Checkable Deposits versus T Bills and CP

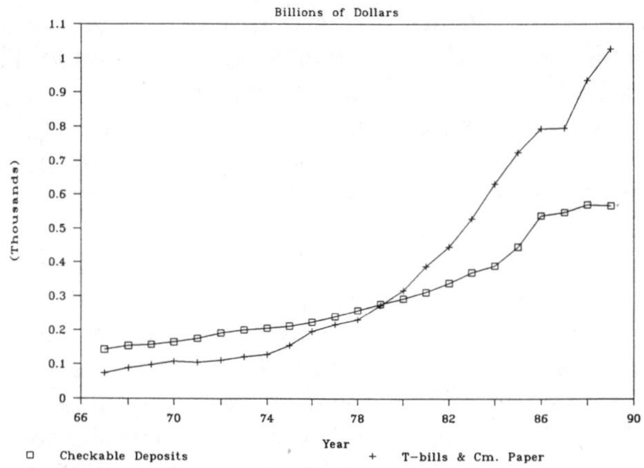

T bills include all marketable federal government debt held by private investors with a maturity of one year or less. Commercial paper excludes bank-related issues.

SOURCE: Board of Governors of the Federal Reserve System.

6.5 is the sum of marketable federal government debt with a maturity of less than one year (largely T bills) held by private investors and nonbank related commercial paper. Interestingly, the sum of Treasury bills and commercial paper was significantly smaller than checkable deposits until the late 1970s. However, in 1980 T bills and commercial paper surpassed the level of checkable bank deposits and is currently almost twice as large, $1,027 billion versus $568 billion in 1989.

General Equilibrium Effects of Introducing an MMMF-Based System

The preceding section was only suggestive of the feasibility of an MMMF-based payments system. Simply showing that the volume of T bills and commercial paper exceeds checkable bank deposits by a wide margin cannot be conclusive evidence. Since these money market instruments may already be satisfying some of the liquidity demands of the economy, the total volume of these instruments cannot be used as backing for newly formed MMMFs. It may, however, be the case that upon introduction of an MMMF-based system, more short-term, relatively riskless, debt would be privately created if there was a demand for it. The private sector may endogenously respond by supplying more. Another possibility is that the government could modify the given outstanding government debt toward shorter term securities.

It is not possible to predict with complete accuracy what would happen in a change to a new payments system, but there is at least some evidence that the amount of privately produced liquidity is elastic or, alternatively, that alterations of the average maturity structure of outstanding government debt would have no deleterious effect on the economy. This evidence comes from a Federal Reserve policy attempted in the early part of 1961 known as "Operation Twist." In this exercise the Federal Reserve attempted to twist the maturity structure of interest rates by raising yields on short maturity securities while simultaneously lowering yields on long-term securities. [18]

The basis of Operation Twist was the view that short-term debt is significantly more liquid than long-term debt and that the supplies of the two types of debt were subject to government manipulation. In other words, the Federal Reserve apparently believed in a version of the Segmented Markets Theory of the term structure of interest rates. The Federal Reserve conducted open market operations aimed at shortening the average term to maturity of the outstanding government debt. An increase in the supply of short-term debt was expected to exert upward pressure on short-term interest rates and the corresponding decrease in the supply of long-term debt was expected to lower long-term interest rates. [19]

Operation Twist was a unique experiment in that there was an exogenous shift in the relative supplies of debt of different maturity. If the government were successful in twisting the term structure, that would provide evidence for the Segmented Markets Theory, that is, for the inability of private markets to supply substitutes for long-term government debt. If the government were unsuccessful in twisting the term structure, then it would provide evidence for either of two, nonmutually exclusive alternatives. First, it could be evidence against the Segmented Markets Theory because the private economy could offset any action the government took through altering its supplies of the different types of securities. Second, perhaps the public might view long- and short-term debt as nearly perfect substitutes (as in the Expectations Theory of the term structure).

The basic conclusion as to the effectiveness of Operation Twist is that the government was unable to effect the term structure. The strategy was,

---

18. The policy was designed to contribute toward reducing the capital outflow from the United States, thus helping to mitigate an undesirable balance-of-payments problem. But, at the same time, by keeping long-term rates low, the policy could increase the flow of private investment. See "Bank Credit and Monetary Developments in 1964," *Federal Reserve Bulletin* 51, February 1955, 214–16.

19. In addition, there was a series of successive increases in the ceiling interest rates commercial banks were allowed to pay on time and savings deposits under Regulation Q.

in the words of Modigliani and Sutch (1966), "a total failure."[20] This implies either that the private economy can offset the effects of government actions through endogenous responses or that a policy of modifying the maturity structure of government debt would have no important effect on the economy. Either of these conclusions is important evidence that the economy is capable of adjusting to create a larger amount of the types of securities necessary to back MMMF liabilities.

Given the financial developments in the United States and around the world during the last two decades, the supply of short-term securities is almost surely even more elastic then it was in the early 1960s. Clearly, there is not only a domestic U.S. dollar-denominated short-term money market but an off-shore market, as well. Domestic and foreign firms issue debt in a variety of Eurodollar instruments.[21] A possible increased demand for money market instruments in the United States, that would begin to lower U.S. short-term rates, will not only induce domestically financed firms to switch from issuing long- to shorter-term debt, but it will also induce foreign and domestic firms to switch from Eurodollar issues to U.S. domestic market issues. Arbitrage opportunities prevent any significant differences in interest rates between these two markets. There is wide agreement among financial economists and practitioners that the domestic and Eurodollar money markets are highly integrated, such that they can really be considered a single market.[22]

Government Policies to Augment Liquidity

Whereas the previous section dealt with the private supply response to an increased demand for money market instruments, we now consider a corresponding government supply response. In particular, we would like to examine the amount of government liquidity that could be created to offset the possible net increase in private demand. Just as with Operation Twist, the government could shorten the maturity structure of its debt. The potential impact of this policy is illustrated in Figure 6.6, where checkable bank deposits are compared to the levels of Treasury bills and Treasury securities of all maturities. The current quantity of T bills is approximately equal to that of checkable deposits, but the supply of T bills could be

---

20. There is a long literature on Operation Twist and some minor disputes as to whether the policy was a total failure or not. See Modigliani and Sutch, 1966, 1967; Van Horne, 1966; Fand, 1966; and Van Horne and Bowers, 1968.

21. Goodfriend (1986) estimates that in December of 1985, the net size of the Eurodollar market was $1,251 billion.

22. As an example, see Kohlhagen, 1983. In addition, the observation that yields on a bank's domestic and Eurodollar CDs differ by, at most, 15 to 20 basis points suggests a high level of integration.

Figure 6.6   Checkable Deposits and Treasuries

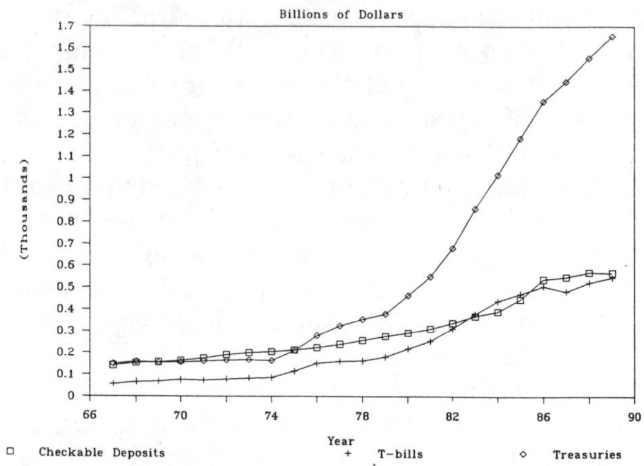

Treasuries include all marketable federal government debt held by private investors. T bills include all marketable federal government debt with a maturity of one year or less held by private investors.

SOURCE: Board of Governors of the Federal Reserve System.

---

increased significantly by converting longer maturity Treasury bonds and notes to T bills. Based on current levels of government debt, there is certainly wide scope for active government liquidity creation, should the supply of private liquidity be inadequate.

The extent of government liquidity creation, however, is not really constrained by the total size of its debt. For example, although few people would lose sleep over the possibility, consider the effect of continued government budget surpluses leading to a shrinkage of the government's debt. Would the amount of government liquidity also have to shrink? Not necessarily. Governments could still create liquidity by issuing T bills that would finance the purchase of (less liquid) private securities. What we have in mind is an operation very similar to that of the Federal National Mortgage Association (FNMA), which buys and holds private mortgages, financing its purchases by issuing its own debt.

THE IMPLICATIONS OF FINANCIAL INNOVATION FOR BANK REGULATION

In the last few decades, technological change and greater competition have spurred enormous financial innovation. New securities and markets are very apparent in many cases, but there seems to be less awareness of how these changes are transforming the banking industry. No doubt this is partly due to the fact that regulation has suppressed some of the manifestations of these changes.[23] We have presented some evidence which suggests that a separation between the two activities of credit enhancement and the production of transactions services appears to be developing. The opening of new markets, and the concomitant creation of new financial instruments, raise the prospect that liquidity can be created using baskets of marketable securities rather than nonmarketable bank loans. Moreover, even if the current amounts of marketable securities available to provide backing for transactions services appear insufficient, there is considerable evidence that the private economy would respond to such a shortfall by creating a greater volume of eligible private securities.

Attempting to understand the effects of financial innovation on banking is essential to any meaningful discussion of public policy toward banks. It is easy for policy reform to be passively reactive by responding to problems as they arise, rather than attempting to foresee them, but this is a mistake. A lesson from the thrift crisis is that policy making should not amount to driving while looking in the rearview mirror. In a regulated environment it is difficult to predict what the world would look like if it were regulated differently. Nevertheless, to judge the impact of regulatory reform, such predictions must be attempted.

Although we have not outlined any details of a proposal for banking reform, we wish to stress that the basis for banking reform ought to be a recognition that the root problem justifying traditional bank regulation is disappearing. Increasingly, credit and liquidity services are being separated, and this trend reflects a movement toward a more stable and efficient financial system. Public policy which assumes that these two services must remain bound together in one heavily regulated institution risks creating future crises.

REFERENCES

Akerlof, George, "The Market for Lemons: Qualitative Uncertainty and the Market Mechanism," *Quarterly Journal of Economics* 84, 1970, 488–500.

Boyd, John and Edward Prescott, "Financial Intermediary-Coalitions," *Journal of Economic Theory* 38, 1986, 211–32.

Calomiris, Charles, and Gary Gorton, "The Origins of Banking Panics: Models, Facts, and Bank Regulation," working paper, The Wharton School, University of Pennsylvania, 1990.

---

23. For example, in the absence of federal deposit insurance and regulations which restrict MMMFs from direct access to established payments networks, we believe that a much greater proportion of transactions would now be carried out through accounts resembling MMMFs rather than through bank demand deposits.

Campbell, Tim, and William Kracaw, "Information Production, Market Signalling and the Theory of Financial Intermediation," *Journal of Finance* 35:4, September 1980, 863–81.

Diamond, Douglas, "Financial Intermediation and Delegated Monitoring," *Review of Economic Studies* 51, 1984.

Fama, Eugene, "What's Different About Banks?" *Journal of Monetary Economics* 15, 1985.

Fand, David, "A Time-Series Analysis of the 'Bills-Only' Theory of Interest Rates," *Review of Economics and Statistics* 48, no. 4, November 1966, 361–71.

Flannery, Mark, "Capital Regulation and Insured Banks' Choice of Individual Loan Default Risks," *Journal of Monetary Economics* 24, 1988, 235–58.

Goodfriend, Marvin, "Eurodollars," in *Instruments of the Money Market,* T. Cook and T. Rowe, eds., Federal Reserve Bank of Richmond, 1986.

Gorton, Gary, and George Pennacchi, "Financial Intermediation and Liquidity Creation," *Journal of Finance* 45(1), 1990a, 49–72.

Gorton, Gary, and George Pennacchi, "Security Baskets and Index-Linked Securities," working paper, The Wharton School, University of Pennsylvania, 1990b.

Gorton, Gary, and George Pennacchi, "Banks and Loan Sales: Evidence of Implicit Contracts," working paper, University of Pennsylvania, 1989.

Gorton, Gary, and Joseph Haubrich, "Bank Deregulation, Credit Markets, and the Control of Capital," *Carnegie-Rochester Conference Series on Public Policy,* vol. 26, Spring 1987, 289–334.

James, Christopher, "The Use of Loan Sales and Standby Letters of Credit by Commercial Banks," *Journal of Monetary Economics* 22, 1988, 395–422.

————, "Some Evidence on the Uniqueness of Bank Loans," *Journal of Financial Economics* 19, 1987, 217–36.

Kohlhagen, Steven, "Overlapping National Investment Portfolios: Evidence and Implications of International Integration of Secondary Markets for Financial Assets," in *Research in International Business and Finance* 3, Hawkins and Levich, eds., JAI Press, 1983, 113–37.

Merton, Robert, "On the Pricing of Corporate Debt: The Risk Structure of Interest Rates," *Journal of Finance* 29, 1974, 449–70.

Modigliani, Franco, and Richard Sutch, "Innovations in Interest Rate Policy," *American Economic Review* 56, May 1966, 178–97.

Modigliani, Franco, and Richard Sutch, "Debt Management and the Term Structure of Interest Rates: An Empirical Analysis of Recent Experience," *Journal of Political Economy* 75, Supplement, August 1967, 569–89.

Pennacchi, George, "Loan Sales and the Cost of Bank Capital," *Journal of Finance* 43(2), 1988, 375–96.

Rowe, Timothy, "Commercial Paper," in *Instruments of the Money Market,* T. Cook and T. Rowe, eds., Federal Reserve Bank of Richmond, 1986.

Van Horne, James, "Interest-Rate Expectations, the Shape of the Yield Curve, and Monetary Policy," *Review of Economics and Statistics* 48, May 1966, 211–15.

Van Horne, James, and David Bowers, "The Liquidity Impact of Debt Management," *The Southern Economic Journal* 34, April 1968, 526–37.

Willemse, Rob, "Large Certificates of Deposits," in *Instruments of the Money Market,* T. Cook and T. Rowe, eds., Federal Reserve Bank of Richmond, 1986.

CHAPTER 7

Aggregate Shocks, Loan Losses, and Portfolio Concentrations: Lessons for Assessing Depository Institution Risk*

Robert S. Chirinko

Graduate School of Public Policy Studies,
University of Chicago

and

Gene D. Guill

Credit Policy,
Bankers Trust Company

The enormous problems facing the banking and thrift industries have concentrated attention on regulatory redesign, but these recent delibera-

---

*The authors would like to acknowledge the helpful comments from Dan Brumbaugh, our discussant, Catherine England, and other participants at the Center for Economic Policy Research Conference, and the expert research assistance by Michael Brien. Partial financial support from the Federal Home Loan Bank Board under Grant No. C88066 is gratefully acknowledged. All errors, omissions, and conclusions remain the sole responsibility of the authors, and do not necessarily reflect the views of the organizations with which they are associated.

tions have not given sufficient attention to the sensitivity of depository institution risk to aggregate (or macroeconomic) shocks. This study offers a quantitative examination of aggregate shocks that impact depository institution risk in two important ways. First, aggregate shocks create covariation between assets held in the portfolio. Our results demonstrate that this covariation is of first order importance; when covariation is ignored, risk exposure can be underestimated by 70 to 800 percent. Second, aggregate shocks will have a direct effect on the economy, and hence on depository institution performance. Based on our empirical evidence, we conclude that current initiatives and deliberations must be more sensitive to the effects of aggregate shocks on depository institutions laid vulnerable by past policy mistakes. Piecemeal approaches to regulatory reform that fail to recognize these interrelationships will ultimately prove inadequate to the tasks of identifying and controlling risk.

INTRODUCTION

The enormous problems facing the banking and thrift industries have focused attention on regulatory redesign. Of particular concern has been the widely discussed incentives for excessive risk taking by depository institutions. Although reform proposals and policy discussions have addressed issues of misdirected incentives, accounting deficiencies, and asymmetric information, these recent deliberations have given too little attention to the sensitivity of depository institution risk to aggregate (or macroeconomic) shocks.[1] In the measurement of the total risk borne by depository institutions and insurers, aggregate shocks play a critical role, a claim that will be substantiated by the empirical evidence presented in this study.

Aggregate shocks affect depository institutions in two ways. First, they create covariation between assets in a portfolio. As is well known, covariation may be an important component of overall portfolio risk. Many proposals have ignored this issue altogether, an approach that may be justified if the covariation between assets is of second-order importance.[2] Second, variations in aggregate policies and variables largely exogenous to the

---

1. See Federal Reserve System, 1989a, and FIRREA, 1989, for recently adopted regulations. A partial list of studies includes Kane, 1985, chap. 6, 1989, chap. 6; Kaufman and Kormendi, 1986, Final Report; the Shadow Financial Regulatory Committee, 1989; and U.S. General Accounting Office, 1989. Brookings Task Force, 1989; Brumbaugh, 1988; and White, 1989, are exceptions in discussing explicitly the role of aggregate shocks. None of these three studies, however, offers quantitative assessments, a lacuna that the present study seeks to fill.

2. For example, in the summary of comments received in response to the then proposed risk-based capital guidelines, no mention is made of portfolio effects (Federal Reserve System, 1989a, 4187–4188).

policy process will have direct effects on the economy, and hence on depository institution performance.

The current study offers a quantitative examination of aggregate shocks, and presents evidence that they have major implications for public policies toward depository institutions. Specifically, we explore the sensitivity of depository institution risk to four types of aggregate shocks—monetary, fiscal, exchange rate, and primary commodity prices. As we shall show, risk estimates are very sensitive to aggregate effects both directly and indirectly in terms of covariation.

Linking aggregate variables to depository institution risk is a difficult task, and the following section presents a new empirical framework for drawing these relationships. Briefly, our method relates the distribution of exogenous variables to the distribution of industry loan losses through a number of estimated econometric relations and assumptions about the values and probabilities for these exogenous variables. A depository institution is characterized by the proportion of its loans extended to firms in different industries. These proportions, in conjunction with the industry loan loss distributions, define the depository institution's loan loss distribution.

The substantive empirical results are then discussed in the next two sections. The calculations presented in the third section quantify the credit risk due to covariation in representative loan portfolios. The following section estimates the response of depository institution risk to variations in monetary and fiscal policy, as well as to shocks in primary commodity prices and exchange rates. These empirical results highlight the substantial—and largely underappreciated—sensitivity of depository institution risk to aggregate influences.

The implications of these findings for regulatory reform are discussed in the final section.

LINKING AGGREGATE SHOCKS AND LOAN LOSSES

The empirical framework used in this study connects the loan loss distribution facing a depository institution with aggregate shocks to the economy. We first present a general overview of this framework. Specific assumptions about loan losses, interindustry relations, and macroeconomic behavior that are the basis for our calculations are then discussed.

The General Framework for Assessing Risk

Our analysis of depository institution risk quantifies the total credit risk arising from lending. From a regulatory perspective, total risk is the appropriate concern because it creates potential demands on regulatory reserves. Apart from credit risk, there are additional sources of risk affecting depository institutions. Risks arising from unscrupulous management practices are likely to be checked only with supervision, but have little relation to aggregate conditions. Interest rate, exchange rate, and liquidity risks are sensitive to macroeconomic influences. With a detailed description of a depository institution's income statement and balance sheet, the framework developed in this paper could assess these additional risks and their relation to credit risk. Construction of such a detailed system, however, is beyond the scope of the current study. By focusing on credit risk, we believe that our framework captures the primary risk facing depository institutions in the 1990s.[3]

Credit risk is measured by the distribution of loan losses associated with the depository institution's loan portfolio. This distribution is calculated as a weighted average of industry loan loss distributions, where the weights equal the proportion of the loan portfolio extended to firms in each industry. Industry loan losses are determined by industry and economy-wide variables that affect profitability. A distribution of loan losses is constructed with different assumptions about possible states of the world, indexed by $s = 1,S$. (It may be easiest to think of the model as atemporal and the states determined by draws from as yet to be specified probability distribution, but it is straightforward to extend the framework to multiple periods.) These considerations lead to the following set of equations for the I industries,

$$\ell_{i,s} = F[Y_{i,s}] + \epsilon_i \qquad i = 1,I \tag{1}$$

where $\ell_{i,s}$ is loan losses in industry i for state s per dollar of outstanding loans, $F[\cdot]$ is an econometrically estimated function (discussed below), $Y_{i,s}$ is a vector of variables affecting loan losses, and ϵ_i is an industry-specific shock.

A depository institution is characterized by the proportion of its loans extended to firms in different industries. It is fundamental to the evaluation of the depository institution that the assets in the loan portfolio respond similarly to the same aggregate shock. In terms of equation (1), this implies that the determinants of loan losses in industry i ($Y_{i,s}$) may be correlated with the loan loss determinants for industry i'. In our framework, this correlation will be induced by fluctuations in macroeconomic variables, such as interest rates, GNP, and its components, to which industries are more or less responsive.[4] A critical step in making our method operational

---

3. In his study of bank holding companies that experienced difficulties, Randall (1989) concluded that the concentration of loans with common risk characteristics "appears to have played a significant role in nearly all of the cases studied" (p. 15). According to an FDIC report (1983, p. II-6), credit risk was the primary cause for three-quarters of bank failures.

4. This view is in contrast to the sectoral shock view of economic fluctuations, which holds that industry-specific stochastic shocks are the key impulse mechanism (for example, Davis, 1987; Long and Plosser, 1983).

is to link the industry-specific variables to macroeconomic outcomes. This link is forged by means of an interindustry model of the U.S. economy that relates industry production to final expenditures, as well as capturing production flows between industries.

The final step is to identify the sources of risk in the macroeconomy, and relate them to the interindustry model. We assume that the macro-economy can be adequately represented by a large-scale, nonlinear econometric model and that risk arises from the diversity of possible outcomes of a subset of exogenous variables. Exogenous variables are divided between those that remain fixed across states (Z) and those that vary among states, such as primary commodity prices (including energy), exchange rates, and monetary and fiscal policies. For each latter variable, we specify a set of possible outcomes $(X_{j,u})$ and the probability that each will occur $(p_{j,u})$, where j refers to an exogenous risk variable and u to a possible outcome. The permutations of the $x_{j,u}$'s are formed (X_{Jxs}), and the probability of any given combination is represented by the probability weights (π_s) that are formed from the $p_{j,u}$'s and sum to unity. The relationship between industry variables, the macroeconometric and interindustry models $(G[\cdot]$, discussed below) and the exogenous variables is represented by the following equation.

$$Y_{i,s} = G[X_{Jxs},Z] \qquad s = 1,S \qquad (2)$$

These $Y_{i,s}$'s enter equation (1), and the $\ell_{i,s}$'s are weighted by the π_s's to determine a vector of loan losses by industry and a matrix of covariances between industries.[5]

To summarize, we compute the loan loss distribution facing a depository institution by selecting possible outcomes for a set of exogenous macroeconomic variables $(X_{j,u})$ and probabilities that each will occur $(p_{j,u})$. The permutations of these variables (X_{Jxs}) and their associated probabilities are computed, and each is simulated through the macroeconomic and interindustry models to obtain a set of industry-specific variables $(Y_{i,s})$. With equation (1) and the probabilities associated with the various states (Π_{sx1}), these $Y_{i,s}$'s are used to compute a vector of expected loan losses by industry $(M[\ell]_{Ix1})$. An important innovation in this study is that we are also able to compute the covariances between loan losses in different industries $(C[\ell]_{IxI})$ induced by fluctuations in aggregate variables.[6]

A depository institution's portfolio is represented by the proportion of

---

5. We have chosen this approach (the $F[\cdot]$ and $G[\cdot]$ functions) for generating information about industry loan losses because it provides a tractable means for using the scarce information that is available and it does not restrict the number of possible outcomes (nor their interactions with the fixed exogenous variables) that may be considered.

6. See the Appendix for a more mathematical statement of the method for calculating the loan loss distribution.

loans extended to firms in these industries, and it is straightforward to calculate the mean (μ) and standard deviation (σ) associated with a particular loan portfolio. For purposes of portraying risk, a critical loan loss rate, ℓ^*, is defined. Loan losses in excess of this rate undermine a depository institution's viability. In our framework, risk exposure is measured by the area under the portfolio's loan loss distribution to the right of ℓ^*, and this critical region is labeled γ.[7] Under the assumption that the depository institution's loan losses are distributed normal, the mean and standard deviation of the loan portfolio completely characterizes the distribution, and the relation between this distribution, ℓ^*, and γ is given in Figure 7.1. The specific assumptions underlying the calculation of loan loss distributions for different depository institutions are discussed below.

The Loan Loss Model

The proposed framework requires that we obtain data on loan losses by industry and that they be linked to variables in the macroeconomic and input/output models. The most readily available source for data on depository institutions is the Call Reports collected by the Federal Financial Institutions Examination Council. Unfortunately, these data are not classified by industry, and hence are not useful for our purposes. Loan loss data from Robert Morris Associates are published by industry, but the collection procedure precludes their analysis by econometric methods.[8] Instead,

Figure 7.1   Loan Loss Distribution

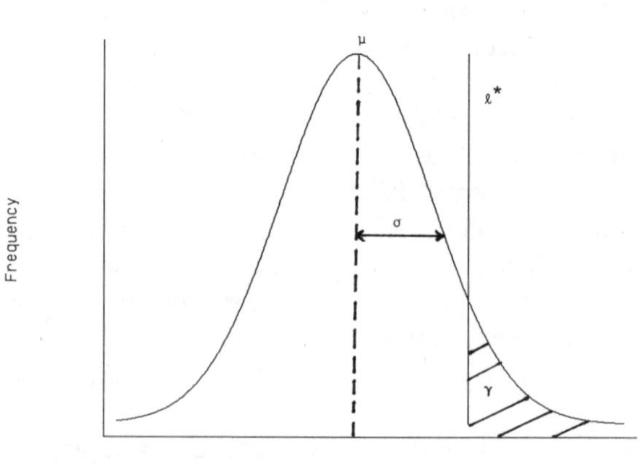

---

7. It would be incorrect to increase ℓ^* because of a perceived increase in risk in the macroeconomy, which will be reflected in the choice of the $x_{j,u}$'s and $p_{j,u}$'s, hence in the computed loan loss distribution.

8. Specifically, the Robert Morris data are based on responses from a sample of banks who provide information about their five largest charge-offs. Thus, for our purposes, the sample is not useful—the sixth largest charge-off by, say, Bank of America, is not counted, while a substantially smaller charge-off from a small bank is included.

we rely on data available from the Shared National Credits (SNC) Program, collected jointly by the Office of the Comptroller of the Currency, the Federal Reserve System, and the Federal Deposit Insurance Corporation. To appear in this sample, loans must be shared by two or more institutions, and their value exceed $20 million. These data are available annually, and are constructed at a two-digit SIC code classification.[9] Loans included in the sample represent roughly one-third of the value of outstanding commercial and industrial loans held by all commercial banks.

Given our interest in identifying problem institutions, the loan loss variable is defined as the percentage of loans in one of the following four criticized categories: Special Mention, Sub-Standard, Doubtful, and Loss. In 1988, loans in these four categories amounted to 7.34 percent of the value of loans in the SNC database; loans classified as Doubtful and Loss amounted to 1.07 percent of the total. For several industries, data are not available for at least one year of the sample. These industries are excluded in the estimation but included in the simulations.[10]

In estimating a loan loss equation, we are guided by two considerations. Statistically, in order to obtain a reasonable amount of variation in the regression, we pool the sample across industries, though the intercepts (α_i's) vary among industries, and estimate the parameters by ordinary least squares. Theoretically, we assume that loan losses are related systematically to the recent growth of cash flows for that industry. We do not have sufficient data to calculate cash flow explicitly, but have available two major components: sales revenues ($R_{i,t}$) and the costs of intermediate inputs and labor services ($C_{i,t}$). The growth rates of these series are entered as four-year moving averages. In addition, to capture the short-run effects brought about by variations in the cost of funds, the federal funds rate (F_t) enters contemporaneously. These considerations lead to the following equation (where the estimated coefficients are standardized):

$$\ell_{i,t} = \alpha_i - \frac{0.549}{(0.120)} \sum_{t-3}^{v=t} (R_{i,v}/R_{i,v-1})/4$$

$$+ \frac{0.431}{(0.131)} \sum_{t-3}^{v=t} (C_{i,v}/C_{i,v-1})/4 \qquad (3)$$

$$+ \frac{0.319}{(0.093)} F_t + \epsilon_{i,t} \qquad \begin{aligned} i &= 1,27 \\ t &= 1985,1988 \\ R^2 \text{ (adj.)} &= 0.276 \end{aligned}$$

where α = a fixed effect that varies across industry i

---

9. The SNC data are published for 84 SIC industries and, for this study, have been aggregated to the 46 industries listed in Table 7.1.

10. See Chirinko and Guill (1990, sec. IV) for further discussion. These industries are included in the simulations by estimating α_i as the difference in the means of the variables in equation (3), weighted appropriately by the estimated coefficients.

$\ell_{i,t}$ = loan losses for industry i at time t, as defined in the text

$R_{i,t}$ = sales revenues for industry i at time t

$C_{i,t}$ = intermediate input and labor costs for industry i at time t

F_t = federal funds rate at time t

$\epsilon_{i,t}$ = an error term for industry i at time t

The Interindustry Model

The loan loss equation (3) depends on industry revenues, industry costs, and the federal funds rate and, conditional on a set of final demands (for example, categories of consumption expenditures), the industry variables are obtained from the DRI Interindustry Model. The structure of this model is based on a Leontief input-output system, and is modified to permit (direct) input coefficients to adjust to technology and product use and to include estimates of industry wages and prices. [11] An important feature of the Interindustry Model for this study is its explicit recognition of the interdependencies among industries. This feature enables the model to capture both the direct and indirect claims on production associated with the delivery of a given set of final demands. Since approximately 50 percent of all production in the United States supports other industry production (that is, indirect claims), it is critical to account for both direct and indirect claims in assessing industry performance. For the purposes of this study, the Interindustry Model has been aggregated to the 46 industries listed in Table 7.1.

The Macroeconometric Model

The concluding step in our calculations is to relate the set of final demands to exogenous macroeconomic variables divided between those that remain fixed across states (Z) and those that vary between states $(X_{J \times S})$. With assigned values for the exogenous variables, we then rely on the DRI Model of the U.S. Economy to relate the $X_{J \times S}$ and Z to the endogenous variables, such as interest rates, prices, and final demands. [12] This model

---

11. See Guill and Kraft, 1985, for a detailed description of the model.

12. See Eckstein, 1983, for further details. Much criticism has been raised against the use of macroeconometric models in quantitative analysis (Lucas, 1976; Lucas and Sargent, 1978). While the parameter instability at the core of the Lucas Critique must be granted, the important question for the current study is whether this instability is sufficiently severe to invalidate the perturbations under consideration. The analysis of Chirinko (1988) indicates that, even in the face of major changes in tax policy, equations for business fixed investment remained relatively stable in the 1980s. Such stability is not inconsistent with forward-looking behavior on the part of public and private economic agents (cf. Sims, 1982; Sargent, 1984).

is highly disaggregated, and has been used and developed in ongoing forecasting exercises. At the core of the DRI Model is a long-term growth model in which productive capacity is determined by the growth in technical progress, the labor force, and the capital stock. Short-term dynamics are determined largely by the data, and are always fully consistent with the circular flow of income and spending and other intrinsic macroeconomic identities. [13]

For reasons of computational expense, four sets of risk variables ($J = 4$) are examined and, for each set, a Basecase and an Alternative set of values are considered. The Basecase assumptions, as well as values for the fixed exogenous variables, are taken from the forecasting project at DRI/McGraw-Hill. Alternative values have been chosen to capture important developments affecting depository institutions. Relative to the Basecase forecast, short-term interest rates rise, the federal deficit falls, the dollar exchange rate appreciates, and primary commodity prices (including energy) rise (further discussion of these alternatives will be provided below).

The permutations of Basecase and Alternatives of the four sets of exogenous risk variables lead to sixteen possible states, a Benchmark (the Basecase value for each of the four risk variables) and fifteen Alternatives. However, from an aggregate perspective, these Alternatives are contractionary relative to the Benchmark. To provide a broader set of possible macroeconomic outcomes and to minimize computational expenses, we assume that the loan loss outcomes are symmetric about the Benchmark solution. This provides us with fifteen additional observations with which to approximate loan loss distributions. The values of these sets of the exogenous variables are represented by $X_{J \times S}$, dimensioned 4 by 31.

To complete the calculations of industry loan losses, the different states must be weighted by probabilities. For each risk variable ($j \epsilon J$), we begin by assuming probabilities of occurrence ($p_{j,u}$) for the Basecase ($u = 1$) and two Alternatives ($u = 2,3$), which sum to unity. The calculations in this study are based on the assumption that the Basecase is 0.80 and that each of the Alternatives is 0.10. [14] These probabilities of occurrence are multiplied together to form the probability for a given state. Calculating the permutations of the $p_{j,u}$'s across J, we obtain the probabilities for the 31 possible states (π_s, $s = 1,31$; $\pi_s \epsilon \Pi_{S \times 1}$). For example, the Basecase probabilities for all four j's are equal to 0.80, and the probability of the Benchmark scenario (which defines the mean outcome) is 0.4096 ($= 0.80**4$).

---

13. The simulations of the macroeconometric and interindustry models begin in 1989, and the results reported in the next section are for 1991.

14. For computational convenience, we assume that the $p_{j,u}$'s are independent across the j's, though it is straightforward to relax this assumption.

Table 7.1 Distribution of Loan Portfolios*

| | Portfolio | | | | |
Industry Description	A	B	C	D	E
1. Ag Production, Crops	0.08	2.17	0.05	0.08	0.11
2. Ag Production, Livestock	0.06	2.17	0.02	0.03	0.05
3. Ag Services, Forest. & Fish.	0.04	2.17	0.01	0.02	0.00
4. Metal Mining	0.67	2.17	0.09	0.57	0.78
5. Coal Mining	0.30	2.17	0.68	0.91	0.42
6. Oil and Gas Extraction	7.44	2.17	5.55	19.72	11.82
7. Nonmet. Minerals, Ex. Fuels	0.07	2.17	0.07	0.05	0.00
8. Contract Construction	1.75	2.17	1.55	0.37	3.90
9. Food & Kindred Products	2.49	2.17	1.55	2.12	3.15
10. Tobacco Manufacturers	2.35	2.17	2.19	1.44	1.25
11. Textile Mill Products	0.54	2.17	0.78	0.11	0.31
12. Apparel & Other Textile Prod.	0.87	2.17	1.03	0.06	0.00
13. Lumber & Wood Products	0.62	2.17	0.85	0.52	0.00
14. Furniture & Fixtures	0.16	2.17	0.30	0.15	0.00
15. Paper & Allied Products	1.74	2.17	3.19	0.63	0.62
16. Printing & Publishing	2.08	2.17	4.32	1.27	1.65
17. Chemicals & Allied Products	4.20	2.17	8.30	2.49	4.77
18. Petroleum & Coal Products	2.58	2.17	3.70	6.70	4.84
19. Rubber & Misc. Plastics Prod.	1.46	2.17	1.13	1.45	1.27
20. Leather & Leather Products	0.17	2.17	0.21	0.22	0.00
21. Stone, Clay, and Glass Prod.	1.60	2.17	1.36	1.79	2.02
22. Primary Metal Industries	2.28	2.17	1.29	2.41	2.95
23. Fabricated Metal Products	1.47	2.17	1.98	1.52	1.93
24. Machinery, Except Electrical	2.60	2.17	2.40	1.97	2.99
25. Electric & Electronic Equip.	1.92	2.17	1.86	2.09	2.47
26. Transportation Equipment	3.88	2.17	2.88	3.51	4.50
27. Instruments & Related Prod.	0.50	2.17	0.77	0.27	0.52
28. Misc. Manufacturing Indust.	0.48	2.17	0.46	0.47	0.34
29. Railroad Transportation	0.83	2.17	1.07	0.72	0.97
30. Local & Interurb Pass. Tran.	0.22	2.17	0.24	0.14	0.00
31. Trucking & Warehousing	0.28	2.17	0.22	0.41	0.54
32. Water Transportation	0.40	2.17	0.28	0.31	0.00
33. Transportation by Air	1.82	2.17	1.46	1.97	2.77
34. Pipe Lines, Ex. Natural Gas	0.10	2.17	0.07	0.13	0.00
35. Transportation Services	0.29	2.17	0.11	0.27	0.00
36. Communications	4.28	2.17	8.92	3.65	4.49
37. Elec., Gas, & Sanitary Serv.	9.21	2.17	7.05	13.01	11.12
38. Wholesale Trade	1.98	2.17	1.41	2.14	1.03
39. Retail Trade	5.86	2.17	6.92	4.71	5.07
40. Banking & Insurance	15.12	2.17	12.81	10.41	10.21
41. Real Estate & Rental	6.68	2.17	3.37	4.11	6.10
42. Personal Services, Ex. Auto	0.04	2.17	0.03	0.00	0.66
43. Business Services	2.11	2.17	2.85	1.71	1.76

Table 7.1 (*Continued*)

Industry Description	Portfolio				
	A	**B**	**C**	**D**	**E**
44. Auto Repair	0.67	2.17	0.95	0.63	0.00
45. Medical Services	2.14	2.17	2.12	1.68	0.63
46. Other Services	3.60	2.17	1.55	1.06	2.01
	100.00	100.00	100.00	100.00	100.00

*Percent.

AGGREGATE SHOCKS AND PORTFOLIO CONCENTRATIONS

This and the following section analyze loan loss distributions facing various depository institutions. Under a normality assumption, these distributions can be represented by their mean (μ) and standard deviation (σ). The importance of portfolio concentrations is assessed by constraining the covariances for loans in different industries to zero, and this restricted standard deviation is represented by σ'. The measure of risk adopted here is the area (γ) under a distribution in excess of a critical loan loss rate (ℓ^*; cf. Figure 7.1). The calculations throughout this paper are based on a value of $\ell^* = 20.55$ percent, which implies a loan charge-off rate of 3.00 percent. [15]

The computations depend on the industry loan loss, interindustry, and macroeconomic models described previously, and the distribution of a depository institution's loan portfolio across 46 industries. Five different portfolios are analyzed, and the corresponding weights are listed in Table 7.1:

- Portfolio A—represents the "average" depository institution, as determined by the proportion of loans held by industries in the SNC database.

- Portfolio B—assigns an equal weight to loans from each of the 46 industries.

- Portfolio C—has concentrations in communications and non-durable manufacturing industries, including paper, printing and publishing, and chemicals.

- Portfolio D—is heavily weighted toward energy and energy-related lines of business.

---

15. The ratio of loans in the Doubtful and Loss categories to all criticized loans (the latter equal to $\ell_{i,t}$) is 0.146, which, when multiplied by 20.55 percent, yields 3.00 percent.

- Portfolio E—has concentrations in energy, construction, and durable manufacturing industries.

The loan loss distributions for each of the five portfolios are calculated with the unrestricted and restricted standard deviations. Figure 7.2 is for Portfolio A, and presents a striking comparison between the unrestricted and the substantially narrower restricted loan loss distributions (drawn with circles and a solid line, respectively). The narrower distribution is representative of one that might be computed by a regulator unable to assess covariation or believing that it is of a second order of importance. The comparisons drawn in Figure 7.2 indicate that such an approach can be highly inaccurate, leading to a substantial underestimation of credit risk.

A convenient statistic for capturing differences in risk is 6, defined as the ratio of the critical regions for the restricted and unrestricted distributions. That is, $6 = \gamma(\sigma')/\gamma(\sigma)$. Since the covariation between industry loan losses is positive for each portfolio, $\sigma > \sigma'$, and $6 < 1$. The further 6 is from unity, the greater the misrepresentation. A graphical representation of 6 is provided in Figure 7.3, which is an enlargement of the right side of the distribution presented in Figure 7.2. The areas under the distributions to the right of ℓ^*, A_1 and A_2, are mutually exclusive, and 6 is defined as $[A_1/(A_1+A_2)]$.

The 6's for the five portfolios are presented in Figure 7.4. This histogram presents the relative changes in the critical regions when the standard deviations are computed with and without the covariance terms, and reveals the substantial variation in the 6's across portfolios. With the restricted covariance, the estimate of risk exposure for the "average" depository institution (Portfolio A) would be only 0.29 of the correct value. The underestimation is greatest for Portfolio C with $6 = 0.11$. Portfolio

---

Figure 7.2 Loan Loss Distributions

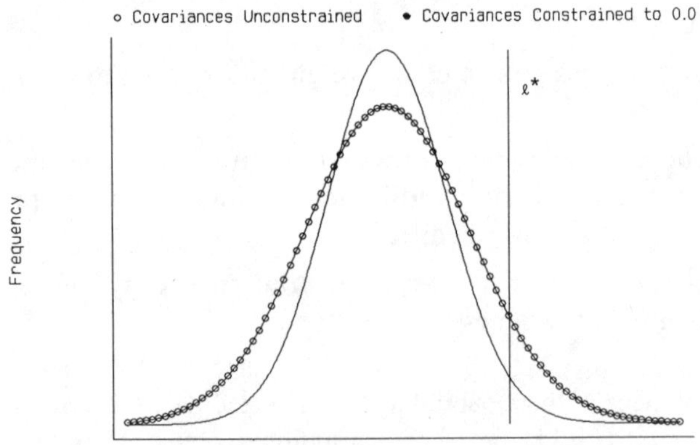

Figure 7.3   Loan Loss Distributions

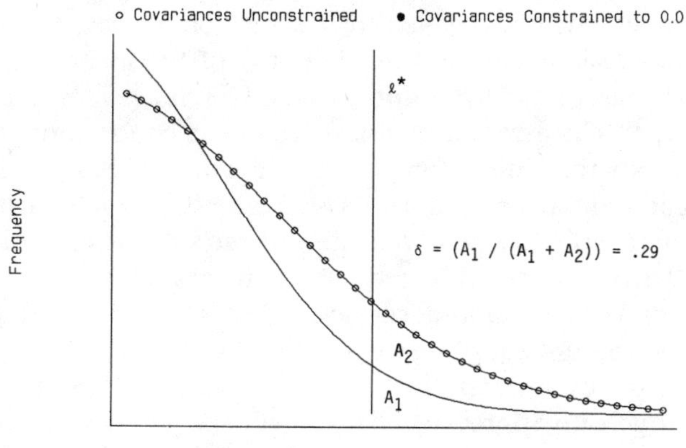

Figure 7.4   Delta Calculated for Portfolios A through E

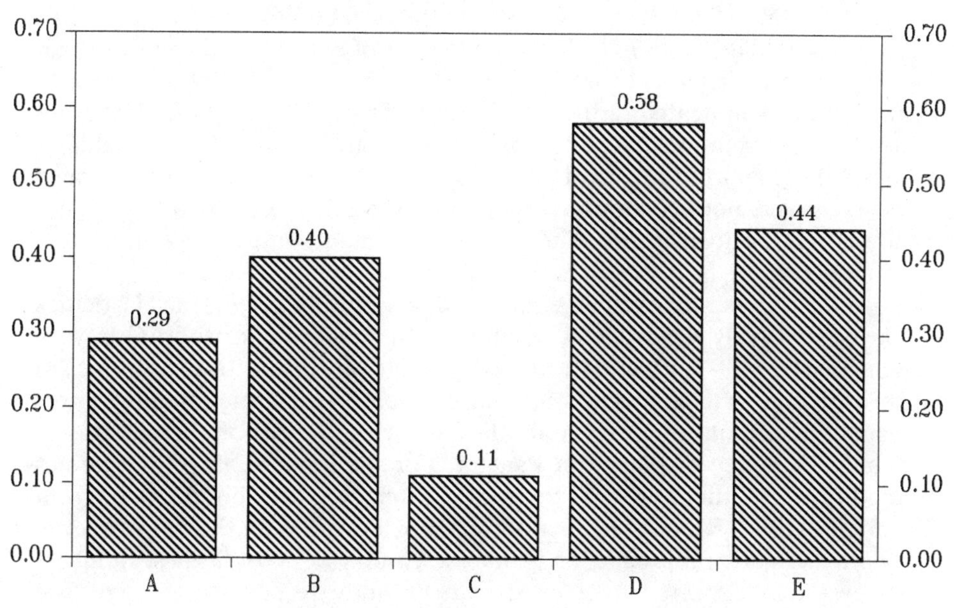

D is the most concentrated, and suffers least from the absence of the
covariation terms. Nonetheless, $\delta = 0.58$, and the inaccuracy associated
with ignoring covariation remains substantial. Thus, not only would risk
assessments based on the constrained variances be too low, they would also
differ widely across depository institutions.

AGGREGATE SHOCKS AND EXPECTED LOAN LOSSES

Aggregate shocks will also have direct effects on expected loan losses and risk, and this section examines the response of the mean and the critical region of the loan loss distribution to isolated changes in each of the four risk variables. [16] The first simulation represents a contractionary monetary policy that raises the federal funds rate an average of 167 basis points over the three-year simulation period. [17] Relative to the Benchmark, this represents a 19.7 percent increase in this interest rate. In the second simulation, the federal deficit is lowered by reducing defense and nondefense spending and increasing personal and corporate taxes. The remaining two simulations examine the impact of aggregate shocks determined largely outside the domestic policy process. In the third simulation, the trade-weighted dollar exchange rate appreciates by 2.3 percent per year. Last, the prices of primary commodities are assumed to rise by 4.5 percent per year, reflecting, among other changes, increases of 6.1 percent in world crude oil prices and 5.0 percent in farm products. All changes are annual averages relative to the Benchmark over the three-year simulation period.

Calculations for these four sets of risk variables for the five portfolios are presented in Table 7.2. The first two rows of each panel display changes in loan losses ($\Delta\mu$) and the elasticity (η) of these changes with respect to the variables indicated in the panel. For aggregate policies, the elasticities are largest for monetary policy, and range from 0.81 to 0.63. The smaller elasticities reported for fiscal policy in Panel 2 occur because the reduced deficit lowers both economic activity and interest rates, which have opposite effects on loan losses. The latter is dominant, and the η's indicate a modest decline in loan losses of between -0.13 to -0.25.

For increases in exchange rates and commodity prices, the elasticities vary extensively across loan portfolios. In Panel 3, Portfolio C is very sensitive ($\eta = -1.10$) and Portfolio B is relatively insensitive ($\eta = -0.24$) to exchange rate appreciation. The elasticities for the remaining three portfolios are quite close (in absolute value) to those for the changes in monetary policy displayed in Panel 1. For the increase in primary commodity prices, the η's for the nonenergy-intensive portfolios fluctuate from 1.57 (Portfolio B) to 0.17 (Portfolio E). For Portfolio D, the rise in energy prices has a favorable effect on loan losses, and $\eta = -0.48$. These numbers suggest that expected loan losses can be quite responsive to aggregate shocks and that these effects differ widely across portfolios.

Changes in risk, as measured by the critical regions, will be in the same

---

16. These four simulations are part of the 31 simulations used in constructing the loan loss distributions in Figure 7.3. (See the Appendix for further discussion.) In effect, the calculations are based on changes in the location parameter (μ) of those distributions.

17. It should be noted that interest rates are an endogenous variable in our framework, and hence will also vary in the other simulations.

Table 7.2   The Response of Expected Loan Losses to Aggregate Shocks, Alternative Portfolios*

	Portfolios				
	A	**B**	**C**	**D**	**E**
	(1)	(2)	(3)	(4)	(5)
1. Interest Rate Increase (Monetary Policy)					
$\Delta\mu$	1.54	1.72	1.45	1.49	1.52
η	.72	.79	.81	.63	.65
ρ	1.52	1.47	1.68	1.40	1.44
2. Deficit Reduction (Fiscal Policy)					
$\Delta\mu$	−.28	−.22	−.34	−.30	−.28
η	−.17	−.13	−.25	−.17	−.16
ρ	.93	.95	.89	.93	.93
3. Exchange Rate Appreciation					
$\Delta\mu$	−.16	−.06	−.23	−.20	−.17
η	−.65	−.24	−1.10	−.72	−.63
ρ	.94	.98	.94	.95	.95
4. Primary Commodity Price Increase					
$\Delta\mu$	.32	.78	.27	−.26	.09
η	.66	1.57	.66	−.48	.17
ρ	1.10	1.21	1.12	.93	1.02

*The simulations begin in 1989, and the reported results are for 1991. $\Delta\mu$ is the change in loan losses, and η is the elasticity of loan losses with respect to the following perturbations: Panel 1, federal funds rate; Panel 2, federal deficit; Panel 3, trade-weighted dollar exchange rate; Panel 4, primary commodity prices. ρ is the ratio of the critical regions for the simulated and Benchmark distributions calculated with $\ell^* = 20.55$.

direction as changes in expected loan losses, but will not be proportional because of nonlinearities associated with the probability distributions. To assess the impact on depository institution risk, we calculate the ρ-statistic, similar to δ but defined as the ratio of the critical regions for the simulated and Benchmark loan loss distributions.[18] The change in risk exposure is considerable. For Portfolio C, credit risk would increase by 68.0 percent with a 19.7 percent (167 basis points) increase in interest rates and 12.0 percent with a 4.5 percent increase in primary commodity prices. A smaller response of 40.0 percent to the interest rate increase would occur under the energy-intensive Portfolio D, but the rise in primary commodity prices would have a salutary impact, leading to a 7.0 percent decrease in risk. The largest response to the commodity price increase is 21.0 percent for Portfolio B. As with changes in expected loan losses, the effects of aggregate shocks on risk are substantial and diffuse.

---

18. Note that, in columns 1 and 2 of Panel 1, the ordering of the η's and ρ's are reversed. The unrestricted standard deviations are used in calculating the ρ's.

In interpreting these statistics, several qualifications should be kept in mind. First, in a nonlinear dynamic model, the elasticities may depend on the size of the change, the base from which the changes are computed, or the specific policies leading to a given change (for example, the deficit may be lowered by different fiscal policy combinations).[19] Second, the measure of risk is only for credit risk from commercial and industrial loans, and does not reflect mortgage lending, regional effects, or all aspects of interest-rate risk. Third, these computations do not permit behavioral responses by depository institutions in the face of aggregate shocks. Accounting for these factors would affect our quantitative estimates, but we believe that they would not alter our qualitative conclusion concerning the importance of aggregate shocks on depository institution risk.

POLICY LESSONS

The empirical evidence presented in this study demonstrates that depository institution risk can be highly sensitive to aggregate shocks. For plausible variations in policy and nonpolicy variables, our calculations showed that expected loan losses on representative portfolios could be affected substantially (Table 7.2). Although such considerations may not be relevant for fundamental structural reforms, they bulk large for the near-term performance of depository institutions laid vulnerable by past policy mistakes.

This sensitivity does not appear to receive sufficient weight in determining aggregate policies. Statements from the Federal Reserve (1989b, 1989c, 1990) give little attention to the difficulties faced by depository institutions. When notice is taken, it concerns how problem institutions might affect the interpretation of monetary aggregates and the flow of funds to select credit markets, not how monetary policy might impact depository institutions. Passing mention is made by the Council of Economic Advisers (1990, p. 99) of the role of the "external environment," but the thrust of the analysis is on structural reform, rather than on the immediate effects of aggregate policies. There exists an important need for coordination between these policy makers and regulators charged with resolving the current difficulties posed by bankrupt and depleted institutions.[20]

Perhaps of more consequence is our demonstration of the significance of portfolio concentrations (Figures 7.2, 7.3, and 7.4). Our evidence indi-

---

19. Furthermore, the elasticity concept is not clearly defined in a dynamic context, as η can be calculated with respect to the current stimuli, previous stimuli, or an average over the previous periods. The latter has been used for the η's presented in Table 7.2.

20. The first wave of the thrift crisis (1980–82) was precipitated by the sharp rise in interest rates due to monetary policy changes (Barth, et. al., 1985; Brumbaugh, 1988).

cates that recent regulations are wholly inadequate to the task of curbing excessive risk exposure by depository institutions. The newly adopted plan by the Federal Reserve System (1989a), along with 11 other central banks, assesses credit risk by the activities in which a depository institution is engaged. Capital standards are determined by allocations among broad asset groups, with commercial and industrial loans taken as a homogeneous aggregate requiring the greatest amount of capital. Portfolio concentrations and asset covariations, however, are of first-order importance. With such broad asset classifications, these regulations will be unable to monitor risk adequately or to impede the actions of adventurous institutions. When covariation is ignored and for the portfolios considered here, the extent of risk underestimation ranges from 70 to 800 percent.

Regulatory reforms and discussions need to be reoriented toward considering depository institutions in a portfolio context.[21] The recently adopted FIRREA regulation—restricting thrifts to holding 70 percent of their loan portfolios in qualifying mortgage-related accounts—proceeds entirely in the wrong direction. Although our calculations shed no direct light on the effects of mortgage lending, they nonetheless suggest that even modest loan concentrations can magnify risk exposure. A possible defense of this regulation is that the increased risk due to portfolio concentrations is outweighed by the benefits of having thrifts specialize in assets in which they have a comparative advantage. The expanding number of alternative suppliers of mortgage funds suggests to us that the latter benefit is likely to be small.

An additional dimension is introduced by bank expansion into international lending and borrowing. Returns from these activities and those on the domestic side will be significantly interrelated by, among other factors, movements in exchange rates. As shown in Table 7.2, domestic loan losses can be very sensitive to exchange rates. Assessments of depository institutions that do not simultaneously account for correlations with foreign operations may thus lead to substantial errors in estimating risk exposure.

The significance of portfolio concentrations suggests added difficulties in implementing market value accounting reforms.[22] As has been often discussed, the major impediment to market-value accounting is the valuation of illiquid assets. Assuming that cash flows can be specified or relations to marketable assets can be drawn, a further problem exists because the value of illiquid assets cannot be determined independently of the pattern of returns to other activities. Our calculations suggest that ignoring the effects of covariation can lead to major biases.

---

21. Such a framework for assessing depository institution risk is developed and illustrated in Chirinko and Guill (1990).

22. See Benston and Kaufman, 1988; Brumbaugh, 1988; and White, 1990, for discussions about market value accounting.

Aggregate shocks affect the fortunes of depository institutions in substantial and complicated ways, and create fundamental risks that heighten the vulnerability of institutions and their insurers. The computations presented in this study indicate that aggregate shocks are quantitatively important. Piecemeal approaches to regulatory reform that fail to recognize these interrelationships will ultimately prove inadequate to the tasks of identifying and controlling risk.

APPENDIX: DETAILS ON COMPUTING THE LOAN LOSS DISTRIBUTIONS

This Appendix presents some of the details pertaining to the computation of the loan loss distribution. We begin by specifying the values of the exogenous variables to be used in the simulations. In the present case, it is useful to distinguish between those exogenous variables for which there is only one assumed value (Z; for example, demographic variables, reserve ratios) and those that assume a range of values with given probabilities. Examples of variables in the latter category are the prices of food and imported oil, the exchange rate, and government spending ($X_{j,u}$'s, $j = 1,J$). The probabilities of occurrence are represented by $p_{j,u}$'s, $j = 1,J$, $u = 1,U$. These probabilities are assumed to be independent and the two possibilities for four sets of exogenous variables leads to sixteen possible states, a Basecase and fifteen Alternatives. The values of these sets of the exogenous variables are represented by $X_{J \times S}$; the probability that any given state will occur is represented by an element in $\Pi_{S \times 1}$, which is determined by permuting the probabilities of occurrence ($p_{j,u}$) across j.

To calculate the distribution of loan losses, we perform S simulations of the models. For a given $s \epsilon S$, the $X_{J,s}$ and Z vectors serve as inputs to the macroeconometric model. The resulting vector of final demands is distributed to the 46 industries by the input/output model. For each industry and each possible state, the industry-specific and macroeconomic information is used to determine loan loss rates for that industry using equation (1). Viewing the macroeconometric, input/output, and loan loss models as one function ($\Gamma[\cdot]$), the first step in our framework performs the following mapping.

$$\Gamma[X_{J,S},Z] \rightarrow \ell_{I \times S} \qquad \text{(A-1)}$$

This latter matrix of loan losses (by industry and by state) forms the basis for all subsequent calculations. From a computational perspective, this recursive structure bestows a substantial advantage since, once the relevant possible outcomes have been identified and simulated, the remaining computations are relatively minor.

In order to obtain the most information from a given number of simulations, we select the Alternatives to be contractionary from a macroeconomic perspective relative to the Benchmark, and assume that the loan loss outcomes are symmetric about the Benchmark solution. This provides us with 15 additional observations with which to approximate the loan loss distribution. With an expanded computer budget, symmetry can be relaxed.

The information contained in the loan loss matrix—dimensioned 46 (industries) by 31 (states)[23]—can be summarized by two scalars. This reduction occurs in two stages. First, the probability of a realization of an individual exogenous variable ($p_{j,u}$, $j = 1,J$, $u = 1,U$) are transformed into the probability of a realization of a particular combination of exogenous variables. This latter realization is referred to as a state, and its probability is denoted by $\pi_s \epsilon \Pi_{S \times 1}$.[24] In turn, this matrix is used to calculate the mean vector of loan losses by industry ($M[\ell]$).

$$M[\ell]_{I \times 1} = \ell_{I \times S} \Pi_{S \times 1} \qquad (A-2)$$

To calculate the covariance matrix, we first compute the deviations of loan losses from their industry means.

$$\ell \#_{I \times S} = \{\ell_{I \times S} - M[\ell]_{I \times S}\} \qquad (A-3)$$

where $M[\ell]_{I \times S} = [M[\ell]_{I \times 1}, M[\ell]_{I \times 1}, \ldots M[\ell]_{I \times 1}]$ with identical columns. The covariance matrix for loan losses is computed as a weighted average of equation (A-3) with the weights reflecting the probability of realizing state s.

$$C[\ell]_{I \times I} = \ell \#_{I \times S} \text{DIAG}[\Pi]_{S \times S} (\ell \#_{I \times S})^T \qquad (A-4)$$

where $\text{DIAG}[\Pi]_{S \times S}$ has nonzero elements only on the diagonal. Equation (A-4) does not fully represent the covariance matrix of loan losses because it does not incorporate the residual variation from $\epsilon_{i,t}$ in equation (3). An additional covariance matrix is calculated from the regression residuals, and added to equation (A-4). Since this latter matrix is fixed across simulations, this adjustment attenuates changes in the variance of the loan loss distribution with respect to changes in macroeconomic scenarios and loan portfolios.

The second step in compressing the information contained in the loan loss matrix (A-1) is to relate the mean and covariance matrices to the loan portfolio chosen by a depository institution. In this framework, a depository institution is characterized by the distribution of its loan portfolio

---

23. The number of states equals the Benchmark plus the permutation of two possibilities for four sets of exogenous variables (less the Benchmark), the latter multiplied by two because of symmetry (1 + 2*[2**4 − 1]).

24. This calculation is based on the assumption that the probabilities of occurrence ($p_{j,u}$'s) are independent. Alternatively, one could specify a more complicated distribution that would be reflected in the calculation of the π_s's, but this change would not alter the structure of the $\Pi_{s \times 1}$ matrix.

among different industries ($\omega_{I \times 1}$), and the mean (μ) and standard deviation (σ) of the depository institution's loan portfolio are calculated as follows.

$$\mu = (\omega_{I \times 1})^T M[\ell]_{I \times 1} \qquad\qquad \text{(A-5)}$$

$$\sigma = (\omega_{I \times 1})^T C[\ell]_{I \times I} \, \omega_{I \times 1} \qquad\qquad \text{(A-6)}$$

In sum, given the macroeconomic, input/output, and loan loss models, our proposed framework relates choices of the values of exogenous variables ($X_{J \times S}, Z$), the probability of their occurrence ($P_{J \times U}$, which leads directly to $\Pi_{S \times 1}$), and the depository institution's loan portfolio ($\omega_{I \times 1}$), to the mean and standard deviation of loan losses (cf. Figures 7.1 and 7.2).

REFERENCES

Barth, James R., R. Dan Brumbaugh, Daniel Sauerhaft, and George H.K. Wang, "Insolvency and Risk-Taking in the Thrift Industry: Implications for the Future," *Contemporary Policy Issues* 3, Fall 1985, 1–32.

Benston, George J., and George G. Kaufman, "Regulating Bank Safety and Performance," in *Restructuring Banking & Financial Services in America,* William S. Haraf and Rose Marie Kushmeider, eds., American Enterprise Institute (Washington), 1988, 63–99.

Brookings Task Force, *Blueprint for Restructuring America's Financial Institutions,* Brookings Institution (Washington), 1989.

Brumbaugh, R. Dan, Jr., *Thrifts Under Siege: Restoring Order To American Banking,* Ballinger (Cambridge), 1988.

Chirinko, Robert S., "Business Tax Policy, The Lucas Critique, and Lessons from the 1980s," *American Economic Review* 78, May 1988, 206–10.

Chirinko, Robert S., and Gene D. Guill, "A Framework for Assessing Depository Institution Risk: Toward Regulatory Reform," University of Chicago, August 1990.

Council of Economic Advisers, *The Annual Report of the Council of Economic Advisers,* U.S. Government Printing Office (Washington), February 1990.

Davis, Steve J., "Fluctuations in the Pace of Labor Reallocation," in *Empirical Studies of Velocity, Real Exchange Rates, Unemployment and Productivity,* Karl Brunner and Allan H. Meltzer, eds., North-Holland (Amsterdam), 1987, 335–402.

Eckstein, Otto, *The DRI Model of the U.S. Economy,* McGraw-Hill (New York), 1983.

Federal Deposit Insurance Corporation, *Deposit Insurance in a Changing Environment,* Federal Deposit Insurance Corporation (Washington), April 15, 1983.

Federal Reserve System, "Capital: Risk-Based Capital Guidelines," *Federal Register* 54, January 27, 1989a, 4185–221.

———, "1989 Monetary Policy Objectives," *Federal Reserve Bulletin* 75, March 1989b, 107–19.

———, "1989 Monetary Policy Objectives: Midyear Review of the Federal Reserve Board," *Federal Reserve Bulletin* 75, August 1989c, 527–39.

———, Statement by Alan Greenspan before the Joint Economic Committee, January 30, 1990, *Federal Reserve Bulletin* 76, March 1990, 128–31.

Financial Institutions Reform, Recovery, and Enforcement Act of 1989 (FIRREA), Public Law 101–73, August 9, 1989.

Guill, Gene D., and Sandra G. Kraft, "The DRI Interindustry Model: Mark III," *The DRI Interindustry Review,* Fall 1985, 23–36.

Kane, Edward J., *The Gathering Crisis in Deposit Insurance,* MIT Press (Cambridge), 1985.

————, *The S&L Insurance Mess: How Did It Happen?* Urban Institute Press (Washington, D.C.) 1989.

Kaufman, George G., and Roger C. Kormendi, *Deregulating Financial Services: Public Policy In Flux,* Ballinger (Cambridge), 1986.

Long, John B., Jr., and Charles I. Plosser, "Real Business Cycles," *Journal of Political Economy* 91, February 1983, 39–69.

Lucas, Robert E., "Econometric Policy Evaluation: A Critique," in *The Phillips Curve and Labor Markets,* Karl Brunner and Allan H. Meltzer, eds., North-Holland (Amsterdam), 1976, 19–46. Reprinted in *Studies in Business Cycle Theory,* MIT (Cambridge), 1981, 104–30.

Lucas, Robert E., and Thomas J. Sargent, "After Keynesian Macroeconomics," in *After the Phillips Curve: Persistence of High Inflation and High Unemployment,* Federal Reserve Bank of Boston (Boston), 1978, 49–72, 81.

Randall, Richard E., "Can the Market Evaluate Asset Quality Exposure in Banks?" *New England Economic Review,* July/August 1989, 3–24.

Sargent, Thomas J., "Autoregressions, Expectations, and Advice," *American Economic Review* 74, May 1984, 408–15.

Shadow Financial Regulatory Committee, "An Outline of a Program for Deposit Insurance and Regulatory Reform," Statement No. 41, Mid America Institute, February 1989.

Sims, Christopher A., "Policy Analysis with Econometric Models," *Brookings Papers on Economic Activity,* 1982:1, 107–64.

United States General Accounting Office, *Troubled Financial Institutions: Solutions to the Thrift Industry Problem,* U.S. Government Printing Office (Washington), February 21, 1989.

White, Lawrence J., "The Reform of Federal Deposit Insurance," *The Journal of Economic Perspectives* 3, Fall 1989, 11–30.

White, Lawrence J., "The Value of Market Value Accounting for the Deposit Insurance System," *Journal of Accounting, Auditing, and Finance,* 6, April 1991.

CHAPTER 8

Lender of Last Resort, Too Large to Fail, and Deposit-Insurance Reform

George G. Kaufman

Loyola University of Chicago

Proposals for deposit-insurance reform to improve the safety and efficiency of the banking system frequently overlook the operation of the lender of last resort (LLR) facility by the Federal Reserve System. In recent years, the Federal Reserve has quietly and almost invisibly become an integral part of the deposit-insurance safety net, along with the more visible FDIC operations, through LLR assistance to economically insolvent or near-insolvent large commercial banks considered too large to fail (TLTF). Thus, the Federal Reserve provided LLR assistance to support the Franklin National Bank in 1974, the First Pennsylvania Bank in 1980, the Continental Illinois National Bank in 1984, almost all major Texas banks in 1987 through 1989, and the Bank of New England in 1990. All these banks but the First Pennsylvania failed economically with large losses to taxpayers. Moreover, the assistance has for the most part been provided at below market rates of interest.

Effective reform of deposit insurance, therefore, needs to include reform of both LLR operations and TLTF policies. That is, deposit-insurance reform requires reform of the Federal Reserve System as well as the FDIC.[1] This paper reviews the history of central bank LLR activities

---

1. An earlier discussion of the interrelationship between deposit insurance and lender of last resort appears in George J. Benston, Robert A. Eisenbeis, Paul M. Horvitz,

and makes recommendations for modifying these operations to make them consistent with effective deposit-insurance reform.

REVIEW OF THE LENDER OF LAST RESORT FUNCTION

Lender of last resort operations by the central bank date back to the activities of the Bank of England at the turn of the nineteenth century. Historians have summarized the traditional role of the central bank as lender of last resort as "averting bank panics and crises. . . . As lender of last resort, it has the responsibility of preventing panic-induced collapses of the money supply."[2]

When the Federal Reserve failed to do so in the United States during the Great Depression from 1929 through 1933, the Federal Deposit Insurance Corporation and sibling institutions were established to prevent panic-induced runs into currency from the banking system as a whole. This reduced the day-to-day importance of the Fed's LLR operations and the operations became more or less dormant until the threatened failure of the large Franklin National Bank in the mid-1970s. Just before its purchase by the European and American Bank in October, borrowings from the Federal Reserve Bank of New York totaled nearly $2 billion and were funding almost one-half of the Franklin Bank's total assets. This assistance was provided with the support of the Comptroller of the Currency and the FDIC and represented the beginning of the TLTF policy.

Why did TLTF breathe new life into Fed LLR operations? Primarily because large deposits are dejure insured for less than their full amount and bank regulators have been reluctant to impose losses on large depositors at insolvent institutions because of fear of undesirable spill-over to other banks and possibly the macroeconomy. The regulators want to give these banks every opportunity to regain solvency before admitting defeat and officially recognizing the failure, which would be viewed as a black mark on their record.

In the first $1-billion bank failure since the Great Depression—the United States National Bank in 1973—the Fed was not a major player. But the Fed changed its role shortly thereafter. In 1973, the Franklin National Bank, with assets of $5 billion, the nation's twentieth largest bank, began to experience serious financial problems. Large depositors and other creditors started to withdraw their funds. The regulatory agencies attempted to find a buyer for the Franklin, but the outflow continued as the search was prolonged. At the time, the FDIC did not believe it could legally declare the bank "essential" within the interpretation of the term, which was

---

Edward J. Kane, and George G. Kaufman, *Perspectives on Safe and Sound Banking,* MIT Press (Cambridge), 1986, chap. 5.

2. Thomas M. Humphrey, "Lender of Last Resort: The Concept in History," *Economic Review,* Federal Reserve Bank of Richmond, March/April 1989, p. 8.

required for it to infuse capital into an open bank and effectively guarantee all its deposits. Thus, the regulators turned to the Fed to offset the deposit outflows until a purchaser could be found. To accomplish this, the Fed progressively liberalized its definition of eligible collateral for discount window assistance as the Franklin's better assets were sold, and even accepted foreign assets to offset deposit outflows from the bank's London office. Between December 1973 and October 1974, when the bank was finally sold, deposits declined by more than 60 percent from $3.7 billion to $1.4 billion. The Fed at one point provided nearly 50 percent of the Franklin's funding. The FDIC assumed the debt to the Fed upon resolution. The Fed provided the assistance at a significant discount from market rates of interest on uncollateralized loans to insolvent or barely solvent banks. Garcia and Plautz estimate the average subsidy at almost 300 basis points, or $20 million. [3]

The next large bank to experience financial difficulties was the First Pennsylvania Bank in 1980. It had incurred large losses from betting on the wrong direction of changes in interest rates. At the time, the bank had assets in excess of $8 billion and was the twenty-third largest bank in the country. In contrast with its decision with regard to Franklin, in this instance the FDIC declared the bank "essential" on the basis of its size and the potentially unfavorable impact of its liquidation on others, and infused sufficient capital to prevent the bank from becoming legally insolvent. The capital was in the form of loans of $325 million by the FDIC and $175 million by large banks. The lenders received warrants which, when exercised, would give them a majority interest in the bank. The bank was also provided with a line of credit on the participating private banks and the Federal Reserve Bank of Philadelphia. During the rescue negotiations, the Fed loaned the bank nearly $1 billion.

In the First Pennsylvania Bank rescue, the Federal Reserve not only was an active participant in the federal safety net by virtue of its substantial lending but attempted to be the controlling participant. Irvine Sprague, who was Chairman of the FDIC at the time, described the intrusion of the Fed as follows:

> The Fed's role as lender of last resort first generated contention between the Fed and FDIC during this period. The Fed was lending heavily to First Pennsylvania, fully secured, and Fed Chairman Paul Volcker said he planned to continue funding indefinitely until

---

3. Because all Fed discount loans are fully collateralized, it can economically charge a risk-free rate. Only if it lends at a lower rate will the Fed suffer an opportunity loss. Full collateralization, however, reduces the availability of the bank's assets to other lenders, particularly to the FDIC, and this increases the rate they must charge. It follows that by lending at below market rates for uncollateralized loans, the Fed increases the ultimate resolution cost to the FDIC. This is equivalent to a subsidy to the banks while in operation. I am indebted to Mark Flannery for clarifying this for me.

> we could work out a merger or a bailout to save the bank. Our
> position was clear. The Fed refuses to lend without impeccable
> collateral, so it is always protected. FDIC, however, is exposed.
> Beyond that, if Fed funding keeps an institution open longer than
> it should be, then uninsured depositors who withdraw their funds
> during this period receive a preference, and the ultimate bank
> failure is more costly to FDIC.[4]

The Fed was learning the advantages of being a "free rider" in participating in the safety net. It could call the shots without bearing the costs.

The Continental Illinois problems arose when the FDIC was in the process of experimenting with imposing losses on uninsured depositors of insolvent smaller banks. Doubts about the Continental's solvency were accompanied by deposit outflows from both domestic and foreign sources. At first, the regulators attempted to encourage other banks to recycle the funds back to the Continental and even assisted in organizing a group of major banks to do so. But the attempt was not successful and the Fed began to provide large amounts of funds through the discount window to prevent the bank from experiencing liquidity problems that would make official reorganization of its insolvency more difficult to postpone. The amount provided peaked at near $8 billion and averaged $6 billion for some three months. Again the funds were provided at substantially below market rates of interest. At the time of the resolution in July 1984, the debt to the Fed was assumed by the FDIC, which injected sufficient capital to recapitalize the bank and guaranteed all funds provided by all depositors and creditors of the bank and its parent holding company.

If the Fed had not provided the LLR assistance, the FDIC would have had to act sooner. The Fed's support may have provided the FDIC with additional time to determine the solvency of the bank but, although this was made academic by the 100 percent guarantee, also provided time for uninsured depositors to flee at face value, if the FDIC was not intent on making all parties whole. As in the First Pennsylvania Bank rescue, the Federal Reserve exerted substantial influence in preventing the failure of the Continental Bank. Some FDIC officials feared that, even if they had wanted to fail the bank, the Fed would have prevented it by providing sufficient assistance through the discount window. Stanley Silverberg, who was Director of Research at the FDIC at the time, has stated, "if the FDIC had wanted to pay off Continental in May [1984], I don't think we could have gotten there. I suspect the Fed would have continued to fund it and the Comptroller would not have closed it."[5]

4. Irvine H. Sprague, *Bailout: An Insider's Account of Bank Failure and Rescues,* Basic Books (New York), 1986, p. 89.

5. Stanley Silverberg, "Resolving Large Bank Failures," paper delivered at Symposium on Issues and Options Dealing with Large Bank Problems and Failures, Dartmouth College, New Hampshire, August 29–30, 1984, p. 2.

More recently, the Fed provided assistance to all large insolvent Texas banks before the FDIC made its final solvency determination. Most recently, starting in January 1990, the Federal Reserve Bank of Boston lent money to the Bank of New England, about the fifteenth largest bank in the country at the time and now closed and reorganized. By April, the loan amounted to more than $1.6 billion, equivalent to about 10 percent of the bank's assets, before declining. The Fed has not only become an integral part of the too large to fail policy, but, as noted earlier, has provided the support at significantly below market interest rates. This has compounded the ultimate cost of its actions to the economy. Indeed, the subsidy flies in the face of one of the oldest and most widely accepted rules in central banking—to lend freely at penalty rates.

Moreover, the need to support large banks in order to prevent contagion to other banks and bank runs is difficult to demonstrate in a world in which credible federal deposit insurance exists, even with less than full account coverage and even in a world in which the Federal Reserve may not be wiser than it was in the 1930s and does not replenish aggregate bank reserves when they are diminished by a currency run on the banking system.[6] As has been amply and continually demonstrated in recent years, runs on individual banks, whether solvent or not, do not turn into runs on the banking system as a whole, characterized by a net outflow of currency from the banking system. Only that type of run that produces the much feared multiple contraction in money and credit, accompanied by large fire-sale losses by banks as they attempt to sell their loans, can ignite a domino reaction among banks. Instead, runs on individual banks are almost certain to channel deposits to other banks either directly as depositors seek safe banks or indirectly as depositors first flee into Treasury securities (flight to quality), the proceeds of which are then redeposited at safe banks.

Indeed, the evidence from American history even before the institution of deposit insurance in 1934 shows that runs on the banking system were infrequent—possibly occurring only in 1893 and 1929–33—and that losses to depositors at insolvent banks were a smaller percentage of total deposits than losses on defaulted bonds were of all bonds.

If decreases in the aggregate money supply are unlikely to follow from the failure of large banks, the primary historical justification for LLR assistance is removed. Under what other circumstances may Federal Reserve LLR assistance be justified to satisfy both safety and efficiency considerations? History suggests that bank crises may be ignited by reasons other than a decline in the aggregate money supply.[7]

---

6. George G. Kaufman, "Are Some Banks Too Large To Fail? Myth and Reality," *Contemporary Policy Issues,* vol. 8, no. 4, October 1990, pp. 1–14.

7. Bagehot differentiated between shocks produced by external drains of specie, which resulted in a decline in the money supply, and internal drains, which did not necessarily reduce the money supply but created liquidity problems.

LENDER OF LAST RESORT AND LIQUIDITY SHOCKS

Humphrey's description of LLR activities quoted earlier emphasizes crises and panics. Webster's *Dictionary* defines crisis as a time "at which the business organism is severely strained and forced liquidation occurs." A financial panic is defined as a "sudden widespread fright concerning financial affairs and resulting in a depression in values caused by . . . the sale of securities or other properties." The key word in this definition is "sudden." This implies the potential for abrupt liquidations and temporary or fire-sale losses resulting in the destruction of real wealth that would not occur, or at least not to the same extent, if there was greater time. That is, a financial crisis or panic exists when there is a liquidity problem in one or more important sectors of the economy. [8]

Correcting a liquidity problem does not mean that equilibrium asset prices may not decline, but only that market prices do not decline so abruptly that there is insufficient time to conduct an efficient search for the highest bidder. For example, although both are likely to produce fire-sale losses, the sudden appearance of an adverse rumor subsequently identified as unfounded would not be expected to depress equilibrium asset values, but a sudden and unexpected military invasion or oil embargo might. Fire-sale reductions in asset prices are of concern to the LLR if they are sufficiently important in themselves to temporarily reduce aggregate real income significantly, even only temporarily, or if they threaten to spill over to other important sectors. How may widespread fire-sale losses arise?

Numerous types of shocks can cause a sudden reevaluation of asset prices either up or down. Some shocks are applicable to one or a very limited number of assets; others may impact prices of a broad array of assets. Some shocks may cause only temporary equilibrium displacements of asset prices and others a more lasting shift in prices. In either case, in perfect markets, the assets to which the shock applies would attain their new postreevaluation prices immediately and without the need for any transactions (sales). But markets are not perfect and some asset owners may wish to sell their assets immediately upon observing the shock. The prices at which they can sell these assets depend on the liquidity of the particular market.

Liquidity may be defined as the costs involved, including time, in searching out the potentially highest bidders and the underlying equilibrium price. The greater the costs, the less liquid the market. Liquidity varies with the characteristics of the asset traded. The more unique the asset, the smaller the volume outstanding, and the smaller the daily trading volume, the less liquid the market and the longer will fire-sale prices be incurred. Thus, liquidity may be expected to differ across markets so that,

---

8. The following discussion is based on my paper, "Lender of Last Resort: A Contemporary Perspective," *Journal of Financial Services Research,* vol. 5, no. 2, June 1991.

for any given time interval after a shock, fire-sale losses will differ from market to market.

Even in the most liquid markets, sudden changes in perceived prices by a sufficiently large number of participants, because of, say, sudden new information, can produce fire-sale prices. In part, this reflects both technological restrictions on trade imposed by the extant mechanics of consummating trades on the particular market and the minimum amount of time necessary for market participants to reassess their strategies in consideration of the new information and place new buy or sell orders. These factors appear to have been the major causes of the fire-sale prices accompanying the breaks in the stock and derivative markets in October 1987 and 1989, among the most liquid of all markets.

Matching buyers and sellers and reassessing strategy require finite time, although both are greatly affected by the technology available. The more advanced the technology, the briefer the time period required. Thus, liquidity is largely a technological characteristic and reflects the potential for a temporary mismatching of supply and demand in a particular market or across markets. For a given state of technology and liquidity, the greater the shock, the greater the resulting volume of transactions and the magnitude of fire-sale losses may be. LLR intervention cannot affect the state of technology, but can offset its adverse implications by effectively providing additional time through stimulating demand.

For market participants, reassessing portfolio strategies in the wake of an adverse shock and new information is likely to be more difficult and time consuming for securities subject to default risk than for default-free securities, such as U.S. Treasury securities. At such times, there is also a likelihood of an immediate flight to quality as some market participants would rather be safe than sorry. This should worsen the liquidity problem for nondefault-free securities and alleviate it for default-free securities. Indeed, prices may even rise and interest rates decline for default-free securities.

It follows that the more liquid a market, the briefer the fire-sale will be, the less will wealth be reduced in the sector, the less are such prices likely to affect other markets and sectors, and the less is the need for support from the LLR. The role of the LLR is thus to provide liquidity temporarily when market failure causes it to dry up. Both theory and evidence suggest that the LLR, or any other monetary assistance, cannot increase real income for extended periods of time and, therefore, should not be provided to attempt to offset lasting real income declines.

In sum, LLR assistance appears appropriate to offset shocks that ignite temporary liquidity problems likely to produce significant fire-sale losses that might reduce aggregate income and wealth temporarily below equilibrium levels or the levels that would exist if the markets were perfectly efficient. What constitutes a sufficiently severe liquidity problem to warrant intervention is difficult to define precisely and, as is argued later, requires a careful and publicly verifiable cost-benefit analysis. Also, there is a strong tendency for the LLR to view crises as more severe than they actually are and the costs of intervention as smaller than they actually are.

WHAT IS THE COST OF LLR ASSISTANCE?

LLR assistance, no matter how apparent the immediate need or by whom provided, is not costless. Any government assistance that reduces losses below those that would occur as a result of market forces in the absence of such assistance incurs the danger of discouraging action by private participants to protect themselves from future market shocks. Thus, unless priced correctly, LLR assistance induces moral hazard problems by encouraging market participants to alter their behavior in a way that shifts risks to the LLR and government. This potential hazard has been described succinctly by Charles Kindleberger:

> Markets generally work, but occasionally they break down. When they do, they require government intervention to provide the public good of stability. . . . [But] if the markets know in advance that help is forthcoming under generous dispensations, they break down more frequently and function less effectively. . . . This paradox is equivalent to the prisoner's dilemma. Central banks should act one way (lending freely) to halt the panic, but another (leave the market to its own devices) to improve the chances of preventing future panics. [9]

The decision whether or not to provide LLR assistance and at what price involves an economic cost-benefit analysis. The benefits are both immediate and obvious. The costs are delayed and thus more likely not to be perceived as associated with the LLR action and to be more diffuse and difficult to measure. For example, LLR provision of liquidity to prevent fire-sale losses in a particular sector at a price below what the private market would charge is unlikely to encourage market participants in that sector to improve the mechanisms for achieving increased liquidity through private means. As a result, the LLR is more likely to be required to provide assistance again in the future and the sector is effectively being subsidized by being permitted to operate less efficiently than otherwise. Moreover, in the process, participants are encouraged to assume greater risk exposure than they would if they had to absorb the full share of the losses, that is, they incur moral hazard with the likelihood of greater losses in the future.

---

9. Charles P. Kindleberger, *Manias, Panics and Crashes,* Basic Books (New York), 1978, pp. 6, 163.

Similarly, assistance to economically insolvent banks encourages the banks to increase their own risk exposures as they have little if any of their own shareholder funds at risk, discourages other banks from reducing their risk exposures, and frequently provides sufficient time for uninsured depositors to shift their funds elsewhere at full par value before the bank is declared legally insolvent and the value of their deposits is reduced. The last effect was demonstrated most vividly in the case of the Franklin National Bank in 1974 where, as noted earlier, deposits decreased by more than 60 percent before its final resolution. Any loss from such resolution delays is borne by the FDIC and the taxpayer. Thus, the potential future costs of current LLR intervention are substantially larger than the benefits of the current intervention. But the discount rate used by policy makers, who are under considerable political pressure to optimize economic performance in the short term and whose terms of office are relatively short and not guaranteed to last until the next crisis, is likely to be overestimated. Thus, the present value of the current benefits of intervention is likely to be found greater than the present value of the future costs and the benefit of any doubts will be resolved in favor of current intervention. In the words of Kindleberger, "actuality inevitably dominates contingency. Today wins over tomorrow."[10]

HOW SHOULD LLR INTERVENTION BE PROVIDED AND PRICED

LLR intervention by the central bank may be provided in either of two ways: through the discount window and through open market operations. The discount window has been the traditional means of providing LLR assistance, both because it was the major tool of central banking before the development of broad financial markets permitted open market operations to be conducted, and because it could direct the assistance more precisely to the particular sector under pressure. As financial markets developed in breadth and resiliency, not only did open market operations preempt the discount window as the major tool of monetary policy, but they reduced the need for the central bank to direct its actions at particular sectors as the market could now efficiently direct funds made available anywhere in the system to the affected sector.

Recent Federal Reserve operations that may be classified as LLR intervention appear to have been divided between open market and discount window assistance. Assistance was provided primarily through the discount window in the Franklin National Bank (1974), the Continental Illinois Bank (1984), and the Texas banks (1987–89) failures and through open market operations in the October 1987 and 1989 stock market

---

10. Kindleberger, p. 163.

breaks.[11] This division may have been determined at least in part by a recognition of the probable insolvency of the banks and the unlikelihood that funds would be directed to them by the private market. Unlike the FDIC, the Federal Reserve is in an enviable position as an LLR. As noted earlier, because it requires full market value collateralization of its discount window loans, it can lend freely to economically insolvent banks, if it so wishes, without fear of suffering losses. Any loss is shifted to the FDIC and, if sufficiently large, to the taxpayer. This moral hazard problem can be reduced by requiring the Fed to obtain permission from the FDIC before extending emergency assistance through the discount window or by not permitting full collateralization of its loans to institutions.[12]

Reliance on open market operations to provide assistance also reduces the political pressures on the LLR to assist directly through the discount window all entities in financial distress, in particular, financially weak but politically strong entities, for example, large commercial banks or (more recently) large savings and loans and even the government Resolution Trust Corporation to avoid recording budget outlays. The private market is less likely to direct additional funds provided by open market operations to such entities.

Last, open market operations eliminate the need to price LLR assistance correctly. By definition, funds provided through open market operations are priced at the current market rate for the particular securities involved. In contrast, funds provided through the discount window need to be priced administratively and, if priced incorrectly, may reduce the effectiveness of the assistance. If the discount rate charged is too low, too much assistance is likely to be provided with resulting subsidies and encouragement to risk taking. If the discount rate is too high, there may be insufficient assistance. Identifying the correct price is not an easy task and unlikely to be achieved at all times.

Only if the central bank has superior or more timely information about the nature of the crisis and the participants involved than does the market, should providing assistance through the discount window dominate open market operations. Because it is unlikely that the Federal Reserve ever has such knowledge, providing LLR assistance through the discount window should be limited to rare occasions, if it is to be provided at all. Moreover, the LLR may not find it easy, particularly on short notice, to differentiate between good and bad security or solvent and insolvent banks. Open market operations make it unnecessary to worry about the correct rate to charge or about the correct borrowers to whom to lend, in particular about

---

11. In the Penn Central failure (1970) the Fed announced its intention to provide liquidity if necessary, but apparently did not have to do so. This is consistent with Bagehot's strategy.

12. George J. Benston, et al., chap. 5.

providing assistance to those experiencing the initial shock, who are likely exerting the greatest pressures on the LLR. [13]

SUMMARY AND CONCLUSIONS

This paper has argued that effective and lasting reform of the federal deposit-insurance and safety net systems requires not only reform of the FDIC, but also of the Federal Reserve's lender of last resort operations. In recent years, the Fed has become a powerful partner with the FDIC in providing a safety net under large banks. Because, in contrast to the FDIC, the Fed does not bear any of the costs of its safety net operations, it is effectively a free rider and reform is likely to prove even more difficult than it is for the FDIC. But for the same reason, it is also more urgent.

Since 1974, the Federal Reserve has provided lender of last resort assistance to prolong the life of insolvent banks deemed too large to fail. [14] Recent research has clearly demonstrated that the severity of the damage

13. The Swiss National Bank (SNB) appears to conduct its lender of last resort operations in conformity with this principle. Two of its research economists have recently described the Bank's operations as follows:

> [T]he Swiss National bank is obliged to act as a lender of last resort to the banking system. It has traditionally interpreted its lender-of-last-resort role restrictively. As a rule, the SNB is only prepared to provide liquidity assistance in exceptional circumstances. It is willing to intervene in the event of major liquidity problems that may threaten the stability of the domestic financial system. In the SNB's view, liquidity problems arising from the interbank payments system do not call for central bank action, at least not in normal circumstances. The banks should maintain sufficiently high cash reserves in order to be able to absorb normal fluctuations in their payments flows. Should the SNB be compelled to intervene, it prefers to provide liquidity assistance to the market as a whole, rather than to individual banks. Its reluctance to deal with individual banks derives from two observations. First, if caught in a liquidity squeeze, a solvent bank should always be able to get the required funds on the money market provided the aggregate supply of liquidity is adequate. Second, owing to the rapid development of financial activities outside the banking system, liquidity problems may erupt increasingly in the nonbank sectors of the economy. Therefore, the SNB should not direct its liquidity assistance exclusively at the banks.

Urs Bircher and Georg Rich, "Switzerland," in *Banking Structures in Major Countries,* George G. Kaufman, ed., Kluwer Academic (Boston), 1991.

14. More recently, the Federal Reserve Bank of Richmond has provided significant assistance through the discount window to the National Bank of Washington, the oldest bank in the District of Columbia. Because the bank has assets of only $2 billion, and was only about the 250th largest bank in the country, it is difficult to classify it as too large to fail. But because the controlling shareholders in its parent Washington Bancorp

done by a large bank failure with pro-rata losses to uninsured depositors is considerably less than the severity of the damage either feared by many policy makers or done by failing to reorganize and recapitalize institutions before their economic net worth turns negative. [15] Decreases in the aggregate money supply are no longer a plausible concern. The LLR assistance provided in recent years has not saved most banks, but has given uninsured depositors time to flee without losses. This has served to increase the potential loss borne by the FDIC. Moreover, the Fed has provided the assistance through the discount window at greatly subsidized interest rates which has added needlessly to the cost of the too large to fail policy. Indeed, had the banks been considered economically solvent by their peers, funds would have been recycled to them in the marketplace. If the policy makers feared that large bank problems might ignite temporary liquidity problems, assistance should have been provided to the market as a whole by open market operations. This would have relieved the Fed of the need both to distribute the funds directly and to take the risk of second guessing the market and pricing the assistance correctly. The Fed appears to have no comparative advantage in either task.

Many years ago, Milton Friedman recommended that the Federal Reserve discount window be closed. [16] Regardless of the desirability of that recommendation at the time, the current state of financial technology and knowledge clearly suggests that the discount window can now be closed for all but a few exceptions: possibly small banks in need of small and brief amounts of adjustment assistance or overnight assistance to large banks in cases of computer or other market technology malfunction, such as the computer breakdown at the Bank of New York in 1985. At minimum, all adjustment assistance through the discount window should be undertaken only with prior FDIC approval in writing. Alternatively, such assistance could be provided on a less than fully collateralized or even uncollateralized basis, so the Fed would bear the cost of subsequent bank failure.

A case can be made for continuing Fed LLR assistance through open market operations to correct severe macro liquidity problems. But because such crises are generally significantly less severe than the policy makers perceive and the assistance introduces costly moral hazard problems, it

---

have long-time national political associations, the lending appears to fit into a new separate category of "too political to fail" or TPTF. (The National Bank of Washington failed in 1991 with large losses to the FDIC.)

15. This is not to argue that bank failures may not entail some special costs. For a review of these costs see Mark Getler, "Financial Structure and Aggregate Economic Activity: An Overview," *Journal of Money, Credit and Banking,* August 1988, Pt. 2, pp. 539–88, and Joseph Stiglitz and Andrew Weiss, "Credit Rationing in Markets with Imperfect Information," *American Economic Review,* June 1981, pp. 393–410.

16. Milton Friedman, *A Program for Monetary Stability,* Fordham University Press (New York), 1959.

should be provided sparingly and be justified by a publicly reproducible cost-benefit analysis. The Fed's LLR operations cannot be viewed in isolation from the rest of the banking safety net. Effective reform of the latter requires reform of the former. The Fed may be granted greater discretion in its LLR operations if we apply early regulatory intervention and recapitalization before an institution's economic net worth erodes completely (as recently proposed by Federal Reserve Chairman Alan Greenspan, the Federal Reserve Bank of New York's Gerald Corregan, and on a mandatory basis by the Shadow Financial Regulatory Committee). Thus, losses would be minimized and would result primarily from fraud and inadequate monitoring. Assistance through open market operations would still be preferred to the discount window, however, to avoid pricing problems and misallocation of financial resources. [17]

---

17. Shadow Financial Regulatory Committee, "An Outline of a Program for Deposit Insurance and Regulatory Reform," Statement No. 41, February 13, 1989; George G. Kaufman, "Deposit Insurance Reform," testimony before the U.S. Senate Committee on Banking, Housing and Urban Affairs, May 22, 1990; Alan Greenspan, testimony before the U.S. Senate Committee on Banking, Housing and Urban Affairs, July 12, 1990.

CHAPTER 9

The Role of Market Value Accounting in the Regulation of Insured Depository Institutions

**William H. Beaver,
Srikant Datar, and
Mark A. Wolfson**

Graduate School of Business,
Stanford University

INTRODUCTION

The call for market value accounting has recently been made by several observers of the thrift crisis and has been seen as an important part of regulatory reform of the deposit-insurance system. In one form or another, market value accounting has been championed by Benston (1989), Benston et al. (1989), Kane (1985), White (1988), Simonson and Hempel (1990), and Mengle (1989), among others. Remarks of White reflect the strength of conviction with which their views are held:

> If there are any readers who remain unconvinced at this point, I can only suggest that they ask themselves the following questions:

> If I were the regulator of the thrift industry and the insurer of $970 billion of its liabilities, how could I properly do my job without having the static and dynamic market value data that would reveal much more information about risks that are present among my insureds?

> If I were a thrift CEO how could I open the doors each morning and not know what my thrift was really worth? How could I fulfill my fiduciary obligation if I had no market-based information for judging the soundness of possible buying or selling transactions that might arise?
>
> I rest my case.

The market value controversy is a long-standing one in the regulation of financial institutions and has an even longer history in accounting. The merits of market value accounting have been eloquently set forth in many sources, including those cited above. It is interesting that the regulators responsible for setting accounting standards have resisted the general call for market value accounting, as have the federal bank and thrift regulators. Generally Accepted Accounting Principles (GAAP), which guide the construction of financial reports, are based primarily on historical costs along with myriad supplemental disclosures. Private sector debt contracts typically base monitoring arrangements on these GAAP-based financial statements; they typically do not call for market value accounting. This suggests that the costs of market value accounting are perceived to exceed the benefits. Indeed, if the arguments for market value accounting were so compelling, we would expect to observe more demand for it, in the case of banks and thrifts as well as for other industrial organizations.

The Financial Accounting Standards Board's (FASB) most ambitious experiment with market value accounting was the adoption of Statement No. 33, which required supplemental disclosures of replacement cost data (one definition or estimate of market value). For the most part, empirical evidence suggests that replacement cost data do not provide incremental explanatory power beyond that provided by historical cost data with respect to the pricing of common shares (see Beaver and Landsman, 1983; Bernard and Ruland, 1987; and DeBerg and Shriver, 1987, among others). This is even true in studies that restrict attention to industries wherein the usefulness of market value data might be expected to be particularly easy to demonstrate. In this regard, Harris and Ohlson (1987) and Ghicas and Pastena (1989) find that current value estimates in the oil and gas industry do *not* provide incremental explanatory power with respect to common share prices beyond that provided by historical cost data.

Of course, estimating the market value of financial assets and liabilities may not face the same difficulties as estimating the current value of oil and gas reserves. In this regard, the evidence indicates that supplemental disclosures with respect to default risk and interest-rate risk are significant factors in explaining the common share prices of banks (Beaver, Eger, Ryan, and Wolfson, 1989, hereafter BEWR). In a similar context, Barth, Beaver, and Stinson (1990) find that supplemental disclosures with respect to default risk are significant determinants of common share prices of thrifts although interest-rate sensitivity data are not.

The evidence cited above on the relation between supplemental disclosures and bank and thrift share prices can be invoked in support of market value accounting. Investors can be characterized as attempting to assess the market value of assets and liabilities using supplemental financial statement disclosures. A market value accounting proposal can be viewed as a call for providing more accurate estimates of what investors are attempting to estimate through crude proxies.

On the other hand, the supplemental data already may be providing the role potentially played by market values. It may well be that market value estimates provide no additional information to the system beyond that provided by the supplemental disclosures. Investors, as well as regulators, might learn nothing beyond what they already know. At a minimum, a comparison of the explanatory power of historical costs (without supplemental disclosures) against that for reported market values is a "myopic" one. Moreover, the negative findings with respect to the explanatory power of interest-rate risk data for thrifts suggests that obtaining market value estimates is an exercise conducted with measurement error. These errors arise in part because of the nature of the markets in which the assets and liabilities of firms arise and the related problems of defining and estimating market values.

The accounting standard setters have long faced a curious paradox. Market value accounting possesses many of its attractive properties under conditions of perfect and complete markets. When these market conditions are relaxed, the desirability of market value accounting is no longer self-evident, even if such information could be generated costlessly.

In perfect and complete markets, the market price captures all the relevant attributes of an asset or liability, including the time value of money and risk, among other factors. However, the market for many firm assets is incomplete. For example, a market for the results of research and development expenditures may be incomplete because revealing the results of the research and development project may destroy its value (i.e., a potential buyer would no longer need to pay in order to obtain the information). In the current context, the depository institution may possess information about default risk on the loan portfolio that the market does not possess. Such information asymmetry can result in the absence of a market in such assets. Such market incompleteness presents obvious difficulties for market valuation (Berger, Kuester, and O'Brien, 1989, make a similar point).

Another reason why valuation of a firm's assets or liabilities may be difficult is imperfection in the markets. With imperfections such as transactions costs, the entry price of an asset (that is, its replacement cost), its exit price (that is, its liquidation value), and its value in use (that is, present value of future cash flows to the current user) typically will not coincide.

In incomplete and imperfect markets, market prices may no longer possess the desirable properties they exhibit under perfect and complete markets. In particular, market prices may not be rich enough to capture the value of all attributes of an asset. Market prices may not be relevant when the items being traded differ in some material respect from the asset or claim of the firm being accounted for (that is, specialized uses of assets). Moreover, market prices may be unreliable where assets are very "thinly" traded. There are many dimensions to thinness. When the time interval between trades is large, there can be substantial disagreement as to what the market price would have been for a trade that would have occurred during that interval (for example, valuing securities at yearend). Moreover, in thin markets, there may be concern as to whether the price at which a small trade takes place can be extrapolated to the price that would result from a larger order at the same time, even when control is not an issue in either transaction. Loans to Less Developed Countries (LDCs) is an excellent example of thinness. The secondary market prices may not come close to reflecting the reservation prices of debt holders (see Shirreff, 1990).

Still further, the claims traded may not be a "random sample" of the claims held by the firm. Information asymmetries and attendant adverse selection issues would be a major reason for selective trading.

There is a fundamental paradox in the current regulatory context. The market conditions under which market value accounting attains desirable properties are essentially the conditions under which there would be no demand for regulation or for mandating the reporting of such information. The markets would be sufficiently rich to handle the economic functions being performed by the regulators. Thus the call for market value accounting in a regulatory context, while not necessarily misdirected, is also not obviously desirable either. The reason is that the very factors which give rise to a demand for regulation in the first place can also impair the usefulness of requiring a system of market value accounting. This is a theme to which we will return.

REGULATION OF DEPOSITORY INSTITUTIONS

Insured depository institutions have primarily played a role of financial intermediation, whereby short-term (riskless to the depositor) liabilities are invested in longer-term (risky) loans. To be sure, intermediation can play a substantive role in the economy and can enhance economic efficiency. Managers of financial institutions can possess specialized experience, skill, and knowledge in assessing credit and interest-rate risk and in monitoring these risks during the term of the loan via collection efforts (see Leland and Pyle, 1977; Fama, 1985; and Diamond, 1984). However, the "magic" by which lead is changed into gold (the default risk and interest-rate risk to the depositors disappear) is federal deposit insurance. The social risk, of course, does *not* disappear but instead gets shifted, in this case to taxpayers and other stakeholders of the financial institution, such as employees and investors.

One can imagine alternative institutional arrangements in which there would be two types of funds (institutions), one invested in default-free and interest-rate-risk free securities (that is, money market funds) and the other invested in portfolios of risky loans. Here the demand for federal "deposit" insurance is not obvious, since those depositors who wish to avoid bearing risk could invest in the riskless fund, and the role of monitoring the agents making the loan portfolio decisions would fall directly on those depositors, and their agents, who choose to invest in the risky fund.

In the absence of a federal presence, one can only speculate about whether deposit insurance would have been privately demanded, whether private insurers would have been willing to provide such insurance, and, if so, what premiums would have been charged relative to those charged by the federal insurers. What level of leverage would private markets have tolerated relative to those permitted by federal regulators? How would those levels have differed as a function of risk?

There are, of course, no easy answers to these questions. Given that the government has chosen to enter the insurance business, however, there is a demand on its part for information regarding the assets that are being insured. The information in part relates to the value of the assets and how these values change over time due to actions of the loan portfolio managers (a strategy to select a given level of default and interest-rate risk) and to factors beyond the control of managers (economywide and local factors that affect the outcomes of the risky loan portfolio). A principal–agent setting naturally comes to mind in characterizing the regulator–manager relationship.

The relationship can be viewed, however, in a broader "three party" context, where there are an owner, a supervisor, and an agent. In this context, the owners are the taxpayers (perhaps represented by Congress), with the federal banking and thrift regulators as supervisors. This relationship is developed in Tirole (1986) and permits a broader set of issues to be examined. For example, now there is not only concern about moral hazard on the part of the agent but on the part of the supervisor as well. In a related vein, the owner is concerned about collusion between the supervisor and the agent. Tirole's analysis suggests that there may be demand on the part of the owner to constrain the behavior of the supervisor so as to mitigate the extent of collusion. Viewed in this context, the call for market value accounting (or any information system, for that matter) is not only to "improve" the ability of the supervisor to monitor the agent, but also potentially to constrain and monitor the behavior of the supervisors as well. For example, the imposition of capital adequacy constraints in terms of market value accounting can be viewed as an attempt to constrain the ability of regulators to exercise discretion in allowing weak banks to continue to operate without granting valuable concessions to the federal insurance agency.

To be sure, in many cases supervisors may be acting in the best interests of taxpayers by granting forbearance. Indeed, if there were no concern about moral hazard on the part of the supervisor, the desirability of constraining supervisor's discretion would not be obvious. After all, the supervisor often has information that is relevant to a determination of whether the government's insurance costs would be reduced by forbearing. More realistically, however, constraining regulatory behavior may be a cost-effective way of mitigating moral hazard and collusion.

At this point, it is possible to illustrate why it is important to be precise about the role of regulation and the role that an accounting information system is to play in that setting. For example, if market value accounting were adopted as a reporting requirement, would such information be public or only available to the regulators? Historically, there are many examples where the data reported to the regulators were kept confidential. Information regarding slow, delinquent, nonaccrual, and restructured loans is a recent example. Such information is now part of the public domain. Even currently, however, information on bank examiners' reports and their CAMEL is regarded as highly confidential.[1] These policies are extremely controversial and are hotly debated after major thrift and bank failures.

To the extent that the role of the information system is to aid the owners in either constraining and/or monitoring regulatory behavior, the issue of public dissemination is an important one. Most discussions of market value accounting are silent on the issue of dissemination and discuss the merits of the system in the abstract without raising the issue of who will observe the signals from the market value information system. The exceptions in this regard are Simonson and Hempel, who raise confidentiality as a possibility, and Mengle, who essentially recommends confidentiality. In an address to the Financial Analysts Foundation in March 1989, Comptroller of the Currency Robert L. Clarke suggested that national banks should be placed on a market value accounting basis but only for purposes of confidential reports filed with regulators.[2]

In addition to the set of issues that arises when market values can be observed "without error," we must face an additional set of issues that recognizes that markets are imperfect and incomplete. Hence, we can think of obtaining estimates of market value that are subject to measurement error, or more fundamentally, we can think of market value not even being

---

1. CAMEL is an analysis conducted by bank examiners based on a consideration of five factors: Capital adequacy, Asset quality, Management, Earnings profitability, and Liquidity. A bank is given a score in each category and an overall score. The CAMEL rating is used for a variety of purposes including assessment of frequency of future bank examinations. Major elements of the process, as well as the findings for a particular bank, are considered highly confidential. As a result, private-sector services have arisen that attempt to proxy the CAMEL rating system (for example, Sheshunoff, 1989).

2. Summary Report of the April 24, 1990, meeting of the Financial Accounting Standards Advisory Committee, Attachment B.

well defined in these settings. In fact, most market value proposals include a variety of estimation methods including discounting cash flows at current interest rates and appraisals, among others.

Informational asymmetries are a major difficulty in estimating market prices. This informational deficiency is likely to be different depending on whether interest-rate risk or default risk is the major source of changes in value of the asset portfolio. To the extent that interest-rate risk is a factor and default-free interest rates of varying maturities are publicly available, the computations of discounted cash flows at current interest rates seem like a relatively straightforward exercise. Even in this case, however, assessing prepayment risk, the effect of caps, floors, and collars on adjustable rate loans, and the tax effects associated with the implied unrealized gains and losses are not straightforward exercises.

For example, the present value of the tax consequences of changes in the market value of interest-bearing securities depends on such factors as when the gains and losses will be recognized for tax purposes (often well within the discretion of the institution's management), the statutory tax rate that applies at that time, the likelihood that the institution will face tax loss or tax credit carryforwards, and the likelihood that the institution will employ special bad debt deductions that are linked to taxable income or be subject to the alternative minimum tax, among a host of others. As for discretion in the timing of gains and losses from the sale of marketable securities, Scholes, Wilson, and Wolfson (1990) document that banks systematically forgo tax benefits when loan loss provisions are higher than usual and when regulatory capital is relatively low.

Beyond the difficulties with measuring the market value of default-free assets, loans with default risk are a major component of the asset portfolio. Relative to regulators, auditors, and especially investors and taxpayers, the institution's management is likely to have vastly superior knowledge of the default risk and the impairment of value due to the default risk and of the assets. Berger, Kuester, and O'Brien (1989) discuss this issue in some detail and assert that changes in credit risk may be more important than market value changes due to unanticipated changes in interest rates.

If the proposed adoption of market value accounting is motivated by the fact that managers have incentives to withhold relevant information with respect to default risk, it is not clear how market value accounting will improve the quality of the information in this regard. In other words, if there is an incentive not to disclose certain information under the existing system, that same disincentive will exist under the proposed system unless something is done to promote incentives to report the private information truthfully. So requiring "market value" accounting may be a change in form but not necessarily in substance.

It is interesting that the Freddie Mac experiment to apply market value accounting relies on the already reported allowance for loan loss accounts (under the current historical cost system) to reflect default risk (FHLMC,

1990). Most advocates of market value accounting adopt a similar recommendation with respect to default risk (Simonson and Hempel, 1990). Moreover, there are a variety of ways to communicate default-risk information, including the currently required schedules on slow, delinquent, nonaccrual, and restructured loans. Berger, Kuester, and O'Brien (1989) recommend the use of such data to supplement the allowance for loan losses. The evidence cited above by BERW and BBS would lend support to that recommendation.

Requiring discounted cash flow computations to estimate market values of nontraded loans will not necessarily enhance the available information. In fact, requiring estimated market values as a replacement for more easily audited historical cost and other supplemental information could make it more difficult for both regulators and other parties to monitor a financial institution's performance. In particular, it is important to determine what the regulators (and managers) will know about the default risk of the loan portfolio that they don't already know under the current system of historical cost accounting with supplemental disclosures. Besides, don't we want to focus on changing the incentives to disclose as well as on the form of the disclosure?

The bottom line here is that requiring the *direct* disclosure of estimated market values and dropping the requirement to report more easily auditable information on attributes of loan portfolios that are correlated with market values may well *impair* the ability of regulators to monitor the regulatees. Equally important, a change to market value accounting may impair the ability of the public to monitor the regulators, especially where an independent auditor has difficulty verifying the market value-related information mutually observable to the regulator and the regulatee.

Once again, the importance of stating the purpose of the proposed information disclosure is apparent. It is in this regard that our analysis of the market value accounting controversy seems to depart most markedly from that of Benston and White. Benston, in particular, argues that regulators have demand for market value accounting to facilitate more efficient regulatory action. Implicit in this view is that regulators seek to act benevolently to maximize social welfare, but in fact, the concern over moral hazard on the regulators' part has been expressed often.

And no wonder. In the late 1970s and early 1980s, an unprecedented number (for the postdepression era) of thrifts became insolvent on a market value basis (that is, as long as the market value of regulatory forbearance was ignored). This was no secret to regulators despite the absence of a market value accounting system. In fact, it was the very recognition of this market value impairment that gave rise to a series of regulatory forbearance measures. These included: *reducing* the capital adequacy requirement from 5 to 3 percent of assets; increasing the insurance coverage per account from $40,000 to $100,000; passing special tax legislation allowing financial institutions to increase the market value of their tax losses; a dramatic relaxation of capital requirements through the creation of a host of imaginative regulatory accounting procedures (RAP) designed to boost capital for regulatory accounting purposes relative to GAAP measures [for example, loss deferral methods on the sale of loans, the creation of so-called net worth certificates issued by the Federal Home Loan Bank Board, an option to mark up certain thrift assets (selectively!) to estimated market value, and special purchase accounting rules that applied to the sale of thrifts]. In the face of these forbearances, the insurance premium charged as a percent of insured deposits remained unchanged at .083 percent per annum.[3]

In fairness to the regulators, their behavior is also affected by broad governmentwide concerns. For one thing, forbearances may have been driven by regulatory concern over bank runs and a loss of public confidence in the banking system (see Benston et al., 1989, for discussion of this issue). An alternative explanation that seems less benign relates to the fact that the movement to RAP overstated net worth (relative to GAAP) and hence understated the potential net liability owed by the government to insured depositors. The reserves of the FSLIC in 1980 amounted to a mere $6.5 billion, far short of what was required to reckon fully with the thrift problem at that time. The forbearance actions undertaken by regulators can be viewed as a form of "off balance sheet" or perhaps more precisely "off income-statement" reporting to taxpayers to minimize the reported or perceived federal budget deficit and implicit national debt.

Indeed, as additional funds are requested for the thrift bail-out a major issue is whether such funds will be treated as part of the federal deficit. To the extent that Congress and others encourage thrift regulators to adopt such a view, the moral hazard issue does not rest solely with the supervisors or with those being supervised. This naturally brings to mind a four-party system with Congress as an agent between the taxpayer-insurers and the depository institution regulators. We will not, however, take on the additional burden of evaluating the consequences of introducing a fourth party into the regulatory setting.

EVALUATION OF A MARKET VALUE PROPOSAL

An evaluation of a market value proposal consists of three elements: an assessment of potential "benefits" or desirable consequences, an assessment of potential "costs" or undesirable consequences, and a consideration of alternatives.

The labeling of consequences as benefits or costs is subjective and

---

3. In light of this evidence on regulatory forbearance, and given the disincentives to disclose truthfully certain private information to regulators, the desirability of adopting risk-sensitive deposit-insurance premiums to be administered by the federal government is far from obvious.

arbitrary. Consequences that involve issues of equity as well as efficiency are obvious examples. Whether a particular consequence is desirable depends on which party's perspective is adopted. Unfortunately, we do not have an objective function that can be invoked noncontroversially to capture social welfare. Instead, our primary motivation is to set forth a general inventory of potential consequences of adopting a market value accounting proposal to facilitate more meaningful public debate.

A consideration of alternatives is important since benefits or costs can only be defined relative to some set of specified alternatives. Selecting a particularly weak alternative can obviously slant the conclusions.

Our discussion in some respects characterizes the status quo more broadly than do prior discussions. In particular, we view the current system primarily as one based on historical cost accounting but with supplemental disclosures that are available to regulators, investors, and the public. A critical issue here is whether the adoption of market value accounting would be more than merely a change in form. What would various parties know under such a proposed system that they do not already know under the status quo?

Moreover, the costs and benefits of altering the mandated reporting system cannot be evaluated in isolation from other features of the proposed changes in the regulation of financial institutions. For example, the desirability of market value accounting is affected by whether greater private-sector monitoring of the depository institutions is encouraged by other features of regulatory reform. Benston and White, among others, have emphasized dramatically the lack of incentives to monitor on the part of the private sector (i.e., depositors) because of the structure of the insurance system. A major alternative is to introduce greater incentives to monitor on the part of the private sector. Such proposals would be operationalized by essentially placing "at risk" a larger portion of the capital supplied to these institutions (including, perhaps, the resources of private insurance companies). A discussion of the exact structure of the proposals is beyond the scope of this paper, but key features of such a system would include a nontrivial reduction in the de jure and de facto insurance coverage to capital suppliers and a nontrivial increase in capital adequacy ratios, defined broadly as the proportion of total capital that is not publicly insured.[4]

In urging a broadening of the alternatives considered we do not intend to prejudge the issue. Whether responsibility for monitoring the risk and performance of financial institutions should be shifted from the public

---

4. It is worth noting that while permanent equity is treated as a more desirable form of capital for regulatory purposes than is subordinated debt, the latter may provide better private incentives for monitoring the performance of bank management in a way that allows intervention at a time that precedes insolvency. Regulators may be able to "free ride" to some degree on this private monitoring by taking remedial action whenever control of the institution is transferred to subordinated debt holders.

sector to the private sector depends in part on who has the comparative advantage in conducting monitoring activities. On the one hand, economies of scale would suggest a centralization of the monitoring functions in the hands of a regulator. On the other hand, concern about moral hazard, among other factors, might lead to decentralization. In this regard, some consideration should be given to changes in the financial markets since the regulatory apparatus was erected in the 1930s. The role of the "sophisticated investor" has increased, markets are more complete in terms of the richness of securities offered, and information technology has changed dramatically. It may well be that private markets are now in a better position to assume a monitoring role than they were at the time of the initiation of the regulatory structure.

It is important for several reasons to broaden the scope of regulatory reform alternatives beyond the consideration of different accounting systems. We believe that altering the private-sector incentives to gather information and monitor activities may in fact dwarf in importance the effects of a proposal to alter the regulatory information system. This is especially so in light of the possibility that the accounting system alternatives may well differ more in form than in substance. Instead, the basic issue, as correctly pointed out by Benston, is the incentives of the various parties to gather and use the data. Changing the form of the disclosure without changing the basic incentive structure is subject to a substantial risk that the change will have limited impact on the behavior of the various parties. It seems at least as important to focus on changing the incentives to gather and act on information as it is to contemplate changes in the form of the information.

Potential Benefits of Market Value Accounting

The arguments in favor of market value accounting have largely focused on the shortcomings of historical cost accounting. For instance White (1988) argues that under historical cost accounting, identical financial assets may be carried on the books at different values (depending on when they were acquired) while different financial assets with different market values may have identical accounting values. A related issue is the distortionary effect of historical cost accounting on the incentives of managers to undertake transactions for accounting benefits even though those transactions may be harmful to the economic worth of the institution. An example of such behavior might be the incentive of thrift managements to sell assets that have appreciated in value while continuing to hold assets that have declined, thereby not recognizing any loss.

As a counterpoint to the criticism that historical cost accounting encourages manipulation of income and capital through judicious choice of asset and liability transactions, it should be noted that market value accounting is hardly immune from such distortions. For example, suppose an institution builds a portfolio of loans of varying quality and that management has vastly superior knowledge, relative to regulators and other third parties, of the default risk of the individual loans in the portfolio. Suppose further that management shared with a buyer its private information on a few of its most valuable (that is, highest risk-adjusted-yield) loans and sells these loans at premium prices. An opportunistic management might use such nonrepresentative transaction prices as a surrogate for the market value of the remaining lower-quality loans. And since only management knows that the retained loans are not equal in value to those that were sold, its capacity to distort income and capital under a market value accounting system could easily exceed its ability to do so on an historical cost basis.

From the point of view of the regulator, market value accounting is intended to provide a better picture of the economic net worth of individual banks and thrifts and consequently of the insurance risks faced by the federal insurance agency. In this context, the benefits of market value accounting can be thought of either from a valuation or an information perspective. As argued earlier, a valuation argument has obvious appeal only in a world of perfect and complete markets, a world in which there is no demand for regulation or the reporting of market value information. Since the market for the assets (and liabilities) of financial institutions is largely imperfect and incomplete, however, we shall concentrate our evaluation of the benefits of market value accounting by adopting an informational perspective.

If market value accounting is to play a valuable role, an important question is the nature of the information it will provide the regulator. Presumably, one benefit of market value accounting is that it provides the regulator with information about default risk and interest-rate risk on the net assets of a bank or thrift. But, as discussed earlier, this information may already be available to the regulator in the form of supplemental disclosures on fixed and variable interest income and schedule information regarding nonaccruing loans. Thus, a case for market value accounting cannot be made only on the basis of the additional information it provides over historical cost accounting. At a minimum, the case for market value accounting must be made in terms of its information advantages over the supplemental disclosures on interest-rate and default risk. In fact, information about default and interest-rate risk is probably available to the regulator on a more timely basis from other sources as well. Where markets exist for the individual assets of banks and thrifts, regulators can use market prices to infer the economic status of individual banks and thrifts.

This suggests that the greatest potential value of market value accounting comes from the information it might provide about assets whose direct market values are not easily determined such as, for example, nonstandardized loans that do not have securitized analogs (consumer and commercial loans), direct equity positions in real estate, and intangible assets, such as franchise value. There are at least three factors, however, that counteract this benefit of market value accounting.

First, the regulatee lacks proper incentives to disclose private information such as that relating to default risks of assets. The heart of any proposal in favor of market value accounting is that thrift managers have the incentives to disclose their private information to regulators. But more realistically, such incentives hardly seem to exist. How will market value accounting change those basic incentives? If incentives for disclosure are unaltered, it is unclear what market value accounting will achieve. Regulatees will disclose "market values" that do not reflect fully what they know about default risks and other valuation relevant information about their assets and liabilities. An evaluation of the informational benefits of market value accounting must simultaneously consider the regulatee's incentives to disclose such information.

Second, measurement problems abound in determining the market value of certain bank and thrift assets (and liabilities) such as nonstandardized loans, real estate, and goodwill. Determining the market value of nonsecuritized loans requires an evaluation of factors such as the quality of the borrower, maturity, and prepayment likelihoods. Even without moral hazard on the regulatee's part, the market values for these assets are likely to be measured with significant error.

Many market value accounting proposals seem to understate the problems here. They argue that the vast majority of assets held by banks and thrifts have easily determinable market values (see, for example, White). Even if this were true (which we doubt), it fails to recognize that market valuation difficulties with a small fraction of total assets can translate into huge problems relative to the market value of an institution's equity. And valuation difficulties relative to the equity base would seem to be the relevant issue for regulatory purposes.

Finally, difficulties in measuring the market value of certain assets create distortionary incentives of their own. Financial institution managers may favor investments in assets whose market values are difficult to measure. For example, instead of holding mortgage-backed securities, financial institutions might find it desirable to retain the mortgages they have originated themselves and introduce contractual features that govern these assets, giving managers an informational advantage over regulators. More generally, the market value accounting system could encourage financial institutions to increase their concentration in assets that have equity-like features where they can manipulate reported values because of market incompleteness and their superior information. The effect of such a strategy is to reduce the informational and evaluative value of market value accounting.

A potential benefit of market value accounting is that it permits an evaluation of the economic risk of a financial institution in the context of its overall portfolio rather than an assessment of individual assets and liabilities. Market value accounting can, in principle, capture covariances in returns among assets by reflecting increases and decreases in asset values that historical cost accounting largely ignores. This information could be used to develop better risk-based minimum capital standards and a risk-based deposit-insurance premium.

It is sometimes argued that market value accounting would commit regulators to a more socially desirable regulatory policy. The argument runs as follows. If the market value of the net assets of thrifts and banks were disclosed publicly, regulators would find it difficult *not* to take regulatory action for those institutions reporting negative net worth. Public disclosure of market value numbers constrains the regulator from exercising discretion with regard to allowing weak banks and thrifts to continue to operate.

There are two qualifications that must be made to this argument. First, the desirability of committing regulators to take certain rule-based actions presumes that regulatory discretion is unwarranted. This is not obvious. Indeed, if regulators sought to maximize social (rather than their own personal) welfare, allowing discretion would be preferred to rule-based action. It is precisely the concern with moral hazard on the part of the regulators that favors reducing their discretionary powers.

Second, the underlying premise that public disclosure of market value numbers guarantees commitment to a particular regulatory strategy is faulty. Many thrifts reported negative net worth positions in the early 1980s based on generally accepted accounting principles (GAAP), which, at the time, formed the basis for regulatory action. Rather than close down "insolvent" thrifts, however, the regulators introduced more liberal regulatory accounting procedures (RAP) that had the effect of substantially increasing the regulatory net worth of thrifts. The move to RAP *may* have been dictated by the lack of funds at the FSLIC (although insufficient funding is also an endogenous factor) and the consequent "inability" of regulators to close down thrifts. Nevertheless, this episode serves to underscore the point that well established, widely adopted principles of GAAP accounting were undone.

Perhaps an argument could be made that market value accounting is different from GAAP in that market value numbers more closely reflect "economic valuations" of certain thrift assets and liabilities that are harder for the regulators to ignore. By why this per se should result in market value accounting generating greater commitment to regulatory action (relative to GAAP accounting) is far from evident.

To the extent that the role of the accounting system is to aid taxpayers in constraining and monitoring regulatory behavior and to help employees and owners monitor financial performance, the issue of which reporting form is easiest to disseminate and understand is an important one. Market value accounting is probably the easiest form of communication for owners to understand because it reports on the economic values of various assets and liabilities. Historical cost accounting requires the application of various accounting principles that owners (taxpayers) may find difficult to comprehend as they may find historical cost-based income statements and balance sheets more difficult to interpret.

Consideration of Potential Costs

Moving to market value accounting involves various costs. The most obvious and direct cost is the out-of-pocket expense of data gathering, computation, summarization, and analysis. Market values of assets are not readily available. Often, asset cash flows and discount rates must be estimated. The computation of market values is a significant task. This point is emphasized by the American Bankers Association (1990).

Besides the direct costs, market value accounting is fraught with measurement errors, reducing the value of information to regulators and owners. Difficulties in measurement can also distort managerial incentives by encouraging investment in assets whose market values are more difficult for regulators and other third parties to determine than for management.

It is sometimes claimed that the implementation of market value accounting will reveal a larger number of insolvencies, causing greater erosion of public confidence in thrifts and widespread closures. It is not clear that this would occur so long as the general public has confidence in the government's deposit-insurance system. Nevertheless, the "too big to fail" perspective adopted by the federal regulators in the case of Continental Illinois Bank, among other institutions, suggests that the potential cost of reduced confidence in the banking system cannot be ignored completely.

Another cost associated with implementing a market value accounting system relates to the fact that the firms are better informed about their financial condition than are the regulators. A market value accounting system will result in regulatees incurring costs designed to convince the regulators that their market value estimates are not misrepresented. In other words, the cost of producing market value numbers only *begins* with the out-of-pocket cost to the regulatee of producing the requisite market value estimates. Historical cost accounting numbers and certain supplemental disclosures are more easily auditable by third parties, a desirable feature. Recent work by Milgrom and Roberts (1990) demonstrates that it may be desirable to close down certain communication channels between regulators and regulatees, even when it blocks communication of information that would be valuable in a setting devoid of incentive problems, if such a restriction discourages overinvestment in informtion that is designed to yield favorable regulatory treatment.

A consideration of costs should include not only those particular to a market value proposal but also those that are generally associated with changes in the regulatory status quo. Such broader costs include those associated with the path dependency of regulatory environments or "transition costs." In other words, the cost of implementing a new system depends on where we are now. Among other factors, costs of changing and adapting to a new system must be considered.

There is a second type of broader cost, introduced by regulatory uncertainty. In this context, the relationship between the regulators and regulatees can be viewed as a set of contracts (implicit and explicit). The coercive power of the state often means the regulators have the power to change unilaterally the terms of the contracts.[5] Changes in the regulatory environment (for example, adoption of market value accounting or reduction in insurance coverage) can effectively negate provisions of prior contracts between the regulators and the private party. Obviously, there can be a "cost," *ex post,* when the regulatory change occurs. However, there is an *ex ante* risk that can affect private parties' behavior, in at least several related respects including their willingness to contract with the regulators, the "price" they charge for bearing such risk, and strategic behavior they may engage in, postcontracting, to mitigate such risk. Each change in regulation has the potential to increase this regulatory risk.

CONCLUDING REMARKS

The stunning failures we have experienced in attempting to regulate the banking industry has given birth to a host of proposed remedies involving regulatory overhaul. Prominent among the features of the regulatory structure that has been denigrated is the historical cost accounting system that allegedly prevents regulators from recognizing when an institution is insolvent on a market value basis.

Many of the calls for market value accounting have been naive in several respects. Some ignore the incentives of financial institutions to be strategic in their reporting of "market value" numbers. Some understate the significance of market imperfections and market incompleteness for the ability to produce market value data that possess desirable properties. Some ignore the fact that historical cost financial statements are supplemented by myriad disclosures that are relevant to assessing market values. Some ignore incentive problems on the part of regulators; they fail to recognize that regulators have been well aware of market value deficits in many of their regulatees despite the seemingly contradicting indications of historical cost accounting valuations.

A crucial step required to reform the industry is to implement a credible means by which regulatory intervention occurs *prior* to insolvency. It is precisely the insolvent, but unforeclosed, entities that have the

---

5. On the other hand, several thrifts have sued the government for allegedly reneging on deals they struck that have been effectively violated by the terms of the Financial Institutions Reform, Recovery, and Enforcement Act of 1989. See "Congress Learns That Even Thrifts Have Constitutional Rights," *Wall Street Journal,* March 28, 1990.

greatest incentives to engage in investment and financing strategies designed to transfer wealth from the taxpayers (via the federal insurance agency) to private suppliers of capital. This suggests that an increased role for private-sector monitoring ought to be given serious consideration in any regulatory reform, along with the implications this has for the desirability of adopting a market value accounting system.

It is by no means automatic that market value accounting would improve the efficiency with which financial institutions are regulated, especially given the regulators' track record on foreclosure. Indeed, while we do not mean to prejudge this issue, we have advanced arguments suggesting that a market value accounting system could actually exacerbate the problem.

REFERENCES

American Bankers Association, *Market Value Accounting*, Washington, D.C., June 1990.

Barth, Mary, William Beaver, and Chris Stinson, "Supplemental Data and the Structure of Thrift Share Prices," *Accounting Review*, vol. 66, January 1991, 56–66.

Beaver, William, Carol Eger, Stephen Ryan, and Mark Wolfson, "Financial Reporting, Supplemental Disclosures, and Bank Share Prices," *Journal of Accounting Research*, Autumn 1989, vol. 27, 157–78.

Beaver, William, and Wayne Landsman, "Incremental Information Content of Statement 33 Disclosures," Research Report: Financial Accounting Standards Board, November 1983.

Benston, George J., "Market Value Accounting: Benefits, Costs, and Incentives," working paper, December 1989.

Benston, George, R. Dan Brumbaugh, Jr., Jack M. Guttentag, Richard J. Herring, George G. Kaufman, Robert E. Litan, and Kenneth E. Scott, *Restructuring America's Financial Institutions*, Brookings Institution (Washington, D.C.), 1989.

Berger, A., K. Kuester, and J. O'Brien, "Some Red Flags Concerning Market Value Accounting," working paper, Board of Governors of the Federal Reserve System (Washington, D.C.), August 1989.

Bernard, Vic, and William Ruland, "The Incremental Information Content of Historical Cost and Current Cost Numbers: A Time Series Analysis," *Accounting Review*, vol. 62, October 1987, 701–22.

DeBerg, Curtis, and Keith Shriver, "The Relevance of Current Cost Accounting Data; A Review and Analysis of Recent Studies," *Journal of Accounting Literature*, vol. 6, 55–87.

Diamond, Douglas, "Financial Intermediation and Delegated Monitoring," *Review of Economic Studies*, vol. 51, no. 3, July 1984, 393–414.

Fama, Eugene, "What's Different About Banks?" *Journal of Monetary Economics*, vol. 15, no. 1, January, 1985, 29–39.

FHLMC (Federal Home Loan Mortgage Corporation), Information Statement, FHLMC (Reston, Va.), March 30, 1990.

Ghicas, Dimitrios, and Victor Pastena, "The Acquisition Value of Oil and Gas Firms: The Role of Historical Costs, Reserve Recognition Accounting, and Analysts' Appraisals," *Contemporary Accounting Research,* vol. 5, Fall 1989, 125–42.

Harris, Trevor, and James Ohlson, "Accounting Disclosures and the Market's Valuation of Oil and Gas Reserves," *Accounting Review,* vol. 62, October 1987, 631–70.

Kane, Edward, *The Gathering Crisis in Federal Deposit Insurance,* MIT Press (Cambridge, Mass.), 1985.

Leland, Hayne, and David Pyle, "Information Asymmetries, Financial Structure, and Financial Intermediation," *Journal of Finance,* vol. 32, May 1977, 371–87.

Mengle, D., "The Feasibility of Market Value Accounting for Commercial Banks," working paper, Federal Reserve Bank of Richmond, October 1989.

Milgrom, Paul, and John Roberts, "Bargaining Costs, Influence Costs, and the Organization of Economic Activity," in *Positive Perspectives on Political Economy,* J. Alt and K. Shepsle, eds., Cambridge University Press, 1990.

Scholes, Myron, G. Peter Wilson, and Mark Wolfson, "Tax Planning, Regulatory Capital Planning, and Financial Reporting Strategy for Commercial Banks," working paper, Stanford University, April 1990.

Sheshunoff, *The Bank Manual,* Austin, Texas, April 1989.

Shirreff, D., "Into the Next Dimension: Making Money Out of Trading LDC Debt," *Risk,* March, 1990.

Simonson, Donald, and George Hempel, "Running on Empty: Accounting Strategies to Clarify Bank and S & L Capital Value," working paper, Southern Methodist University, 1990.

Tirole, J., "Hierarchies and Bureaucracies: On the Role of Collusion in Organizations," *Journal of Law, Economics, and Organization,* Fall 1986, 181–214.

White, Lawrence, "Market Value Accounting: An Important Part of the Reform of the Deposit Insurance System," in Association of Reserve City Bankers. *Capital Issues in Banking* (Washington, D.C.), 1988, pp. 226–242.

CHAPTER 10

Market Value versus Historical Cost Accounting: Evidence from Southeastern Thrifts*

George J. Benston

John H. Harland Professor of Finance, Accounting, and Economics, Emory University

Mike Carhill

Financial Economist, Office of the Comptroller of the Currency

and

Brian Olasov

Financial Institutions Specialist, Long, Aldridge, and Norman, Atlanta, Georgia

For the deposit insurer, the value of the insured's equity investment determines the value of the "deductible," while the value of the insured's assets (relative to insured liabilities) determines the insurer's potential loss. These

*Benston's research was supported, in large part, by Grant 5-29355 from the Federal Home Loan Bank Board, which is gratefully acknowledged. The authors would like to thank Rocky Rhodes for expert programming assistance and Richard G. Fritz for useful advice on various econometric issues. Comments from seminar participants at a conference sponsored by the Center for Economic Policy Research are also gratefully acknowledged. The views expressed here are those of the authors and should not be interpreted as representing the views of the Office of the Currency.

facts suggest that sound estimates of both values are a prerequisite to sound deposit insurance. The delay in recognizing the high incidence of insolvency among thrift institutions, and the ultimate financial distress of the Federal Savings and Loan Insurance Corporation (FSLIC), were undoubtedly aggravated by the inability to determine the value of the insureds' "deductible" and potential loss.

Partly in response to the insolvency of the FSLIC, the 1989 FIRREA legislation included stiff penalties for fraudulent financial reporting.[1] Many commentators have suggested that reform should go further and include the imposition of market value accounting for financial institutions.[2] To examine the practicality and validity of this suggestion, we constructed a computer model which uses the *Thrift Financial Reports* (*TFR*s) to derive estimates of Fourth District (Southeastern) thrifts' market values.[3] Although *TFR*s have been produced for many years, it was not until March 1984 that these reports included (in "Section H") information on the amounts and timing of cash flows expected from various groups of assets and liabilities. We use these data to estimate market values.

To construct market values from the *TFR* data, we must use effective (as opposed to contract) maturity, appropriate discount rates, and determine credit quality. Because the data reported on the *TFR*s are for aggregates of generally similar assets and liabilities, with some exceptions we had to use discount rates and base our procedures on general rather than thrift-specific assumptions. Consequently, our market value estimates are inferior to those that would be generated by individual thrifts, if market value accounting were adopted. In contrast, traditional accounting is thrift- and individual asset- and liability-specific. Thus, we believe that a test of market value accounting using our estimates is biased against the market value approach. Nevertheless, we test our market value estimates against traditional accounting values for predicting thrift failures, and find that our estimates are superior.

This paper is organized as follows. The first section describes the methodology and assumptions used in estimating market values. Some of these assumptions would be unnecessary for an on-site auditor, while others relate to theoretical difficulties which market value accounting must confront. The second section describes the effect of market valuation on various assets and liabilities.

---

1. See *Financial Institutions Reform, Recovery, and Enforcement Act: Conference Report to Accompany H.R. 1278,* U.S. Government Printing Office (Washington, D.C.), 1989, p. 314. Maximum penalties for "false or misleading" reports range up to $1 million per day.

2. See, for example, Lawrence J. White, "Problems of the FSLIC: A Former Policymaker's View," *Contemporary Policy Issues,* vol. 8, no. 2, April 1990, p. 62–81.

3. The Fourth District is composed of Federal Home Loan Bank of Atlanta members (almost all FSLIC-insured thrifts) in Alabama, the District of Columbia, Florida, Georgia, Maryland, North Carolina, South Carolina, and Virginia.

OVERVIEW OF METHODOLOGY

The value of a financial asset or liability depends on its duration, its contract rate of interest vis-à-vis current market rates of interest, the extent to which contracted payments are expected to materialize ("credit quality"), and the administrative costs involved in making and collecting those payments. Nonfinancial assets are similarly valued: the expected net cash flows from their use in the enterprise over their economically useful lives are discounted by the firm's cost of capital to obtain their present values. Thus, market values refer to values in use, or the values of assets and liabilities to going concerns. In general, accounting (or book) values reflect the price paid or received at the time an asset or liability was acquired or created. As conditions change unexpectedly, the market values of the assets or liabilities fluctuate, but except for items that are sold these fluctuations generally are not reflected by book values. Consequently, to estimate market values, we had to adjust book values for unexpected changes in durations, market rates of interest, and credit quality.

Expected changes, however, should be reflected in the initial price paid for an asset (or received for a liability) and in the cash flows expected. For example, if market rates of interest are expected to change, the interest rate charged for a fixed-rate mortgage loan should equal the geometric mean of the interest rates expected over the time the funds are lent, weighted by the amounts outstanding. Similarly, expected credit-quality losses on loans should be compensated for by higher gross interest rates. In adjusting book values to market values, then, we were concerned with unexpected changes in the key variables.

Source of Data

We estimated yearend market values from data reported in the Office of Thrift Supervision's (formerly Federal Home Loan Bank Board) *TFR*s, which are filed quarterly (semiannually before 1984). The study covers the 517 southeastern thrifts which held membership in the Federal Home Loan Bank of Atlanta on December 31, 1984.

The high interest rates of the late 1970s and early 1980s caused large losses for the thrift industry. It was in response to these losses that Section H was introduced in 1984. This section reports the contracted nominal annual rates and maturities of several categories of assets and liabilities. The information given allows us to make reasonably sophisticated, although generic, estimates of market values for the financial assets and liabilities held by thrifts.

Maturities and Contractual Cash Flows

Section H reports the contractual cash flows for seven groups of financial assets and five groups of financial liabilities. The assets include four types of mortgage loans: balloon and adjustable first mortgages, fixed-rate first mortgages (including mortgage-backed securities), other residential and nonresidential first mortgages, and second mortgages. Nonmortgage assets include consumer loans, commercial loans, and investment securities. The liabilities distinguish among fixed-maturity deposits (certificates of deposit), transaction accounts (including NOWs and SuperNOWs), passbook accounts, FHLB advances, and other borrowings.

Each asset or liability is classified according to its contractual maturity, or in the case of an adjustable-rate instrument, its repricing date. There are seven maturity classifications, or "buckets": zero-to-six months, six-to-twelve months, one-to-three years, three-to-five years, five-to-ten years, ten-to-twenty years, and more than twenty years. We assumed that the maturity of the instruments was the midpoint of each bucket, thus approximating average maturities as three months, nine months, twenty-four months, forty-eight months, eighty-four months, [4] one hundred eighty months, and three hundred months.

Although some items always fall in one bucket (for example, transactions and passbook accounts are all placed in the zero-to-six-month bucket), most may fall into any of the seven. For example, thrifts are instructed to assign each of their fixed-rate mortgages to the bucket corresponding to that mortgage's years remaining to contractual maturity. Adjustable-rate mortgages and commercial loans are assigned to the bucket corresponding to the loan's months remaining to interest-rate adjustment.

Cash Flow Assumptions

The cash flow patterns of interest and principal payments may be characterized as "bullet," "balloon," and "self-liquidating."

Bullet securities, such as the standard corporate bond, pay interest through the contracted maturity date with no interim principal payments. At the contracted maturity date, the principal plus the final coupon is received or paid in a "bullet." We treat commercial loans and all investment securities as bullet securities, with interest received semiannually. All liabilities except passbook savings accounts were treated as bullet securities, with quarterly interest payments.

Balloon securities have payment schedules which amortize principal over n periods, but require lump-sum repayment of the outstanding principal balance at an earlier time. We value adjustable-rate mortgages (ARMs) as balloon securities, with the principal amortized over 300 months and the remaining balance (original principal minus scheduled amortization and prepayments) ballooning at the ARMs' scheduled adjustment (repricing)

---

4. To achieve consistency with readily available seven-year market rates of interest, the "midpoint" of the five-to-ten-year bucket was taken to be 84 rather than 90 months.

dates.[5] We lacked information on ARM interest-rate caps; to the extent that the ARMs' adjustments to market rates are constrained by such caps, we tend to overstate the value of the ARM portfolios.

Self-liquidating instruments completely amortize the principal as part of the scheduled periodic payments, where the size of the payments is fixed over the instruments' lives. In addition to the scheduled payments, these instruments are assumed to prepay a constant proportion each period, as we explain next. Self-liquidating instruments include fixed-rate mortgages, other residential mortgages, second mortgages, and consumer loans.

Prepayment Assumptions

Because consumers always have the option to prepay loans, actual maturities need not equal contracted maturities. When market rates are below contract rates, consumers have incentives to prepay, particularly on longer-maturity loans such as fixed-rate mortgages. Consequently, discounting cash flows that would be determined by contractual maturities significantly overstates market values. Thus, we must introduce more realistic effective maturity structures.

The OTS has estimated prepayments for all mortgage instruments, given in Schedule 9, but this schedule includes only the mortgages' coupon rates and not the market rate to which prepayments are supposed to respond. We ran experiments which showed that the value of mortgage portfolios is very sensitive to the prepayment specification. Thus we had to estimate our own fixed-rate-mortgage prepayment function.

We estimated prepayment rates from data kindly provided by the Federal Home Loan Mortgage Corporation (FHLMC). These data give the FHLMC's monthly prepayment experience, by mortgage-coupon class, for the period February 1985 to February 1989 (243 observations in all). Once determined as a function of the spread, prepayments are assumed to be constant over the mortgages' lifetimes (the so-called "constant prepayment rate" or CPR). After considerable experimentation, we found the following regression to provide the best estimate of the prepayment function:

$$\text{LOGPREPAY} = -2.53 \text{ when LOGSPREAD} < -0.11 \ (n = 58)$$
$$\text{LOGPREPAY} = -2.09 + 4.57 \ (\text{LOGSPREAD}) \text{ when}$$
$$-0.11 \leq \text{LOGSPREAD} < 0.26$$

where the T-statistics are -41.6 (intercept) and 12.4 (LOGSPREAD), the $R^2 = 0.64$, and the F value equals 153.724 ($n = 90$).

---

5. This method marks to market only those payments remaining to repricing, valuing subsequent payments at par. We would have used the actual term remaining to maturity (instead of 300 months) had the required information been available.

$$\text{LOGPREPAY} = -0.95 \text{ when } \text{LOGSPREAD} \geq 0.26 \ (n = 95)^6$$

where LOGSPREAD = log(coupon rate/current FHLMC committed rate), and LOGPREPAY = log(annualized prepayment rate).

The antilogarithm of the intercept provides an estimate of the average annual prepayment rate and the coefficient of LOGSPREAD measures the responsiveness of prepayments to the spread. Our function predicts that prepayments range from 7.5 percent (annualized), when the coupon is more than roughly 100 basis points below the FHLMC rate, to 41.5 percent (annualized), when the coupon is more than roughly 300 basis points above the FHLMC rate.

For ARMs and second mortgages we used the rate-independent CPRs provided by Schedule 9: 12 percent for ARMs, and 14 percent for second mortgages (annualized). We assumed that effective maturity equals contract maturities for commercial loans, investment securities, and other mortgages. Prepayments are not relevant for consumer loans, since we valued those loans at par (see below).

Discount Rates

We discounted the cash flows (contracted payments implied by Section H adjusted for prepayments or decays) by rates which, where possible, reflect the market consensus expectation for obligations with similar durations. This discounting procedure has the effect of capitalizing firm-specific advantages and disadvantages in pricing, administration, and credit-quality control. Because the cash flows reflect loan-specific differences in credit risk, we also adjusted the data for credit losses (as described later).

The appropriate discount rates corresponding to the full range of maturities are not always available. We calculated the term structure for each rate as a direct function of the bond-equivalent yields on U.S. Treasury obligations, published in the *Federal Reserve Statistical Release; H.15(519)* [after 1987, *G.13(415)*]. Even for the Treasury series, yields for 9-month and 48-month obligations were not available. Hence, we interpolated these yields as the geometric mean from surrounding available rates.[7]

We use asset- and liability-specific discount rates. Yield curves for each discount rate then were constructed by using the relationship estimated by regressing Treasury yields on the available maturities for each discount rate.

---

6. In order to estimate a continuous function, we used the middle expression's values of -2.59 for the low and -0.88 for the high spreads, rather than the actual estimates of -2.53 and -0.95.

7. The 9-month yield (Y_9 was interpolated as $[(1+Y_6)\ (1+Y_{12})]^{\frac{1}{2}}-1$ and the 48-month yield (Y_{48}) as $[(1+Y_{36})\ (1+Y_{60})]^{\frac{1}{2}}-1$, with the subscripts denoting months.

Mortgage Loans and Contracts.   To discount the cash flows on mortgage loans, we used the FHLMC committed rate, which represents the 30-day forward rate at which Freddie Mac will pay par for conforming 30-year fixed-rate first mortgages on residential property. Freddie Mac assumes most of the credit risk and administrative costs on the mortgages, so the FHLMC rate captures these components of mortgage interest rates.

For calculating the term structure, we assumed that the 30-year FHLMC rate most closely corresponds to a 10-year Treasury rate because, with normal prepayments, the effective maturity of a 30-year mortgage loan is roughly equivalent to that of a 12-year security.[8] For the same reason, we assumed that the 15-year committed rate is equivalent to 7-year Treasury notes. To derive the rest of the Freddie Mac term structure, we ran a log-linear regression based on the 30-year and 15-year FHLMC committed rates. We presumed a five basis point spread of 3-month mortgages over 3-month Treasury bills.[9] Using the spreads over Treasury rates at these three points on the term structure, we derived the remainder of the yield curve via the log-linear equation. This term structure was applied against first mortgage products including balloon and ARMs, one-to-four-family fixed rate, and other mortgage loans.

It is well known that second mortgages involve higher administrative expenses than adjustable-rate or fixed-rate mortgages. We were unable to find a secondary market rate for second mortgages, but interviews with market participants led us to conclude that the market rate on second mortgages was approximately 200 basis points higher than the Freddie Mac committed rate.

Consumer Loans.   Section H aggregates all types of consumer loans into one category. This is unfortunate, because these loans are very heterogeneous in terms of credit quality and administrative costs, with typical yields (in 1986) ranging from 18.3 percent on credit card debt to 9.4 percent on car loans.[10] Since no single discount rate can capture the differing administrative costs and credit risk, we decided that book values provide the best estimate of the value of consumer loan portfolios.

Commercial Loans.   Commercial loans represent a special problem, in that there are almost no sources as to their proper discount rate. We could

---

8. *The Handbook of Mortgage-Backed Securities,* Frank Fabozzi, ed., p. 652, 1988.

9. Inspection of term structures for various discount rates reveals very little spread over Treasury bills at 3-month maturities. Conversely, a linear equation using the 15- and 30-year FHLMC rates produced a substantial spread over the Treasury rate at 3-month maturities. The counterfactual results of the linear approach led us to impute the 3-month spread and use log-linear estimation.

10. *Federal Reserve Bulletin,* November 1987, Table 1.56.

locate only surveys conducted by the Federal Reserve, which reports the average commercial loan rate for various maturities and sizes of commercial loans. [11] From these surveys, we selected the short-term floating rate as the appropriate discount rate for short-term commercial loans. We assumed that these short-term loans carry negligible credit risk, and that the difference between the short-term floating rate and the 3-month T bill rate was due entirely to administrative costs. Therefore, to discount longer-term loans, we added this administrative premium to the T bill term structure. (The Federal Reserve survey provides rates for longer-term commercial loans, but it is impossible to separate the administrative from the credit-quality components of those rates.)

Investment Securities. The *TFR* provides almost no information on the composition of securities portfolios, but the Federal Home Loan Bank has a safekeeping program which we believe reflects typical thrift portfolios. The composition of these portfolios indicated that the bond-equivalent rate on the Federal National Mortgage Agency debentures is appropriate. [12]

Liabilities. Rates paid on certificates of deposit (CDs) represent the marginal cost of attracting wholesale funds. National index CD rates are quoted on the front page of the yearend report of the *Bank Rate Monitor.* Beginning in 1984, this publication reports the 6-month, 12-month, 30-month, and 60-month CDs' yields as effective annual rates. We extrapolated the missing yield curve points from the ratio of 60-month CDs to 60-month Treasury notes. These discount rates were applied against all liabilities.

Credit Quality

For financial assets, there is some probability that the contracted payments will not be made or will be made at dates later than contracted. At the time an asset is created, that cost of these expected losses should be included in the contract rate of interest. While the probability of loss may not be predicted accurately for individual loans, the expected loss rate usually can be well estimated for portfolios. Hence, if a given pool of assets experiences the credit quality expected, the book value of the pool need not be adjusted for credit risk. (The only adjustment required would be for unexpected changes in market interest rates, as described above.)

---

11. This survey's results are reported in the *Federal Reserve Bulletin,* June 1985, p. A70 (February 1985 survey); May 1986, p. A70 (February 1986 survey); May 1987, p. A70 (February 1987 survey); May 1988, p. A70 (February 1988 survey); and June 1989, page A84 (February 1989 survey).

12. The Federal Reserve does not report an agency rate, so we relied on the *Wall Street Journal* (January 2, 1985, 1986, 1987, 1988, 1989) for the FNMA debenture yields.

Two primary forces cause a portfolio's credit quality to differ from that expected when the pool is created. One is changes in economic conditions, such as the unexpected deterioration in the borrowers' personal (in the case of corporate borrowers, business) economic situations or, for mortgage loans, reductions in the value of the collateral. The other is the skill and honesty of a given institution's management, which may misestimate the default rates and costs.

When a borrower fails to meet the loan payments required, the loan becomes delinquent. A delinquent borrower usually is charged a late fee, both to compensate the lender for the administrative costs of special handling and to provide an incentive to borrowers to avoid delinquency. When the delinquency is not cured, the loan either is restructured or goes into default. Thus, there are three categories into which problem loans fall: delinquency, default, or restructuring.

If the delinquent loan is restructured, usually by allowing given payments to be made over a longer maturity, a market-value loss is generally suffered. [13] Such losses are not recognized by traditional accounting methods, but Section H will reflect the restructuring in a lower contract yield on the loan, so our market valuation method captures the loss. If a borrower defaults, pledged collateral is seized. The book value of the loan (principal plus accrued interest) is subtracted from the loan portfolio and the lower of the collateral's appraised value or the loan's book value is added to the "Real Estate Owned" asset on the balance sheet. The net decline in asset values that usually results is recorded as an expense, which reduces retained earnings. Therefore, if appraisals of the values of repossessed assets are accurate, losses on foreclosure will be measured correctly by us because we take the book value of repossessed assets as equal to their market value. For these reasons, resolved credit-quality problems pose no problems for market valuation. The treatment of ongoing problems is more difficult, however.

If thrift accountants and auditors performed their tasks in accordance with GAAP, the book values of problem loans and other assets would be periodically adjusted to their net realizable values. (This is not the present value amount, as neither GAAP nor RAP allows for changes in market rates of interest.) The amounts of specific loans that the thrift expects will not be collected should be recorded in a "contra asset" account, called "specific valuation allowance," which reduces the asset balance. For the balance of the loan portfolio, experience and expectations indicate that a certain percentage will not be collected; that is, a certain percentage of "good" loans will eventually go "bad." According to GAAP, expected losses on these currently good loans should be estimated and recorded in

---

13. For example, a loan with a $100 payment due in one year might be restructured into a loan with four annual payments of $25 per year. If the market rate of interest is currently 10 percent, the market value of the loan will fall from $90.91 to $79.25.

a "general reserve or allowance for loans losses," which also reduces the asset balance. [14] However, GAAP does not permit accountants to increase asset balances when unexpectedly improved economic conditions or above-average skill in managing credit risk raises the value of an asset.

The discounting procedure we use requires that general valuation allowances be deducted, because the prepayment-adjusted cash flows include amounts expected to compensate a thrift for its expected credit losses, and we discounted these cash flows with rates that reflect general rather than thrift-specific expected losses. [15] We believe, though, that reported valuation allowances are inadequate for our purposes, for three reasons. First, GAAP does not permit assets to be revalued upward. Second, we have reason to believe that some thrifts fail to follow GAAP procedures for reserving credit losses on loans. This belief is based on extended discussions with market participants, on the experience of one of the authors in a project which estimated liquidation costs for thrifts, and on the perusal of numerous thrift balance sheets (which reveal a frequent absence of reserves). Furthermore, the *FSLIC/AED Policy Manual* (OTS, 1988, p. E4–21) recommends the use of GAAP values only as an upper limit for the value of the assets. The analyst is encouraged to review certain confidential data to find the degree to which GAAP values understate credit-quality losses. Procedures are then prescribed for improving the GAAP values. Third, the *TFR* instructions do not include specific directions as to when general valuation allowances should be established, although the instructions for specific valuation allowances are more precise. [16]

We measure credit quality by the amount of delinquent loans. In

---

14. Because the federal income tax law before 1986 permitted banks and thrifts to deduct as an expense against taxable income amounts recorded as "provision for loan losses" that were considerably more than the losses actually expected, general valuation allowances were considered to be overstated and were counted as a part of equity. With the new capital regulations, effective December 7, 1989, general valuation allowances are excluded from equity or "core" capital. However, general valuation allowances are still included in "supplementary" capital, in an amount up to 1.5 percent of total assets.

15. Institutions marking their assets to market using the interest rates they charge for loans should not deduct general valuation allowances from the asset balances, as the cash flows and discount rates already include these expected losses.

16. We abstract here from minor changes in reporting instructions over the years. These instructions can be found in the OTS's *Instructions for the Thrift Financial Report Industry Condition Report System,* various years, various months (1984–88). The April 1988 instructions on valuing repossessed assets can be found on pages A23–A24. The April 1988 instructions on classifying delinquent loans can be found on pages F (M–2&3)–24 and F (M–2&3)–25. The April 1988 instructions for establishing general loan-loss reserves (which implicitly reveal the optional nature of these reserves) are found on page A–15 (mortgage loans) and page A–22 (nonmortgage loans). The reader is warned that these instructions are a minefield through which the wise novitiate will tread lightly or not at all.

contrast to the *TFR* instructions for reporting asset valuation allowances, the instructions for reporting delinquent loans are specific and obligatory. Thrifts are required to report permanent one-to-four-family mortgage loans, commercial loans, and consumer loans as delinquent when they are two or more months past due. Mortgage loans other than permanent one-to-four family are reported as delinquent when past due. Unfortunately, delinquency reporting is subject to some manipulation by a thrift. For example, there is reason to believe that some highly risky borrowers initially borrow sufficient funds to keep their payments current, or are loaned additional funds for this purpose even when the probability of expected repayment has deteriorated. Delinquency also can be deliberately misreported, although this type of misrepresentation is likely to be uncovered by examiners.[17] Nevertheless, we expect that thrifts' reporting of delinquency rates is more accurate, and certainly more uniform, than their establishment of valuation allowances.

We attach a zero value to delinquent loans, and a 100 percent value to performing loans. This procedure overvalues performing loans and undervalues delinquent loans, but can be justified under the assumptions that (1) a loan either is fully performing or is delinquent, (2) delinquent payments and late penalties for delinquencies are never collected, (3) the size of the loan portfolio is constant, and (4) the ratio of nonperforming to total loans currently reported will persist indefinitely into the future. Given these assumptions, the cash flows generated by the portfolio are equal to the contracted cash flows times one minus the delinquency rate (the value of delinquent loans divided by the loan portfolio's total value). Since the delinquency rate and portfolio size are constant through time, loans replacing retiring assets also generate cash flows equal to their contracted cash flows times one minus the delinquency rate, regardless of whether loans are retired through repricing, amortization, repossession, or prepayment.

Our assumptions clearly are unrealistic, but should be understood as representing a starting place for the issue of the proper markdown of a given portfolio for a given delinquency rate. (At least the biases are somewhat offsetting: performing loans are overvalued and delinquent loans are undervalued.) If adopted, market value accounting could continue to use the current method of establishing contra-asset valuation allowances, though this approach creates a lack of uniformity across thrifts. If our delinquency-based approach were used, further investigation should be able to improve the estimate of the relationship between portfolio values and delinquency rates.

The mortgage discount rates we use include a component for the

---

17. The Financial Institutions Reform, Recovery and Enforcement Act (FIRREA, passed in 1989) establishes what could be described as draconian penalties for false reporting, but there were no such penalties prior to the passage of this bill. The only means for disciplining managers who misreported delinquencies was the possibility of a regulatory cease-and-desist order or of deeper and extended examinations.

average expected credit risk. Therefore, the delinquency rate priced into these discount rates should be subtracted from the thrift-specific delinquency rate. The delinquency rate implicit in the FHLMC committed rate averaged 0.64 percent, with slight variation, from 1984 through 1988 (*Freddie Mac 1988 Annual Report,* p. 50). Consequently, we assumed that mortgages at a thrift with a mortgage delinquency rate of 0.64 percent had no additional losses, because discounting its cash flows by the FHLMC rates accounts for these normal losses. Mortgage balances of thrifts with no delinquencies were adjusted upward by 0.64 percent. No such adjustment was made for commercial loans, since the Federal Reserve's survey does not report the delinquency rate. It was for this reason that we assume that short-term commercial loans are risk-free.

The Core-Deposit Intangible Asset

Passbook savings accounts have a contract maturity of one month, and so are assigned to the zero-to-six-month bucket. In reality, passbook savings tend to remain with a bank for a relatively long time. They are withdrawn primarily as a result of a depositor dying, relocating, investing elsewhere, or consuming. An intangible asset results when passbook savings pay depositors interest rates below the institution's opportunity cost of funds. Calculation of the value of this core-deposit intangible asset requires an estimate of the rate at which passbook deposit balances flow out of the bank or into accounts paying market rates of interest, termed their "decay rates."

Firm-specific passbook account decay rates could be estimated from each institution's past experience, but we cannot obtain the requisite data. The OTS has developed generic decay rates, however, which it uses in estimating the effective maturity of passbook accounts. The 1988 Schedule 9 shows the percentage of passbooks expected to be withdrawn at each of the seven Section H time buckets:

Average Maturity

	3	9	24	48	84	180	300
Decay Rate:	16.05	13.47	13.39	10.85	18.93	17.78	09.53
Cumulative Decay:	16.05	29.52	42.91	53.76	72.69	90.47	100.00

Thus, 16.05 percent of passbooks are expected to have a 3-month maturity, 13.47 percent to have a 9-month maturity, and so on. In the absence of more refined data, we used these assumed rates of decay to calculate the value of the core-deposit intangible asset.

Mortgage Servicing Rights

The *TFR* reports loans owned by others but serviced by the institution and loans owned by the institution but serviced by others. The fees paid for loans serviced by others (for example, 50 basis points per year on a given loan balance) are not subtracted from the coupon rates reported on Section H. Therefore, it is necessary to include the present value of these servicing rights as a contra asset. In addition, the present value of mortgage servicing rights on loans owned by others should be included as an asset.

The value of mortgage servicing rights is a function of two or three dozen separate variables. At a minimum, a good ballpark estimate would demand five or six variables, including remaining time to maturity, underlying mortgage coupons, location of the mortgage property, escrow requirements, and appropriate discount rates. Unfortunately, the *TFR* gives only the outstanding principal balance of the serviced mortgages. Consequently, we had to make some simplifying assumptions.

A comprehensive literature search uncovered little published research on valuing mortgage servicing. We then interviewed public and private sector specialists in mortgage servicing sales. This investigation revealed that there is no established data base containing the variables needed to value mortgage servicing rights. Nor could we find data on the prices paid for these rights. However, a consensus developed that the majority of mortgage servicing packages priced, on average, between 1.50 and 2.00 percent of the mortgages' outstanding principal balances, although any given year might see the packages range from below 1.00 percent to above 3.00 percent. Since the consensus seems to suggest a price of about 1.75 percent, we used this figure to value net mortgage servicing rights.

Effects of Market Valuation

Table 10.1 reports the differences between market values and traditional book values for selected assets and liabilities over the five years in our study. Section A shows equity measured according to RAP (regulatory accounting principles), as a percentage of RAP total assets. It differs from GAAP primarily in that it includes as assets (and hence, as equity) deferred losses on mortgages sold and upward revaluation of buildings and land (the "appraisal increment"), and as part of equity the claims of subordinated debt holders and the FSLIC. For the comparisons in Table 10.1, we included subordinated debt and FSLIC claims in market value. The median and 25th percentile RAP ratios are 4.19 and 2.68 percent in 1984, rising to 5.99 and 4.12 percent by 1988. Over this period, the range between the 25th and 75th percentiles is about 4 percent. Thus, by this measure, most of the thrifts appear solvent.

Section B shows equity measured according to our market values, as a percentage of market value total assets. The median and 25th percentile equity percentage is 0.68 and −2.08 percent in 1984. These percentiles increase to 4.64 and amd 1.87 percent in 1985 (reflecting declining interest rates) and then gradually rise to 5.75 and 2.14 percent by 1988. The range of the equity/asset ratios is about 6 percent from the 25th to the 75th percentiles, due primarily to lower ratios for the 25th percentiles.

Section C gives the difference between the market value and RAP

Table 10.1   Net Worth: RAP Book Value, Market Value, and Market Less Book Value*

	1984	1985	1986	1987	1988
No. of Obs.	517	509	497	474	454

A. RAP Book Value To Book—Value Total Assets

Percentiles	1984	1985	1986	1987	1988
99	31.64	14.83	14.15	15.55	16.83
75	6.10	6.39	7.17	7.93	8.13
50	4.19	4.68	5.26	5.92	5.99
25	2.68	3.26	3.67	3.98	4.12
1	−4.82	−7.88	−12.27	−14.65	−19.84
Mean	4.98	4.90	5.22	5.64	5.70
Std Error	0.23	0.16	0.22	0.25	0.31

B. Market Value to Market—Value Total Assets

Percentiles	1984	1985	1986	1987	1988
99	31.59	17.56	17.27	17.85	18.90
75	4.01	7.17	8.38	8.58	8.49
50	0.68	4.64	5.96	5.67	5.74
25	−2.08	1.87	2.61	1.91	2.14
1	−14.00	−11.32	−21.55	−16.38	−22.05
Mean	1.33	4.28	4.87	4.48	4.54
Std Error	0.32	0.25	0.33	0.35	0.37

C. Market Less Book Value to Book—Value Total Assets

Percentiles	1984	1985	1986	1987	1988
99	4.07	5.83	5.70	5.64	5.34
75	−1.51	1.36	1.76	1.11	0.85
50	−3.41	−0.08	0.56	−0.26	−0.38
25	−5.24	−1.83	−1.71	−2.32	−2.62
1	−14.98	−12.10	−13.50	−15.51	−12.09
Mean	−3.66	−0.62	−0.35	−1.17	−1.15
Std Error	0.16	0.15	0.18	0.17	0.15

*All values in percentages.

equity divided by RAP assets at each thrift, in percentages. Reflecting sections A and B, the median difference is −3.4 percent in 1984, and negligible thereafter. Excepting 1984, the top 25 percent of thrifts by market value were better capitalized than the top 25 percent by RAP values, while the bottom 25 percent by market values were much more poorly capitalized than the bottom 25 percent by RAP values. The mean difference between market and RAP capitalization was significantly negative in every year.

Selected assets and liabilities are reported in Table 10.2. Our estimates are that, for the median thrift, the market values of mortgage portfolios (shown in section A) were 95 cents on the RAP dollar in 1984, rose to 102 cents on the dollar by 1986, and then declined to 98 cents on the dollar by yearend 1988. The mean markdowns (markups) of mortgage portfolios are similar to the median values, and significantly different from zero in every year except 1985. The market values of most thrifts' mortgage portfolios are much less affected by delinquencies than by interest rate movements. From 1984 through 1988, the median mortgage delinquency rate ranged between 1.23 and 1.67 percent (section A1). Since the FHLMC delinquency rate is about 0.6 percent, our median markdown for mortgage credit quality ranged from 0.63 percent to 1.07 percent. Therefore, the movement in the value of the median thrifts' mortgage portfolios was mostly due to movements in interest rates.

The market values of commercial loans (shown in section B) tell a different story. At the median thrift, commercial loans were about at par in 1984, and their values relative to par declined by 3.59 percent through 1987. This decline in values was due to credit quality. For the median thrift the nonmortgage delinquency rate was below 1.0 percent in every year, but the distribution of delinquency rates, and therefore the distribution of markdowns for delinquencies, is highly skewed (section B1). In any given year 10 percent delinquency rates afflict about 10 percent of the thrifts, and delinquency rates above 20 afflict about one or two percent of the thrifts. Although the reported nonmortgage delinquency rate includes both consumer loans and commercial loans, an econometric investigation we conducted showed that high nonmortgage-delinquency rates are almost always a function of commercial as opposed to consumer lending. Furthermore, depending on the year, less than one-half of the Southeastern thrifts engaged in commercial lending at all. Therefore, the 75th percentile of nonmortage-delinquency rates, rising from 1.00 percent in 1984 to 2.52 percent in 1988, gives more insight into the median values of commercial loan portfolios than does the median nonmortgage-delinquency rate.

Passbook accounts gave rise to a core deposit intangible asset that reduced the liability by 25.56 percent at the median thrift in 1984 (section D). As interest rates decreased through 1986, this reduction in liability values fell to 11.29 percent; subsequent rate increases increased the reduction in the liability value to 17.4 percent by 1988. Since the level of passbooks (as a percent of liabilities) showed relatively little change over the period, we have prima facie evidence of rate stickiness on passbook deposits. This shows that the OTS was correct in assigning decay rates to these deposits, though of course the precise decay rates chosen are a matter for dispute.

Other financial liabilities were not much affected by rate changes (section E). Even the few thrifts at the extreme percentiles were little affected; the greatest percentage change was the 5.29 increase in liability value recorded for the 99th percentile in 1986.

Table 10.2   The Effect of Market Valuation on the Book Values of Selected Assets and Liabilities*

	1984	1985	1986	1987	1988
A. Total Mortgages, Market Less Book Value to Book Value of Mortgage Loans					
Percentiles					
99	2.90	4.49	6.30	2.74	1.50
75	−3.12	1.46	2.88	−0.05	−0.76
50	−5.12	0.30	1.96	−1.24	−1.89
25	−6.70	−0.92	0.72	−2.61	−3.36
1	−11.86	−8.97	−14.87	−15.44	−13.59
Mean	−4.78	0.00	1.29	−1.90	−2.38
Std Error	0.13	0.13	0.17	0.16	0.13
A1. Mortgage Delinquencies to Book Value of Mortgage Loans					
Percentiles					
99	12.44	17.67	18.80	19.58	17.58
75	2.37	2.90	3.12	3.23	3.27
50	1.23	1.49	1.67	1.57	1.57
25	0.54	0.68	0.78	0.75	0.70
1	0.19	0.00	0.00	0.00	0.00
Mean	1.80	2.36	2.83	2.90	2.58
Std Error	0.09	0.15	0.20	0.19	0.15
B. Commercial Loans, Market Less Book Value to Book Value of Commercial Loans					
Percentiles					
99	7.84	6.71	2.17	0.61	2.10
75	1.04	0.15	−0.73	−1.39	−0.87
50	0.24	−0.80	−2.20	−3.59	−2.62
25	−1.24	−3.25	−6.01	−6.46	−6.48
1	−28.22	−43.67	−53.33	−29.31	−35.19
Mean	−0.92	−2.81	−4.91	−5.15	−4.67
Std Error	0.23	0.33	0.37	0.27	0.30
B1. Nonmortgage Delinquencies to Book Value of Nonmortgage Loans					
Percentiles					
99	20.04	22.71	38.36	2.26	25.30
75	1.00	1.71	2.12	2.52	2.52
50	0.12	0.31	0.52	0.71	0.85
25	0.00	0.00	0.00	0.00	0.06
1	0.00	0.00	0.00	0.00	0.00
Mean	1.31	1.93	2.51	2.26	2.49
Std Error	0.16	0.24	0.28	0.23	0.24

Table 10.2 (*Continued*)

	1984	1985	1986	1987	1988
C. Investment Securities, Market Less Book Value to Book Value of Investments					
Percentiles					
99	4.62	13.02	15.24	5.71	6.35
75	1.33	2.54	2.36	0.45	0.09
50	0.70	1.23	1.18	0.11	−0.41
25	0.22	0.54	0.30	−1.44	−1.67
1	−10.79	−5.65	−5.66	−13.27	−11.37
Mean	0.37	1.74	1.72	−0.89	−1.17
Std Error	0.11	0.12	0.15	0.19	0.15
D. Passbook Deposits, Market Less Book Value to Book Value of Passbooks					
Percentiles					
99	−17.74	−13.19	−7.78	−13.47	−10.38
75	−25.09	−19.85	−11.19	−17.80	−17.33
50	−25.56	−20.41	−11.29	−17.80	−17.37
25	−25.56	−20.41	−11.29	−17.85	−17.42
1	−26.39	−21.39	−15.42	−20.77	−20.66
Mean	−25.14	−20.09	−11.28	−17.94	−17.31
Std Error	0.18	0.06	0.07	0.05	0.08
E. Other Financial Liabilities, Market Less Book Value to Book Value of Other Fin. Liabs.					
Percentiles					
99	2.77	3.77	5.29	2.51	1.87
75	1.25	1.82	2.16	0.71	0.27
50	1.00	1.38	1.59	0.38	0.05
25	0.79	1.05	1.11	0.18	−0.09
1	0.11	0.38	0.40	−0.29	−0.39
Mean	1.07	1.52	1.80	0.51	0.15
Std Error	0.02	0.03	0.05	0.03	0.02

*All values in percentages.

The percentage effects of individual asset and liability market valuations on total book-value assets is given in Table 10.3. (The percentage effect on book-value net worth could not be shown meaningfully because book-value net worth often is very small—giving rise to very large percentages—and negative.)

On average, thrifts hold about 50 percent of their assets in one-to-four-family mortgage loans (including mortgage-backed securities), 20 percent in the various other mortgages, 2 percent in commercial loans, and 10

Table 10.3   The Effect of Market Valuation of Selected Assets and Liabilities Market Less Book Value as Percentages of Book Value Total Assets

	1984	1985	1986	1987	1988
A. Total Assets					
Percentiles:					
99	2.46	5.38	6.74	4.22	4.43
75	−2.77	1.15	2.47	−0.15	−0.51
50	−4.56	−0.24	1.25	−1.45	−1.80
25	−6.15	−1.81	−0.69	−3.11	−3.54
1	−13.96	−12.09	−11.26	−13.46	−11.75
Mean	−4.58	−0.65	0.52	−2.10	−2.35
Std Error	0.14	0.13	0.15	0.15	0.13
B. Total Mortgages					
Percentiles:					
99	1.90	3.25	4.16	1.75	1.29
75	−2.39	1.11	2.10	−0.04	−0.59
50	−3.84	0.22	1.40	−0.95	−1.40
25	−5.22	−0.69	0.55	−1.85	−2.41
1	−9.07	−6.85	−11.54	−11.05	−11.52
Mean	−3.71	0.00	0.94	−1.40	−1.77
Std Error	0.10	0.10	0.12	0.13	0.09
C. Commercial Loans					
Percentiles:					
99	0.15	0.08	0.01	0.00	0.02
75	0.00	0.00	0.00	0.00	0.00
50	0.00	0.00	−0.03	−0.03	−0.03
25	0.00	−0.04	−0.12	−0.12	−0.10
1	−0.54	−1.95	−3.11	−1.41	−1.38
Mean	−0.02	−0.11	−0.17	−0.12	−0.10
Std Error	0.00	0.03	0.03	0.01	0.01
D. Investment Securities					
Percentiles:					
99	0.90	2.03	2.06	1.28	1.08
75	0.15	0.27	0.31	0.04	0.00
50	0.06	0.11	0.13	0.01	−0.03
25	0.01	0.04	0.03	−0.10	−0.14
1	−1.04	−0.63	−0.86	−2.61	−2.22
Mean	0.07	0.23	0.23	−0.12	−0.11
Std Error	0.01	0.02	0.03	0.03	0.03

Table 10.3 (*Continued*)

	1984	**1985**	**1986**	**1987**	**1988**
E. Mortgage Servicing					
Percentiles:					
99	1.85	2.67	3.34	4.16	3.82
75	0.24	0.26	0.32	0.35	0.33
50	0.00	0.03	0.05	0.07	0.10
25	−0.03	−0.03	−0.01	0.00	0.00
1	−0.90	−1.04	−1.20	−1.15	−1.10
Mean	0.11	0.14	0.21	0.27	0.26
Std Error	0.02	0.02	0.03	0.04	0.05
F. Total Liabilities					
Percentiles:					
99	1.60	3.23	4.13	1.50	1.20
75	−0.07	0.57	1.15	−0.35	−0.60
50	−0.84	0.00	0.53	−0.94	−1.08
25	−1.69	−0.71	0.07	−1.58	−1.69
1	−6.60	−4.48	−2.27	−4.36	−4.54
Mean	−1.01	−0.12	0.68	−1.01	−1.19
Std Error	0.07	0.06	0.05	0.05	0.05
G. Passbook Deposits					
Percentiles:					
99	−0.02	−0.02	−0.02	−0.06	−0.06
75	−1.14	−0.83	−0.50	−0.85	−0.79
50	−1.71	−1.26	−0.78	−1.28	−1.17
25	−2.50	−1.84	−1.07	−1.83	−1.65
1	−7.30	−5.30	−2.83	−4.55	−4.69
Mean	−1.95	−1.44	−0.87	−1.45	−1.32
Std Error	0.07	0.05	0.03	0.04	0.05
H. Other Financial Liabilities					
Percentiles:					
99	2.46	3.49	4.68	2.25	1.70
75	1.09	1.60	1.85	0.60	0.23
50	0.87	1.21	1.35	0.32	0.04
25	0.67	0.90	0.96	0.16	0.08
1	0.06	0.32	0.35	−0.23	−0.32
Mean	0.93	1.31	1.54	0.44	0.13
Std Error	0.02	0.03	0.04	0.02	0.02

percent in investment securities. Of thrift liabilities, about 10 percent are in passbook accounts, 70 percent in other types of deposits, and 15 percent in nondeposit borrowings. Thus, most of the difference between market and book values is due to the revaluation of mortgages. In particular, marking total mortgages to market reduced total assets by 3.84 percent at the median thrift in 1984; more than three-quarters of the thrifts suffered reductions in total assets due to revaluation of mortgages. As interest rates decreased, the market value of mortgages increased substantially; by yearend 1985, mortgage markups increased the value of most thrifts' total asset portfolios. By yearend 1987, rising interest rates and mortgage delinquencies had reversed this favorable development, resulting in a markdown of total assets of 1.40 percent.

Although the revaluation of commercial loans had a substantial effect on the book-value amounts (Table 10.2, section B), for most thrifts the net effect on total assets is slight because commercial loans are a small percentage of assets. Indeed, as shown in section C of Table 10.3, commercial loan revaluations have almost no effect on total assets at the median thrift. However, the markdown in some thrifts' commercial loans was such that total assets are significantly affected. For example, for the 99th percentile in 1986, commercial loan markdowns resulted in a reduction of total assets of 3.11 percent.

The effect of revaluing investment securities and mortgage servicing is similar to that of revaluing commercial loans (Table 10.3, sections D and E). Market valuation of these items results in mean and median changes that are not minor, though for the extreme percentiles market valuation does have a significant effect.

The revaluation of total liabilities (section F) is the sum of the revaluations of passbook deposits and other liabilities. Even though passbooks are a small percentage of liabilities, passbook-deposit revaluation is considerable; in 1984 the application of passbook decay rates resulted in a passbook markdown equal to an average of 1.95 percent of total assets (1.71 percent of assets at the median thrift) (section G). This percentage effect continued throughout the five years of our study, although at somewhat lower levels. Liabilities other than passbooks were marked up, but except in 1986 this markup was less than the passbook markdown. Only in 1986 did the total market value of liabilities exceed the total book value. In 1984, 1987, and 1988, the market valuation of liabilities resulted in mean and median markdowns of about one percent of total assets.

In summary, revaluation to market in the five-year studies has significant effects on the net worth of southeastern thrifts. The largest effects are on mortgages and passbook deposits, and these, in turn, had the largest effects on total assets. Revaluations of commercial loans, investments, mortgage servicing, and other liabilities, although of lesser importance, can significantly affect the total assets and net worths of some thrifts, as shown by observations at the extreme percentiles. As a result of not making such revaluations to market, the supervisory authorities could underestimate the risks that some thrifts pose to the insurance fund.

Failure Prediction

We tested the usefulness of our market revaluations by comparing the ability of market value, tangible, RAP, and GAAP equities to predict thrift failures.[18] (For this test, we do not include the subordinated debt and FSLIC claims in market value equity, as we did in Tables 10.1, 10.2, and 10.3.) The Federal Home Loan Bank of Atlanta provided us with a list of 1988–89 failures (eight thrifts which failed in the first quarter of 1990 were defined as 1989 failures). Failure is defined as liquidation, sale with FSLIC assistance, or assignment to a conservatorship. It should be noted that the authorities have used RAP net worth as their principal measure of insolvency. Furthermore, GAAP and tangible values can easily be calculated from data reported to the supervisory authorities, while market values have not formally been calculated until now. Hence the tests are biased in favor of traditional accounting values and against market value.

To test failure prediction, we calculated percentile rankings for each of the four measures of equity, for each thrift in our study (517 in 1984, declining to 455 by yearend 1988). The percentile rankings of those thrifts that failed can then be compared across each of the different accounting equities. For example, we can test the hypothesis that accounting measures have no value in predicting failure by testing the hypothesis that the failures' mean percentile rankings are not significantly different from 50. Even at a five-year lag (1984 equities predicting 1989 failures), the failures' mean percentile ranking for all four of the accounting measures is significantly lower than 50 (Table 10.4).

At lags of one year, we test 1987 equities predicting 1988 failures and 1988 equities predicting 1989 failures. At the two-year lag, we test 1986 equities predicting 1988 failures and 1987 equities predicting 1989 failures, and so on. At lags of one, two, or three years market values provide the failures' lowest mean percentile ranking (denoting better failure prediction); at lags of four and five years the failures' lowest mean percentile ranking was by RAP and tangible capital, respectively. Mean percentile GAAP ranking was highest at all five of the feasible lags.

The most appropriate test for statistical significance of these results is

---

18. We used the OTS's May 1990 definition of tangible capital. This definition includes purchased mortgage servicing rights as an asset, even though these are usually considered to be intangible assets.

Table 10.4   Predictions of 1988—First Quarter—1990 Failures in Terms of Accounting Methods' Mean Net Worth Percentile Rankings for Lags of One to Five Years

	Mean of 1-Year Lag (Std Error)	Mean of 2-Year Lag (Std Error)	Mean of 3-Year Lag (Std Error)	Mean of 4-Year Lag (Std Error)	Mean of 5-Year Lag (Std Error)
Tangible	6.25 (.69)	16.33 (2.31)	20.07 (2.99)	24.59 (3.38)	28.07 (4.08)
GAAP	6.41 (.86)	15.59 (2.29)	21.40 (3.03)	26.75 (3.39)	32.08 (3.91)
RAP	5.81 (1.00)	13.13 (2.09)	19.46 (2.95)	24.14 (3.29)	29.26 (3.95)
Market Model	5.43 (.63)	10.49 (1.70)	18.31 (2.82)	26.10 (3.76)	31.49 (4.92)

the pair-wise t-test. This test is conducted by calculating, for each failure, the differences between each traditional measure and the market value measure of equity. The mean difference and the standard deviation of the differences can then be used to calculate a t-statistic.[19] To reduce the number of ties, milltile rankings of equity were used instead of percentiles. The results of this test are reported in Table 10.5. Market value is significantly superior (95 percent or better confidence) to all three measures at the two-year lag, and to tangible and GAAP at the one-year lag. At other lags, statistical significance diminishes, particularly when comparing market value to RAP.

Given the hypothesis that all four measures of equity have equal predictive power, binomial significance levels can also be calculated. GAAP is obviously inferior; the probability that any one measure would finish last at all five lags is less than one-tenth of one percent. The probability that any one measure would finish first more than twice is 10.4 percent; thus, binomial probabilities suggest 90 percent confidence in the superiority of market values at randomly selected lags.

The statistically significant (at the 92-percent level) superiority of tangible over market values at the five-year lag may be due to the particular period studied here; the five-year lag involves 1984 equities predicting 1989 failures. The thrifts with the lowest 1984 market values took the largest interest-rate gambles, and benefited the most from the 1985 and 1986 interest-rate rallies.[20]

It is worth pointing out that, until recently, a negative RAP capital was a prerequisite for failure, as thrifts with "positive equity" could not be

---

19. William Mendenhall and James E. Reinmuth, *Statistics for Management and Economics,* Duxbury Press (North Scituate, Mass.), 1978, p. 279–97.

20. See Benston, Carhill, and Olasov, "The Failure of Thrifts: Evidence From the Southeast," in *Financial Markets in Financial Crisis,* R. Glenn Hubbard, ed., National Bureau of Economic Research, University of Chicago Press, 1991.

Table 10.5   Paired Difference t-Tests for Failures Milltile Rankings by Traditional Values Less Ranking by Market Values of Net Worth 1988—First Quarter—1990 Failures

	No. of Obs.	50 1-Year Lag	50 2-Year Lag	50 3-Year Lag	50 4-Year Lag	37 5-Year Lag
RAP	Mean Diff.	3.78	26.42	11.54	19.58	−22.24
	Std Dev	55.86	98.04	139.18	154.41	229.96
	Std Error	7.90	13.86	19.68	21.84	37.81
	t-test	0.47	1.91**	0.59	−0.90	−0.58
GAAP	Mean Diff.	9.84	51.04	30.88	6.50	5.95
	Std Dev	44.21	113.49	140.33	158.97	205.86
	Std Error	6.25	16.05	19.85	22.48	33.84
	t-test	1.57*	3.18***	1.56*	0.29	0.18
Tangible	Mean Diff.	8.20	42.38	17.62	−15.16	−34.14
	Std Dev	30.55	108.99	101.70	114.52	137.95
	Std Error	4.32	15.41	14.38	16.20	22.68
	t-test	1.90**	2.75***	1.22	−0.94	−1.51*

*t-test significant at the 10 percent level when t=1.28.

**t-test significant at the 5 percent level when t=1.65.

***t-test significant at the 1 percent level when t=2.33.

seized.[21] In view of this fact, the difference in predictive power between RAP and GAAP is not surprising, and should not be taken as an indication of the relative merits of RAP versus GAAP accounting. Rather, the fact that RAP fails to excel in a test so biased in its favor could be taken as a condemnation of RAP accounting.

CONCLUSIONS

This study has explored the assumptions required for market value accounting for thrifts.[22] If market value accounting were to be imposed by regulators or the Financial Accounting Standards Board, these assumptions could and should be standardized in much the same manner as GAAP rules currently are. The relative predictive power of differing assumptions should be investigated; such an investigation would require a considerable investment of research resources.

The results reported here show that market valuation applied generically is superior to traditional accounting methodologies applied on thrifts specifically. This conclusion is also supported by a behavioral study using the FHLB-Atlanta Market Value Model, in which market values are found to predict risk-taking.[23] Given the extent to which an on-site accountant could improve our market value estimates, the potential benefits of market value accounting seem appealing.

There are also costs to adopting market value measures, as historical cost accounting is considerably easier than determining the correct contract rates, discount rates, and effective maturities of the various assets and liabilities. Furthermore, some of the market value assumptions can only be made subjectively, and market value accounting could increase the number of ways in which troubled institutions can overstate their values.[24]

The weighing of the costs and benefits of market value accounting will

---

21. The regulators seized Lincoln Savings in 1989 and Centrust Savings in early 1990. At the time of seizure, both thrifts had negative tangible and (at least in the case of Centrust) negative market value capital but positive RAP capital. American Continental Corporation (parent of Lincoln) challenged the legality of this seizure, seeking to regain control (Lincoln Savings and Loan Association v. Wall). On August 22, 1990, Judge Sporkin ruled that "the Bank Board was fully justified in taking the actions it did." To avoid such challenges from obviously but not RAP-insolvent thrifts in the future, FIRREA gave the regulators explicit authority to seize thrifts regardless of RAP solvency.

22. For a discussion of market-value accounting for commercial banks, see David L. Mengle, "The Feasibility of Market Value Accounting for Commercial Banks," Federal Reserve Bank of Richmond Working Paper 89-4, February 1990.

23. See Benston, Carhill, and Olasov, op. cit.

24. For further analysis, see George J. Benston, "Market-Value Accounting: Benefits, Costs, and Incentives," *Proceedings: Conference on Bank Structure and Competition,* Federal Reserve Bank of Chicago, 1989, pp. 547–69.

inevitably prove to be a political process. However, we feel this paper provides the beginnings of an empirical case for market valuation, and that the making of that case is worthy of the expenditure of research resources.

APPENDIX: MARKET VALUE EQUATIONS

In this appendix we describe how we used our methodology to estimate the market values of the financial assets and liabilities. We used the SAS programming language. We do not report the actual program used, but those interested in replicating our study should be aware that the programming itself is fairly sophisticated. It should require about two months of skilled programming, not including the programming required to create a usable data set.

Note: N (the final letter in the mnemonic variable names) refers to the number of months remaining to maturity; $N = 3, 9, 24, 48, 84, 180,$ and 300.

Discount Rates:

FMRN   = The Freddie Mac committed rate with N months remaining to maturity.

COMN   = The commercial loan rate for commercial loans with N months remaining to maturity.

AGRN   = The Agency rate.

Outstanding Principal Balances:

BVFRMN   = The book value of the fixed-rate mortgage portfolio with N months remaining to maturity (outstanding principal balances excluding accrued interest receivable and loans-in-process).

BVARMN   = The book value of the adjustable-rate mortgage portfolio.

BVSECN   = The book value of second mortgages.

BVOTHN   = The book value of "other mortgages" (for example, commercial mortgages).

BVCOMN   = The book value of commercial loans.

BVSECN   = The book value of securities.

DELMORT   = Delinquency rate on mortgage loans.

DELNON   = Delinquency rate on nonmortgage loans.

PREPAY   = Prepayments expressed as a periodic rate. See above for calculation of prepayments.

RESSEC   = Valuation allowances on securities expressed as a proportion of total securities.

PAYMENT   = Contracted payments. Calculated by the SAS payment function as a function of the contract rate, term to maturity or repricing, and outstanding principal balance.

REMBAL   = The outstanding principal balance (amortized balance less projected prepayments) for each type of loan at the time each payment or prepayment is made.

The following equations were calculated for $N = 3, 9, 24, 48, 84, 180,$ and 300. Equation (1) calculates the market value of an institution's portfolio of fixed rate mortgages. [25]

$$\text{PVFIXMORT} = \sum_{T=1}^{N} [\text{PREPAY} + (1 - \text{DELMORT} + 0.0064) \ \text{PAYMENT}]/[(1 + \text{FMRN})^T] \tag{1}$$

where $\text{PREPAY} = \text{f}(\text{REMBAL}_T)$, $\text{PAYMENT} = \text{f}(\text{REMBAL}_{T-1})$, and $\text{REMBAL} = \text{F}(\text{BVFRMN})$.

Let PVADJMRT refer to the present value of the institution's portfolio of adjustable-rate mortgages (ARMs). Let PPADJMRT represent the prepayment rates for adjustable mortgages. Equation (2) calculates the present value of an institution's ARM portfolio.

$$\text{PVADJMORT} = \left\{ \sum_{T=1}^{N} [\text{PREPAY} + (1 - \text{DELMORT} + 0.0064) \ \text{PAYMENT}]/[(1 + \text{FMRN})^T] \right\}$$

$$+ \ \frac{[(\text{REMBAL}_N - \text{PREPAY}_N)/}{(1 + \text{FMRN})^N]} \tag{2}$$

where $\text{PREPAY} = (1 - .12)^{(1/12)}$, $\text{PAYMENT} = \text{f}(\text{REMBAL}_{T-1})$, and $\text{REMBAL} = \text{F}(\text{BVARMN})$.

Equation (3) calculates the market value of an institution's second mortgage portfolio.

$$\text{PVSECMORT} = \sum_{T=1}^{N} [\text{PREPAY} + (1 - \text{DELMORT} + 0.0064) \ \text{PAYMENT}]/[(1 + \text{FMRN} + .001652)^T] \tag{3}$$

where $\text{PREPAY} = (1 - .14)^{(1/12)}$, $\text{PAYMENT} = \text{f}(\text{REMBAL}_{T-1})$, and $\text{REMBAL} = \text{F}(\text{BVSECMN})$.

Mortgages for five-plus family dwellings, commercial property, and

---

25. Section H includes mortgage-backed securities among fixed-rate mortgages; mortgage-backed securities cannot be separated from portfolio mortgages without extremely arbitrary assumptions as to their maturities. Our techniques should accurately value the portfolios, whatever their composition of mortgage-backed securities versus fixed-rate loans. Relative to portfolio mortgages, mortgage-backed securities carry both lower coupons (relative to their market value) and lower delinquency rates. Provided that portfolio mortgages' higher coupon rates compensate for their additional delinquency costs, they can be merged with mortgage-backed securities in calculating a portfolio's value. For the same reason, we use the overall mortgage delinquency rate in calculating the market value of all types of mortgage loans. The one element of value which our approach misses is the higher administrative costs incurred in maintaining portfolio mortgages.

other real estate are grouped together by Section H in the category "other mortgage loans."

$$PVOTHMORT = \sum_{T=1}^{N} \frac{(1 - DELMORT + 0.0064)\,PAYMENT]}{[(1 + FMRN)^{T}]} \tag{4}$$

where $PAYMENT = f\,(REMBAL_{T-1})$ and $REMBAL = F\,(BVOTHMN)$.

Commercial and Investment Securities were valued similarly to other mortgages, as expressed in equations (5) and (6).

$$PVCOMMLOAN = \sum_{T=1}^{N} \frac{[(1 - DELNON)\,PAYMENT]}{[(1 + COMN)^{T}]} \tag{5}$$

where $PAYMENT = f\,(REMBAL_{T-1})$ and $REMBAL = F\,(BVCOMLN)$.

$$PVINVSEC = \sum_{T=1}^{N} \frac{[(1 - RESSEC)\,PAYMENT]}{[(1 + AGRN)^{T}]} \tag{6}$$

where $PAYMENT = f\,(REMBAL_{T-1})$ and $REMBAL = F\,(BVSECN)$.

Liabilities were all treated as quarterly paying instruments, and all were discounted at the CD rate. Let

CDRN	=	The CD rate.
PASS	=	Passbook balances.
DECAY	=	Percentages of passbooks assumed to decay at each quarter.
PASPAY	=	The quarterly yield reported for passbook accounts.
OTHLIABN	=	Other interest-bearing-liability balances with n quarters remaining to maturity.
OTHLIABPAY	=	The contracted interest payments on other interest-bearing liabilities, calculated using the weighted average of quarterly yields reported for these interest-bearing liabilities.

$$PVPASS = [(PASS)\,(DECAY)]/[(1+ CDRN)^{N}] \tag{7}$$

$$PVOTHLIAB = \left\{ \sum_{T=1}^{N} [OTHLIABPAY]/[(1 + CDRN)^{T}] \right\}$$
$$+ [OTHLIABN/[(1 + CDRN)^{T}] \tag{8}$$

Note that all items not prefixed by PV are valued at net book value.

Other Balance-Sheet Accounts:

We valued several balance sheet items at net book value because the information needed to estimate market values is not available. These items include fixed assets, consumer loans, real estate held for investment,[26] investment in service corporations, miscellaneous non-interest-bearing liabilities, miscellaneous assets, accrued interest receivable and payable, and net position in financial futures. Naturally, cash and non-interest-bearing liabilities are also valued at book. Recorded intangible assets were assigned a zero value.

To summarize, the market value of a given firm is calculated by equation (9):

$$
\begin{aligned}
PVFIRM = [\,&PVFIXMORT + PVADJMORT + PVSECMORT \\
&+ PVCOMMLOAN + PVINVSEC \\
&+ VALUE\ OF\ ALL\ OTHER\ ASSETS \\
&+ 0.0175\ (\text{loans serviced for others less} \\
&\qquad\qquad \text{loans serviced by others})] \\
-[\,&PVPASS + PVOTHLIAB \\
&+ VALUE\ OF\ ALL\ OTHER\ LIABILITIES]
\end{aligned}
\tag{9}
$$

---

26. Banks' Call Reports use the term "real estate held" to refer to repossessed assets. The thrift industry uses the term "real estate held" to refer to real estate development projects and equity participations in real estate development projects. Service corporation investment includes everything from repossessed assets to mortgage servicing operations. GAAP dictates that repossessed assets, investment in service corporations, and real estate held be valued at lower of cost or market.

Index